Essays on Nonconceptual Content

edited by York H. Gunther

A Bradford Book
The MIT Press
Cambridge, Massachusetts
London, England

This book was set in Palatino by SNP Best-set Typesetter Ltd., Hong Kong and was printed and bound in the United States of America.

Library of Congress Cataloging-in-Publication Data

Essays on nonconceptual content / edited by York H. Gunther.
     p.   cm.
"A Bradford book."
Includes bibliographical references and index.
ISBN 0-262-07239-4 (pbk.: alk. paper)—ISBN 0-262-57161-7 (pbk.: alk. paper)
1. Concepts. 2. Content (Psychology). I. Gunther, York H.

BD181 .E87   2003
121'.4—dc21   2002069300

Contents

Acknowledgments

I am indebted to Akeel Bilgrami, Arthur Danto, Martin Kusch, and Crispin Wright for their encouragement and comments on various stages of the project. Both the book and my own work on nonconceptuality have benefited immeasurably from their attentiveness and criticism.

Anthony Everett, Lance Hickey, Henry Jackman, Ronald McIntyre, and Takashi Yagisawa offered detailed suggestions for the improvement of the general introduction, for which I am most grateful. And many thanks to José Bermúdez, Ronald Chrisley, Tim Crane, Adrian Cussins, David Hamlyn, Sean Kelly, and Christopher Peacocke for their feedback on the anthology's contents.

I must also express my appreciation to Carolyn Anderson, without whose support the project would not have seen the light of day, Adam Hoffman, who came through in a time of need, and to Judy Feldmann and Tom Stone for their advice on all things editorial and press-related. And for enabling the project's development, I am grateful to Stanford University for granting me a Fellowship in the Humanities from 1999 to 2001, and to California State University at Northridge, where the philosophy department has made me feel so very welcome.

And finally, I want to thank Michael, Roger, Nick, Schwiggy, and Dick for making the summer of 2001 so very congenial and nonconceptual. For their friendship and *joie de vivre*, I dedicate the collection to them.

Contributors

José Luis Bermúdez: Professor of Philosophy, University of Stirling

Andy Clark: Professor of Philosophy and Director of the Cognitive Science Program, Indiana University, Bloomington

Tim Crane: Reader in and Chair of Philosophy, University College, University of London

Adrian Cussins: A philosopher sailing around the world on his boat, *tj Haecceia.* He can be reached at adrian@haecceia.com or at his website, www.haecceia.com.

Fred Dretske: Bella and Eloise Mabury Knapp Professor Emeritus of Philosophy, Stanford University

Gareth Evans: Late Wild Reader in Mental Philosophy, Oxford University

York H. Gunther: Assistant Professor of Philosophy, California State University, Northridge

David W. Hamlyn: Professor Emeritus of Philosophy, Birbeck College, University of London

Sean D. Kelly: Assistant Professor of Philosophy, Princeton University

Michael Martin: Lecturer in Philosophy, University College, University of London

John McDowell: University Professor of Philosophy, University of Pittsburgh

Christopher Peacocke: Professor of Philosophy, New York University

Robert Stalnaker: Professor and Chair of Philosophy, Massachusetts Institute of Technology

Michael Tye: Professor of Philosophy, University of Texas, Austin

To my musical brethren

General Introduction

The word "concept" is used in various ways; its sense is sometimes psychological, some-times logical, and sometimes a confused mixture of both. Since this license exists, it is natural to restrict it by requiring that when once a usage is adopted it shall be maintained.
—Frege, "Concept and Object"

1 A Historical Prelude

In his slogan, "Thoughts without content are empty, intuitions without concepts are blind," Kant sums up the doctrine of conceptualism. While he specifically pro-posed the restriction for transcendental psychology, the latter half of the slogan neatly sums up the doctrine in any of its forms: religious, existential, aesthetic, epistemological, psychological, and so forth. According to the conceptualist, no intentional content, however portentous or mundane, is a content unless it is structured by concepts that the bearer possesses.

Resistance to conceptualism has arisen on many fronts. Although the focus of this anthology is on the contemporary debate in the philosophies of mind and psychology, it is instructive to review briefly ways in which the greater tradition has characterized and contrasted the conceptual and nonconceptual. This will not only enable us to recognize that the views of past and present writers are similar but suggest that their concerns may not be as different as one might initially suppose.[1]

In mystical writings from East to West, for example, we find an emphasis on the immediacy of nonconceptual experience. Lao Tsu taught that "integral wisdom involves a direct participation in every moment: the observer and the observed are dissolved in the light of pure awareness, and no mental concepts or attitudes are present to dim that light" (*Hua Hu Ching*, p. 26). Stressing the sub-jectivity of concepts, Ockham regarded them as stand-ins for reality and explained that "We cannot know in themselves either the unity of God . . . or His infinite power of the divine goodness or perfection; but what we know immediately are concepts, which are not really God but which we use in propositions to stand for God" (Ockham 1967–1979, 3, 2, F). We can, however, immediately apprehend God through faith, something theologians and mystics have sharply contrasted with discursive thought and inferential reasoning, which, as Bonaventure insisted, are apt to mislead: "a philosopher necessarily falls into some error, unless he is aided by the light of faith" (Bonaventure 1882–1902, *Sentences* 18, 2, 1, ad 6–280). And Buddhists, in addition to underscoring the indeterminate and ineffable character of mystical experience, regard the path from worldly suffering to *nirvana* as a liberation from the fallibility of conceptual thought: "Anything we define as *it* is not it," explains the Third Patriarch of Zen Buddhism, Chien-chih Seng-ts'an, "So let go of all concepts and all definitions" (Seng-ts'an 1991, p. 79).

While existentialists reject absolute truths, their characterization of the dread experienced by an individual encountering an absurd universe is fundamentally similar. In *Fear and Trembling*, Kierkegaard emphasizes the utter isolation and silence distinctive of Abraham, the "knight of faith." According to Kierkegaard, Abraham's faith is not "the content of a concept," but "the prodigious paradox . . . which no thought can grasp [since] . . . faith begins precisely where thought stops" (1843, pp. 249 and 53). In *Nausea*, Sartre describes the failure of Roquentin's words to fix determinately the experience of existence:

> I thought without words, *on* things, *with* things. . . . And without formulating anything clearly, I understood that I had found the key to Existence, the key to my Nauseas, to my own life. In fact, all that I could grasp beyond that returns to this fundamental absurdity. Absurdity: another word; I struggle against words; down there I touched the thing. But I wanted to fix the absolute character of this absurdity here. (1938, p. 129)

Like Ockham, Sartre regarded concepts as subjective, as inadequate stand-ins for reality. "To him," Simone de Beauvoir wrote, "general laws and concepts and all such abstractions were nothing but hot air: people, he maintained, all agree to accept them because they effectively mask a reality which men found alarming" (1989, p. 30).

Aesthetic experiences have been identified in much the same way. Schopenhauer, for example, insisted that while music is "an entirely universal language, whose distinctness surpasses even that of the world of perception itself," its message is "infallible," the expression of "the immediate knowledge of the inner nature of the world unknown to [the] faculty of reason; it cannot be an imitation brought about with conscious intention by means of concepts, otherwise the music does not express the inner nature of the will itself" (1819, vol. 1, §52). Comparable descriptions abound in nineteenth and twentieth century art criticism and aesthetics. In his review of Beethoven's *Fifth Symphony*, E. T. A. Hoffmann suggested that the "music opens up an unknown realm to man . . . in which he leaves behind all the feelings which are determinable by concepts in order to devote himself to the unsayable" (1810). Dewey proposed a more general distinction between the content of the arts and discursive language, explaining that "If all meanings could be adequately expressed by words, the arts of painting and music would not exist" (1934, p. 74). And even Kant, that preeminent champion of the Enlightenment, conceded that aesthetic ideas are not contained by concepts, explaining that they "cannot become cognition because it is an *intuition* (of the imagination) for which an adequate concept can never be found" (1790, p. 342).

In epistemology, we find writers from Locke to Quine attempting to rest knowledge on something more fundamental than concepts, for example, "raw sensations," "blind intuitions," "simple impressions," "sense-data," the "Tribunal of Experience," the "Given." Our experience of them is allegedly "immediate" and "infallible" and to be sharply distinguished from inferential and abstract knowledge. As Berkeley maintained, "the senses perceive nothing which they do not perceive *immediately*: for they make no inferences . . . deducing therefore of causes or occasions from effects and appearances . . . entirely relates to reason" (Berkeley 1713, p. 587). "I know the colour *perfectly and completely* when I see it," explained Russell, "and no further knowledge of it itself is even theoretically possible. Thus the sense-data which make up the appearance of my table are things with which I have acquaintance, things *immediately* known to me just as they are" (1912, p. 47; my emphasis). And even Wittgenstein, in his suggestive distinction between sense and nonsense, especially as it bears on religious, aesthetic, and ethical discourses, describes nonsense (*Unsinn*) in ways reminiscent of the nonconceptual: it is indeterminate and indefeasible because it lacks genuine truth conditions and its ineffability is, of course, famously summed up in the last line of the *Tractatus*: "Whereof one cannot speak, thereof one must be silent" (1921).

Contemporary philosophers of mind and psychology offer similar characterizations of the nonconceptual. Consider, for instance, perceptual experience. Many proponents of nonconceptuality are deeply impressed by the specificity of its content, its richness of detail, and fineness of grain (see essays 1, 3, 5, 6, 9). Through vision, for example, we are capable of discriminating shades of color and shapes of objects that seem to outrun the descriptions and categories available to us. Or when we hear a sound coming from a certain direction, we tend to turn our heads to look for its source without thinking or calculating, inferring or deducing where to turn (see essays 2, 6, 7, 12). Like our perception of color and shape, our experience of space is believed not only to be immediate but indeterminate and even inexpressible. Comparable claims are made about subpersonal states, which are presumed to have contents that are individuated nonsubjectively, in other words, independently of an individual's cognitive resources (essays 4, 7, 8). And there's also the case of pain (essays 6, 13), an experiencer's judgment of which is commonly considered infallible, as well as the direct referential character of indexical and demonstrative thought (essays 2, 3, 5, 6, 9, 11), and the failure of emotional content to exhibit full logical complexity (essay 14).

Although well-entrenched, the intuitions that move writers to regard the contents of thoughts and experiences as nonconceptual are often vague. Two factors contribute to this. First, a variegata of features (properties) are loosely associated with the possession of conceptual content. Without a clearer understanding of how it is determinate or how it renders an individual fallible, of the sense in which it is subjective, of its relationship to inferential reasoning or linguistic expressibility and communication, to claim that certain thoughts and experiences have nonconceptual content will surely sound glib to anyone seeking clarity on the issue. Second, "*non*conceptual" is a negative term, defined against "conceptual." Even if the features we associate with conceptual content were identified clearly, there remains an ambiguity in how the "non" should be rendered. For example, the content of a state may be nonconceptual if it *cannot* be represented conceptually or if an individual *does not grasp* or *exercise* the concepts involved in its articulation. To make the claims of the nonconceptualist more explicit and her debate with the conceptualist more tractable, different ways of fixing the conceptual and of rendering "non" should be considered. And this, it seems to me, can serve to clarify not only the contemporary debate in the philosophy of mind and psychology but analogous debates in religion, existentialism, aesthetics, epistemology, and so forth.

2 Content and Semantic Normativity

Yet before fixing the conceptual and identifying renderings of "non," something needs to be said about the genus to which the conceptual and nonconceptual belong, namely, intentionality, or what I'll also call "intentional content" or simply "content." The notion was re-introduced to modern philosophy by Franz Brentano who suggested that intentionality is essential to the mental and serves to distinguish it from the physical (Brentano 1874). Since then, it has also been attributed to sentences and utterances as well as various kinds of artifacts such as books, computers, and artworks. While there is some question about whether their intentionality is original rather than merely derived from entities with minds (see, e.g., Chisholm 1958, Searle 1980, Dennett 1996), for a state (event, experience, activity, object, and so forth) to have intentional content is for it to be *about* something; for example, I hope to visit the Chrysler Building, believe that 751 multiplied by 512 equals 384,512, am outraged at purchasers of fuel-inefficient vehicles, assert that King Lear is mad, and I may even play chess against a computer that wants to take my queen, and own a painting about the futility of human creativity in the face of an ever-changing universe. In this way, my hope, belief, outrage, and assertion, and perhaps also the computer (that is, its desire) and my painting, are directed at things (objects, events, state of affairs, and so on), whether concrete or abstract, real or fictional, particular or universal.

We must, however, take care not to confuse intentionality with intention. Where the former is a property of different kinds of mental states, an intention, for instance, to fly to the moon, is but one kind of mental state with intentionality—hopes, beliefs, emotions, desires, and wishes are others. Moreover, a distinction should be acknowledged between intentionality and intentional content on the one hand and propositions or propositional content on the other. The reasons for this concern the latter's association with Platonic entities, states of affairs, and truth. Let me explain.

To begin with, "proposition" is often used to denote an abstract, Platonic entity (see Church 1956, pp. 4ff). Although it may turn out that identifying intentional contents with such entities constitutes the most promising metaphysical account of them, this remains controversial. It is, for example, not easy to accept that there would be intentional contents even if there were no thinkers or, for that matter, no physical world.

Moreover, propositional content is generally assumed to be about states of affairs, possible or impossible, actual or not (see Sosa 1995, p. 765). For example, the propositional content of Pierre's belief that the Chrysler Building is in New York, expressed by the *that*-clause, is about the Chrysler Building's being in New York. Yet many intentional contents are about something other than a state of affairs: Pierre sees the Chrysler Building, you fear the approaching dawn, I hear the buzzing of a mosquito, and Anna desires the company of a friend. Perceptions, emotions, and desires are commonly about objects and events rather than states of affairs. And according to many philosophers, those things to which maps, pictures, artworks, and practical knowledge (to name a few) are directed have an altogether different ontological (logical) structure than states of affairs.[2]

Finally, it is not uncommon to claim that propositions have truth conditions essentially (see Stalnaker 1999, p. 131). Even if we set aside difficulties involving the contents about fictional characters and non-existent entities, the claim remains problematic. For example, it isn't apparent that an intentional state, event, or object about something other than a state of affairs should be evaluated in terms of truth/falsity,—a perception, emotion, map, or artwork, for example. Furthermore, while the contents of beliefs and assertions have truth conditions, the contents of commands, hopes, and wishes do not—they have compliance, realization, and fulfilment conditions, respectively. Of course, one might suggest that these and other nontruth conditions can be reduced to or identified with truth conditions; or one might contend that compliance, realization, and fulfilment conditions (to name a few) are conditions that govern psychological states bearing propositional content, whereas truth conditions govern propositions *in themselves*. But it isn't evident that any of this is actually defensible.[3] And as such, because not all contents have truth conditions essentially (not even those regarded as propositional), and due to the tendency to associate Platonic entities and states of affairs with "proposition" and "propositional content," I will speak instead of "intentionality" or "intentional content."

With that said, one might wonder whether intentionality has some distinctive feature or mark. What is noteworthy, what is true of any state (event, experience, and so forth) with content, is that it is governed by semantic normativity. For whether its content is conceptual or nonconceptual, propositional or not, an intentional state presents the world as being a certain way; and intrinsic to this presentation, to its content, is a set of (semantic) conditions under which it does this correctly, truthfully, satisfactorily, appropriately, skillfully, and so on. Although Pierre's belief that the Chrysler Building is in San Francisco is false, intrinsic to its content is a set of conditions that prescribes what the world would be like if the belief were true, namely, the Chrysler Building would be in San Francisco. Similarly, Anna's desire for the company of a friend or my outrage at purchasers of fuel-inefficient vehicles has normative conditions, prescriptions for what it would be like for Anna's desire to be satisfied or my outrage to be calmed, whether it, in fact, is or is not.

In this way, the debate between conceptualists and nonconceptualists is about states with semantic normativity. If a state lacks such normative conditions, we can assume that it doesn't have intentional content and is thus not to be attributed the property of conceptuality or nonconceptuality.[4] For example, it would be mistaken to regard qualitative states like pains and itches as having either conceptual or nonconceptual content if, as is widely assumed, they lack normative conditions. (This assumption, however, is challenged in essay 13.) Given that semantic normativity is the mark of intentionality, only states with it are the legitimate subjects of debate between conceptualists and nonconceptualists.

Are there perhaps other norms that govern intentional states in this way? In addition to semantic normativity, philosophers, psychologists, social scientists,and so forth, often speak about "rational normativity" (see, e.g., Elster 1985). The latter encompasses a rather wide range of norms under its heading, from those governing formal rationality—cognitive or motivational consistency— to those governing more substantial types of rationality—autonomy or self-determination. However, while these norms bear on various aspects of the mental (including value and attitudes), it's not evident that any govern all intentional states in the way semantic normativity does.[5] This, it seems to me, is an open question, as is the question of whether there are any other distinctive features of intentionality. (See essay 8, pp. 193–201 for further discussion of the issue.)

3 Fregean Sense

With the genus thus identified, we now need a way of distinguishing conceptual from nonconceptual content. To this end, it is natural to appeal to Frege. Although much of his focus was on the philosophy of language and logic, there are several reasons that his characterization of linguistic content as sense (*Sinn*) is particularly useful for fixing conceptual content. First, from his model of sense, we can derive several principles that bear specifically on conceptual content, as opposed to some other aspect of the mental. Second, the framework in which Frege developed this model has had significant influence on twentieth century Anglo-American philosophers who invoke his principles, whether explicitly or implicitly, in the course of fixing conceptual content. (It is noteworthy that Frege's own use of "concept" (*Begriff*), intended to indicate the reference of a predicative expression, should not be confused with contemporary uses of "concept" or "conceptual content.") Third, as the primary focus of this anthology is on the interpretation of mature human beings, Fregean sense is generally presumed to be better suited for explaining thought and action than reference-based models of content such as Mill's. And finally, Frege's tendency to identify senses with Platonic entities, and to regard them as having truth conditions and being directed at states of affairs, can be bracketed. The principles we derive from his work can be formulated independently of these commitments.

Among the considerations that led Frege to his characterization of sense is a well known puzzle about identity statements (Frege 1892). If the content of a proper name were its reference as Mill believed, certain statements of the form $a = a$ should have the same content as statements of the form $a = b$. For example, since both "Hesperus" and "Phosphorus" refer to Venus, the statements "Hesperus is Hesperus" and "Hesperus is Phosphorus" should both be trivially true given that they identify proper names with the same reference and, according to Mill, the same content. Frege, however, recognized that while "Hesperus is Hesperus" is trivially true, "Hesperus is Phosphorus" expresses information that may genuinely be instructive to anyone who doesn't know that the evening star and the morning star are one and the same. And this, Frege believed, suggests that "Hesperus" and "Phosphorus" express different contents. Similar considerations have led to the distinction between the contents of co-extensive predicates and relations.

To account for the possibility that co-referential or co-extensive expressions have different contents, Frege distinguished the sense of an expression from its reference. The reference (extension) of an expression is a function of the reference of its parts (the thing[s], property[ies], relation[s], state of affairs, and so forth) and is considered to be what the expression is about (its normative, truth, correctness, etc., conditions). By contrast, an expression's sense (content, thought) is a function of the senses of its parts (names, predicates, relations), which are the cognitive values available to anyone in command of the language. Senses are *modes of presentation* that are like directions specifying the route to a referent. In fact, given that sense is distinct from reference, even expressions lacking reference have sense, for instance, statements about fictional entities.[6] In this way, an expression's sense *determines* its reference, what it's about. The same reference, however, may be determined differently by more than one sense, which is what the puzzle about identity statements underscores. While "Hesperus" and "Phosphorus" are co-referential, the sense of the latter is *the morning star* and the sense of the former is *the evening star*. The terms thereby specify unique routes to Venus. Yet as the example illustrates, to grasp two senses of a single reference does not imply that one must recognize that they are different routes to the same reference. And it is this feature of sense and reference that can make identity statements of the form $a = b$ genuinely informative.

Frege's model naturally extends from language to thought, from the linguistic to the mental. Consider an individual, Pierre, who believes that Phosphorus appears before sunrise in the east and Hesperus after sunset in the west. Assume that Pierre believes that Hesperus and Phosphorus are different planets and that when queried he readily agrees that Hesperus appears after sunset in the west and Phosphorus does not. We take him at his word and consider him to be balanced and rational. Now, were we to fix Pierre's conceptual contents along Millian lines, it seems we would have to attribute to him a contradictory belief, namely, a belief that Venus appears after sunset in the west and does not appear after sunset in the west. In other words, since on the Millian view "Hesperus" and "Phosphorus" express the same content, we seem compelled to attribute to Pierre a belief of the form *Fa* and *not-Fa*. However, on the Fregean model, since "Hesperus" and "Phosphorus" express different conceptual contents, this contradiction is easily defused by attributing to Pierre a belief of the form *Fa* and *not-Fb*. In matters of interpretation, many have found that the Fregean model is more compelling because it seems better suited to capturing Pierre's viewpoint and in greater accord with the Principle of Charity, which states that by minimizing an individual's inconsistency one maximizes her intelligibility, arguably the point of interpretation (see, e.g., Davidson 1973).[7]

Just as Frege's puzzle about names led to a distinction between sense and reference, the adaption of his puzzle to thought suggests a distinction between conceptual content and its reference (extension). A conceptual content, we may suppose, is like a set of directions that determines a thing(s), property(ies), relation(s), or state of affairs—in a word, a set of normative conditions. And just as senses may direct one to things (objects, events, states of affairs, and so on) that don't exist or don't exist as they're represented, a conceptual content may direct one to fictional or incorrect (false, unsatisfactory, inappropriate, etc.) things. A distinction between conceptual content and reference (extension) makes it possible to interpret Pierre as believing of a planet that it is Hesperus but not Phosphorus since *Hesperus* and *Phosphorus*, though co-referential, are different conceptual contents.

4 Fixing the Conceptual

From a Fregean characterization of conceptual content, four principles can be derived:

> (1) Compositionality
> (2) Cognitive Significance
> (3) Reference Determinacy
> (4) Force Independence

The first states that complex conceptual contents are functionally determined by their constituents, the second illustrates how conceptual contents are distinguished from one another, the third concerns their relation to their reference or normative conditions, and the fourth claims that they are individuated independently of their force. Each principle presents a necessary condition for conceptual content, capturing features that have traditionally been associated with the conceptual.

Consider first the Principle of Compositionality:

> If content c is conceptual (and complex), then c's constituents functionally determine c.

As stated, the principle says nothing about what the constituents of conceptual contents—concepts—are. Without offering a theory of concepts, which would certainly be a formidable task—as is attested to by the numerous competing theories (e.g. the prototype theory, theory-theory, conceptual atomism) and the array of challenges facing each (see, e.g., Margolis and Laurence 1999)—for the present let us merely accept that concepts stand to complex conceptual contents as Fregean senses to Fregean thoughts.

To begin with, Compositionality enables us to account for *communicability*, in particular how language can be systematic and productive. To explain, for instance, how an ability to understand the assertions "Pierre studies astronomy" and "Anna studies philosophy" implies an ability to understand the assertions "Pierre studies philosophy" and "Anna studies astronomy," we must assume that the assertions express contents that are functions of the concepts *Anna*, *Pierre*, *studies astronomy*, and *studies philosophy*. Without such an assumption, it's doubtful that systematicity could be explained. The same is true of productivity, the alleged ability to form and grasp any of infinitely many novel expressions. Given the finite mental capacity of human beings, our manifestation of productivity seems to depend on an ability to understand a finite set of basic concepts. If contents weren't compositional, human beings would require an infinite mental capacity to form and grasp novel expressions.

It is noteworthy that similar claims are often made about thought under the heading of "The Generality Constraint" or "Recombinability." By adopting Evans's characterization, it is not uncommon to adapt the constraint to conceptual content and formulate it along the following lines:

> For any two thoughts, Fa and Gb, and for any thinker, s, if the contents of Fa and Gb are conceptual, then (if s understands both Fa and Gb, s also understands Fb and Ga).

In other words, if I believe that Pierre studies philosophy and believe that Anna studies astronomy, it is within my capacity to believe that Anna studies philosophy and Pierre studies astronomy. Obviously, this doesn't mean that I have to believe the latter if I believe the former—it only suggests that it is within my ability as a thinker to grasp the contents of the latter if I grasp the contents of the former. Moreover, while there are differences between the properties of systematicity and recombinability,[8] both presuppose compositionality.

Compositionality also accounts for the *inferential structure* of language and thought. Inferential reasoning presupposes, for example, that expressions share constituent contents as do intentional states. Suppose someone believes that if Pierre studied astronomy, then Anna was his teacher; and suppose that same individual believes that Pierre studied astronomy. Then, ceteris paribus, that individual will believe that Anna was Pierre's teacher. The inference is, of course, valid since it conforms to the schema of modus ponens: $F \supset G$, F, therefore G. And of course to conform to the schema, the person's beliefs must share the same contents, namely, F and G. Without shared contents, modus ponens would have no way of sinking its formal teeth into the contents of the intentional states (or expressions), preventing one from logically inferring the conclusion that Anna was Pierre's teacher.

The second principle, Cognitive Significance, can be construed in at least two ways. On the weak construal, the kind of content a mental state has is determined by whether it leads the individual in question to have a corresponding belief. Several assumptions evidently inform the principle thus construed. First, the elicitation of a corresponding belief must occur in normal conditions, which should be specified in a ceteris paribus clause. Second, the state in question is generally taken to be a perceptual experience (or some other low-level mental state such as an emotion or desire) as opposed to a supposition or contemplation. And third, the contents of the corresponding belief are considered conceptual because they are assumed to be governed by principles of rationality, which are loosely associated with conceptuality. With this in mind, the weak construal might be formulated as follows:

> If the content c of a mental state m is conceptual, then s believes that c in normal conditions.

If s does not believe that c, then m's content is nonconceptual. In other words, when a perception, emotion, or desire is belief-independent its content is, according to the principle, nonconceptual. Consider the Müller-Lyer Illusion (see Evans 1982, pp. 122–129). Although perception often leads to belief, in the case of the illusion it generally does not. I say "generally" since there are undoubtedly circumstances (ones the normalcy conditions are meant to rule out) in which an individual perceiving the illusion might believe that the lines are different lengths—for whatever reason she may consciously believe that they're the same length but unconsciously believe that they're different lengths.

While suggestive, the weak construal is vague. For even if the normalcy conditions could be specified explicitly, the construal rests on an assumed distinction between higher and lower mental states that is unmotivated. The assumption, of course, is needed to deal with cases where mental states (usually higher cognitive states) don't elicit corresponding beliefs, for example, when I contemplate that $7 + 5 = 11$ but don't believe it. In such cases, it seems counterintuitive to regard the content of the state as nonconceptual. But the question is, why? Without motivating the distinction between higher and lower mental states, the weak construal seems question begging. Moreover, as formulated, the principle also depends on a rather vague commitment to the rationality of belief and the assumption that perceptions and other lower mental states aren't governed by rationality. But here again clarity and motivation are required. What is the relevant principle of rationality at work in this case? Why suppose that the contents of perceptions and other lower mental states violate it? The problem is that the weak construal seems merely to air intuitions about nonconceptuality rather than to ground them.

By contrast, the strong construal of Cognitive Significance is more explicit about its commitment to rationality:

> If content c is conceptual, then F and G, which are constituents of c, are different concepts if an individual could have an intentional state[9] about a thing, a, with the content a is F and a is not-G.

As stated, the principle implies the consistency of conceptual content. For from the strong construal, it follows that someone could not have a belief, hope, wish, perception, or so forth, about, say, a planet that it both appears and does not appear in the west at sunset. To recognize this, assume for a moment that an individual could believe a logical contradiction, namely, have a belief of a thing, a, that Fa and not-Fa. With this assumption and an instance of Cognitive Significance,

> If an individual could have a belief about a thing, a, with the content Fa and not-Fa, then F and F are different concepts,

we could infer that F is different from itself, a clear violation of the Principle of Identity. However, since Identity is not a principle most of us will want to abandon, we can agree that it is *not* the case that F is different from itself. Consequently, with the enlisted help of the Principle of Identity and by modus tollens, we can infer from Cognitive Significance that an individual could not have a belief (or any other intentional state) with a contradictory content.[10]

In addition to linking conceptuality to rationality, Cognitive Significance on either construal reflects the *subjective* or *mediating* character of the conceptual. The move from the Millian to the Fregean paradigm can be regarded as a move from an objective to a subject-dependent model. On the latter, conceptual content is fixed partially by an individual's personal-level states—whether beliefs, judgments, hopes, or so forth—suggesting that her epistemic capacities mediate what her experiences and thoughts are about. Of course, to associate subjectivity and mediation with the conceptual in this way is not to present the latter as a Lockean veil that keeps an individual from an inaccessible reality, as Ockham maintained, or an absurd and alarming universe as Sartre alleged. Nor does their subjectivity imply that conceptual contents are fictional or false as noncognitivists and error theorists maintain. While associations of this sort are common, there is nothing about Cognitive Significance itself that suggests this. By linking subjectivity and indirectness to the conceptual, I only mean to emphasize that an individual's conceptual contents are fixed partially by her personal-level states or epistemic capacities, broadly construed.

3

The Principle of Reference Determinacy, of course, captures the *determinateness* of conceptual content to which so many writers allude. An intentional state with conceptual content is one where the bearer of the content is able to grasp what her state is about, that is, its semantic value (reference, normative conditions). Reference Determinacy, as a necessary condition of conceptual content, may be formulated thus:

> If content c is conceptual, then a subject, s, can determine the semantic value of c.[11]

In general, to determine the semantic value involves a knowledge of, or an ability to identify, classify, and/or recognize the referent of c. However, as there is a discrepancy about what this comes to, let's distinguish three common ways of construing the principle's consequent:

> (a) metaphysical construal: . . . s knows the *essence* of the referent of c
> (b) descriptive construal: . . . s is able to *locate* or *identify* the referent of c
> (c) recognitional construal: . . . s is able to *recognize* or *re-identify* the referent of c

While the construals offer different interpretations of the principle, it is noteworthy that the first two are intimately linked with *verbal expression*. For example, knowing the essence of a referent involves having knowledge of a scientific or ontological theory that is undoubtedly language-dependent. On the descriptive construal, the determinate character of concepts is based on an ability to formulate a description that uniquely locates or identifies the referent. Admittedly, an ability to recognize or re-identify may not involve language.

The principle also makes room for *error*, which Schopenhauer, Bonaventure, and others have associated with concepts. By distinguishing content from reference, the Fregean model suggests an explanation for how false and fictional contents are possible.[12] Since conceptual contents are like directions that specify a route to a thing (object, event, state of affairs, and so on), there is no guarantee that the directions are correct (true, satisfactory, appropriate, etc.), or that they lead to anything. The thing may not exist or it may exist not in the way it is specified. Error and fiction are afforded entry by the cognitive limitations of individuals themselves. Because the specification or determination of reference is an epistemic feat undertaken by an imperfect individual, a gap between what is right and what seems right forms. And this gap enables the Fregean to account for the possibility of false and fictional contents.

4

The final principle, Force Independence, concerns the distinction and separation of content and force that is commonly acknowledged in both language and thought:

> If content c is conceptual, then c can be individuated independently of its force.

In language this involves distinguishing between the mood of a sentence (e.g., indicative, optative, imperative) or the use of an utterance (e.g., to make an assertion or wish, to issue an order or command) and its content; and in thought it involves distinguishing a mental state's content from its attitude (e.g., belief, desire, hope, wish).

There is good reason for heeding this distinction and individuating content independently of force. To begin with, the principle enables us to explain *communication* and *linguistic expressibility*. Suppose for a moment that force were indistinguishable from content (see, e.g., Fodor 1978, p. 326f). In such a case, if I were to assert (or believe) that Anna is a philosopher and you were to question (or doubt) that she is, my assertion and your question would not merely reflect differences in the way we said things, they would reflect differences in what we said. In addition to radically multiplying the number of contents you and I have, our very ability to disagree and, for that matter, to communicate would be undermined. Your questions and my assertion, your doubts and my beliefs, would fail to express the same contents (or at least ones with a principled connection to one another). Moreover, if force were indistinguishable from content, even my own thought and language would potentially be out of synch. My belief that Pierre studies astronomy and my assertion that he does would have different contents (assuming, of course, that belief and assertion are regarded as different types of force), suggesting that I could not in principle express what I think or think what I say.

Force Independence also helps us to explain how content can exhibit certain forms of *logical complexity*. For example, as Frege observed, an utterance's assertoric force cannot be part of its content (sense) because, if it were, then whenever the utterance appeared in the antecedent of a conditional, it would have to be *asserted* rather than *entertained* (Frege 1891, p. 34). But this is clearly not the case. For example, while one may assert "Anna is a philosopher," one can also entertain the content expressed by the assertion, "If Anna is a philosopher, she studied philosophy." Similarly, to believe that if Pierre is an astronomer, he studied astronomy doesn't require believing that Pierre is an astronomer. The antecedent content in this case can be entertained rather than believed. By contrast, if force were an indissoluble aspect of content, the contents of assertions, beliefs, and so forth, could not be made conditional. And the same seems true of disjunctions and negations. Hence, to individuate content independently of force enables us to exhibit the logical complexity that both language and thought exhibit.

While the principles may not allow us to capture all that writers have associated with the conceptual, they do enable us to reflect features such as rational consistency, logical complexity, subjectivity and mediation, determinateness, expressibility, communicability, and fallibility. And while there is room to dispute the accuracy of these characterizations, any level of arbitrariness that remains is, I believe, offset by the relative clarity that the principles offer. I don't thereby mean to suggest that these are the only principles that can capture these features. Other principles might do as well. However, as far as I can tell, these are among the most common principles which have been invoked, whether explicitly or implicitly, in discussions of concepts and conceptual content.

5 Rendering "Non"

Just as there are different ways of fixing conceptual content, there are different ways of rendering "non." As I suggested, "nonconceptuality" is a negative term, one defined against "conceptuality." A nonconceptualist could have any one of at least three renderings in mind: the content of a state might be *nonconceptual*,

(1) if it *cannot* be represented conceptually;

(2) if an individual *does not grasp* the concepts involved in its articulation; or

(3) if an individual *does not* or *cannot exercise* the concepts involved in its articulation.[13]

Depending on how "non" is rendered, very different notions of nonconceptuality emerge, even when the principle for fixing conceptual content is explicitly identified.

Consider Reference Determinacy. On the first rendering of "non," to say that a content is nonconceptual is to say that an individual *cannot* know its semantic value. This is a stringent claim, one suggesting that no individual can know what a state with nonconceptual content is about. The claim can be sharpened by considering a particular construal of Reference Determinacy. For example, on the metaphysical construal, a content is nonconceptual if an individual cannot know the essence of its referent, a position reminiscent of a metaphysical realism, including the views of certain mystics about experiencing the Absolute. In the papers included in this collection, only essay 14 seems to advocate this rendering.

On the second rendering, a content is nonconceptual if an individual *does not* grasp its semantic value. This is a more common way of rendering "non" that underlies the discussion of many of the contributions in the anthology. The first and second renderings are distinguishable in the following way. Assume for a moment that one doesn't know the semantic value of a thought about Hesperus. On the second rendering, this would constitute an intentional state with a non-conceptual content. More specifically, if knowing the semantic value involved knowing the essence of Hesperus (as it does on the metaphysical construal), an individual's ignorance of this fact might lead one to conclude that the individual has a nonconceptual content about Hesperus. By contrast, in order for the same content to be considered nonconceptual on the first rendering, we would have to assume that an individual *couldn't*—in fact, that no one in principle *could*—have knowledge of Hesperus's essence, a view that seems implausible. As such, insisting that a content is nonconceptual on the first rendering is a much stronger claim than insisting that it is nonconceptual on the second.

However, the most flexible and perhaps weakest rendering is the third. Here it is not presupposed that the individual *cannot* have or *does not* have the concepts required to articulate the content's semantic value. An individual may have a content that is nonconceptual even if she possesses the requisite concepts. What makes the content nonconceptual is that the individual in question does not or cannot exercise them on the content. One may therefore know what Hesperus's essence is without exercising this knowledge in certain instances on contents. What might account for a failure to exercise concepts? Informational theorists, often moved by naturalistic motivations, insist that concepts are irrelevant for the individuation of contents. Some subpersonalists believe that concepts are not exercised by individuals on the contents of their computational states. And others, informed by empiricism, maintain that concepts are exercised on the contents of cognitive but not perceptual states.

6 *Intentional Psychology*

Once a principle for fixing conceptual content and a rendering of "non" are settled on, the nonconceptualist's next step is to identify a mental state (event, experience, etc.) whose content violates the principle. What is crucial, what should be apparent from the outset, is that the state in question is genuinely explanatory. For without an explanatory value, the use and reality of nonconceptual content itself would be questionable.

To judge whether a mental state has explanatory value depends not only on what is being explained but on the discourse on which one is focused. For example, since what a mystic will find explanatorily relevant will surely differ from what an existentialist, aesthetician, or epistemologist will, it is necessary to restrict one's inquiry from the outset, which is precisely what I do. The articles and excerpts collected herein focus exclusively on intentional psychology.

The restriction is motivated by two considerations. First, it is natural to begin an inquiry with the ordinary and then move from it to the extraordinary. Unlike religion, existentialism, or aesthetics, intentional psychology focuses on mundane experiences of, for example, color, spatiality, and emotion—experiences that are more commonplace than those discussed by mystics, existentialists, and aestheticians, and that don't require a commitment to metaphysical absolutes, the absurdity of existence, the truth of art, and so forth. However, it is noteworthy that while such basic intentional states are used in developmental and animal psychology as well, the papers generally focus on the interpretation of mature human beings. In fact, each author can be seen as addressing the question, Do any of the contents used in the explanation of mature human beings violate any of the aforementioned principles?

The restriction is also motivated by the fact that intentional psychologists, more than mystics, existentialists, aestheticans, and so forth, have exploited the explanatory tools (principles) of Frege most extensively and prominently. This, of course, isn't surprising since these tools were developed in the philosophies of language and mind, which have had considerable influence on philosophical discussions of intentional psychology. What is significant about this is that nonconceptualists working within intentional psychology provide new and perhaps more rigorous ways of approaching the issue, ones that might be adopted by theorists in other fields.

It is therefore noteworthy that, although the debate is framed in distinctly Fregean terms, one need not be an intentional psychologist to stake a position in it. In fact, one need not even be a Fregean. After all, following neo-Millians like Fodor and Burge, one could claim that no contents heed all of these principles. Fodor, for reasons concerning the naturalization of intentionality, and Burge, for reasons concerning externalism, deny that Fregean senses have a place within intentional psychology (see Fodor 1995 and Burge 1979). Rather than undermine the framework, their positions merely suggest the possibility of a global nonconceptualism. Unlike the prosaic nonconceptualist (or "content dualist") who believes that intentional psychology requires both conceptual and nonconceptual content, the global nonconceptualist believes that only the latter is needed.

Of course, while the explanatory value of conceptual content (senses) may be denied, the nonconceptualist is committed to the explanatory value of the genus, namely, content. In the absence of such a commitment, her debate with the conceptualist would be pointless. It would be like arguing for a distinction between witchcraft and sorcery without believing in magic. Who, then, might be excluded from the debate? The most obvious candidate is the eliminative materialist (see, e.g., Churchland 1981 and Churchland 1986). Eliminativists, at least those who claim that minds are nothing but functioning brains and that behavior can be explained without recourse to any intentional contents, regard mental states with content as relics of an outmoded folk theory. This theory, they contend, will eventually be replaced by a mature psychology based on developments in neurophysiology, cognitive science, and so on. If the eliminativist's claims were correct, the debate would be undermined since any content, whether conceptual or nonconceptual, would be considered a fiction or falsehood and thus denied an explanatory value. Of course, if eliminativism were true, the very moral, political, and social framework in which we live, including the honor we bestow on authors, athletes, and scientists for the books they write, the records they break, and the cures they discover, would be undermined. It would be an upheaval that, as Fodor puts it, "would be, beyond comparison, the greatest intellectual catastrophe in the history of our species" (Fodor 1987, p. xii).

This is not to say that the conceptualist and nonconceptualist must be committed to the reality of contents. It is enough to grant them an explanatory value (see, e.g., Wright 1993, p. 317). The gap between reality and explanatory value is occupied by noncognitivists who maintain that a discourse may have a value without making claims about reality. Emotivists, for example, maintain that our moral practices can be made sense of without positing moral facts. The significance of ideas like right and wrong, according to an emotivist, has nothing to do with the denotation of properties and everything to do with the expression of attitudes or feelings. Instrumentalists similarly maintain that intentional idioms don't denote actual properties. Their value is wholly linked to the role they play in explaining human action (see Dennett 1981b and 1987a).

While instrumentalists are not without problems (see, e.g., Stich 1981, Fodor and Lepore 1993, Baker 1994), their unwillingness to endorse the reality of intentional content doesn't prevent them from staking a position in the conceptual/nonconceptual debate. Within the context of an instrumentalism, the emphasis of the debate merely shifts from the ontological to the pragmatic. Hence, rather than set out to establish the reality of contents that violate one of Frege's principles, a nonconceptualist would instead attempt to illustrate the explanatory value of adopting the "nonconceptual stance." It is, of course, unlikely that an instrumentalist would try to demonstrate this in the course of naturalizing intentionality in the way realists like Stalnaker and Peacocke do. But this need not keep an instrumentalist from considering nonconceptual content indispensable. As long as the explanatory value of intentionality is recognized, a contrast between the conceptual and nonconceptual is potentially significant.

Although the focus of the anthology is on intentional psychology, anyone participating in analogous debates should likewise be committed to either a realism or instrumentalism about content. In other words, whether one's focus is on intentional psychology, mysticism, existentialism, aesthetics, or so forth, one must reject content eliminativism. With that said, the Fregean framework I've outlined can be utilized irrespective of one's disciplinary focus. For, as I hope is now apparent, any argument should

(1) fix a principle for conceptual content and a rendering of "non,"
(2) cite an intentional state (event, experience, etc.) whose content violates the principle, and
(3) ensure that the intentional state (event, experience, etc.) in question has an explanatory value.

Hence, to extend the framework to, for example, the philosophy of art involves, first, settling on a principle for fixing concepts and a rendering of "non," next, considering whether the content of an aesthetic experience—of natural beauty, music, or tragedy—violates the principle on which one's settled, and finally, justifying the existence and/or significance of this experience.

The Fregean framework is, I believe, one rather compelling way of making the claims of the nonconceptualist more explicit and her debate with the conceptualist more tractable. It is a way of not only airing but grounding the intuitions that many of us share with those of the greater tradition.[14]

Notes

1. I say "suggest" because, given the cultural, temporal, and linguistic distance of many of these texts, far greater sensitivity and care to issues of translation and interpretation (historical, socio-political, philosophical, etc.) would be required for anything more.

2. While "ontological" and "logical" are often freely substituted in this context, strictly speaking the former concerns the structure of what the content is about and the latter the structure of the content itself. Generally, to say that a content has a propositional (logical) structure is to say that it exhibits or can be expressed by a subject-predicate form. Although different in kind, ontological and logical structures are often assumed to be isomorphic (an assumption, though, rarely supported). For claims about ontological and/or logical structures that allegedly differ from those involving propositions, see Tye 1991 on maps, Wollheim 1993 and Lopes 1996 on pictures, Heidegger 1936 and Langer 1953 on artworks, and Heidegger 1927, Ryle 1949, and Dreyfus 1991 on practical knowledge.

3. I am not suggesting that there aren't practical considerations that have led philosophers to focus on truth conditions. In part, the focus is due to the prioritization of indicatives (sentences that have truth conditions), which itself is motivated by their integral role in communication and predicate calculus, as well as the tradition's fixation on metaphysical truth. Yet, while this may help to explain why philosophers focus on truth conditions, it doesn't warrant the claim that all propositional contents have truth conditions essentially.

4. A word about terminology. Occasionally, participants in this debate speak about the conceptuality or nonconceptuality of intentional *states* rather than *contents*, using locutions like "conceptual state" or "nonconceptual representation." As I hope is clear, the debate between conceptualists and nonconceptualists concerns the kinds of contents such states bear, not, strictly speaking, the kinds of states (representations, attitudes, etc.) that they are. In cases where locutions like "conceptual state" or "nonconceptual representation" are used, they are best treated as shorthand for "intentional state with conceptual content" or "representation with nonconceptual content."

5. While consistency is a norm governing content, there is a debate about whether it governs all or merely some content. For a defense of the latter, see Crane's "The Waterfall Illusion" (essay 10); for a defense of the former, see Gunther 2001.

6. Evans and McDowell offer an alternative reading of Frege which interprets the relationship between sense and reference more intimately. Senses are regarded as object-dependent and thus inseparable from their reference. See Evans 1982, chapters 1–3 and McDowell 1986. While intriguing, the view is problematic for various reasons and is unlikely to have been held by Frege himself. See, e.g., Bell 1990.

7. While the controversy between Fregeans and Millians is far from resolved, it need not directly concern us here. After all, the appeal to Frege is intended as a way of fixing the conceptual and distinguishing it from the nonconceptual, *not* as the paradigm for individuating intentional content generally.

8. There are at least two fundamental differences between systematicity and recombinability. First, systematicity is more often than not treated as an empirical property, whereas recombinability is considered metaphysical. And second, those who advocate a Language of Thought thesis tend to cite systematicity as something the thesis is uniquely able to explain (see, e.g., Fodor and Pylyshyn 1988) By contrast, those who speak about recombinability tend to avoid any specific commitment to the thesis by identifying compositionality with structured mental abilities or capacities rather than symbols or elements. As Evans puts it, "I should prefer to explain the sense in which thoughts are structured, not in terms of their being composed of several distinct *elements*, but in terms of their being a complex of the exercise of several distinct conceptual *abilities*" (Evans 1982, p. 101; essay 2, p. 67).

9. This intentional state is generally regarded as a personal-level as opposed to a subpersonal-level state. See Dennett 1969, pp. 93ff. for the distinction.

10. Admittedly, the rational constraint that the strong construal places on conceptual content is limited. For example, from the principle it does not follow that an individual could not have two separate contradictory beliefs, viz. a belief that *Fa* and a belief that *not-Fa*, or mixed contradictory states, e.g., a belief that *Fa* and a hope or perception that *not-Fa*. Nor does it rule out cases involving a single belief with contrary predicates, e.g., *a* is green all over and *a* is red all over, or logically contradictory predicates, e.g., *a* is a triangle and *a* is not a trilateral.

11. Compare this to Peacocke's Identification Principle: "Possessing a concept is knowing what it is for something to be its semantic value" (1992b, p. 23).

12. I don't thereby mean to suggest that contemporary Millians don't have accounts of error.

13. (3) could be divided into two principles, viz. (3a) . . . if an individual *does not exercise* the concepts involved in its articulation; and (3b) . . . if an individual *cannot exercise* the concepts involved in its articulation. I've chosen not to distinguish (3a) and (3b) because nonconceptualists are generally unclear about why concepts are not exercised. Moreover, further distinctions between different senses of "cannot" could be made in both (1) and (3), e.g., between a logical and physical impossibility. In fact, if Sidney Morgenbesser is right, there are seventeen senses of "can," and thus at least as many senses of "cannot."

14. For the sake of consistency in this anthology, all spelling has been Americanized and all instances of "non-conceptual" have been replaced with "nonconceptual."

Part I

Preliminaries

The essays in the opening section have had considerable influence in shaping the contemporary debate on nonconceptual content. As among the earliest proponents of nonconceptualism, Dretske and Evans adopt approaches that later theorists have amended, supplemented, and even embraced outright. On the other hand, as its most prominent and outspoken critic, McDowell presents an alternative model of experience and thought with which nonconceptualists (and conceptualists alike) have been forced to reckon. In many respects, the tone of today's debate has been set by these three philosophers.

Dretske's contribution offers a suggestive distinction between two ways of "coding" information (content), the digital and the analog. A signal (state, event, etc.), according to Dretske, carries information that s is F in digital form if, and only if, it carries no additional information about s, no information that is not already nested in s's being F. If information other than s is F is contained in a signal, information more fine-grained than or distinct from it, then the information is considered analog in form. Thus, while both a picture and a sentence may tell us that Patricia has brown hair, a picture may also reveal its length, style, coarseness, and so on, suggesting an analogical encoding of information. Dretske claims that the digital/analog distinction helps to explain the difference between the contents of higher cognitive states and those of perceptions. Like pictures, perceptions carry a richness of information that, in the course of mental processing, is "pruned away and discarded," leaving higher cognitive states with information digital in form.

Analogically encoded content is nonconceptual because an individual cannot or does not recognize or classify all of what she perceives. In short, the richness of perceived detail suggests that the perceptual content violates the Principle of Reference Determinacy, recognitionally construed. Moreover, Dretske seems to have the third rendering of "non" in mind. For example, it isn't that what one perceives cannot be conceptualized nor is it that one necessarily lacks the conceptual apparatus to discriminate or recognize it (although, admittedly, these may be factors). Rather, the nonconceptuality of our perceptual content results from our inability to apply our conceptual apparatus to everything we perceive. If all of our perceptual contents were (wholly) conceptual, we would "require gigantically large storage and retrieval capabilities," which of course, as human beings, we lack.

In the excerpt from *Varieties of Reference*, Evans attempts to clarify and secure Russell's distinction between demonstrative and descriptive identification. He is specifically concerned with showing how perception makes "pure" demonstrative thought possible, that is, the recognition or identification of spatiotemporal particulars independently of *any* descriptions. According to Evans, perception is necessary though not sufficient for an object's demonstrative identification. In addition to perceiving it, an individual must be able to locate it. For example, in hearing a sound, one hears it coming from a specific direction or position in space. The location of the sound's source, however, is not identified by an individual who calculates the sound's trajectory or formulates a description of its origin. Rather, Evans believes that its location is fixed to a set of axes relative to the individual's body, for example, left/right, front/behind, and up/down.

Nonconceptual content is a feature of the perception that makes pure demonstrative identification possible. Since the location of the referent (of the demonstrative thought) is part of the perceptual content and since it is not determined by either a belief or description, the content violates Cognitive Significance, weakly construed, and Reference Determinacy, descriptively construed. Unlike Dretske, however, Evans does not claim that perceptual content violates the recognitional construal of Reference Determinacy. Such a violation effectively constitutes a breech in Russell's Principle, which Evans assumes is a constraint on all content, whether conceptual or nonconceptual (see 1982, p. 89). As for the rendering of "non", he isn't clear whether an individual with nonconceptual content lacks the requisite descriptive resources or whether she cannot or does not exercise them.

In lecture 3 of *Mind and World*, McDowell strives to reestablish a Kantian model of perception that emphasizes the passive operation of concepts in experience. Intent on thwarting the appeals by nonconceptualists to the "Myth of the Given," he identifies and criticizes three arguments for the nonconceptuality of perceptual content presented in *Varieties of Reference*. The first, the argument for fineness of grain, claims that experience presents us with details (e.g., shades of color, shapes of objects, timbres of voices) for which individuals often lack the requisite descriptive resources. The claim is that the contents of perceptual experience violate Reference Determinacy, descriptively construed, along the lines of the second rendering of "non." However, McDowell denies this, suggesting that an adult's mastery of demonstratives such as "this" and "that" can capture (determine) the content of any perceptual experience, however fine-grained.

The second argument McDowell considers is based on belief-independence. The contents of perceptions are thought to differ from those of beliefs or judgments, Evans claims, since the latter are independent of the former. (In this regard, he relies on the weak construal of Cognitive Significance, although he doesn't identify the relevant rendering of "non.") For example, in the Müller-Lyer Illusion, an individual sees one line longer than the other even though she believes they are the same length, suggesting that her perception couldn't merely be a disposition to believe or judge. McDowell agrees that a distinction between belief and perception is in order, that the former involves receptivity and the latter spontaneity: "an active undertaking in which an individual takes rational control of the shape of her thinking." However, he denies that the receptivity/spontaneity distinction should be understood in terms of nonconceptual and conceptual content. According to him, we can acknowledge that perceptions belong to receptivity without abandoning the idea that concepts operate passively in perceptual experience.

The third argument is based on the fact that both human beings and animals have an ability to perceive and that perceptions have content. Like Evans and McDowell, many assume that animals don't have concepts (although the relevant principle and rendering are generally not identified) and that therefore they perceive the world nonconceptually. In light of this, one may be tempted to isolate what we share with animals by factoring out what is unique to us, namely, our possession of conceptual capacities. But McDowell encourages us to resist the temptation, claiming that the view inevitably leads to a dilemma. On the one hand, the nonconceptuality of perceptual content compels the coherentist rightly to deny that states with nonconceptual content can justify beliefs with conceptual content but only at the risk of losing epistemic touch with the world. On the other hand, while the nonconceptualist rightly insists that perception can justify belief, she mistakenly assumes that states with nonconceptual content can do this. McDowell believes that the way out of the dilemma is to insist that perceptual content is conceptual and that perceptions can justify beliefs.

Whether one agrees with McDowell's views about perception or not, his objections and Kantian model of experience pose a worthy challenge to anyone claiming that perceptual content is nonconceptual.

Chapter 1

Sensation and Perception (1981)

Fred Dretske

Information-processing models of mental activity tend to conflate perceptual and sensory phenomena on the one hand with cognitive and conceptual phenomena on the other. Perception is concerned with the pickup and delivery of information, cognition with its utilization. But these, one is told, are merely different stages in a more or less continuous information-handling process.[1] Recognition, identification, and classification (cognitive activities) occur at every phase of the perceptual process. Seeing and hearing are low-grade forms of knowing.

I think this is a confusion. It obscures the distinctive role of *sensory experience* in the entire cognitive process. In order to clarify this point, it will be necessary to examine the way information can be delivered and made available to the cognitive centers without itself qualifying for cognitive attributes—without itself having the kind of structure associated with knowledge and belief. For this purpose we must say something about the different ways information can be coded.

1 Analog and Digital Coding

It is traditional to think of the difference between an analog and a digital encoding of information as the difference between a continuous and a discrete representation of some variable property at the source. So, for example, the speedometer on an automobile constitutes an analog encoding of information about the vehicle's speed because different speeds are represented by different positions of the pointer. The position of the pointer is (more or less) continuously variable, and each of its different positions represents a different value for the quantity being represented. The light on the dashboard that registers oil pressure, on the other hand, is a digital device, since it has only two informationally relevant states (on and off). These states are discrete because there are no informationally relevant intermediate states. One could, of course, exploit the fact that lights have a variable intensity. This continuous property of the signal could be used to represent the *amount* of oil pressure: the brighter the light, the lower the

From *Knowledge and the Flow of Information* (Cambridge, MA: The MIT Press, 1981), pp. 135–153. Reprinted with the kind permission of the author and The MIT Press.

oil pressure. Used in this way the light would be functioning, in part at least, as an analog representation of the oil pressure.

The analog-digital distinction is usually used to mark a difference in the way information is carried about a variable property, magnitude, or quantity: time, speed, temperature, pressure, height, volume, weight, distance, and so on. Ordinary household thermometers are analog devices: the variable height of the mercury represents the variable temperature. The hands on a clock carry information about the time in analog form, but alarm clocks convert a preselected part of this into digital form.

I am interested, however, not in information about properties and magnitudes and the various ways this might be encoded, but in information about the instantiation of these properties and magnitudes by particular items at the source. I am interested, in other words, not in how we might encode information about temperature, but in how we might represent the *fact* that the temperature is too high, over 100°, or exactly 153°. What we want is a distinction, similar to the analog-digital distinction as it relates to the representation of properties, to mark the different way *facts* can be represented. Can we say, for example, that one structure carries the information that *s* is *F* in digital form, and another carries it in analog form?

For the purpose of marking an important difference in the way information can be encoded in a signal or structure, I propose to use the familiar terminology— analog vs. digital— in a slightly unorthodox way. The justification for extending the old terminology to cover what is basically a different distinction will appear as we proceed.

I will say that a signal (structure, event, state) carries the information that *s* is *F* in *digital* form if and only if the signal carries no additional information about *s*, no information that is not already nested in *s*'s being *F*. If the signal *does* carry additional information about *s*, information that is *not* nested in *s*'s being *F*, then I shall say that the signal carries this information in analog form. When a signal carries the information that *s* is *F* in analog form, the signal always carries more specific, more determinate, information about *s* than that it is *F*. Every signal carries information in both analog and digital form. The most specific piece of information the signal carries (about *s*) is the only piece of information it carries (about *s*) in digital form.[2] All other information (about *s*) is coded in analog form.

To illustrate the way this distinction applies, consider the difference between a picture and a statement. Suppose a cup has coffee in it, and we want to communicate this piece of information. If I simply *tell* you, "The cup has coffee in it," this (acoustic) signal carries the information that the cup has coffee in it in digital form. No more specific information is supplied about the cup (or the coffee) than that there is some coffee in the cup. You are not told *how much* coffee there is in the cup, *how large* the cup *is*, *how dark* the coffee is, what the shape and orientation of the cup are, and so on. If, on the other hand, I photograph the scene and show you the picture, the information that the cup has coffee in it is conveyed in analog form. The picture tells you that there is some coffee in the cup by telling you, roughly, how much coffee is in the cup, the shape, size, and color of the cup, and so on.

I can say that A and B are of different size without saying how much they differ in size or which is larger, but I cannot picture A and B as being of different size without picturing one of them as larger and indicating, roughly, how much larger it is. Similarly, if a yellow ball is situated between a red and a blue ball, I can state that this is so without revealing where (on the left or on the right) the blue ball is. But if this information is to be communicated pictorially, the signal is necessarily more specific. Either the blue or the red ball must be pictured on the left. For such facts as these a picture is, of necessity, an analog representation. The corresponding statements ("A and B are of different size," "The yellow ball is between the red and the blue balls") are digital representations of the same facts.

As indicated, a signal carrying information in analog form will always carry some information in digital form. A sentence expressing *all* the information a signal carries will be a sentence expressing the information the signal carries in digital form (since this will be the most specific, most determinate, piece of information the signal carries). This is true of pictures as well as other analog representations. The information a picture carries in digital form can be rendered only by some enormously complex sentence, a sentence that describes every detail of the situation about which the picture carries information. To say that a picture is worth a thousand words is merely to acknowledge that, for most pictures at least, the sentence needed to express all the information contained in the picture would have to be very complex indeed. Most pictures have a wealth of detail, and a degree of specificity, that makes it all but impossible to provide even an approximate *linguistic* rendition of the information the picture carries in digital form. Typically, when we describe the information conveyed by a picture, we are describing the information the picture carries in analog form—abstracting, as it were, from its more concrete embodiment in the picture.

This is not to say that we cannot develop alternative means of encoding the information a picture carries in digital form. We could build a device (a buzzer system, say) that was activated when and only when a situation occurred at the source that was *exactly* like that depicted in the picture (the only variations permitted being those about which the picture carried no information). The buzzer, when it sounded, would then carry exactly the same information as the picture, and both structures (the one pictorial, the other not) would carry this information in digital form. Computer recognition programs that rely on whole-template matching routines approximate this type of transformation. (See Uhr 1973, chap. 2.) The incoming information is supplied in pictorial form (letters of the alphabet or geometric patterns). If there is an exact match between the input pattern and the stored template, the computer "recognizes" the pattern and labels it appropriately. The label assigned to the input pattern corresponds to our buzzer system. The output (label) carries the same information as the input pattern. The information the picture carries in digital form has merely been physically transformed.

As everyone recognizes, however, such template-matching processes have very little to do with genuine recognition. As long as what comes out (some identificatory label) carries *all* the information contained in the input pattern, we have nothing corresponding to stimulus generalization, categorization, or classification. What we want, of course, is a computer program that will "recognize," not just a letter A in *this* type font, in *this* orientation, and of *this* size (the only thing the stored template will *exactly* match), but the letter A in a variety of type fonts, in a variety of orientations, and a variety of different sizes. For this purpose we need something that will extract information the input pattern carries in *analog* form. We want something that will disregard irrelevant features of this particular A (irrelevant to its being an instance of the letter A) in order to respond to those particular features relevantly involved in the pattern's being an instance of the letter A. We want, in other words, a buzzer system that is responsive to pieces of information the pictures (patterns) carry in analog form.

To understand the importance of the analog-to-digital conversion, and to appreciate its significance for the distinction between perceptual and cognitive processes, consider the following simple mechanism. A variable source is capable of assuming 100 different values. Information about this source is fed into an information-processing system. The first stage of this system contains a device that accurately registers the state of the source. The reader may think of the source as the speed of a vehicle (capable of going from 0 to 99 mph), and the first stage of our information-processing system as a speedometer capable of registering (in its mobile pointer) the vehicle's speed. This information is then fed into a converter. The converter consists of four differently pitched tones, and a mechanism for activating these different tones. If the source is in the range 0 to 14, the lowest-pitched tone is heard. A higher-pitched tone occurs in the range 15 to 24, a still higher pitch from 25 to 49, and the highest at 50 to 99. These different ranges may be thought of as the approximate ranges in which one should be in first, second, third, and fourth gear, and the converter a device for alerting novice drivers (by the differently pitched tones) of the need to shift gears. The flow of information looks something like figure 1.1. What I have labeled the "Analog Representation" (the speedometer) carries all the information generated by the variable source. Since the source has 100 different possible states (all equally likely), the speedometer carries 6.65 bits of information about the source. It carries the information that the vehicle is going, say, 43 mph. This information is fed into a converter, and (assuming a speed of 43 mph) the third tone is activated. Since the third tone is activated when, and only when, the vehicle has a speed in the range 25 to 49, this tone carries 2 bits of information about the speed of the vehicle (a reduction of 100 equally likely possibilities to 25).

The output of this system is always less, quantitatively, than the input. Although 6.65 bits of information get in, something less than this comes out. What is gained

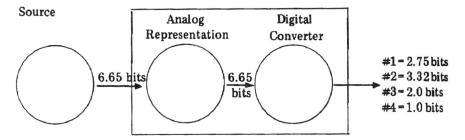

Figure 1.1

by this loss of information is a *classification* (in the various tones) of the *significant ranges* of the input variable. This is a form, albeit a fairly primitive form, of *stimulus generalization*. The output of this system ignores the difference between 43 mph and 32 mph. Both these values are treated as essentially the same. Both activate tone 3. From the point of view of the information the system is designed to communicate, the internal speedometer is an analog representation of the source because it carries more specific, more determinate information about the source than is required to control the system's output. The speedometer "says" that the vehicle is going 43 mph. Nested within this piece of information is the information that the vehicle is going *between* 25 and 50 mph. The digital converter is interested only in the latter piece of information. It "throws away" the more specific piece of information and passes along a piece of information (that the vehicle is going somewhere between 25 and 50 mph) that the speedometer carries in analog form. Of course, the speedometer carries the information that the vehicle is going 43 mph in digital form (since it carries no more specific information about the vehicle's speed), but relative to the information this system is designed to communicate (e.g., whether the speed is between 15 and 24 or between 25 and 49) the speedometer constitutes an analog representation of the state of the source. It is the information the speedometer carries in analog form that the system is *acting* on, that *drives* its motor centers (the various buzzers). The more specific pieces of information it carries are systematically ignored in order to achieve a uniform response to *relevant similarities*.

   To describe a process in which a piece of information is converted from analog to digital form is to describe a process that necessarily involves the *loss* of information. Information is lost because we pass from a structure (the speedometer) of greater informational content to one of lesser information content. Digital conversion is a process in which irrelevant pieces of information are pruned away and discarded. Until information has been lost, or discarded, an information-processing system has failed to treat *different* things as essentially the *same*. It has failed to classify or categorize, failed to generalize, failed to "recognize" the input as being an instance (token) of a more general type. The simple system just described carries out this process in a completely mechanical way. Nevertheless, although it lacks some of the essential features of a genuine perceptual-cognitive system, it illustrates the information-theoretic processes underlying all forms of stimulus generalization, classification, and recognition.

2 Sensory vs. Cognitive Processes

The contrast between an analog and a digital encoding of information (as just defined) is useful for distinguishing between sensory and cognitive processes. Perception is a process by means of which information is delivered within a richer matrix of information (hence in *analog* form) *to* the cognitive centers for their selective use. Seeing, hearing, and smelling are different ways we have of getting information about *s* to a digital-conversion unit whose function it is to extract pertinent information from the sensory representation for purposes of modifying output. It is the successful conversion of information into (appropriate[3]) digital form that constitutes the essence of cognitive activity. If the information that *s* is *F* is never converted from a sensory (analog) to a cognitive (digital) form, the system in question has, perhaps, seen, heard, or smelled an *s* which is *F*, but it has not *seen that* it is *F*—does not *know* that it is *F*. The traditional idea that knowledge, belief, and thought involve *concepts* while sensation (or sensory experience) does not is reflected in this coding difference. Cognitive activity is the *conceptual* mobilization of incoming information, and this conceptual treatment is fundamentally a matter of ignoring differences (as irrelevant to an underlying sameness), of going from the concrete to the abstract, of passing from the particular to the general. It is, in short, a matter of making the analog-digital transformation.

Sensation, what the ordinary man refers to as the look (sound, smell, etc.) of things, and what the psychologist refers to as the *percept* or (in some contexts) the sensory information store (SIS),[4] is informationally profuse and specific in the way a picture is. Knowledge and belief, on the other hand, are selective and exclusive in the way a statement is. "The tapestry of awareness is rich, but the pattern recognition process, dependent on classification, is relatively impoverished in the detail with which it operates" (Pribram 1971, p. 136). Our sensory experience embodies information about a variety of details that, if carried over in toto to the cognitive centers, would require gigantically large storage and retrieval capabilities. (See Anderson and Bower 1973, p. 453.) There is more information in the sensory store than can be extracted, a limit on how much of this information can be exploited by the cognitive mechanisms.[5]

I do not mean to suggest by my comparison of sensory experience to pictures (or cognitive structures with statements) that our sensory experience is always (or *ever*) pictorial or imagistic in character—that the perception of things involves having little images (sounds, smells, tastes) in the head, or that cognitive activity is a linguistic phenomenon. It may be that the acquisition of language is essential to an organism's having the capacity to convert sensory information into digital form (hence the capacity to have beliefs and knowledge), but this, if so, is an empirical question, a question to which I will return in section 3 [not included herein]. For the moment I merely wish to develop the idea that the difference between our perceptual experience, the experience that constitutes our seeing and hearing things, and the knowledge (or belief) that is normally consequent upon that experience is, fundamentally, a coding difference. In this respect the relation between sensory processes and cognitive processes is like the relation between the preliminary analog representation and the subsequent digital representation described in figure 1.1. The speedometer carries the information that the vehicle is going between 25 and 50 mph, and it carries this information in analog form (embedded in the more specific information that the vehicle is going 43 mph), but the particular state of the system that carries this information (the position of the pointer) is not a picture of the vehicle's speed. It does not *resemble* the state of affairs about which it carries information. And the third tone, the one that carries (in digital form) the information that the vehicle is going between 25 and 50 mph, is not a *statement* or *linguistic representation* of the vehicle's speed. The conversion of information from analog to digital form *may* involve a conversion from picture to statement, but it need not. From a neurological point of view the transformation from sensory to cognitive coding takes places in the complete absence of either pictures or statements.

Unlike the simple, mechanical converter described in figure 1.1, however, living systems (most of them anyhow) are capable of modifying their digital-conversion units. As the needs, purposes, and circumstances of an organism change, it becomes necessary to alter the characteristics of the digital converter so as to exploit *more*, or *different*, pieces of information embedded in the sensory structures. Shifts of attention need not (although they may) involve a change in the kind of information made available in the sensory representation. There need not be any change in the way things look, sound, or smell. It may only involve a change in what pieces of information (carried in analog form) are extracted from the sensory representation.

Similarly, learning a concept is a process in which there is a more or less permanent modification of a system's ability to extract analogically coded information from the sensory store. What the simple mechanical system already described lacks is the capacity to change its response characteristics so as to exploit more, or different, pieces of information embodied in the speedometer's registration. It cannot *learn*. There is no way for it to modify the way it digitalizes information so as to respond, say, with tone 3 (or an altogether different tone) when and only when the vehicle is going between 30 and 35 mph. This more specific piece of information is being picked up, processed, and fed into the converter (by the speedometer), but the system is incapable of "attending to" this fact, incapable of extracting this piece of information and "acting" on it. Contrast this with a young child, one whose receptor systems are fully matured and in normal working order, learning to recognize and identify items in her environment. Learning to recognize and identify daffodils, say, is not a process that requires the pickup of more information from (or about) the daffodils. Given the child's keen eyesight, she may already (before learning) be receiving more information from daffodils than her more experienced, but nearsighted, teacher. Still, the teacher *knows* that the flower is a daffodil and the child does not. The child knows only that it is a flower of some sort (perhaps not even this much). What the pupil needs is not more information of the sort that could be supplied by the use of a magnifying glass. She is not *perceptually* deficient. The requisite information (requisite to identifying the flower *as* a daffodil) is getting in. What is lacking is an ability to extract this information, an ability to decode or interpret the sensory messages. What the child needs is not more information about the daffodil but a change in the way she codes the information she has been getting all along. Until this information (viz., that they are daffodils) is recoded in digital form, the child *sees* daffodils but neither knows nor believes that they are daffodils.

The process of digitalization, and how it is related to learning and cognitive activity in general, will be examined at greater length in section 3. For the moment our concern is with the perceptual delivery systems—those systems whose function it is to make available, in our sensory experience, the information on which such cognitive activity depends.

It should perhaps be noted that I am greatly oversimplifying the process by means of which sensory information is extracted from the physical stimulus, integrated with collateral information, and coded in sensory form. I ignore the details of this process in order to highlight an important *difference* in the way this information is coded: a sensory (analog) form and a cognitive (digital) form. In particular, I simply ignore the fact that much of the information embodied in the sensory representation (our sensory experience) is the result of a temporal integration:

> evolution has tuned the human perceptual system to register not the low-grade information in momentary retinal images but rather the high-fidelity information in *sequences of images* or in simultaneous complexes of images—the kind of information given by motion parallax and binocular parallax [Dretske's emphasis].[6]

James Gibson has argued persuasively that much of the information we manage to extract from our environment depends on a strategy of detecting higher-order invariants in a temporal series of signals—the kind of information we are able to pick up by *moving around* and registering the systematic alteration in patterns, textures, and relative positions.[7] To understand how certain sorts of information are registered, it is important to understand the way a sensory representation may be the result of a temporal summation of signals. To think of the processing of sensory information in static terms, in terms of the kind of information embodied in the stimulus *at a particular time,* is to completely miss the extent to which our sensory representations depend on an integrative process *over time.* Even a simple tachometer (depending, as it does, on the *frequency* of pulses) can be used to illustrate the importance of this phenomenon.

I am also ignoring the fact that our sensory representations often carry information derived from a number of different sensory channels. If we considered *only* the stimulus reaching the eyes (even if understood relative to some *temporal interval*), the conclusion would be inevitable that the stimulus is (very often at least) *equivocal*. It would be a mistake, however, to conclude from this that the sensory representation of the source is itself equivocal. For there is no reason to think that our visual experience of the source relies exclusively on the information arriving in the light reaching our *visual* receptors. Quite the contrary. Information about the gravitational orientation of objects is available in the sensory experience because the visual input is processed *jointly* with body-tilt information from proprioceptive sources. Signals specifying the position of the head in relation to gravity, the angular position and movement of the eyes in relation to the head, and the relative position and movement of all other relevant body parts play a role in determining *how* we experience what we experience. The wealth of information available in our sensory experience is to be explained, in part at least, by the fact that this experience embodies information gleaned *over time* from a *variety* of sources.

Important as it is for understanding the actual processes by means of which our sensory experience is produced, and the sorts of mechanisms responsible for the information to be found therein,[8] the details are not directly relevant to our characterization of the result—the sensory experience itself—and the manner in which it codes information. It will be necessary, later in this chapter [not included herein], to look more closely at the machinery for delivering information in order to clarify the nature of the perceptual object and, in particular, the way the constancy mechanisms help to determine *what* we see, hear, and smell. But for present purposes these details can be set aside. Our immediate concern is with the analog character of our sensory experience.

Consider vision. You are looking at a fairly complex scene—a crowd of youngsters at play, a shelf full of books, a flag with all the stars and stripes visible. A reaction typical of such encounters, especially when they are brief, is that one has seen more than was (or perhaps *could be*) consciously noticed or attended to. There were (as it turns out) 27 children in the playground, and though you, perhaps, *saw them all, you* are unaware of how many you saw. Unless you had the time to count, you do not *believe* you saw 27 children (although you may certainly believe something less specific—e.g., that you saw *many* children or *over a dozen* children). You saw 27 children, but this information, precise numerical information, is not reflected in what you know or believe. There is no cognitive representation of this fact. To say one *saw* this many children (without realizing it) is to imply that there was *some* sensory representation of each item. The information *got in*. It was *perceptually* coded. Why else would it be true to say you saw 27 children rather than

26 or 28? Therefore, the information that is cognitively extracted from the sensory representation (the information, namely, that there are *many* children in the yard, or *over a dozen* children) is information that the sensory structure codes in *analog* form. The relationship between your *experience of* the children and your *knowledge of* the children is the same as that between the speedometer and the tone in figure 1.1.

I do not mean to be suggesting that there is a psychophysical correspondence between the information contained in the physical stimulus (or temporal sequence of stimuli) and the information contained in the sensory experience to which that stimulus gives rise. There is obviously a *loss* of information between the receptor surfaces and the internal representation. And conversely, there occurs something that is called "restoration"—an insertion into the sensory experience of representationally significant features that have no counterpart in the physical stimulus (closure of boundaries, restoration of missing sounds, etc.) (Warren 1970, p. 167). If, for example, one saw all 27 children but saw some of them only peripherally (or at dusk), it seems unlikely that information about the color of their clothes would be available in the visual experience. If such color information, contained in the stimulus (light reaching the retina), does not fall on the color-sensitive cones of the fovea, it will obviously not be available in the resulting sensory experience.[9] But even with these peripherally seen children, information about their (rough) relative location, size, spacing, and number *will* be perceptually coded. We may suppose, along with many psychologists, that the preliminary operations associated with the preattentive processes (those which occur prior to the more elaborate perceptual processing associated with focal attention) yield only segregated figural units, units that lack the richness of information available in those portions of the visual field to which attention is given.[10] Still, there is certainly more information embodied in this configuration of "figural units" than we normally extract—information about the spacing, relative size, and position of the objects represented. Typically, the sensory systems overload the information-handling capacity of our cognitive mechanisms so that not all that is given to us in perception can be digested. What is digested are bits and pieces—information the sensory structure carries in analog form.

There is a rule of seven which tells us that there is a certain limit to the rate at which subjects can process information.[11] When information arrives at a rate that exceeds this "capacity," the organism fails to process it. We have already seen ["The Proper Measure of Information" of chapter 2 in Dretske 1981] that the idea of "channel capacity" has no direct application to the amount of information that can be carried by a *particular* signal. It applies only to the *average* amount of information an ensemble of signals can carry. Nevertheless, understood in the correct way, this rule seems to have some rough empirical validity. Its significance should not be misinterpreted, however. If the rule applies at all, it must be understood as applying to our capacity for *cognitively* processing information. It does not apply, and there is no evidence to suggest that it applies (quite the reverse), to our *per-*

ceptual coding of information. The rule represents some kind of limit to how much information we can extract *from* our sensory experience, not a limit to how much information can be contained *in* this experience. It assigns a limit to our capacity to convert information from analog to digital form. Recall the speedometer-buzzer system. A similar limitation applies to this system considered as a whole. Although the input contains 6.65 bits of information about the speed of the vehicle, the output contains, at most, 3.32 bits. The average output is something less than this. But this limit on the information-processing capabilities of this system is a limit that arises as a result of the analog-to-digital conversion mechanism. A full 6.65 bits of information *gets in*. There is an *internal representation* of the speed of the vehicle at all times. Nevertheless, this information is selectively utilized in order to obtain, in the output, a digital representation of certain relevant features of the input. If the rule of seven applies at all, it applies to the input-output relationship. It does not apply to that stage in the process which occurs prior to digital conversion. It does not apply to the sensory coding of information.

J. R. Pierce (1961, pp. 248–249) makes the same point in discussing the informational processing capacity of human subjects.

> Now, Miller's law and the reading rate experiments have embarrassing implications. If a man gets only 27 bits of information from a picture, can we transmit by means of 27 bits of information a picture which, when flashed on a screen, will satisfactorily imitate any picture? If a man can transmit only about 40 bits of information per second as the reading rate experiments indicate, can we transmit TV or voice of satisfactory quality using only 40 bits per second? In each case I believe the answer to be no. What is wrong? What is wrong is that we have measured what gets *out* of the human being, not what goes *in*. Perhaps a human being can in some sense only notice 40 bits second worth of information, but he has a choice as to what he notices. He might, for instance, notice the girl or he might notice the dress. Perhaps he notices more, but it gets away from him before he can describe it.

Pierce is making the point that to measure the amount of information that can flow *through* a subject is to measure the limitation on the *joint* operation of the perceptual and the cognitive mechanisms (not to mention the performative mechanisms). Whatever limits are arrived at by this technique will tell us nothing about the informational limits of our sensory mechanisms. It will give us, at best, the capacity of the *weakest link* in the communication chain, and there is no reason to think that sensation constitutes the weakest link. As Pierce notes, we cannot imitate a picture with only 27 bits of information even though 27 bits of information is about the most that one can *cognitively* process. Our own perceptual experience testifies to the fact that there is more information *getting in* than we can manage to *get out*.

The same point is revealingly illustrated by a set of experiments with brief visual displays (Sperling 1960; see also Averbach and Coriell 1960 and 1961).

Subjects are exposed to an array of nine or more letters for a brief period (50 milliseconds). It is found that *after* removal of the stimulus there is a persistence of the "visual image." Subjects report that the letters appear to be visually present and legible at the time of a tone occurring 150 milliseconds after removal of the stimulus. Neisser has dubbed this iconic memory—a temporary storage of sensory information in perceptual form (Neisser 1967, chap. 2). We need not, however, think of this as the persistence of *an image*. What persists is a structure in which incoming information *about* a pictorial array is coded in preparation for its cognitive utilization. For it turns out that although subjects can identify only three or four letters under brief exposure, *which* letters they succeed in identifying depends on the nature of a later stimulus, a stimulus that appears only 150 milliseconds after removal of the original array of letters. The later stimulus (a marker appearing in different positions) has the effect of "shifting the subject's attention to different parts of the lingering icon." The later stimulus changes the analog-to-digital conversion process: different pieces of information are extracted from the lingering sensory representation.

What these experiments show is that although there is a limit to the rate at which subjects can *cognitively* process information (*identify* or *recognize* letters in the stimulus array), the same limitation does not seem to apply to sensory processes by means of which this information is made available to the cognitive centers. Although the subjects could identify only three or four letters, information about *all* the letters (or at least *more* of the letters) was embodied in the persisting "icon."[12] The sensory system has information about the character of all nine letters in the array while the subject has information about at most four. The availability of this information is demonstrated by the fact that after removal of the stimulus the subject can (depending on the nature of later stimulation) still extract information about *any* letter in the array. Hence, information about *all* the letters in the array must be available in the lingering icon. The visual system is processing and making available a quantity of information far in excess of what the subject's cognitive mechanisms can absorb (i.e., convert to digital form). Our sensory experience is informationally rich and profuse in a way that our cognitive utilization of it is not. Relative to the information we manage to *extract* from the sensory representation (whatever beliefs may be occasioned by having this kind of sensory experience), the sensory representation itself qualifies as an *analog* representation of the source. It is this fact that makes the sensory representation more like a *picture* of, and the consequent belief a *statement about*, the source.[13]

Consider, finally, an example from developmental studies. Eleanor Gibson in reporting Klüver's studies with monkeys describes a case in which the animals were trained to respond to the larger of two rectangles (1969, p. 284). When the rectangles were altered in size, the monkeys continued to respond to the larger of the two—whatever their absolute size happened to be. In the words of Klüver:

If a monkey reacts to stimuli which can be characterized as belonging to a large number of different dimensions, and if in doing so he reacts consistently in terms of one relation, let us say in terms of the "larger than" relation, he may be said to "abstract."

Klüver's monkeys succeeded in abstracting the larger-than relation. But how shall we describe the perceptual situation *before* they learned to abstract this relation. Did the rectangles *look* different to the monkeys? If not, how could they ever learn to distinguish between them? What possible reinforcement schedule could get them to react differently to perceptually indistinguishable elements? It seems most natural to say in a situation of this sort (and the situation is typical of learning situations in general) that prior to learning, prior to successful abstraction of the appropriate relation, the monkey's perceptual experience contained the information that it only later succeeded in extracting. It is possible, I suppose, that the rectangles only *began* to look different to the monkeys after repeated exposures, that the reinforcement schedule actually brought about a perceptual (as well as a cognitive) change.[14] This would then be a remarkable case of perceptual learning (change in the *percept* or sensory representation as a result of training) (Epstein 1967). Perceptual learning may certainly take place, especially with the very young and the newly sighted, and in mature subjects with ambiguous figures[15] but there is no reason to suppose that it is occurring in *every* learning situation with mature subjects. What is taking place here is very much like what takes place with the young child learning to recognize daffodils. The flowers do not look any different; the subject merely learns how to organize (recode) the information already available in its sensory experience.

The situation becomes even clearer if we present the monkeys with three rectangles and try to get them to abstract the "intermediate-size" relation. This more difficult problem proves capable of solution by chimpanzees, but the monkeys find it extremely difficult.[16] Let us suppose that they are incapable of this more sophisticated type of learning. What shall we say about the perceptual situation with respect to the monkeys? Since they have already abstracted the larger-than relation, it may be assumed that they are receiving, and perceptually coding, the information that rectangle A is larger than B, and that B is larger than C. In ordinary terms this is a way of saying that the intermediate rectangle (B) *looks* smaller than the larger (A) and larger than the smaller (C). But information about which rectangle is intermediate, though obviously embedded (in analog form) in the perceptual experience itself, is not (and apparently cannot be) cognitively extracted by the animal. To say that the monkey cannot abstract the intermediate-size relation, therefore, is *not* to say anything about the way it perceptually codes information about figures. Rather, it is to say something about its cognitive limitations. The information is available in analog form in the experience the animal is having of the three rectangles, but the animal is unable to generate an appropriate on-off response, the kind of response characteristic of recognition or identification, to this piece of information. It does not *know* (think, believe, judge) that B is of interme-diate size, even though this information is available in its sensory representation of A, B, and C.[17]

Although our speedometer-tone system cannot learn, its limitations can be use-fully compared with those of the monkey. This simple mechanical system can receive, process, and generate an internal (analog) representation of the fact that the vehicle is going between 30 and 35 mph. The speedometer's registration of (say) 32 mph is an analog encoding of this information. As originally conceived, however, the system as a whole cannot be made to "respond" to this piece of infor-mation. We get the same tone whether the vehicle is going between 30 and 35 mph, slower (down to 25 mph), or faster (up to 49 mph). The problem lies in the system's built-in limitation for converting information from analog to digital form. It can "recognize" a speed as between 25 and 50 mph because this fact, the fact that the speed is within this interval, is information the system is designed to convert into digital form (a distinctive tone).[18] But the system is unable to "rec-ognize" finer details, unable to make more subtle discriminations. It has no *concept* of something's being between 30 and 35 mph, no *beliefs* with this content, no inter-nal structure with this kind of *meaning*.

To summarize, then, our perceptual experience (what we ordinarily refer to as the look, sound, and feel of things) is being identified with an information-carrying structure—a structure in which information about a source is coded in analog form and made available to something like a digital converter (more of this in section 3) for cognitive utilization. This sensory structure or representation is said to be an analog encoding of incoming information because it is always information *embedded in* this sensory structure (embedded within a richer matrix of information) that is subjected to the digitalizing processes characteristic of the cognitive mecha-nisms. Until information has been *extracted from* this sensory structure (digitaliza-tion), nothing corresponding to recognition, classification, identification, or judgment has occurred—nothing, that is, of any *conceptual* or *cognitive* significance.

If perception is understood as a creature's *experience* of his surroundings, then, perception itself is cognitively neutral.[19] Nevertheless, although one can see (hear, etc.) an s which is F (sensorily encode information about s and, in particular, the information that s is F) without believing or knowing that it is F (without even having the concepts requisite to such beliefs), perception itself depends on there *being* a cognitive mechanism able to utilize the information contained in the sensory representation. In this sense, a system that cannot know cannot see; but if the system is capable of knowing, if it has the requisite cognitive mechanisms, then it can see without knowing.[20] A sensory structure that carries the informa-tion that s is F is not to be confused with a belief about s, a belief to the effect that s is F, but to qualify as a *sensory* representation of s (an experience of s), this struc-ture must have a certain function within the larger information-processing enter-prise. It must make this information available to a suitable converter for possible cognitive utilization. . . .

Notes

1. The following is typical: "Sensation, perception, memory and thought must be considered on a continuum of cognitive activity. They are mutually interdependent and cannot be separated except by arbitrary rules and momentary expediency." R. N. Haber, "Introduction" in Haber 1969.

2. The parenthetical "about *s*" is necessary at this point since, as we shall see in chapter 7 of Dretske 1981 [not included herein], information *about s* that is coded in digital form may nonetheless be nested in information about some other item.

3. It is not *merely* the conversion of information from analog to digital form that qualifies a system as a perceptual-cognitive system. The speedometer-buzzer system described above neither *sees* nor *knows* that the vehicle is going between 25 and 49 mph when the third tone is activated. To qualify as a genuine perceptual system, it is necessary that there *be* a digital-conversion unit in which the information can be given a cognitive embodiment, but the cognitive embodiment of information is not *simply* a matter of digitalization. What additional conditions must be satisfied to qualify a structure as a *cognitive* structure (besides digitalization) will be discussed in section 3 [not included herein, see Dretske 1981, chap. 6].

4. It has also been called the *Precategorical Acoustic Store* by R. G. Crowder and J. Morton (1969). Roberta Katzky (1975) notes that the term precategorical is important "because it implies that information held in the registers is not held there as recognized, categorized items, but in raw, sensory form . . . That the sensory registers are precategorical deserves emphasis here, because a central problem in research relating to the registers is the separation of true effects of sensory storage from possible effects of recognized information" (pp. 39–40).

5. In commenting on the SIS (sensory information storage), Lindsay and Norman (1972, p. 329) note that this "discrepancy between the amount of information held in the sensory system and the amount that can be used by later stages of analysis is very important. It implies some sort of limit on the capacity of later stages, a limit that is not shared by the sensory stages themselves."

6. Bower 1972, p. 357. Ulric Neisser also notes that the progressive deletion of microtexture at an edge yields a compelling perception of one surface going behind another and that this kind of information comes into existence only when something moves (it does not exist in the frozen array) (1977, p. 22).

   In a summary of kinetic-size constancy Gunnar Johansson concludes that even under extremely impoverished stimulus conditions the sensory system is capable of extracting sufficient information (for the constancy effect) from *changing* patterns (1977, p. 382).

7. See Gibson 1966 and 1950. There may be some question of whether Gibson's notion of information is the same as that with which we are operating in this work [Dretske 1981]. In a conference on philosophy and psychology (Cornell University, April 2–4, 1976), Ulric Neisser claimed that Gibson's concept of information could be identified with Shannon's. David Hamlyn denied this, and if I understood him correctly, so did Gibson. Yet, the following passage is revealing:

   > Let us begin by noting that *information about* something means only *specificity* to something. Hence, when we say that information is conveyed by light, or by sound, odor, or mechanical energy, we do not mean that the source is literally conveyed as a copy or replica. The sound of a bell is not the bell and the odor of cheese is not the cheese. Similarly the perceptive projection of the faces of an object (by the reverberating flux of reflected light in a medium) is not the object itself. Nevertheless, in all these cases a property of the stimulus is univocally related to a property of the object by virtue of physical laws. This is what I mean by the conveying of environmental information. (Gibson 1966, p. 187)

   This, it seems to me, fully justifies Neisser's judgment. It is, moreover, in reasonably close agreement with the concept of information developed in chapter 3 of the present work [Dretske 1981]. See Neisser 1977 and Hamlyn 1977.

8. The underlying sensory mechanisms may even involve what some investigators (following Helmholtz) are pleased to describe as *computational* or *inferential* processes. Although I see nothing

wrong with using this terminology to describe sensory processes, I think it a mistake to be (mis)led by it into assigning *cognitive* structure to such processes. We may describe sensory phenomena in informational terms, in terms that involve (to this extent at least) a structure's having a *propositional content*, but a structure's having a propositional content we associate with knowledge, belief, and judgment. I return to this point in chapter 7 [Dretske 1981].

9. Which is not to say that peripherally seen things will *look* colorless. This may be viewed as a case of perceptual restoration. The point is, however, that this restoration does not carry *information* about the color of the objects. Similarly, there is a spot on the retina (the blind spot) where the optic nerve leaves the eye which is incapable of picking up information from the stimulus. Nevertheless, if a homogeneous field (e.g., a sheet of white paper) is fixated (with one eye), we do not see a black spot. One should not suppose, however, that this sensory "interpolation" carries information about the stimulus. For, obviously, if there happened to be a black spot at this point in the field, then (under rigorously constricted viewing conditions) we would not see it. This information would be lost.

10. See, for example, Neisser 1967, pp. 94–104. Also see Hebb 1974 (pp. 140–41): "The primitive unity of a figure is defined here as referring to that unity and segregation from the background which seems to be a direct product of the pattern of sensory excitation and the inherited characteristics of the nervous system on which it acts. The unity and distinctiveness of such figures from their background, then, are independent of experience, or 'primitive.'"

11. Miller 1956. The number seven is an index to our capacity for making accurate absolute judgments of unidimensional stimuli. Our common ability to accurately identify any one of several hundred faces, any one of several thousand words, etc., should not be taken as an exception to this "rule." For faces, words, and objects are *multidimensional* stimuli.

12. "It appears as if all of the information in the retinal projection is available in this iconic storage, since the perceiver can extract whichever part is asked for" (Haber and Hershenson 1973, p. 169).

13. Irvin Rock interprets these experiments as suggesting that "in some sense of the term perception, all items in the array are perceived. Some sensory representation of each item endures for a fraction of a second. Perception during that brief period is based on the persistence in the visual system of the neural discharging triggered by the retinal image of the letters even after the letter display is turned off. Unless the items are further processed, however, these sensory representations will quickly fade away" (1975, p. 359). For the sense of the term "perception" in which all items are perceived, see "The Objects of Perception" (Dretske 1981, chapter 6, section 3).

14. But how then explain the different responses? "If experience is to have an effect, there nevertheless must first be a perception of the pattern that is itself *not* a function of experience, and through that perception the relevant memory traces can be activated on the basis of similarity" (Rock 1975, p. 361).

15. See, for example, Steinfeld 1967, pp. 505–522. Also Irvin Rock, "But there is a genuine perceptual change when in viewing potentially familiar figures one goes from an initial 'nonsense' organization to a subsequent 'meaningful' organization. The figure looks different when it is recognized" (Rock 1975, p. 348).

16. E. Gibson 1969, p. 292.

17. In his excellent introductory text, Irvin Rock (1975) is careful throughout to distinguish perceptual and cognitive issues. As a case in point: "learning a discrimination entails more than just perception; cognitive factors are also involved. An animal might perceptually distinguish a triangle and circle from the start, but nevertheless requires training to learn that response to one stimulus is followed by reward whereas response to the other stimulus is not. A human subject might require several trials before realizing that a triangle is always rewarded and a circle is not. *But no one would argue from this fact that on these first few trials the subject did not perceive the forms veridically*" (p. 369) [Dretske's emphasis].

18. I put the word "recognition" in scare quotes because this is *not* a genuine cognitive achievement. No *beliefs* are produced by this simple mechanical system—nothing having the intentional struc-

ture of *knowledge*. For more about what constitutes the distinguishing features of a belief state, see section 3.

19. The word "perception" is often reserved for those sensory transactions in which there is some cognitive uptake (identification, recognition, etc.). The sense of the term I allude to here is the sense in which we can see, hear, and smell objects or events (be aware or conscious *of* them) without necessarily categorizing them in any way. This point is more fully discussed below (next note and the following section of this chapter [latter note included herein]).

20. In *Seeing and Knowing* I argued that seeing *s* (a dog, a tree, a person) was essentially nonepistemic: no *beliefs* were essential to the seeing. Although we (adults) typically acquire a variety of beliefs about the things we see, seeing a dog, a tree, or a person is itself a relationship that is independent of such beliefs—one *can* see *s* without believing that it is *F* (for any value of *F*). My present way of expressing this point is different, but the point remains the same. The only modification consists in the requirement that in order to qualify as a perceptual state (see *s*) a structure must be *coupled* to a cognitive mechanism capable of exploiting the information held in the sensory representation. In this respect my present view is somewhat closer to Frank Sibley's (1971). I am indebted to David Ring for helpful discussion and clarification of this point.

Chapter 2

Demonstrative Identification (1982)

Gareth Evans

---

1 Demonstrative Identification and Perception

Russell introduced us to the idea that demonstrative identification is a mode of identification quite unlike descriptive identification, and to the idea that it is apt to underlie the use of Russellian singular terms. Certainly, as we concentrate upon the standard cases, in which we identify objects in our immediate vicinity, his first contention seems plausible. But in order to go further we must discover what exactly demonstrative identification involves.

It is natural to think that it involves perception. Strawson writes that a subject can identify an object demonstratively if he "can pick out by sight or hearing or touch, or otherwise sensibly discriminate" that object.[1] There must be something correct in what Strawson says, but I do not think we can regard it as a complete account of the notion of demonstrative identification.

In the first place, we need an explanation of exactly how it is that perceiving something makes a thought of a certain kind possible. And as I have urged before (4.1), such an explanation must enable us to understand what unifies demonstrative identification with other modes of identification.

But, secondly, even if we were incurious about this theoretical unification, we should still need to go beyond Strawson's formulation, because the ordinary concept of perception is vague. The core idea is clearly that of an information-link between subject and object, which provides the subject with (nonconceptual)[2] information about the states and doings of the object, over a period of time.[3] But it is quite undetermined by the ordinary concept what kinds of spatial circuitousness and time-lags in the information channel are consistent with the subject's being said to perceive the object. We speak of seeing someone on the television, or hearing him on the radio. We speak of seeing someone in a mirror as well as of seeing his reflection—but only of seeing someone's shadow, not of seeing him in a shadow. We speak without qualification of seeing stars, despite

From *The Varieties of Reference* (Oxford: Oxford University Press, 1982), pp. 143–179, 100–105. Reprinted with the kind permission of Antonia Phillips. Wavy parentheses indicate John McDowell's editorialization, square brackets indicate York Gunther's. Unless otherwise noted, references are to chapter and section number in *The Varieties of Reference*.

the long delay that the channel involves; but we could not speak without qualification of hearing Caruso when we listen to a record.

There is another continuum, one which worried G. E. Moore (see Moore 1918–1919). Moore was fairly sure that if someone pointed in the direction of a beach from a little way offshore, and said "This island is uninhabited," he would have to be understood as referring to the island of which the beach is a part. Continuing this line of thought, Moore arrived at the position that an ordinary demonstrative like "this chair" would have to be understood as referring, "by description," to the chair of which something one could strictly refer to as "this" is a part. The idea was that pure demonstrative identification is possible only of something of which one is aware; and that one cannot, strictly speaking, be aware of something unless one is aware of all of it. Although Moore never gave a very compelling argument for this latter principle, he certainly raised a difficulty, and demonstrative identification must be located on this continuum. Can a person demonstratively identify the room or house in which he is sitting, or the city in which he lives?

When we consider the vagueness of the ordinary concept of perception, we may be unclear what the deliverances of Strawson's formulation are (what its content is). But when we bear in mind the complexity and variety of information-links, we may cease to be sure even of its truth. We do certainly use demonstrative expressions of natural language when watching television or listening to the radio together, but are they to be taken at face value? After all, we use demonstrative expressions very widely to effect what Quine calls "deferred ostension," as when we indicate a man by pointing to his car (Quine 1969, pp. 40–41). "That man is going to be sorry," we say, pointing to a car burdened with parking tickets. Here, surely, the identification is "by description." Is this the model we should follow in the case of the radio and television? It cannot be right, in answering this question, to be content to allow the concept of demonstrative identification to follow wherever the ordinary concept of perception, for whatever obscure reason, leads. The concept of identification is a theoretical concept, connected, via Russell's Principle, to the concepts of thought and judgment. A decision on its extension must take account of these ties. So we are brought back to the question "How does perception make a thought possible?"[4]

2 Information-links Are Not Sufficient

I think that an information-link between a subject and an object is a crucial necessary condition of the mode of identification we are trying to characterize. A demonstrative thought is clearly an information-based thought (one might say, the mother and father of all information-based thoughts); the subject's thinking is governed by a controlling conception[5] he derives from the object. If the question were raised "How do you know there is such a thing as the thing you take yourself to be thinking about" he would answer "I can see" (or "hear," or "taste," or "feel") "that there is." More distinctively, demonstrative thoughts take place in the context of a *continuing* informational link between subject and object: the subject has an evolving conception of the object, and is so situated *vis-à-vis* the object that the conception which controls his thinking is disposed to evolve according to changes in the information he receives from the object. This already imports an element of discrimination, and it rests upon certain very fundamental perceptual skills which we possess: the ability to keep track of an object in a visual array, or to follow an instrument in a complex and evolving pattern of sound.[6]

It is a consequence of this necessary condition that a subject who has a demonstrative Idea of an object has an *unmediated* disposition to treat information from that object as germane to the truth and falsity of thoughts involving that Idea [see note 48]. (When I say that his disposition is unmediated, I mean that it is not the product of any more general disposition to treat as germane to the truth and falsity of those thoughts information received from an object satisfying some condition, together with a recognition that the object satisfies that condition.)[7] To put this in the context of the interpretation of utterances (where it is anyway destined to belong), we can say that a subject who interprets a singular term in an utterance as referring demonstratively to an object will have an unmediated disposition to treat certain present and future informational states, derived from that object, as germane to the truth or falsity of the utterance.[8]

It is very tempting to suppose that the existence, and discriminatory employment, of such an information-link between subject and object is not merely a necessary condition of demonstrative identification, but a sufficient condition of identification; and given that, it would be natural to adopt the view that being based on such an information-link is constitutive of a theoretically well-motivated conception of *demonstrative* identification. The opposing view would be that the sheer existence of an information-link is not sufficient for identification; that even when there is such a link, the object with which the subject has the link can, in certain cases, be thought of only *as* the object serving as input to the information channel: for instance, as the object of which *this* is a photograph, or the object which is responsible for *these* television images. On this opposing position, these thoughts, although dependent on an information-link, do not have the conceptual simplicity of a genuine demonstrative thought: a conceptual element, requiring an idea of the informational situation, must be present. But why (we might wonder) must it be present? Surely, if a person is selectively disposed, *vis-à-vis* an object, to treat its states and doings as uniquely relevant to the truth-value of a proposition, then he thereby shows himself to know which object is in question, whether or not there are circuits and time-lags in the information channel on which this sensitivity depends?[9]

I do not deny that this conception of demonstrative identification is an attractive one, especially if we remember what it is like to watch the television or to listen to the radio. The situation is so like the ordinary one that "this" and "that" pop out without the slightest sense of strain. If the nature of our thoughts could be settled by introspection, the present issue would be settled. Furthermore, if we do not accept this conception of identification, and do suppose that the thought of the information channel must be in the background in cases like the television and radio case, then we are obviously faced with the question why no such thought need be present in the standard case.[10]

Nevertheless, the sheer existence of an information-link between subject and object does not guarantee the possibility of demonstrative thought about the object. So long as we concentrate upon propositions about the object which can be decided as true or false by information accessible via the information channel, there might seem to be no difficulty: the subject's knowledge of what it is for a proposition to be true can be equated, we might suppose (but see section 4), with his practical capacity to decide its truth. But the Generality Constraint must be remembered, and the consequences that were seen to follow from it (4.3) [see the appendix]. If the subject has an adequate Idea of an object, it must be capable of sustaining indefinitely many thoughts about that object. Not only thoughts like "That player has committed a foul," or "That player is good-looking," as a man watches a game of football on the television, must be accounted for, but also thoughts like "That player has influenza," "That player will die of cancer," "That player weighs 20 stone," "That player was born in Liverpool."

I argued in chapter 4 that for our thoughts to have this productive quality, an Idea of an object would need either to be a fundamental identification of that object, or to consist in a knowledge of what it is for an identity proposition involving a fundamental identification to be true. In the case of a spatiotemporal particular, this means that an adequate Idea of an object involves either a conception of it as the occupant of such-and-such a position (at such-and-such a time), or a knowledge of what it is for an object so identified to be the relevant object (or, equivalently, what it is for the relevant object to be at a particular position in space and time).

Now the sheer existence of an information channel does not seem to me to guarantee either of these conditions. It certainly does not by itself provide the subject with a fundamental conception, for it may well not enable him to *locate* the object; while its sheer existence cannot provide the subject with a knowledge of what makes it the case that an object, distinguished as the occupant of a position in space, is that object. The truth of an identity-proposition of the form $\ulcorner \delta = $ that man$\urcorner$ (where "that man" is used of a man seen on television or heard on the radio) can consist in nothing but the fact that δ is a fundamental Idea of a man who is causally responsible for the sounds or images which the subject is perceiving; and so a knowledge of which man is in question can exist only in the presence of the idea of tracing the immediate objects of perception back to their causal source. (I am not suggesting that this idea requires knowledge of the technicalities of wireless transmission.) It is when an information-link *does not provide the subject with an ability to locate the object* that a conceptual element is needed for identification.[11]

It is reported that certain primitive people, when they first heard a radio, were convinced that there was a man inside it whom they could hear. Laboring under this misapprehension, they would naturally attempt to identify the man they thought they could hear, in the standard demonstrative way. Their identification would have no complexity, but nor, in this circumstance, would it be adequate. If they were totally mystified by the apparatus when it was explained to them, and could not understand the idea that they might be hearing a man very distant from them in space (and possibly in time), then I should say that, in this situation, they could form no adequate Idea of the man they could hear at all. They would simply not know what it meant to say, of a man identified at another, possibly distant place, that he was *that* man (the man they heard). To attribute an Idea of an object to someone in this situation would involve attributing to him a totally unmanifestable Idea of the kind against which I railed in 4.6. Of course, we know which man he *means*, which man he has *in mind*, as he gesticulates at the radio, but we shall not be misled by these idioms into thinking that he has the capacity to have particular-thoughts about him. (See *ibid.* 1982, 5.3.)[12]

Given that the existence of an information-link between subject and object is not by itself sufficient for identification, what makes it possible to have, in the standard cases of demonstrative identification, a mode of identification that is free of the conceptual element we have been considering? The answer is that in the standard cases, not only is there an information-link, but also the subject can, upon the basis of that link, *locate the object in space*. I shall now turn to the spelling out of this thought, in order to explain how demonstrative identification in the ordinary case constitutes an adequate Idea of an object. This will require being much more specific about the fundamental level of thought about material objects than I have been up to now.

Before doing so, however, I want to clarify what I have said about thoughts which rely on informational channels involving circuitousness and time-lags. Although a "descriptive" component is required in the Idea involved in such a thought, it would be quite wrong to attempt to assimilate these thoughts to thoughts involving a wholly descriptive identification of an object—even to those thoughts of this kind which are information-based, involving memory and testimony. (See 5.4.) These thoughts constitute a *sui generis* category, which combines features of both kinds of thought—both purely demonstrative thoughts and (information-based) descriptive thoughts. It is thoughts of this *sui generis* kind—requiring the existence and exploitation of an information-link between subject and object—that are required for the understanding of utterances using demonstratives, in the kind of situation we have been considering; such utterances cannot be regarded as just another case of deferred ostension.[13]

3 Egocentric Spatial Thinking: "Here"

We must first understand what is involved in the identification of places. The places which we think about are differentiated by their spatial relations to the objects which constitute our frame of reference. (We here take note of a well-known interdependence between what differentiates objects from one another and what differentiates places from one another.) (See Strawson 1959, p. 37.) Hence a fundamental identification of a place would identify it by simultaneous reference to its relations to each of the objects constituting the frame of reference. A place would be thought about in this way if it was identified on a map which represented, simultaneously, the spatial relations of the objects constituting the frame of reference. This identification has a holistic character: a place is not identified by reference to just one or two objects, and so the identification can be effective even if a few objects move or are destroyed.

Our identification of places has this holistic character whenever we rely, in our thinking about places, upon what has come to be called a "cognitive map": a representation in which the spatial relations of several distinct things are simultaneously represented.[14] It is essential to the existence of a genuine concept of space, and of objects existing in space independently of perception, that the thinker have the capacity to form and employ representations such as these. As we grow up, and as we are educated, the scope of the representations of this kind that we are able to form greatly increases. Of course, we are not able to form fundamental identifications of all the places in the universe—especially in view of the fact that our conception of the world comprises the idea of vast numbers of microscopic objects simultaneously occupying distinct places. But what matters is that we should have the idea of what a fundamental identification of a place involves.

To say that the fundamental level of thought about the spatio-temporal world—the level of thought to which all our other thinking directs us—is thought which would be sustained by a cognitive map of that world is to stress that our fundamental level of thinking is, in a certain sense, "objective." Each place is represented in the same way as every other; we are not forced, in expressing such thinking, to introduce any "here" or "there."[15] (It is often said that in such thinking we are taking the third-person, or God's-eye, point of view, but for a reason I have explained (4.2), I reject this way of looking at the matter. This formulation expresses ideal verificationism; whereas in fact the thinking is truly objective—it is from no point of view.)

With this background, let us turn to those thoughts about places which we typically express with, and require in the understanding of, utterances containing the word "here." One is struck immediately by an important difference between "here"-thoughts and demonstrative thoughts of the kind we have been considering. While the latter are information-based thoughts *par excellence*, the former do not seem to depend necessarily either upon the subject's actual possession of information from the place, or upon the actual existence of an information-link with the place. Thus one can think "I wonder what it is like here" when one is blindfolded, anaesthetized, and has one's ears blocked.[16] I think this observation has led some people to think that the special way of gaining knowledge which we have in virtue of occupying a place is irrelevant to our "here"-thoughts about it, and that in those thoughts we identify the place by description, roughly as *the place I occupy*.

This seems to me to be wrong. Where there is no *possibility* of action and perception, "here"-thoughts cannot get a grip. Consider the philosophers' fantasy of a brain in a vat: a person's thinking organ kept alive and capable of sustaining thoughts, yet with no avenue of perception or mode of action. We can perhaps imagine being the person whose thoughts are sustained in this way (but see 7.6); but in the perpetual darkness and silence of our existence, we could surely have no use for "here." If we knew what had become of us, we could certainly think of a place as the place where the brain which sustains our thoughts is located— but this is a mode of identification of a place quite unlike that expressed by "here."

The suggestion is wrong, anyway, in giving a primacy to "I" over "here." It is not the case that we *first* have a clear conception of which material object in the world we are (or what it would be to establish that), and *then* go on to form a conception of what it is for us to be located at a particular place. It is true that $\ulcorner p =$ here$\urcorner$ is the same thought as $\ulcorner$I am at $p \urcorner$; but this does not mean that I identify *here* as *where I am*. This would raise the question "How do I identify myself, and make sense of my being located somewhere?" but—if we had to keep the capacity to grasp "here"-thoughts out of the picture—would make it impossible to answer it. (See 6.6 and 7.3.)

To understand how "here"-thoughts work, we must realize that they belong to a system of thoughts about places that also includes such thoughts as "It's F *over there*," "It's F *up there to the left*," "It's F *a bit behind me*." "Here"-thoughts are merely the least specific of this series. We may regard this as an *egocentric* mode of thought.

The subject conceives himself to be in the center of a space (at its point of origin), with its co-ordinates given by the concepts "up" and "down," "left" and "right," and "in front" and "behind." We may call this "egocentric space," and we may call thinking about spatial positions in this framework centering on the subject's body "thinking egocentrically about space." A subject's "here"-thoughts belong to this system: "here" will denote a more or less extensive area which centers on the subject.

Egocentric spatial terms are the terms in which the content of our spatial experiences would be formulated, and those in which our immediate behavioral plans would be expressed. This duality is no coincidence: an egocentric space can exist only for an animal in which a complex network of connections exists between perceptual input and behavioral output. A perceptual input—even if, in some loose sense, it encapsulates spatial information (because it belongs to a range of inputs which vary systematically with some spatial facts)—cannot have a spatial significance for an organism except in so far as it has a place in such a complex network of input-output connections.

Let us begin by considering the spatial element in the nonconceptual content of perceptual information. What is involved in a subject's hearing a sound as coming from such-and-such a position in space? (I assume that the apparent direction of the sound is part of the content of the informational state: part of the way things seem to the subject, to use our most general term for the deliverances of the informational system.)

I have already claimed that it is not sufficient for an organism to perceive the direction of a sound that it should be capable of discriminating—that is, responding differentially to—sounds which have different directions. As T. G. R. Bower writes:

> An organism could perfectly well discriminate between values on all the proximal variables that specify position in the third dimension, and yet have no awareness of position in the third dimension *per se*.[17]

When we envisage such an organism, we envisage an organism which can be conditioned to respond differentially to those different values of the proximal stimulus which code the direction of sound, for instance by pressing a button, but in which the difference in stimulus is not connected to any difference in spatial *behavior*. When we hear a sound as coming from a certain direction, we do not have to *think* or *calculate* which way to turn our heads (say) in order to look for the source of the sound. If we did have to do so, then it ought to be possible for two people to hear a sound as coming from the same direction (as "having the same position in the auditory field"), and yet to be disposed to do quite different things in reacting to the sound, because of differences in their calculations. Since this does not appear to make sense, we must say that having spatially significant perceptual information consists at least partly in being disposed to do various things.[18]

This point also comes out very clearly if we reflect upon how we might specify the spatial information which we imagine the perception to embody. The subject hears the sound as coming from such-and-such a position, but how is the position to be specified? Presumably in *egocentric* terms (he hears the sound as up, or down, to the right or to the left, in front or behind). These terms specify the position of the sound in relation to the observer's own body; and they derive their meaning in part from their complicated connections with the subject's *actions*.

Some people, including, apparently, Freud, are able to understand the word "right" only via the rule linking it to the hand they write with. (I suppose a similar defect might force someone to rely on the connection between "down" and the earth's surface—though such a person ought not to travel into space.) But when the terms are understood in this way, they are not suitable for specifying the content of the information embodied in directional perception. No one hears a sound as coming from the side of the hand he writes with, in the sense that in order to locate the sound he has to say to himself "I write with this hand" (waggling his right hand) "so the sound is coming from over there" (pointing with his right hand). Rather, having heard the sound directionally, a person can immediately say to himself "It's coming from over there" (pointing with what is in fact his right hand), and may then reflect as an afterthought "and that's the hand I write with." As Charles Taylor writes:

> Our perceptual field has an orientational structure, a foreground and a background, an up and down. . . . This orientational structure marks our field as essentially that of an embodied agent. It is not just that the field's perspective centers on where I am bodily—this by itself doesn't show that I am essentially agent. But take the up-down directionality of the field. What is it based on? Up and down are not simply related to my body—up is not just where my head is and down where my feet are. For I can be lying down, or bending over, or upside down; and in all these cases "up" in my field is not the direction of my head. Nor are up and down defined by certain paradigm objects in the field, such as the earth or sky: the earth can slope for instance. . . . Rather, up and down are related to how one would move and act in the field.[19]

We can say, then, that auditory input—or rather that complex property of auditory input which encodes the direction of sound—acquires a (nonconceptual) spatial *content* for an organism by being linked with behavioral output in, presumably, an advantageous way. In the case of adult human beings at least, the connection is very complex, for the appropriate behavior in response to a sound at such-and-such a position is, when described in muscular terms, indefinitely various. This is not merely because the behavior may involve the movement of different parts of the body: one can run, walk, crawl, or—as in the case of rats in a famous experiment—swim to a target position. Even if we focus on a particular kind of behavior, such as reaching out with the hand for a rattle heard in the dark, there is a similar kind of complexity, since an indefinite range of reaching responses (identified in muscular terms) will be appropriate, depending on the starting position of the limb and the route it follows (which need not, and often cannot, be the most direct).

It may well be that the input-output connections can be finitely stated only if the output is described in explicitly spatial terms (e.g., "extending the arm," "walking forward two feet," etc.). If this is so, it would rule out the reduction of the egocentric spatial vocabulary to a muscular vocabulary.[20] But such a reduction is certainly not needed for the point being urged here, which is that the spatial information embodied in auditory perception is specifiable only in a vocabulary whose terms derive their meaning partly from being linked with bodily actions. Even given an irreducibility, it would remain the case that possession of such information is directly manifestable in behavior issuing from no calculation; it is just that there would be indefinitely many ways in which the manifestation can occur.[21]

My use of the term "egocentric" is close to its literal meaning, but I do not intend to link my views with any others which have been expressed with the use of the term. Notice that when I speak of information "specifying a position in egocentric space," I am talking not of information about a special kind of space, but of a special kind of information about space-information whose content is specifiable in an egocentric spatial vocabulary. It is perfectly consistent with the *sense* I have assigned to this vocabulary that its terms should *refer* to points in a public three-dimensional space. (Indeed I shall be claiming that that is what they refer to, if they refer to anything at all.)

So far I have been considering the nonconceptual content of perceptual informational states. Such states are not *ipso facto* perceptual *experiences*—that is, states of a conscious subject. However addicted we may be to thinking of the links between auditory input and behavioral output in information-processing terms— in terms of computing the solution to simultaneous equations[22]—it seems abundantly clear that evolution could throw up an organism in which such advantageous links were established, long before it had provided us with a conscious subject of experience. If this point is not immediately obvious, it can be brought out by reflection on the following possibility. A conscious adult may display fairly normal responses to stimuli (including directional responses to spatially varying stimuli), and yet have no associated conscious experience (he might sincerely deny that he is perceiving anything at all). A dramatic illustration is provided by the case of the brain-damaged patient, studied by L. Weiskrantz, who was able to point to a source of light despite claiming that he could not see anything at all.[23]

Reflecting upon this kind of case, philosophers and psychologists have thought that what is required for the application of our intuitive concept of conscious experience is that the subject be able to ascribe the experience to himself—to say or think "I am having such-and-such an experience." If one looks at matters in this way, it is understandable that one should find the distinction between (mere) informational state and conscious experience to be of little interest; for surely, one might think, the experience can antedate thoughts about it.

But although it is true that our intuitive concept requires a subject of experience to have *thoughts*, it is not thoughts about the experience that matter, but thoughts about the world. In other words, we arrive at conscious perceptual experience when sensory input is not only connected to behavioral dispositions in the way I have been describing—perhaps in some phylogenetically more ancient part of the brain—but also serves as the input to a *thinking, concept-applying, and reasoning system*; so that the subject's thoughts, plans, and deliberations are also systematically dependent on the informational properties of the input. When there is such a further link, we can say that the person, rather than just some part of his brain, receives and possesses the information.

Of course the thoughts are not epiphenomena; what a conscious subject does depends critically upon his thoughts, and so there must be links between the thinking and concept-applying system, on the one hand, and behavior, on the other. After all, it is only those links which enable us to ascribe content (conceptual content now) to the thoughts. Further, the intelligibility of the system I have described depends on there being a *harmony* between the thoughts and the behavior to which a given sensory state gives rise. (This will seem adventitious only to those who forget that the concepts exercised in the thoughts are learned by an organism in which the links between sensory input and behavior have already been established.)

I do not mean to suggest that only those information-bearing aspects of the sensory input for which the subject has concepts can figure in a report of his experience. It is not necessary, for example, that the subject possess the egocentric *concept* "to the right" if he is to be able to have the experience of a sound as being to the right. I am not requiring that the content of conscious experience itself be conceptual content. All I am requiring for conscious experience is that the subject exercise some concepts—have some thoughts—and that the content of those thoughts should depend systematically upon the informational properties of the input.[24]

We have not yet built in, or required, in this sketch of the spatial significance of auditory perception, that the subject should be able to hear sounds from different positions simultaneously. But even in the absence of this requirement, we have, in the kind of informational state we have described, a "simultaneous" spatial representation;[25] for the subject hears a sound as coming from one among indefinitely many, simultaneously existing positions which define egocentric space. Moreover, it is easy to understand what is involved in the subject's having a simultaneous spatial representation in the stronger sense that he simultaneously hears two sounds coming from different positions: this requires him to be in a complex informational state the content of which entails the egocentric location of two distinct sounds.

Of course, the spatial information embodied in purely auditory perception is very thin (though we have seen that the input-output connections involved are already very complex). We can enrich the content we have to deal with, and approach closer to an appreciation of the complexity of the input-output connections underlying an ordinary conception of egocentric space, by considering tactile-kinesthetic perception. Although the spatial information which this yields is richer than that available by hearing, and quite different perceptible phenomena are spatially located by it, there is a fundamental point of similarity: the spatial content of tactile-kinesthetic perception is also specifiable in egocentric terms. Indeed, when he uses his hand, a blind person (or a person in the dark) gains information whose content is partly determined by the disposition which he has thereby exercised—for instance, the information that if he moves his hand forward such-and-such a distance and to the right, he will encounter the top part of a chair. And when we think of a blind person synthesizing the information he received, by a sequence of haptic perceptions of a chair, into a unitary representation (a simultaneous spatial representation), we can think of him ending up in a complex informational state which embodies information concerning the egocentric location of each of the parts of the chair: the top *over there to the right* (connected with an inclination to reach out or to point), the back running from *there* to *there*, and so on. Each bit of this information is directly manifestable in his behavior, and is equally and immediately influential (since he is a conscious subject) upon his thoughts. (One, but not the only, manifestation of the latter state of affairs would be his judging that there is a chair-shaped object in front of him.)

The spatial content of auditory and tactile-kinesthetic perceptions must be specified in the same terms—egocentric terms. (Though less of the vocabulary is drawn on in specifying the content of auditory perception.) It is a consequence of this that perceptions from both systems will be used to build up a unitary picture of the world. There is only one egocentric space, because there is only one behavioral space (see Freedman and Rekosh 1968).

Now suppose we have a conscious subject with a conception of egocentric space. We have been considering thoughts with egocentric spatial content, directly linked to the subject's perceptual input; but, given the conceptual equipment whose underpinnings we have been discussing, it seems a clear possibility that a subject might entertain a thought about a position or region in egocentric space whether or not he is currently perceiving it. Consider, for instance, a subject who has placed a bottle of whisky by his bed, and who thinks, in the dark, "There's a bottle of whisky *there*." We are prepared to suppose that there is a determinate thought here—that the subject has a definite place in mind—because we know that subjects do have the capacity to select one position in egocentric space, and to maintain a stable dispositional connection with it. If the subject does have an Idea of a place (does know which place his thought concerns), this will be manifestable only in manifestations of that stable dispositional connection: thus, in his treating certain perceptions from that place as unmediatedly germane to the evaluation and appreciation of any thought involving the Idea, and in his directing actions towards that place[26] when thoughts involving the Idea, together with other circumstances, indicate that this is a good thing to do. These would be manifestations of a complex dispositional connection with the place, and the subject's capacity to entertain thoughts about the place rests upon this dispositional connection with it.[27]

This holds not only for thoughts about specific places and regions in egocentric space, but also for thoughts about the space itself (vaguely conceived)—thoughts expressible with the use of "here," on one interpretation. It is difficult to see how we could credit a subject with a thought about *here* if he did not appreciate the relevance of any perceptions he might have to the truth-value and consequences of the thought, and did not realize its implications for action (consider, for instance, thought like "There's a fire here").

We now have to enquire what makes such Ideas of places in egocentric space adequate Ideas of positions in *public* space. Such an Idea, *p*, is adequate provided the subject can be credited with a knowledge of what it would be for $\ulcorner \pi = p \urcorner$ to be true—where π is a stand-in for an arbitrary *fundamental*, and hence holistic, identification of a place. And it seems that we can presume upon such knowledge. For any subject who is able to think "objectively" about space—any subject who can be credited with a cognitive map of any region—must know what is involved in making precisely such an identification—in imposing his knowledge of the objective spatial relations of things upon an egocentric space. Someone who has a cognitive map of Oxford, for example, must be able to contemplate the imposition of the map in the course of his travels (perhaps in a very dense fog). "If I am here, midway between Balliol and the Bodleian, then that must be Trinity, and so the High must be down there." In such a situation, one may have to choose between several ways of effecting a coincidence between egocentric space and one's conception of objective space. Each way of effecting a coincidence would generate hypotheses about what one should be able to observe if oriented in this or that direction, and what one would observe if one moved in this or that direction. At the same time, of course, each way of effecting the coincidence would entail an identification between every discriminable point in egocentric space and some point in objective space.

It is, then, the capacity to find one's way about, and to discover, or to understand how to discover, where in the world one is, in which knowledge of what it is for identity propositions of the form $\ulcorner \pi = p \urcorner$ to be true consists.

The capacity has some important features and presuppositions. The subject must move continuously through space (if at all); and the course of that movement must (together with how things are disposed in space) determine, and hence be determinable on the basis of the course of the subject's perceptions. It must be possible for the subject to engage in the kind of reasoning exemplified by the following: "If I am between Balliol and Blackwell's (if here = between Balliol and Blackwell's), then that must be Trinity; and if I went on a bit in this direction, then I would be able to see the High" (see, further, 7.3).

It certainly seems that we must be able to attribute this capacity to anyone who has the ability to think about an objective spatial world at all.

On the one hand, such thought presupposes the ability to represent the spatial world by means of a cognitive map. But nothing that the subject can do, or can imagine, will entitle us to attribute such a representation to him if he cannot make sense of the idea that *he* might be at one of the points representable within his map. We say that the subject thinks of himself as located in space (in an objective world that exists independently of him, and through which he moves); only if this is so can the subject's egocentric space be a *space* at all. But what does this thinking of himself as located mean except that the subject can in general regard his situation "from the objective point of view"? And this means that in general he has the ability to locate his egocentric space in the framework of a cognitive map.[28]

On the other hand, the network of input-output connections which underlie the idea of an egocentric space could never be regarded as supporting a way of representing space (even egocentric space) if it could not be brought by the subject into coincidence with some such larger spatial representation of the world as is constituted by a cognitive map. For instance, the subject must be able to think of the relation in which he stands to a tree that he can see as an instance of the relation in which (say) the Albert Hall stands to the Albert Memorial. That is, he must have the idea of himself as one object among others; and he must think of the relations between himself and objects he can see and act upon as relations of exactly the same kind as those he can see between pairs of objects he observes. This means that he must be able to impose the objective way of thinking upon egocentric space.[29]

In view of this, it seems to me that, provided that the subject does maintain a stable dispositional connection with a place, there is just one proposition of the form $\ulcorner \pi = p \urcorner$ (where p is an egocentric spatial Idea) that is true, and the subject knows what it is for it to be true. The qualification is important: if the subject, unbeknownst to himself, is moving in relation to his frame of reference, then there is no one place which he is disposed to regard as germane to the truth of his p-thoughts, or to direct his actions towards on the basis of those thoughts; and so no thought that he might entertain using Ideas from his egocentric repertoire has an object. In this case, the subject's general knowledge of what it is for propositions of the form $\ulcorner \pi = p \urcorner$ to be true would not determine just one proposition of that form as true. (We shall return to this kind of situation shortly.)

For the subject to have a single place in mind, it is not necessary that he remain immobile. We have the ability to *keep track* of a place as we move around; a stable dispositional connection can be maintained, despite changes in circumstances. (The parallel here is with a thought about an object which is moving around, or relative to which one is oneself moving.)

We are now in a position to see why an information-link with a place does not constitute by itself an adequate basis for a knowledge of which place is in question, and this will bring us most of the way to an answer to our question concerning ordinary demonstratives.

There is a possible position about "here"-thoughts which parallels the position we considered in 6.2 [section 2] about demonstrative thoughts. This position would hold that an information-link with a place constitutes an adequate basis for a "here"-identification of a place. One envisages, for example, a television screen showing pictures sent back from a remotely controlled submarine on the sea bed. Some straggly bits of seaweed appear, and so on. It seems that we can throw ourselves into the exploration: "What have we here?," we say, or "Here it's mucky." (We might equally use "there".) The attraction and naturalness of the position matches that of its parallel considered in 6.2 [section 2]. But we are now in a position to see the crucial difference between this and the ordinary case of "here"-thoughts. (This will provide us with the basis of an answer to the question "What makes demonstrative identification possible?")

We have seen that, in the ordinary case, the subject can be said to know which place is in question because he locates it in egocentric space, and his general capacity to find his way about—to unify egocentric and public space—ensures that his knowledge constitutes an adequate Idea. If the subject, in this non-ordinary case, knows that the information does not concern his immediate environment, he will not locate the place in egocentric space, and so some other mode of identification will be in question. He will think of the place as *where the submarine is*, or *where these pictures are coming from.*[30] If, on the other hand, the information is presented in such a way that the subject is taken in, so that he purports to identify the place in egocentric space, as the natives purported to identify a man in the radio (6.2) [section 2], then, clearly, he will not know which place is in question. The skills he can bring to bear would certainly not lead to the place on the sea bed; at best they would lead to the room in the psychological laboratory, or the cabin in the surface vessel, in which the experiment is being conducted. (We would not need to say that his thoughts concerned this place: this is a case of a thought which is not well-grounded (5.4, case (2).)

It might be thought that what is missing from this case which forces the conclusion that either the thoughts are not well-grounded, or else they include a conceptual ingredient that is no part of ordinary "here"-thoughts—is something corresponding to the *action* element in the underpinnings of an ordinary "here"-Idea. (With this in mind, one might say: a subject's identification of places in egocentric space depends upon a harmony which exists in the normal case between his perceptions and his actions, but which has been distorted in the experiment, just as it has been in a case in which a subject wears inverting prisms. On this view the conceptual ingredient would be required because any plan of action *vis-à-vis* the place in question—and, equally, *vis-à-vis* the objects there—would have to incorporate a conception of what it would be to go there—to encounter them.)

But I do not think this is correct. Let us elaborate the story, so that the submarine is equipped with limbs, excavators, etc.; and a means of propulsion remotely controllable by the subject. And let us consider a highly trained subject, who can manipulate the limbs thousands of feet below him like the experienced driver of a mechanical excavator. By making this addition, we have certainly added to the strength of the subject's tendency to use "here" and "there." (And equally "this" and "that": "That's a remarkable fish.") The tendency would be especially strong if we insulated the subject from the sounds, smells, sights, and so on around him. Even so, I should want to deny that such a subject is so situated *vis-à-vis* a place that he can think of it with the conceptual simplicity of a "here"-thought.

The subject can *play at* being where the submarine is ("Here it's mucky"); he can *play at* having that mechanical contrivance for his body ("I'll pick up that rock"). But really *he* is (say) in the bowels of a ship on the surface of the water. This is not just one view he can adopt if he likes; it is the view to which everything in his thinking points. And from this perspective a question arises about the place where the objects that he can perceive and manipulate are: a question he need not *permanently pose*, but which he must understand how to answer. Somewhere *out there*, down there—somewhere in a space that has him as its origin—there is a place (a rock, a fish) that he is thinking about. What is it for a place to be *that place*? And it is here—in answering a question that cannot even arise for a subject normally located, perceptually and behaviorally, in his egocentric space—that the extra conceptual ingredient is required.

If *that place* is conceived by him to be real—so that what appears to be happening there is really happening somewhere in a unified space which also contains himself and his actual environment—then it must in principle have a designation in his system of egocentric spatial relations: it must be *down there*, or *far away behind me*, or . . . (and so on indefinitely).[31] And if these are possibilities which he can genuinely grasp, then he must know what it is for a place identified in one of these ways to be *that place*—a knowledge which must bring in a conception of the spatially extended causal processes that underlie his afferent and efferent connections with the place.

By contrast, when a place is located in one's egocentric space—within the space of the possibilities of one's action—its position within the world as one conceives it to be is already known. There is no further question, and hence no need for any conceptual ingredient to enable one to understand how a further question might be answered.

Perhaps we can tell the story of the submarine in such a way that the subject's location in the surface vessel becomes less and less important to him. He does not move; he becomes insensitive to the sounds and smells around him. It might be possible (with enough of this sort of thing, and perhaps some surgical changes) for us to think of the submarine as *his body*. Then the center of his world would be down on the sea bed, and his utterances of "here" and "this" could go direct to their objects without the need for conceptual supplementation. The precise details of this case do not matter; nor does its ultimate coherence. Let us grant that it is coherent; it does not affect the point I am trying to make. For now, of course, any information he received from the surface vessel—some sounds breaking through, say—would have to be thinkable from that vantage point (if incorporated into his thoughts at all). He would think *"Somewhere up there someone is whispering,"* and his grasp of the thought would have a conceptual ingredient (involving the notion of *where my computing center is*). (For more on this sort of case, see 7.6.)

It is not possible for a single subject to think of two (or more) separate places as "here," with the conceptual simplicity of normal "here"-thoughts. The point is not that the attempt to do so will lead to *confusion*. (A subject might simply have the *de facto* capacity to keep his "heres" apart, and to act appropriately, rather as we have a *de facto* capacity to keep our right and left arms apart in thought, and to move them appropriately. We might imagine a switch enabling him to shut out information from one place or the other.) The point is not a practical point but a conceptual point: the subject is supposed to be able to *think*, for instance, "It's warmer here$_1$ than here$_2$," (where both "heres" have the conceptual simplicity of a "here"-Idea), and claim that this is not coherent. The subject must conceive himself to *be* somewhere—at a point in the center of an egocentric space capable of being enlarged so as to encompass all objects. Any position not explicitly conceived in this system of relations must have its location in this system of relations *thinkable*. And this applies to the putative second "here." No single subject can simultaneously perceive and think of the world from two points of view. (The world cannot be *centered* on two different points.) We may imagine that we can understand the envisaged scheme of thought by oscillating between taking *this* place as *here* and taking *that* place as *here*; but, as David Wiggins once said (in a different context), wavering between two options does not constitute a third option (see Wiggins 1967, p. 17).

Let us now take stock. A thought about a position in *egocentric* space (including the utterly non-specific *here*) concerns a point or region of *public* space in virtue of the existence of certain indissolubly connected dispositions, on the part of the subject, to direct his actions to that place, and to treat perceptions of that place as germane to the evaluation and appreciation of the consequences of the thought. This dispositional connection with a place rests upon a vastly complex network of links between perception and action which allows us to speak of the existence of a unified egocentric space, and in this context, the subject may be said to have an adequate Idea of a point in public space in virtue of his general capacity to impose a conception of public space upon egocentric space.

I speak of a *dispositional* connection for full generality, but it must be understood that one is employing precisely the same Idea of a place when the links are merely potential, on the one hand, and when one is in fact receiving information from it and this information is controlling one's thinking (in the sense of 5.1), on the other—i.e. when the disposition is actualized.

This should put in perspective the apparently considerable difference between demonstrative thoughts proper and thoughts about points and areas of egocentric space with which we began this section. In the first place, there are dispositional elements in the case of demonstrative thoughts too. Secondly, the crucial idea of thought being controlled by information received from something (an object, a place) has a part to play in both cases. And the basis for the difference between "this" and "here" is not difficult to find. Conceivably, one might be so related to a material object that one is disposed to treat information from it as peculiarly relevant to certain sorts of thought about it, even though one has at present no information from it. One might, in the dark, be struck with the thought that there is something immediately in front of one's nose: if this was correct, then one might be disposed to respond in a certain way to information one would receive from it if the lights went on. But obviously it is not, in general, possible to *know* that one is dispositionally so related to an object—still less to know that one is remaining dispositionally so related to the same object over a period of time—

without perceiving the object. Places, however, being—how shall we say?—so much thicker on the ground than objects, a subject cannot fail to have a single place as the target of his "here"-dispositions at an instant; and, since it is possible for a subject to know whether or not he is moving (relative to the earth's surface, or something comparable which provides the framework for identifying the place), a subject can know that his "here"-dispositions over a period have concerned the same place, without needing to have perceived the place during the period.

It seems clear that the way in which a subject identifies a place in egocentric space cannot be regarded as a species of *descriptive* identification. The point is implicit in everything that we have said, and does not need to be labored. Thoughts of this kind rest upon dispositions to react in certain ways in, and to events in, one's immediate environment, and these dispositions cannot be guaranteed by the apprehension of any thought involving a descriptive mode of identification—not even an information-based thought of that kind (see 5.4). The only possible doubt that might arise is over "the place where I am," as a candidate formulation of a descriptive mode of identification to be regarded as employed in "here"-thoughts; but we have dealt with this. In the first place, if this is not just the same Idea dressed up in different words, it wrongly suggests a priority of "I" over "here." Secondly, we have insisted that "here"-thoughts are part of a general system of thought, which includes thoughts about any position in egocentric space. Once we see that no descriptive reduction is generally available, there will be little point in adopting this contentious descriptive treatment for just one element in the system.

We seem, therefore, to have in these thoughts the first clear examples of thoughts whose content can be regarded as Russellian. If there is no place thought about, there is no thought at all—no intelligible proposition will have been entertained. If, for example, the subject is moving, unbeknownst to himself, so that there is no one place which he is disposed to treat as the object of his thought, then it will be quite impossible to excogitate, out of, for instance, his gestures, any intelligible thought content for the "here"-thoughts he essays. To do this would require us to be able to formulate a *condition* for a place to be the object of his thought, even though no place is the object of his thought, and to suppose that his thought is that *the place that meets that condition is F.* But this would be possible only if he identified the place by description, which, as we have seen, he does not do.[3?]

4 Demonstrative Identification of Material Objects

We are now in a position to answer the question what makes demonstrative identification of spatially located material objects possible. In the ordinary perceptual situation, not only will there be an information-link between subject and object, but also the subject will know, or will be able to discover, upon the basis of that link, where the object is. Given the subject's general knowledge of what makes propositions of the form $\ulcorner \pi = p \urcorner$ true, for arbitrary π, when p is an Idea of a position in his egocentric space, and given that he has located, or is able to locate, the object in his egocentric space, he can then be said to know what it is for $\ulcorner$This $=$ the object at π now$\urcorner$ to be true (for arbitrary π). Hence he can be said to have an adequate Idea of the object.

Now that we can see that an information-link does not suffice, we may give up any pretense that a knowledge of what it is for "This is F" to be true is—at least in the case of properties assessable on the basis of the information channel—*constituted* by one's ability to decide the proposition's truth-value. Even in these cases one has a clear understanding of the possibility of error. (See, further, 6.5.) [See section 5.]

We can also see more clearly now that a *communicative* notion of "knowing which"—a notion explained in terms of the ability to tell others which (in the sense that they can gain knowledge of which object is in question)—is a superficial notion. Here, and indeed in general, the notion of *understanding* a reference of a certain type is a more fundamental notion than the notion of making a reference of that type, because of the possibility of exploiting an established device of reference in order to manifest the intention to be understood in a certain way, when one is not in a position to understand one's own words in that way (see 3.2, 4.1). Someone may make a demonstrative reference to one of a circle of people surrounding him even when he is blindfolded, simply by pointing in the direction of that person while saying "That person is F." If we focused upon the notion of *making* a demonstrative reference, and took account of this case, we should not even be able to discern any essential connection between demonstrative identification and information-links (see n. 1 above). But if we focus rather on what is involved in *understanding* a demonstrative reference, then that connection—which seems pretty much at the heart of any interesting notion of demonstrative identification—can be preserved. (The description we then give of the blindfolded person's utterance, as one which he is not in a position fully to understand, is neither contrary to reason nor without precedent.)

The importance which being able to locate the object has may encourage the idea that the demonstrative identification of spatially located things can be *reduced* to the identification of positions in egocentric space, so that "this G" would be equivalent to "the G (now) at p." But this does not seem to me to be generally possible. First of all, in a great many cases a subject may make a demonstrative identification of an object without actually knowing where it is. The information-link with the object may *enable* the subject effectively to locate the object without providing very specific information about its location, for example, when one is able to home in upon the beetle eating away in a beam. (The information-link places the subject in a position rather like that of the man who feels something tugging at the end of his fishing line. In such cases we are placed in a position in which we have the *practical ability* to locate the object; it is not necessary to construct some *concept* "the one at the end of my line" in order to allow the subject's thought to reach out to its object, when he can so effectively do so himself.)[33] Secondly, to define "this *G*" in terms of "the *G* now at *p*" would be wrong anyway, because we are certainly able to identify an object upon the basis of perception even when it is moving too rapidly for there to be any question of assigning it a position in egocentric space.

If the suggestion was expressive of the hope that some clear *descriptive* thought can be ascribed to a subject who essays a demonstrative identification but is not in fact perceiving anything, then it is misconceived for another reason. For such egocentric spatial descriptions of objects to be adequate, they would have to be pretty precise. A subject can demonstratively identify and think about one object in an enormous array of closely packed and indistinguishable objects provided, as we say, he keeps his eye upon it. For example, a subject may confront a table-top covered with indistinguishable colored pills, and have the thought that the one that *X* touched is *that* one. Now, in the absence of an object to anchor our dispositions, we can make only rather gross discriminations of areas or regions in egocentric space. Try to concentrate upon a pill-sized region on a white wall in front of you: even if you keep looking, do you have any confidence, at the end of fifteen seconds, that you are still looking at the same region you began with? The Idea of a point *p* in egocentric space, precise enough to be adequate to individuate the pill, exists only because there is something at *p*—the pill—for the subject's perception to latch on to. Consequently it matters little whether we say that the object is thought about primitively, or that it is thought about by the description "the pill at *p*," when we realize that the Idea of *p* depends upon the perception of the pill, and hence is equivalent to the Idea "where that pill is."

I have already anticipated my conclusion: a demonstrative Idea of an object is not reducible to any other sort of Idea, and in particular cannot be regarded as a species of descriptive identification. One has an adequate Idea in virtue of the existence of an information-link between oneself and the object, which enables one to locate that object in egocentric space. (That the Idea is adequate depends on one's ability to relate egocentric space to public space.) Consequently, demonstrative thoughts about objects, like "here"-thoughts, are Russellian. If there is no one object with which the subject is in fact in informational "contact"—if he is hallucinating, or if several different objects succeed each other without his noticing—then he has no Idea-of-a-particular-object, and hence no thought. His demonstrative thought about a particular object relies upon the *fact* of an informational connection of a certain kind, not upon the thought or idea of that connection; hence it is unconstruable, if there is no object with which he is thus connected.[34]

The situation is really very complex, for the information-link on which demonstrative identification proper depends is really serving three functions. In the first place, its previous and present deliverances provide the subject with his governing conception of the object: this is something in common with, for example, thoughts based upon the memory of a perceptual encounter. Second, the subject remains "in contact" with the object, and is thus (unmediatedly) disposed to alter his governing conception in response to certain future information received from the object: this is something in common with the case where the object is identified via a circuitous channel. But, finally, and crucially, the subject is able, upon the basis of the link, to *locate* the object in egocentric space, and thereby in objective space.

I remarked earlier (6.2) [section 2] that demonstrative thoughts (about material objects) take place in the context of a *continuing* information-link between subject and object; and this is the second of the three points I have just mentioned. A demonstrative Idea of an object is something essentially spanning some period of information-gathering. At any moment at which someone has a demonstrative Idea of an object, he will already have some information from the object; he will be currently receiving information from it; and he will be suitably sensitive to future information from it. (A demonstrative Idea looks both backwards and forwards in time.) The special informational relationship in which the subject stands to the object can be manifested in the way he responds to some thoughts of the form "This was *F* a fraction of a second ago," to some thoughts of the form "This is *F* now," and to some thoughts of the form "This will be *F* in a fraction of a second."[35] (In the case of the first of these, the manifestation will consist in the subject's having a view as to the truth or falsity of the thought, on the basis of stimulations received from it a moment before; in the case of the third the manifestation will consist in the subject's being *disposed* to regard certain later stimulations received from the object as germane to the truth or falsity of the thought.)

The fundamental basis, then, of a demonstrative Idea of a perceptible thing is a capacity to attend selectively to a single thing *over a period of time*: that is, a capacity to *keep track* of a single thing over a period of time—an ability, having perceived an object, to identify later perceptions involving the same object over a period of continuous observation. In this respect, a demonstrative Idea of a currently presented material object is quite different from the sort of past-oriented demonstrative Idea that might underlie a thought of something as *that flash* or *that bang*. (If one could construct a present-oriented version of the Idea "that bang," it would constitute a bad model for ordinary demonstrative Ideas.)[36]

The expectations to which the belief "This will be *F*" gives rise (where being *F* is decidable in the sensory modality relevant to the "this"-Idea involved, and the relevant time is in the immediate future) are expectations (as to the occurrence of *F*-relevant sensations) which concern a particular object *directly*. A way of explaining what I mean by "directly" here is as follows: when the expectation is fulfilled, it will not be possible to break down the subject's belief state, manifested now in the judgment "This is *F*," into two components: ⌜This is *F*⌝ and ⌜This = *a*⌝, where *a* is the Idea occurring in the original prediction (or a different Idea suitably related to it). On the contrary, the later judgment manifests the same persisting belief (reinforced by the stimulations in virtue of which the expectation is fulfilled); and it employs the same Idea.

I do not deny that there may be some arbitrariness in arriving at a decision as to when the subsequent verification of a future tense judgment involving a demonstrative does have such an articulation, and when it does not. Perhaps we should discern this articulation when the gap is a matter of minutes. Similarly, when a past-tense judgment is made after a long enough period of observation: in such a case we might see ⌜This was F⌝ as based on ⌜That was F⌝ and ⌜This = that⌝. But what is important is that we cannot apply this procedure generally, supposing our demonstrative Ideas of objects to cover only momentary slices of the objects' histories. Whenever we discern this sort of articulation in the basis for a judgment, we must be prepared for the possibility of error in either component of the articulate basis, and in particular for a case where there is misidentification. But if, in an attempted demonstrative identification, the subject has not maintained contact with a single object over a reasonable period, then we have not a case of misidentification but a case where the subject has no thought at all. He has not momentarily identified a series of different objects, but failed to identify any object at all.

It is important to understand that the ability to keep track of an object must allow both subject and object to move during the period of observation. Note also that it would be quite arbitrary to deny that the same ability can be exercised in cases in which the object disappears momentarily behind an obstacle. (It follows that demonstrative Ideas will shade off, without a sharp boundary, into Ideas associated with capacities to recognize objects. These capacities are discussed in chapter 8.)

We have seen that a demonstrative identification of an object is part of a scheme of thought which also allows for a place to be identified as *here*, and that both must be explained in terms of the position of a subject in a spatial world; hence both are connected with the subject's identification of himself. There should be no fear that we are explaining simple Ideas ("here" and "this") in terms of a less simple one ("I"). Any subject at all capable of thought about an objective spatial world must conceive of his normal experiences as simultaneously due to the way the world is and to his changing position in it (see 6.3, 7.3) [see section 3]. The capacity to think of oneself as located in space, and tracing a continuous path through it, is necessarily involved in the capacity to conceive the phenomena one encounters as independent of one's perception of them—to conceive the world as something one "comes across." It follows that the capacity for at least some primitive self-ascriptions—self-ascriptions of position, orientation, and change of position and orientation—and, hence, the conception of oneself as one object among others, occupying one place among others, are interdependent with thought about the objective world itself.

5 *Some Consequences*

In the light of this analysis, we can answer certain questions which have been raised about demonstrative identification, and draw out certain consequences.

In the first place, we can understand where to locate demonstrative identification on Moore's continuum (see 6.1) [see section 1]. It is certainly not true that we can demonstratively identify only parts of the surfaces of physical things—the remainder having to be identified descriptively, in terms of relations to those parts. We can know, upon the basis of perception, that we are confronting a solid body, and not merely a thin layer (even though we cannot always tell the two situations apart perceptually). Further, and connectedly, we can receive information via perception about the entire solid body: we can come to know that it satisfies predicates like "rolling," "wobbling," "being given to John," "being pre-Columbian." We are therefore not in informational contact solely with the part. Finally, we can certainly often locate the *whole* body in egocentric space; it would not be right in all cases to say that we can be said to know which other parts are in question only *conceptually*, as we should if we attempted to identify a family by reference to one of its members.

Nevertheless, Moore was right, it seems to me, to think that there is some connection between demonstrative identification and awareness (if by this we mean information), and hence that there are limits to demonstrative identification, of the kind which he attempted to impose. Sitting in a room in a house, a subject is not in informational contact with *a city*; if he believes there is a city around him, this belief cannot be based solely upon what is available to him in perception, nor can he make judgments about the city on that basis (save, perhaps, judgments which hold good of it in virtue of the condition of its parts).[37] The first two informational elements (6.4) [section 4] drop out, and only the third—location in egocentric space—applies. So there is no resistance to regarding a thought which might be expressed in the words "This city is F" as equivalent to a thought which might be expressed in the words "The city here is F," which of course has a perfectly determinate content, whether the room is in a city or not. (There need not be a sharp line between those cases which may be regarded as genuinely demonstrative, and those which are to be analyzed on these lines.)

Secondly, it does not appear to be true that demonstrative identification must be accompanied by a *sortal* which sets the boundaries of the thing in space and time. I have allowed (4.3) [see appendix] that a fundamental Idea of an object will involve such a sortal, but a demonstrative identification need not itself constitute a fundamental Idea. It will be adequate, without being fundamental, so long as the subject knows what makes an identity proposition of the form ⌜This = the G at π, t⌝ true, and he can know what makes such propositions true without actually knowing the sort of the thing, provided there is such a thing as *discovering* the sort of a thing, and he knows how to do it.

There is certainly such a thing as discovering the *extent* of a thing—its spatial boundaries. For instance, one sees something half buried in the sand, and wonders

"What is this?" In determining its extent, one will be executing a general routine which reckons a single thing as, roughly, a bounded piece of matter which moves as a piece. Is this the exercise of a sortal concept? Perhaps that of a material body? But if it is, the concept is certainly not one which provides boundaries in time. Moreover, one is not forced to identify such objects as wholes: one can decide to think of a part. And here again, though the boundaries may be delivered by some sortal, they need not be: they can be set quite arbitrarily, as when one focuses upon an area of someone's arm.[38]

The idea of discovering the sort of a thing, identified demonstratively, would not make sense if there was not some ranking of sorts. As Trinculo goes along the beach and espies Caliban for the first time, he asks "What is this?" It must be presumed that "This is a living animal" is (at least) a better answer than "This is a collection of molecules." Similarly, when the fisherman wonders what he has at the end of his line, the answer "A statue" is a better answer than "A piece of clay." Since we seem to know this ranking, it is not important for us to enquire into its principles: a determinate answer can be given to the question "What kind of thing is this?" provided a definitely extended object is indicated, and such an indication does not by itself presuppose any sortal.[39]

It follows that one can discover oneself to be radically mistaken about the object of one's thought. And—thirdly—this point applies not only to mistakes about the sort of thing it is, but also to mistakes resulting from faulty perception. Our conditions for demonstrative identification do not require that the subject's information-link be functioning well—so long as it provides an effective route to the object. He can misperceive its color, or its shape, or get altogether quite a wrong view of the thing, while still having a perfectly clear Idea of which thing is in question. A proposition about a material object, $\ulcorner a$ is $F\urcorner$, where a is a demonstrative Idea, is conceived to be rendered true by the truth of a pair of propositions of the form $\ulcorner \delta$ is $F\urcorner$ and $\ulcorner a = \delta\urcorner$, where δ is a fundamental Idea. That is to say that the object of the demonstrative thought must be conceived to be part of the objectively describable, spatially-ordered world (which is not to say that the object of the thought can be specified, in a content-giving account of the thought, other than demonstratively). But anyone who has the conception of the objective spatial world must know that no experience of his own can suffice for the truth of any proposition of the form $\ulcorner \delta$ is $F\urcorner$, where being F is an objective property;[40] and consequently that no experience of his own can suffice for the truth of the corresponding proposition of the form $\ulcorner a$ is $F\urcorner$. This is so even though someone who essays a "this"-thought must assume that some present experience of his is an experience *of* something, for his "this" to have a referent: he need not assume that the experience is veridical. . . .

Appendix: The Generality Constraint

In discussing the nature of our conceivings we have little enough to go on, but there is one fundamental constraint that must be observed in all our reflections: I shall call it "The Generality Constraint."

It seems to me that there must be a sense in which thoughts are structured. The thought that John is happy has something in common with the thought that Harry is happy, and the thought that John is happy has something in common with the thought that John is sad. This might seem to lead immediately to the idea of a language of thought, and it may be that some of the proponents of that idea intend no more by it than I do here. However, I certainly do not wish to be committed to the idea that having thoughts involves the subject's using, manipulating, or apprehending *symbols*—which would be entities with nonsemantic as well as semantic properties, so that the idea I am trying to explain would amount to the idea that different episodes of thinking can involve the same symbols, identified by their semantic and non-semantic properties. I should prefer to explain the sense in which thoughts are structured, not in terms of their being composed of several distinct *elements*, but in terms of their being a complex of the exercise of several distinct conceptual *abilities*.[41] Thus someone who thinks that John is happy and that Harry is happy exercises on two occasions the conceptual ability which we call "possessing the concept of happiness." And similarly someone who thinks that John is happy and that John is sad exercises on two occasions a single ability, the ability to think of, or think about, John.[42]

Although I think the cases are quite different (for reasons I shall give shortly), we can shed some light on what it means to see a thought as the result of a complex of abilities by appealing to what is meant when we say that the understanding of a sentence is the result of a complex of abilities. When we say that a subject's understanding of a sentence, "Fa," is the result of two abilities (his understanding of "a," and his understanding of "F"), we commit ourselves to certain predictions as to which other sentences the subject will be able to understand; furthermore, we commit ourselves to there being a common, though partial, explanation of his understanding of several different sentences. If we hold that the subject's understanding of "Fa" and his understanding of "Gb" are structured, we are committed to the view that the subject will also be able to understand the sentences "Fb" and "Ga."[43] And we are committed, in addition, to holding that there is a common explanation for the subject's understanding of "Fa" and "Ga," and a common explanation for his understanding of "Fa" and "Fb." Each common explanation will center upon a state—the subject's understanding of "a" or his understanding of "F"—which originated in a definite way, and which is capable of disappearing (an occurrence which would selectively affect his ability to understand all sentences containing "a," or all sentences containing "F").

Similar commitments attach to the claim that the thought that a is F and the thought that b is G are structured. If we make that claim, then we are obliged to maintain that, if a subject can entertain those thoughts, then there is no conceptual barrier, at least, to his being able to entertain the thought that *a* is *G* or the thought that *b* is *F*. And we are committed in addition to the view that there would be a common partial explanation for a subject's having the thought that *a* is *F* and his having the thought that *a* is *G*: there is a single state whose possession is a necessary condition for the occurrence of both thoughts.

The language case is useful also for illustrating this point: each of the abilities involved in the thought that *a* is *F*, though they are separable, can be exercised only in a (whole) thought and hence always together with some other conceptual ability. This is the analogue of the fact that the understanding of a word is manifested only in the understanding of sentences, and hence always together with the understanding of other words.[44]

Although the language case yields these useful analogies, there is a crucial difference, which we might put like this: while sentences need not be structured, thoughts are *essentially* structured. Any meaning expressed by a structured sentence could be expressed by an unstructured sentence. (Think of a one-word sentence introduced by stipulation to have such-and-such a meaning.) But it simply is not a possibility for the thought that *a* is *F* to be unstructured—that is, not to be the exercise of two distinct abilities. It is a feature of the thought-content *that John is happy* that to grasp it requires distinguishable skills. In particular, it requires possession of the concept of happiness—knowledge of what it is for a person to be happy; and that is something not tied to this or that particular person's happiness. There simply could not be a person who could entertain the thought that John is happy and the thought that Harry is friendly, but who could not entertain—who was conceptually debarred from entertaining—the thought that John is friendly or the thought that Harry is happy. Someone who thinks that John is happy must, we might say, have the idea of *a happy man*—a situation instantiated in the case of John (he thinks), but in no way tied to John for its instantiation.[45]

This is a point that Strawson emphasized when he wrote:

> The idea of a predicate is correlative with that of a range of distinguishable individuals of which the predicate can be significantly, though not necessarily truly, affirmed. (Strawson 1959, p. 99)

It is perhaps easier to see the point I am making in the sort of context Strawson was concerned with. We should surely be reluctant to assign the content "I am in pain" to any internal state of a subject unless we were persuaded that the subject possessed an idea of what it is for someone—not necessarily himself—to be in pain, and unless we were persuaded that the internal state in question involved the exercise of this idea.

What we have from Strawson's observation, then, is that any thought which we can interpret as having the content *that a is F* involves the exercise of an ability—knowledge of what it is for something to be *F*—which can be exercised in indefinitely many distinct thoughts, and would be exercised in, for instance, the thought that b is F. Similarly for the thought that a is G. And this of course implies the existence of a corresponding, kind of ability, the ability to think of a particular object. For there must be a capacity which, when combined with a knowledge of what it is in general for an object to be F, yields the ability to entertain the thought that a is F, or at least a knowledge of what it is, or would be, for a to be F. And this capacity presumably suffices to yield a knowledge of what it is, or would be, for a to be G, when combined with a knowledge of what it is for an object to be G for any arbitrary property of being G.[46]

Thus, if a subject can be credited with the thought that a is F, then he must have the conceptual resources for entertaining the thought that a is G, for every property of being G of which he has a conception. This is the condition that I call "The Generality Constraint."[47]

Using what I hope is a harmless piece of convenient terminology, I shall speak of the Ideas a subject has, of this or that particular object, on the model of the way we speak of the concepts a subject has, of this or that property.[48] And I shall allow myself to say that this or that particular thought-episode comprises such-and-such an Idea of an object, as well as such-and-such a concept. This is simply a picturesque way of rephrasing the notion that the thought is a joint exercise of two distinguishable abilities. An Idea of an object, then, is something which makes it possible for a subject to think of an object in a series of indefinitely many thoughts, in each of which he will be thinking of the object in the same way.[49]

It is not difficult to find work which infringes the Generality Constraint.[50] There is a danger of infringing it whenever attention is focused exclusively upon the question "What makes it the case that a person's *belief* is about such-and-such an object?" For example, Keith S. Donnellan has proposed an answer to that question along these lines: a belief state naturally expressed in the words "a is F" is about the object x if and only if x is the object causally responsible—in an appropriate way—for this belief of the subject's that something satisfies "F" (see Donnellan 1972). Presumably a thought expressive of this belief state would also be about the object the belief is about; and this might clearly yield a violation of Russell's Principle, interpreted as requiring discriminating knowledge. However, if we take Donnellan's line, we shall have treated only of a very restricted class of thoughts, namely those expressive of beliefs; and this in itself is an infringement of the Generality Constraint. Whenever we consider putative counter-examples to Russell's Principle, we must remember that we are concerned not with a single thought, still less with a single belief, but with an Idea of an object which is to be capable of yielding indefinitely many thoughts about it, entertained in other modes than as expressive of belief.[51]

Perhaps it ought to be conceded that the Generality Constraint is an ideal, to which our actual system of thoughts only approximately conforms. But the possibility of vagueness and indeterminacy is not important for present purposes.

Notes

1. *Individuals*, p. 18. John Wallace has recently challenged this connection. He writes: "Most of us are inclined to suppose that there are close connections between demonstration and perception; some of these could be brought out by principles of the form: If conditions are C, then if a person makes a statement which demonstrates an object, the person perceives that object. But I do not know how to spell out the conditions. One has to remember that one can point out distant objects with eyes closed and ears plugged, that blind people can point out the moon, etc." (Wallace 1979, p. 319). But the connection between demonstrative singular terms and perception comes out if we ask what is required in order to *understand* an utterance accompanied by one of these pointing gestures. It is necessary to perceive the object pointed out (to make it out), and to have the thought, about the object thus distinguished, that the speaker is saying of it that it is thus and so. Here again (see 4.1), the central concept is not that of *making* a reference of such-and-such a kind, but that of *understanding* one.

2. For the distinction between conceptual and nonconceptual information, see 5.2, 6.3 [section 3], 7.4.

3. See Austin 1962. Austin seems to make it a necessary condition of perceiving an object that the link be continuous over a period and capable of yielding information about changes in the object.

4. I find little in recent work on the theory of reference which can assist us with this question. Some philosophers have thought to look to the notion of pointing; but this produces a notion of demonstrative identification of extreme heterogeneity and of questionable theoretical interest. Other philosophers have been content to rest upon an unexplained notion of "demonstration"; but this can hardly be satisfactory.

5. On the idea of a controlling conception, see 5.1. Remember (5.2) that we are concentrating on pure cases for the moment: we should think of cases in which the subject's identification of the object of his thought is wholly demonstrative (he neither recognizes it, nor identifies it as something of which he has heard).

6. The notion of an information-link, broad though it is, does place certain restrictions on the application of the notion of demonstrative identification, in view of the *belief-independence* of information (see 5.2) [see also essay 3, pp. 84–87]. This means that we cannot speak of an information-link when there is any process of *inference* on the part of the subject (even though the cognitive state that results in such cases may be causally dependent upon an object, and count as knowledge of it). Gilbert Harman (see *Thought*, chap. 11) would say that what I call "belief-independence" is the consequence of certain inferential processes being automatic and not (or no longer) subject to a person's control. However, it seems to me to be entirely proper to refuse to ascribe such inferences to the *subject*, even if, for whatever reason, one wishes to ascribe them to his brain or nervous system. This distinction is all-important when one wants to give an account of what it is that the *subject* is thinking.

7. {If we take the condition of being such-and-such a particular object as a limiting case of a condition, this rules out the case where the disposition is mediated by the operation of a recognitional capacity.}

8. In fact, in many cases demonstrative interpretation will require the subject to appreciate the relevance, to the truth of a remark, of certain past informational states. A remark may come in the middle of a period of observation of an object. If the subject does not have the capacity to interpret it in the light of past informational states from that object, but takes account of past informational states from another object, then we shall want to deny that he knows which object is in question. (We should realize that we have made a slight alteration to our conception of information-based thoughts. A thought should be seen as information-based, not just when it rests on a certain body of information, but when it rests on a certain information-link. An Idea of an object rests upon, or is associated with, an information-link just in case the subject is so disposed that bits of information delivered by the link will enter the conception that controls thoughts involving the Idea.)

9. Notice the similarity to the verificationist conception of demonstrative identification sketched in 4.2.

10. Russell, as we know, thought it had to be present in all cases in which the object identified was not a private, mind-dependent item. He thought this because in all such cases error, and hence doubt, is possible, and where doubt is possible, the thought "Does this G really exist?" must be intelligible. (See 2.2.) He held that a genuine demonstrative Idea of an object could not exist if there were no object of which it was an Idea; consequently any employment of such an Idea commits the thinker to there being an object of which it is an Idea. It would follow that the Idea involved in the thought "Does this G really exist?" could not be a genuine demonstrative Idea. Russell's diagnosis of the situation seems to me to be entirely correct: the Idea involved in the thought "Does this G really exist?" cannot be a demonstrative Idea. But we do not need to suppose that it must be this Idea (whatever it is) that is employed when there is no question of doubt—when one throws oneself into one's thoughts and one's words. (It is true that one thereby exposes oneself to a grave liability of thinking, which we have seen that Russell did not accept as a possibility. But I have dealt with this: see *ibid.*, 2.2.) Throughout this chapter we shall be concerned with ordinary "committed" thoughts. (I discuss existential thoughts in chapter 10.)

11. {The phrase "ability to locate" perhaps contains the germ of an answer to the question why a *visual* information-link is not precisely analogous to a *radio* information-link, given the plausibility of the thought that a subject in visual contact with something cannot be wholly without a conception of the perceptual mechanism involved, just because the object is to some extent spatially remote from him. (Evans raised this as a problem for himself.)}

12. If it is correct that there is an important distinction between the cases of standard and circuitous information-links, then it constitutes a sort of defense of Russell's Principle that we have been able to bring it out. If it is agreed that a sheer information-link is not sufficient for demonstrative identification, how is this thesis to be defended without Russell's Principle? (Notice that the competing position on demonstrative identification, according to which an information-link is sufficient, is a special application of the Photograph Model.)

13. These cases are very similar to what Strawson calls "story-relative identification" (1959, p. 18), where one can identify an object with respect to a framework, but cannot locate the framework.

14. There is a useful survey of the recent literature on this idea in O'Keefe and Nadel 1978. (But for our purposes the psychological literature, which is in general indifferent to the distinction between conceptual and nonconceptual content, needs to be taken with some caution.)

15. It is true that someone can think in this way only if he has a recognitional capacity for the objects and places constituting the framework. {And that if we are not to fall into a difficulty over the possibility of massive reduplication, this must involve his identification of those objects and places being to some extent "egocentric." See chap. 8, appendix and chap. 7, appendix, §3.}

16. We have now what might be regarded as a limiting case of information-based thoughts: the subject's thinking is not necessarily controlled by any conception, but it rests upon an information-link in that the subject is so disposed that his thinking involving the Idea in question will be controlled by information yielded by the link *if any emerges*. (In 5.5 these cases were spoken of as not information-based at all.) For a parallel with "I," see 7.2.

17. Bower 1975, p. 34. Bower credits the point to Irving Rock.

18. The connection of position in the auditory field with dispositions to behavior is well brought out by George Pitcher (1971, p. 189). (Of course the dispositions to behavior are complex: the behavior will be conditional also on other beliefs and desires.)

19. Taylor 1978–1979, p. 154. (Notice that spatial positions are not identified, in the egocentric mode of thought we are considering, by descriptions like "the position three feet in front of my nose." For something that occupies a position so identified, after one has rotated, is not thought of as occupying the same position as something that was three feet in front of one's nose before one rotated. One would have to think in terms of such descriptions if one were free-floating in space; but it is not our usual mode of egocentric spatial thinking.)

20. For the idea of such a reduction, see Poincaré 1958, p. 47.
21. Egocentric spatial terms and spatial descriptions of bodily movement would, on this view, form a structure familiar to philosophers under the title "holistic." For a study of concepts interrelated in this way, see Peacocke 1979.
22. For the mechanism of auditory localization, see, e.g., Lindsay and Norman 1972, pp. 178–188. For an expression of addiction, see Fodor 1975, pp. 42–53. One of the disadvantages of the addiction is that it tends to blur the distinction I am trying to explain.
23. Weiskrantz, Warrington, Saunders and Marshall 1974. "But always he was at a loss for words to describe any conscious perception, and repeatedly stressed that he saw nothing at all in the sense of "seeing," and that he was merely guessing" (p. 721).
24. On perception and conscious experience, see also 7.4.
25. For the distinction between simultaneous and serial spatial concepts, see my "Things Without the Mind," p. 109.
26. A place is the object of one's action (one's action is directed towards the place) just in case the success of one's action depends upon some characterization of that place.
27. The complex dispositional connection involves a sensitivity of thoughts to information from the place, and a disposition to action directed towards the place when one's thoughts make it appropriate. These are two separate prongs of equal status, neither reducible to the other. Both prongs may become, as it were, *merely* dispositional. We have already met the point that the informational connection still obtains even if the subject's senses are not operating; it is a precisely parallel point that the behavioral connection still obtains even if the subject is paralyzed. {For more about how these dispositional connections would figure in a fully explicit account of an Idea, see §2 of the appendix to chap. 7.}
28. "Has the ability" only. Notice that I am not saying that for a subject to be thinking of a particular place as *here*, he must be *exercising* mastery of a cognitive map. (This would rule out an evident possibility of amnesia.) The point is just that the capacity to think of a place as *here* requires the *ability* to apply cognitive maps.
29. A parallel to the point made here is provided by kinaesthetic perception of a limb, and in fact by the subject's body image in general. We might speak of the body image as representing a space— the body space. But certainly we have no right to speak of a space here unless the subject can impose upon the data of bodily perception his capacity to think objectively about space, so that we have reason to say that he knows that the state of affairs that he feels, when he feels that his leg is bent, is a state of affairs of the very same kind (in the relevant respect) as the state of affairs he observes when he observes a bent stick.
30. Notice that with "where the submarine is," the place is identified by reference to its occupant. This is certainly not how we identify *here* (which would raise the question parallel to "Which submarine?"—"Which person?").
31. The Generality Constraint (4.3) [see appendix of this chapter] is operative here. We shall not attribute "here"-Ideas to a subject who has been trained, e.g., to say "It's hot here" whenever he feels hot. To be credited with the capacity for "here"-thinking he would need to be able to make sense of, e.g., "Was it hot here an hour ago?" (which is not the same question as "Was it hot an hour ago?"). And this will not be possible unless he has the idea of a persisting spatio-temporal world through which he moves continuously.
32. Notice that there are two parts to this point. It is not enough that we be able to formulate, in a vocabulary that we can understand, what it would have been for his thought to have had an object. (No doubt we shall be able to do this: "had he been stationary, . . .") Not only must there be a formulable condition; it must be a condition which can be regarded as being part of the content of the subject's thought.
33. Another case of this kind arises when the subject wears prisms which distort his field of vision— either shifting it to one side or inverting it. In such a situation the subject can give no definite location to an object in egocentric space. Nevertheless he can be said to know which object is in

question—as long as he keeps his eye on it—because he has an effective method for locating the object.

34. Desperate remedies have been adopted to resist this conclusion. For instance, considering a case rather like the one of the pills, Stephen Schiffer (1978, pp. 195–196) suggests that the object would be identified by means of some such description as "the one I have my gaze fixed on." But surely this gets things completely the wrong way round: it is the fact that I have my gaze fixed upon the thing, not the idea that I have my gaze fixed upon something, that determines which object is the object of my thought. And we can drive this point home by a simple dilemma. Either the applicability of the concept "having one's gaze fixed upon ξ" entails the applicability of the concept "thinking of ξ" or it does not. If having one's gaze fixed upon something *does* entail thinking of that thing, then, while it is true that I cannot intelligibly raise the question—in the sort of case Schiffer is considering—"Is this the one I have my gaze fixed on?", the fact is useless; for it cannot be offered as an answer to the question "What makes my thought concern the object it does?" that something is the object of my thought just in case it satisfies the description "the one I am thinking of." If, on the other hand, I can have my gaze fixed upon objects I am not thinking of, then the suggestion falls victim to an Open Question argument; for I can intelligibly raise the question "Is this *the* one I have my gaze fixed on?" (perhaps I have my gaze fixed upon others as well). After one has lost visual contact with the pill, one must surely think of it, if at all, by means of its one distinguishing property: that one was attending to it, or thinking of it, just before. Here there is no circularity; but surely the contrast between the two cases is obvious enough.

35. The thoughts are those that involve suitable replacements for "F": namely, predicates decidable (in a broad sense, accommodating defeasibility) on the basis of the sensory modality involved in the information-link.

36. The difference between keeping track of an object and keeping track of a place underwrites the failure of reducibility between demonstrative Ideas of objects and demonstrative Ideas of places.

37. The situation is different when we are aloft in some high building and can survey the city beneath us.

38. A rather similar case arises when one *sees* something as having certain boundaries. (One does not impose them.) This does affect the question what one is thinking of. Consider a case in which one sees what is in fact the corner of a buried trunk as a pyramid lying on the sand. Demonstrative thoughts based on this perceptual link will not be about the trunk but only about the corner. (We shall not say "He thinks that the trunk is a tiny pyramid.")

39. There is perhaps another reason here for regarding "this city" as not expressing a genuine demonstrative identification; for here the sortal concept is essential to the determinacy of the thought.

40. This is so even if being F is an *observational* property relative to the sensory modality on which the demonstrative Idea in question is based. So it would be a mistake to suppose that the conception of thoughts as being made true by the truth of thought at the fundamental level is involved only when the information-link in question does not prompt a view about the ascription of the relevant predicate.

41. See Geach 1957, esp. chaps. 5, 14.

42. When two thought-episodes depend on the *same* ability to think of something, we can say that the thing is thought about *in the same way*; see the explanation of Frege's notion of sense in 1.5.

43. With a proviso about the categorial appropriateness of the predicates to the subjects; but the substantive point is not affected. A similar proviso is needed at various places below.

44. Waiving qualifications about one-word sentences. Notice that it follows from the point in the text that it is not sufficient, for the claim that a given thought is structured, that it should admit of separate descriptions on the lines of "John is thinking of Harry" and "John is thinking of happiness." It would follow from the applicability of those descriptions that John has the ability to think of Harry and the ability to think of happiness; but it would not follow that he has separate abilities to think of those things.

45. It cannot, therefore, represent any conceptual advance to move to the thought that *some* man is happy—a thought in which the same conceptual ability is exercised in a different thought.

46. We thus see the thought that *a* is *F* as lying at the intersection of two series of thoughts: on the one hand, the series of thoughts that *a* is *F*, that *b* is *F*, that *c* is *F*, and, on the other hand, the series of thoughts that *a* is *F*, that *a* is *G*, that *a* is *H*, . . .

47. Even readers not persuaded that *any* system of thought must conform to the Generality Constraint may be prepared to admit that the system of thought we possess—the system that underlies our use of language—does conform to it. (It is one of the fundamental differences between human thought and the information-processing that takes place in our brains that the Generality Constraint applies to the former but not the latter. When we attribute to the brain computations whereby it localizes the sounds we hear, we *ipso facto* ascribe to it representations of the speed of sound and of the distance between the ears, without any commitment to the idea that it should be able to represent the speed of light or the distance between anything else.)

48. The terminology is borrowed from Geach (1957, pp. 53ff). What are here called "concepts" will also sometimes be called "Ideas." I capitalize the initial letter as a reminder that we are dealing with a technical use of the term.

49. We cannot *equate* an Idea (a particular person's capacity) with a Fregean sense, since the latter is supposed to exist objectively (independently of anyone's grasp of it). But there is a very close relation between them. Two people exercising their (numerically different) Ideas of an object may thereby "grasp" the same Fregean sense. What this means is that they may think of the object in the same way. (And the way of thinking would be available even if no one ever thought of the object in that way.)

50. Note that it is a merit of Dummett's model of sense that it clearly conforms to the Generality Constraint. (See, e.g., *Frege*, p. 238: ". . . to give an account of the sense expressed by such a phrase as 'the author of these works' must be to give a uniform means by which the contribution of that phrase to the determination of the truth-conditions of a sentence in which it occurs can be construed. This will be . . . to fix some route to the determination of the truth-value of any such sentence as in some way preferred . . .")

51. Thoughts not expressive of belief are particularly evident in prudential or moral reasoning. Consider, for instance, a situation in which one contemplates the state of affairs of so-and-so's going around in ignorance of such-and-such, and realizes that one cannot stand the idea. It is worth remembering also that Russell's Principle would apply to desire: one cannot desire that *a* be *F* unless one has a way of distinguishing *a* from all other things.

Chapter 3

Nonconceptual Content (1994)

John McDowell

---

1. I have been talking about a pair of opposing pitfalls: on the one side a coherentism that does not acknowledge an external rational constraint on thinking and therefore, I claim, cannot genuinely make room for empirical content at all; and on the other side a recoil into the Myth of the Given, which offers at best exculpations where what we need is justifications. I have urged that the way to stop oscillating between those pitfalls is to conceive empirical knowledge as a cooperation of sensibility and understanding, as Kant does. To avoid making it unintelligible how the deliverances of sensibility can stand in grounding relations to paradigmatic exercises of the understanding such as judgments and beliefs, we must conceive this cooperation in a quite particular way: we must insist that the understanding is already inextricably implicated in the deliverances of sensibility themselves. Experiences are impressions made by the world on our senses, products of receptivity; but those impressions themselves already have conceptual content.

This unqualified claim that the content of perceptual experience is conceptual will have been raising some eyebrows since my first lecture. Here I am going to defend it against some doubts.

Before I start, let me note that the issue cannot be defused as just a matter of idiosyncratic terminology on my part—as if I am merely affixing the label "conceptual" to the content of experience, although I regard the content of experience in the very way that my opponents express by saying that it is not conceptual, at least not through and through. It is essential to the picture I am recommending that experience has its content by virtue of the drawing into operation, in sensibility, of capacities that are genuinely elements in a faculty of spontaneity. The very same capacities must also be able to be exercised in judgments, and that requires them to be rationally linked into a whole system of concepts and conceptions within which their possessor engages in a continuing activity of adjusting her thinking to experience. Indeed, there can be other elements in the system

From *Mind and World* (Cambridge, MA: Harvard University Press, 1994), pp. 46–65. Reprinted with the kind permission of the author and Harvard University Press. Unless otherwise noted, all references McDowell makes to his own work are to *Mind and World*, and those he makes to Evans's work are to *Varieties of Reference*.

that are not capable of figuring in experience at all. In my last lecture, I claimed that it is only because experience involves capacities belonging to spontaneity that we can understand experience as awareness, or apparent awareness, of aspects of the world at all. The way I am exploiting the Kantian idea of spontaneity commits me to a demanding interpretation for words like "concept" and "conceptual." It is essential to conceptual capacities, in the demanding sense, that they can be exploited in active thinking, thinking that is open to reflection about its own rational credentials.[1] When I say the content of experience is conceptual, that is what I mean by "conceptual."

2. To focus the discussion, I am going to consider what Gareth Evans says about this question.

Evans makes the equally unqualified claim that the content of perceptual experience is nonconceptual. According to Evans, conceptual content first comes into play, in the context of perception, in judgments based on experience. When one forms a judgment on the basis of experience, one moves from nonconceptual content to conceptual content.

> The informational states which a subject acquires through perception are *nonconceptual,* or *nonconceptualized* judgments *based upon* such states necessarily involve conceptualization: in moving from a perceptual experience to a judgment about the world (usually expressible in some verbal form), one will be exercising basic conceptual skills. . . . The process of conceptualization or judgment takes the subject from his being in one kind of informational state (with a content of a certain kind, namely, nonconceptual content) to his being in another kind of cognitive state (with a content of a different kind, namely, conceptual content).[2]

These nonconceptual informational states are the results of perception's playing its role in what Evans calls "the informational system" (p. 122). The informational system is the system of capacities we exercise when we gather information about the world by using our senses (perception), receive information from others in communication (testimony), and retain information through time (memory). (See pp. 122–129.)

It is central to Evans' view that "the operations of the informational system" are "more primitive" than the rationally interconnected conceptual skills that make room for the notion of judgment and a strict notion of belief (p. 124).[3] To put the thought in the terms I have been using: the operations of the informational system are more primitive than the operations of spontaneity. This point is straightforward in the case of perception and memory, which, as Evans says, "we share with animals" (p. 124); that is, with creatures on which the idea of spontaneity gets no grip. Strikingly, he insists on the point for testimony too: "the mechanism whereby we gain information from others . . . is already operative at a stage of human intellectual development that pre-dates the applicability of the more sophisticated notion" (p. 124). His thought here is that for much of the knowledge that one has by virtue of having been exposed to statements of it, one was not in a position to understand the statements at the time.

Evans, then, identifies perceptual experiences as states of the informational system, possessing content that is nonconceptual.[4] According to Evans, conceptual capacities are first brought into operation only when one makes a judgment of experience, and at that point a different species of content comes into play. Contrast the account I have been urging. According to the picture I have been recommending, the content of a perceptual experience is already conceptual. A judgment of experience does not introduce a new kind of content, but simply endorses the conceptual content, or some of it, that is already possessed by the experience on which it is grounded.[5]

It is important not to misconceive this divergence. In Evans' view, experiences are states of the informational system, and as such they have content that is non-conceptual. But he does not equate the idea of an experience with the idea of a perceptual informational state, produced independently of spontaneity by the operations of the informational system. On the contrary, he insists that perceptual informational states, with their nonconceptual content, "are not *ipso facto* percep-tual *experiences*—that is, states of a conscious subject" (p. 157) [essay 2, p. 52]. According to Evans, a state of the perceptual informational system counts as an experience only if its nonconceptual content is available as "input to a *thinking, concept-applying*, and *reasoning system*" (p. 158) [essay 2, p. 52]; that is, only if its nonconceptual content is available to a faculty of spontaneity, which can ratio-nally make or withhold judgments of experience on the basis of the perceptual state. So a nonconceptual informational state, produced by the perceptual element of the informational system in a creature that lacks a faculty of spontaneity, does not count as a perceptual experience, even though a state that does count as a per-ceptual experience, by virtue of its availability to spontaneity, is in itself just such a nonconceptual informational state, endowed with its nonconceptual content independently of the coming into play of the faculty of spontaneity.

3. Near the end of my first lecture (§7), I noted a difficulty it would be natural to feel when one sets out to apply to "inner experience" the picture I have been rec-ommending of experience in general, according to which experiences are states or occurrences in which conceptual capacities are drawn into operation. I have been claiming that it is essential to conceptual capacities that they belong to spontane-ity, that is, to a faculty that is exercised in actively self-critical control of what one thinks, in the light of the deliverances of experience. But that means we cannot attribute the conceptual capacities that would figure in the account of "inner expe-rience" I have endorsed—for instance, a capacity to use the concept of pain—to many creatures of which it could be outrageous to deny that they can feel pain. It is not just active self-critical thinkers that can feel pain. Whatever it may be that is true of a creature without spontaneity when it feels pain, it cannot be that it

has "inner experience," according to the picture of experience I have been recommending.

This point is obviously not peculiar to "inner experience." The application to "outer experience" is similar: "outer experience" that supports to disclose that things are thus and so is, according to the account I am recommending, a state or occurrence involving the operation of the conceptual capacities that would be actively exploited in judging that things are thus and so. In that case "outer experience" can be attributed only to a creature that could engage in such active thinking. So we have a parallel point in this case: I am committed to denying "outer experience" of features of their environment to some creatures, even though it would be outrageous to deny that they are perceptually sensitive to those features. It is not just active self-critical thinkers that are perceptually sensitive to features of their environment.

At this stage I am simply acknowledging this twin discomfort, not aiming to alleviate it; I shall make an attempt at that later (lecture 6). One straightforward response would be to conclude that the notion of experience needs to be completely detached from anything on the lines of the notion of spontaneity. Then we would not be committed to having different stories to tell about the sentient lives of rational and non-rational animals. My point now is just that anyone who is tempted by this course cannot easily enrol Evans as an ally. In his picture as in mine, the concept of experience has a restricted use, governed by a link of a broadly Kantian sort to what is in effect the idea of spontaneity.

4. I have been concerned in these lectures with a standing threat of falling into philosophical anxiety. If we focus on the freedom implied by the notion of spontaneity, what was meant to be a picture of thinking with empirical content threatens to degenerate into a picture of a frictionless spinning in a void. To overcome that, we need to acknowledge an external constraint on the exercise of spontaneity in empirical thinking. But now we come to the other side of the standing difficulty: we must avoid conceiving the external constraint in such a way that it could at best yield exculpations where we needed justifications. One might simply refuse to address this difficulty, by refusing to give any place, in an account of experience, to anything like the idea of spontaneity. But as I have just stressed, that is not a line that Evans takes.

To acknowledge the required external constraint, we need to appeal to receptivity. I have urged that the way to introduce receptivity without merely tipping the seesaw back to the Myth of the Given is this: we must not suppose that receptivity makes an even notionally separable contribution to its co-operation with spontaneity.

Now Evans does not respect this rule. In Evans' account of experience, receptivity figures in the guise of the perceptual element of the informational system, and his idea is that the perceptual system produces its content-bearing states independently of any operations of spontaneity. It is true that the content-bearing states that result count as experiences, in the somewhat Kantian restricted sense that Evans employs, only by virtue of the fact that they are available to spontaneity. But spontaneity does not enter into determining their content. So the independent operations of the informational system figure in Evans' account as a separable contribution made by receptivity to its co-operation with spontaneity.

In that case, the way experiences are related to conceptual capacities in Evans' picture is just the way intuitions are related to concepts in the picture of empirical knowledge that Kant, as I am reading him, displays as hopeless, at least as a picture of how things are from the standpoint of experience. It is true that Kant tries to allow a kind of correctness for a picture with that shape at the transcendental level, but Evans' account of experience is not meant to be only transcendentally correct, whatever indeed that might mean. So unless there is something wrong with the Kantian considerations I rehearsed in my first two lectures, Evans' account of experience ought to be demolished by them.

It may be hard to believe that Evans' view of experience is a version of the Myth of the Given. Evans' smoothly naturalistic account of perceptual informational states shows no sign of the epistemological obsessions that are usually operative in motivating the Myth of the Given. What usually underlies the Myth is a worry that spontaneity's involvement in our picture of empirical thought makes it mysterious how we can be picturing something that is in touch with reality at all, and there is no sign of that in Evans.

Moreover, there may seem to be a more specific problem about attributing the Myth of the Given to Evans. If experiences as Evans conceives them are intuitions without concepts, in a sense that would make his position vulnerable to the Kantian attack on the Myth of the Given, they ought to be blind. But Evans takes care to credit experiences with representational content, even independently of the availability to spontaneity in virtue of which they count as experiences. The content is nonconceptual, certainly, but one might wonder how that could warrant the image of blindness. Surely, one might think, something that is blind would have to be totally devoid of representational content?

The structure of Evans' position is comparable to the structure of a position I considered in my first lecture (§5), when I was trying to avert a misinterpretation of what I was recommending. That position purported to accept that conceptual capacities are drawn into operation in experience. But it treated the states and occurrences that it described in those terms as insulated from spontaneity. The aim was to ensure that they were not subject to the potentially unnerving effects of the freedom that the idea of spontaneity implies.

What I said about that position was that in the context of the insulation from spontaneity, the talk of concepts is mere word-play. The point of the claim that experience involves conceptual capacities is that it enables us to credit experiences with a rational bearing on empirical thinking. But the point of the strategy of insulation is that it confines spontaneity within a boundary that leaves experiences outside it. That means that the putatively rational relations between experiences, which this position does not conceive as operations of spontaneity, and judgments, which it does conceive as operations of spontaneity, cannot themselves be within the scope of spontaneity liable to revision, if that were to be what the self-scrutiny of active thinking recommends. And that means that we cannot genuinely recognize the relations as potentially reason-constituting. We cannot put limits on the self-scrutiny of reason. If we want to be able to take it that the operations of conceptual capacities in experience impinge rationally on our thinking, as we must if they are to be recognizable as operations of conceptual capacities at all, we must acknowledge that those rational relations fall within the scope of spontaneity. And it is hard to see how we could acknowledge that while refusing to accept that the perceptual states and occurrences that lie at one end of the relations involve capacities of spontaneity in operation.

Evans' account of experience is not guilty of *that* fraudulent labeling; exactly not, since he keeps concepts out of the content of experience. But the word "content" plays just the role in Evans' account that is played in that position by the fraudulent use of the word "conceptual": that is, to make it seem that we can recognize rational relations between experiences and judgments, so that we can say, as Evans does, that judgments of experience are "based upon" experience (p. 227), even though these relations are supposed to hold across a boundary that encloses spontaneity. The same point should apply here too. If these relations are to be genuinely recognizable as reason-constituting, we cannot confine spontaneity within a boundary across which the relations are supposed to hold. The relations themselves must be able to come under the self-scrutiny of active thinking.

Evans' position has a deceptively innocent look. It can seem obvious that a possessor of one piece of representational content, whether conceptual or not, can stand in rational relations, such as implication or probabilification, to a possessor of another. But with spontaneity confined, we lose the right to draw the conclusion, as a matter of routine, that one term in such a relation can be someone's reason for another. If experience is pictured as input to spontaneity from outside, then it is another case of fraudulent labeling to use the word "content" for something we can even so take experience to have, in such a way that reason-constituting relations can intelligibly hold between experiences and judgments. The label serves to mask the fact that the relations between experiences and judgments are being conceived to meet inconsistent demands: to be such as to fit experiences to be reasons for judgments, while being outside the reach of rational inquiry.[6]

I am claiming that although Evans does take care to credit experiences with content, that does not save them from being intuitions in a sense that entitles us to apply the Kantian tag to them: since they are without concepts, they are blind. And actually there is an interpretation of that claim under which Evans would not dispute it. It was wrong to suggest that experiences as he conceives them cannot possibly be blind, since he equips them with content. It makes all the difference that the content is supposed to be nonconceptual.

How should we cash out the image of blindness? To say that an experience is not blind is to say that it is intelligible to its subject as purporting to be awareness of a feature of objective reality: as a seeming glimpse of the world. And Evans himself insists that that can be so only against the background of an understanding of how perception and reality are related, something sufficient to sustain the idea that the world reveals itself to a perceiving subject in different regions and aspects, in a way that depends on the subject's movement through the world.[7] Such a background can be in place only for a subject with a self-conscious conception of how her experience relates to the world, and we cannot make sense of that in the absence of conceptual capacities in a strong sense, a faculty of spontaneity.[8]

So when Evans says that experiences, considered in themselves, have nonconceptual content, he is not thereby preempting my suggestion that experiences as he conceives them are blind, because they are intuitions without concepts. What makes it intelligible, in his view, that the eyes of empirical thought are opened is not the claim that, even considered in abstraction from any connection with spontaneity, experiences have (nonconceptual) content. It is the claim that that content is available to spontaneity: that it is a candidate for being integrated into the conceptually organized world-view of a self-conscious thinker. I am only stressing an aspect of Evans' own view when I say that, according to him, the item that an experience is, considered in itself (in abstraction from the availability to spontaneity in virtue of which it acquires the title "experience"), is blind.

This would be all right if we could make sense of the potential for rational linkage with a world-view that is supposed to make the item an experience, something that is not blind. But although crediting the items that experiences are with content, independently of their availability to spontaneity, gives the appearance of making room for this connection, I have urged that when the content is said to be nonconceptual, the appearance stands revealed as illusory.

I am not saying there is something wrong with just any notion of nonconceptual content. It would be dangerous to deny, from a philosophical armchair, that cognitive psychology is an intellectually respectable discipline, at least so long as it stays within its proper bounds. And it is hard to see how cognitive psychology could get along without attributing content to internal states and occurrences in a way that is not constrained by the conceptual capacities, if any, of the creatures whose lives it tries to make intelligible. But it is a recipe for trouble if we blur the distinction between the respectable theoretical role that nonconceptual content has in cognitive psychology, on the one hand, and, on the other, the notion of content that belongs with the capacities exercised in active self-conscious thinking—as if the contentfulness of our thoughts and conscious experiences could be understood as a welling-up to the surface of some of the content that a good psychological theory would attribute to goings-on in our cognitive machinery.[9]

5. Why does Evans think he has to locate experiences outside the sphere of the conceptual? If his position is indeed a case of lapsing into the Myth of the Given,

it is a special case. As I said, it does not issue from the usual epistemological motivation, the recoil from a picture that threatens to leave empirical thinking out of touch with reality, and so not recognizable as empirical thinking at all.

One consideration that impresses Evans is the determinacy of detail that the content of experience can have. He claims that this detail cannot all be captured by concepts at the subject's disposal. "Do we really understand the proposal that we have as many color concepts as there are shades of color that we can sensibly discriminate?"[10] Others besides Evans have taken this kind of consideration to require crediting experience with nonconceptual content [see, e.g., essays 1, 5, 6, 9]. This formulation includes people who do not follow Evans in relegating the content of experience completely to the nonconceptual, but aim to accommodate the phenomenological point Evans makes here by saying that the content of experience is *partly* nonconceptual.[11]

When Evans suggests that our repertoire of color concepts is coarser in grain than our abilities to discriminate shades, and therefore unable to capture the fine detail of color experience, what he has in mind is the sort of conceptual capacities that are associated with color expressions like "red," "green," or "burnt sienna." Such words and phrases express concepts of bands on the spectrum, whereas Evans' thought is that color experience can present properties that correspond to something more like lines on the spectrum, with no discernible width.

But why should we accept that a person's ability to embrace color within her conceptual thinking is restricted to concepts expressible by words like "red" or "green" and phrases like "burnt sienna"? It is possible to acquire the concept of a shade of color, and most of us have done so. Why not say that one is thereby equipped to embrace shades of color within one's conceptual thinking with the very same determinateness with which they are presented in one's visual experience, so that one's concepts can capture colors no less sharply than one's experience presents them? In the throes of an experience of the kind that putatively transcends one's conceptual powers—an experience that *ex hypothesi* affords a suitable sample—one can give linguistic expression to a concept that is exactly as fine-grained as the experience, by uttering a phrase like "that shade," in which the demonstrative exploits the presence of the sample.

We need to be careful about what sort of conceptual capacity this is. We had better not think it can be exercised only when the instance that it is supposed to enable its possessor to embrace in thought is available for use as a sample in giving linguistic expression to it. That would cast doubt on its being recognizable as a conceptual capacity at all. Consider undertaking to give expression to a thought in a way that exploits the availability of a sample, by saying (possibly to oneself) something like "My visual experience represents something as being of *that* shade." Suppose we try to hold that this attempted expression of a thought contains an expression of a color concept that is restricted to this occasion of utterance. This looks like Wittgenstein's case of the person who says "I know how tall

I am," putting his hand on top of his head to prove it.[12] The putative thought—"I am *this* tall," "It looks to me as if something is of *that* shade"—is being construed so as to lack the distance from what would determine it to be true that would be necessary for it to be recognizable as a thought at all.

We can ensure that what we have in view is genuinely recognizable as a conceptual capacity if we insist that the very same capacity to embrace a color in mind can in principle persist beyond the duration of the experience itself. In the presence of the original sample, "that shade" can give expression to a concept of a shade; what ensures that it is a concept—what ensures that thoughts that exploit it have the necessary distance from what would determine them to be true—is that the associated capacity can persist into the future, if only for a short time, and that, having persisted, it can be used also in thoughts about what is by then the past, if only the recent past.[13] What is in play here is a recognitional capacity, possibly quite short-lived, that sets in with the experience. It is the conceptual content of such a recognitional capacity that can be made explicit with the help of a sample, something that is guaranteed to be available at the time of the experience with which the capacity sets in. Later in the life of the capacity it can be given linguistic expression again, if the course of experience is favorable; that is, if experience again, or still, presents one with a suitable sample. But even in the absence of a sample, the capacity goes on being exploitable as long as it lasts, in thoughts based on memory: thoughts that are not necessarily capable of receiving an overt expression that fully determines their content.

If such recognitional capacities are conceptual, Evans' question does not have the answer he thinks it does. It is true that we do not have ready, in advance of the course our color experience actually takes, as many color concepts as there are shades of color that we can sensibly discriminate. But if we have the concept of a shade, our conceptual powers are fully adequate to capture our color experience in all its determinate detail.

What reason could there be for refusing to accept that such recognitional capacities are conceptual? They seem perfectly suited to figure in an understanding of how experience takes hold of aspects of the world, on the lines I sketched in my first two lectures. I claimed that we can make sense of this image of experience taking hold of the world, or being open to it, if we suppose that experience involves the operation of capacities that are conceptual, in the sense that they are rationally integrated into spontaneity at large. Evans' phenomenological point is that the world as experience takes hold of it is more finely grained than we could register by appealing only to conceptual capacities expressible by general color words and phrases. Now it is true that the fine-grained capacities I have appealed to have a special character, which is marked by how demonstrative expressions would have to figure in linguistic expressions of them. But why should that prevent us from recognizing them as rationally integrated into spontaneity in their own way, so that they can simply take their place in my general framework? Why, in fact, are they not so much as considered in Evans' argument, and in the appeal by many others to the consideration about fineness of grain that drives Evans' argument?[14]

The very identity of one of these possibly short-term recognitional capacities is tied to a particular case of the kind of impact on sensibility that is supposed to be captured by the associated concept. A capacity to embrace a shade within one's thinking (as *that* shade, we can say in favorable circumstances) is initiated by the figuring of an instance of the shade in one's experience.[15] There is no saying which capacity it is in abstraction from the activating experience itself. That is how these capacities permit the fine-grained sensuous detail that figures in the actual course of visual life to be taken up into the conceptual content of visual experience.

This means that from the standpoint of a dualism of concept and intuition, these capacities would seem hybrids. There is an admixture of intuition in their very constitution, and that might explain why they do not even figure as candidates for being recognized as conceptual. But if that is why Evans' thinking takes the course it does, it is obviously damaging. Evans is trying to enforce a distance between the conceptual, on the one hand, and the world's impact on the senses, on the other. If it is assumed in advance that the role of intuition in their constitution prevents us from counting these capacities as (purely) conceptual, the distance is being presupposed, not argued for. And obviously this ground for refusing to accept that these capacities are conceptual is equally illicit for those who use the fine-grained character of experience to recommend a mixed position, in which the content of experience is partly conceptual and partly nonconceptual.

Evans thinks intuition and concept, dualistically conceived, need to be shared out between experience and judgment. Proponents of the mixed position differ from Evans in thinking intuition and concept can be juxtaposed in experience. In so far as the claim that intuitions, conceived as nonconceptual, must figure in experience is based on the argument from fineness of grain, this mixed position shares its shakiness of foundation with Evans' view. Moreover, by simply juxtaposing the two species of content in experience, the mixed position makes it difficult for itself to accommodate the strong point of Evans' view, the Kantian insight that we need to appeal to conceptual capacities in order to make it intelligible that experience is not blind.[16]

6. A second consideration that Evans appeals to is that states of the informational system are, as he puts it, "belief-independent" (p. 123). The content of a perceptual experience cannot be explained as the content of an appropriate actual belief, since there may be no belief with a suitable content; a familiar visual illusion continues to present its illusory appearance even though the subject does not believe that things are as they look. Some people try to preserve a definitional connection between informational content and belief content, while acknowledging this point, by suggesting that the content of an experience can be captured as something that the experience gives its subject "a *prima facie* inclination to believe"

(p. 124). Evans responds (*ibid.*): "I cannot help feeling that this gets things the wrong way round. It is as well to reserve 'belief' for the notion of a far more sophisticated cognitive state: one that is connected with (and, in my opinion, defined in terms of) the notion of *judgment*, and so, also, connected with the notion of *reasons.*" That is, to put it in the terms I have been using: we should reserve the idea of belief for something that can be understood only in the context of the idea of spontaneity, the idea of an active undertaking in which a subject takes rational control of the shape of her thinking. Not that all one's beliefs are the result of actively making up one's mind. But there is a point in reserving the title of belief for a kind of cognitive state that is essentially within the scope of one's powers of actively making up one's mind; even in the case of a belief that one simply finds oneself with, the question of one's entitlement to it can always be raised. We can sum up what Evans is suggesting about belief by saying that belief is a disposition to make judgments, and judging is essentially an act of spontaneity.

Evans is here insisting that the active business of making up one's mind is the proper context in which to place conceptual capacities, and that is something I have been urging throughout these lectures. But he uses the point as an argument that the content of experience cannot be conceptual, and by my lights that betrays a blind spot. The point does not tell against the conception of experience I have been recommending: a conception according to which capacities that belong to spontaneity are already operative in receptivity, rather than working on something independently supplied to them by receptivity. Evans does not argue against that conception; it simply does not figure among the possibilities he contemplates.

Someone who holds that the content of experience is conceptual, and who places the idea of the conceptual in the right context, must register a link between the conceptual capacities that she takes to be at work in perception and the active exercise of spontaneity in judgments. Evans considers only one way in which one might try to register the link: namely, by identifying experiences with dispositions to make judgments. The idea would be that these dispositions are realized in actual judgments only when an "other things being equal" clause is satisfied. That is how the position accommodates the fact that experience is "belief-independent": other things fail to be equal in the presence of known illusions, and in any other circumstances in which there is experience without the associated belief.

Evans objects that this picture falsifies the phenomenology of perception (p. 229): "The proposal is implausible, because it is not the case that we simply find ourselves with a yen to apply some concept—a conviction that it has application in the immediate vicinity. Nothing could more falsify the facts of the situation." The picture interposes a distance between experience itself and the active employment of concepts in judgment, a distance that is supposed to be bridged by the idea of dispositions. Evans' protest is that, even so, the picture connects the content of experience too closely to active thinking for it to be able to do justice to experience. Suppose the "other things being equal" clause is satisfied, and there is an inclination to apply some concept in judgment. This inclination does not just inexplicably set in. If one does make a judgment, it is wrung from one by the experience, which serves as one's reason for the judgment. In a picture in which all there is behind the judgment is a disposition to make it, the experience itself goes missing.

This is very perceptive, and I think it is devastating to the suggestion that we can bring experience within the scope of a faculty of spontaneity by conceiving experiences as dispositions to make judgments. But the point does not touch the position I am recommending. According to the position I am recommending, conceptual capacities are already operative in experience itself. It is not that actual operations of conceptual capacities first figure only in actualizations of dispositions to judge, with which experiences are identified—so that experience is connected with concepts only by way of a potentiality. Having things appear to one a certain way is already itself a mode of actual operation of conceptual capacities.

This mode of operation of conceptual capacities is special because, on the side of the subject, it is passive, a reflection of sensibility. In the context of that claim, it takes work to ensure that the capacities are recognizable as genuinely conceptual capacities—that the invocation of the conceptual is not mere word-play. What is needed is that the very same capacities can also be exploited in active judgments. And what secures this identification, between capacities that are operative in appearances and capacities that are operative in judgments, is the way appearances are rationally linked into spontaneity at large: the way appearances can constitute reasons for judgments about objective reality—indeed, do constitute reasons for judgments in suitable circumstances ("other things being equal").

Now this link between experience and spontaneity is similar in some ways to the link that is effected, in the position Evans attacks, by conceiving experiences as dispositions to judge. But the link I envisage, unlike that one, is a link that connects experiences to judgments as reasons for them. That means my picture does not have the feature that Evans complains of: that when there is an inclination to make a judgment of experience, the inclination seems to float mysteriously free of the situation, taking on the look of an unaccountable conviction that some concept "has application in the immediate vicinity." On the contrary, when one does have such a conviction, my picture allows it to be satisfactorily grounded in how things appear to one.

In my first lecture (§6), I suggested that Davidson's coherentism reflects an obstacle in the way of seeing that operations of conceptual capacities can be passive. The same obstacle seems to be at work in Evans' argument from the fact that experience is "belief-independent." In fact Davidson and Evans represent the two horns of a dilemma posed by that obstacle. If one fails to see that conceptual capacities can be operative in sensibility itself, one has two options: either, like Davidson, to insist that experience is only causally related to empirical thinking, not rationally; or else, like Evans, to fall into the Myth of the Given, and try to credit experience, conceived as extra-conceptual, with rational relations to empirical thinking. Davidson holds that the Myth of the Given can be avoided only by denying that experience is epistemologically significant. Evans, for good reasons, cannot stomach that denial, and he shows that he shares Davidson's view of the possibilities by accordingly embracing a form of the Myth of the Given. My point is that we need not confine ourselves within this framework of possibilities. I shall return to this in the next lecture (lecture 4).

7. I have already mentioned a third consideration Evans appeals to. This is the fact that we share perception (like memory) with "animals" (p. 124); that is, with creatures that cannot be credited with conceptual capacities, in the demanding sense Evans and I agree on.

This brings me back to the area of the twin discomforts I mentioned some time ago (§3). Both Evans and I are committed to there being different stories to tell about perceptual goings-on in creatures with spontaneity and in creatures without it. In the one case we can apply the notion of experience, in a strict sense that connects it with conceptual capacities, and in the other case we cannot. But it may seem that Evans' position makes this implication less embarrassing, because the position supplies us with something we can conceive as straightforwardly common to the two cases: namely, states of the informational system, with their nonconceptual content.

We can shake this impression somewhat by considering the third element of the informational system, the testimony system. According to Evans, we have knowledge derived from operations of the testimony system that took place before we were in a position to understand the linguistic performances in question. So the testimony system is, in itself, "more primitive" than understanding. And that is a partial parallel to the fact that we share perception and memory with mere animals. Now suppose our sharing perception with creatures that lack spontaneity were a good reason for crediting our perceptual experience with content that is not conceptual, on the ground that if we said that the content of our experience is conceptual, that would put this kind of content out of reach of those other perceivers. In that case, by parity of reasoning, the partially parallel fact about the primitive operations of the testimony system should be a good reason for supposing that nonconceptual content is involved in our mature dealings with the testimony system, when we do understand the linguistic performances we witness. But understanding language is surely a matter of conceptual capacities if anything is. So what is the role of these conceptual capacities in our mature dealings with the testimony system, if the content involved is nonconceptual? A straightforward parallel to Evans' picture of the role of conceptual capacities in experience would be this: the conceptual capacities exercised in understanding a linguistic performance do not enter into determining the content with which one takes oneself to be presented, but serve only to account for one's access to that content, which is independently determined by the operations of the informational system. But that is surely a quite unattractive idea.

If we share perception with mere animals, then of course we have something in common with them. Now there is a temptation to think it must be possible to isolate what we have in common with them by stripping off what is special about us, so as to arrive at a residue that we can recognize as what figures in the perceptual lives of mere animals. That is the role that is played in Evans' picture by informational states, with their nonconceptual content. But it is not compulsory to attempt to accommodate the combination of something in common and a striking difference in this factorizing way: to suppose our perceptual lives include a core that we can also recognize in the perceptual life of a mere animal, and an extra ingredient in addition. And if we do take this line, there is no satisfactory way to understand the role of the supposed core in our perceptual lives. We are confronted with the dilemma whose horns are embraced by Davidson and Evans, each of them, I claim, deceived in the thought that his position is satisfactory.

We can avoid the dilemma. We do not need to say that we have what mere animals have, nonconceptual content, and we have something else as well, since we can conceptualize that content and they cannot. Instead we can say that we have what mere animals have, perceptual sensitivity to features of our environment, but we have it in a special form. Our perceptual sensitivity to our environment is taken up into the ambit of the faculty of spontaneity, which is what distinguishes us from them.

I think we ought ultimately to be able to take something on those lines in our stride. But perhaps such formulations begin to uncover the character of the obstacle I have been alluding to: the intelligibly powerful influence over the cast of our thinking that tends to obliterate the very possibility of the right picture. The difficulty comes out in questions like this: how can spontaneity permeate our lives, even to the extent of structuring those aspects of them that reflect our naturalness—those aspects of our lives that reflect what we share with ordinary animals? The thought is that the freedom of spontaneity ought to be a kind of exemption from nature, something that permits us to elevate ourselves above it, rather than our own special way of living an animal life. . . .

Notes

1. It is worth noting, since it helps to bring out how demanding the relevant idea of the conceptual is, that this openness to reflection implies self-consciousness on the part of the thinking subject. But I relegate the point to a footnote at this stage, since issues about self-consciousness will not be in the foreground until later (lecture 5).

2. Evans 1982, p. 227 (emphasis in the original). I want to make it clear immediately that I believe the thesis on which I shall be taking issue with Evans here is inessential to the main claims of Evans' profoundly important book. I shall come back to Evans' main claims in lecture 5 (§6).

3. I shall say something about the strict notion of belief in §6.

4. It would be easy to complicate Evans' account so as to accommodate the fact that "experience" can fit occurrences as well as states.

5. Note that grounding need not depend on an inferential step from one content to another. The judgment that things are thus and so can be grounded on a perceptual appearance that things are thus and so. This does not obliterate the characteristic richness of experience (especially visual

experience). A typical judgment of experience selects from the content of the experience on which it is based; the experience that grounds the judgment that things are thus and so need not be exhausted by its affording the appearance that things are thus and so. Selection from among a rich supply of already conceptual content is not what Evans takes judgment to effect, a transition from one kind of content to another.

6. Why can we not acknowledge that the *relations* between experience and judgments have to be rational, and therefore within the scope of spontaneity, without being thereby committed to a concession about experience itself? I have claimed that it is hard to see how this combination could work, but as long as Evans' position looks innocent it will seem quite easy. Rather than radically recasting this lecture from the form in which I delivered it, I postpone further discussion of this matter to the Afterword [of McDowell 1994b].

7. See p. 176 [essay 2, p. 64]: "Any subject at all capable of thought about an objective spatial world must conceive of his normal experiences as simultaneously due to the way the world is and his changing position in it. . . . The capacity to think of oneself as located in space, and tracing a continuous path through it, is necessarily involved in the capacity to conceive the phenomena one encounters as independent of one's perception of them—to conceive the world as something one 'comes across'." See also p. 222: "Any thinker who has an idea of an objective spatial world—an idea of a world of objects and phenomena which can be perceived but which are not dependent on being perceived for their existence—must be able to think of his perception of the world as being simultaneously due to his position in the world, and to the condition of the world at that position. The very idea of a perceivable, objective, spatial world brings with it the idea of the subject as being *in* the world, with the course of his perceptions due to his changing position in the world and to the more or less stable way the world is." Evans elaborates this thought in "Things without the Mind." The thought is central to Strawson's reading of Kant; see Strawson 1966, chap. 2, especially p. 104.

8. In "Things without the Mind" Evans argues that the idea of an object of experience "cannot stand on its own, stand without any surrounding theory" (p. 88). The required theory is a theory of the conditions under which something perceptible is actually perceived (pp. 88–89). If we make sense of the Kantian notion of spontaneity, we must surely suppose that the possession of spontaneity marks the difference between creatures that can intelligibly be thought to have such a theory, even if only implicitly, and creatures that cannot.

9. For a clear and engaging exposition of this welling-up picture, see Dennett 1981a. Dennett suggests that the role of content at the personal level is to be understood in terms of our access to some of the content that figures in a sub-personal story about our internal machinery. I think Dennett's own discussion strongly suggests that something is wrong with this picture: it leads Dennett into the highly implausible claim that perceptual awareness is a matter of presentiments or premonitions, differing from what are ordinarily so called only in that they are not isolated (see pp. 165–166). I discuss this in McDowell 1994a.

10. *The Varieties of Reference*, p. 229. Obviously color figures here as representative of a number of features of experience.

11. Christopher Peacocke takes this view in recent work; for an overview see *A Study of Concepts* [also see essay 5].

12. Wittgenstein 1951, §279.

13. Obviously people differ in the retentiveness of their memory for precise shades. No doubt it can be cultivated, as a memory for flavors is cultivated by aspiring connoisseurs of food or wine.

14. Peacocke is an exception; see *A Study of Concepts*, pp. 83–84. But notice that even though Peacocke there in effect acknowledges that fineness of grain is no threat to the thesis that the content of experience is conceptual, he is not above claiming, in an earlier passage, an advantage for his different view in the fact that "writers on the objective content of experience have often remarked that an experience can have a finer-grained content than can be formulated by using concepts possessed by the experiencer" (p. 67) [essay 5, p. 111]. If this claim that writers have often made is false, why should accommodating it be an advantage for Peacocke's view?

15. In another sense, the capacity to have that particular shade in mind is a standing one, which requires no more than possession of the concept of a shade together with the subject's standing powers of discrimination. Experience raises this standing potential to a degree of actuality; the capacity to have that shade in mind as *that* shade is actually operative in the experience, and potentially operative subsequently in thoughts that exploit recall of the experience.

16. The main lines of what I say in this section date from a seminar I gave in Oxford in 1986 (with Colin McGinn). But my thinking on these issues has since been enriched by discussions with Sonia Sedivy, who independently arrived at similar thoughts, in reaction to the Sellarsian idea that the sensuous specificity of perceptual experience needs to be accounted for in terms of impressions as opposed to concepts. See her 1990 University of Pittsburgh dissertation, "The Determinate Character of Perceptual Experience."

Part II

Naturalism and Computation

The essays of the second section are informed by attempts to naturalize intentionality or to characterize its computational structure.

Naturalism is the view that intentional contents can be accounted for by the explanations of and entities posited by the sciences. This, according to many philosophers, is the primary advantage of appealing to informational states. In his contribution, Stalnaker suggests that the contents of such states are nonconceptual. As he explains, "one thing contains information about another if there are causal and counterfactual dependencies between the states of one and the states of the other." For example, a cross-section of a tree reveals rings that indicate the age of the tree. If there are 64 rings, the tree is generally thought to be 64 years old—each ring representing a completed year in the tree's life cycle. Similarly, a thermometer carries information about temperature, a fuel gauge about the amount of gasoline in a tank, and a retina about various features of the visible world. In fact, according to Stalnaker, beliefs are also informational states and their contents, like those of tree trunks, thermometers, fuel gauges, and retinas, should be considered nonconceptual.

Informational content is nonconceptual because it violates the weak construal of Cognitive Significance as well as Reference Determinacy, irrespective of how it's construed. Moreover, Stalnaker has both the second and third rendering of "non" in mind. In the case of thermometers, fuel gauges, tree trunks, and retinas, it's obvious that the second rendering applies. However, in the case of beliefs, it is the third. For whether an individual has the requisite conceptual capacities or not, the contents of her beliefs remain nonconceptual because they are fixed *external* to anything she knows or believes. In this way, Stalnaker seems to embrace a global nonconceptualism since conceptual contents allegedly play no role in explaining human action. As he puts it, "McDowell argued . . . [that] content is conceptual all the way down. I am inclined to agree with McDowell that different kinds of states have the same kind of content, but I am suggesting that it is nonconceptual all the way up."

In "Scenarios, Concepts and Perception," Peacocke adopts a form of naturalism without embracing global nonconceptualism. Recognizing the explanatory value of concepts, he attempts to naturalize them, specifically those intimately connected with experience, for example, *square, cubic* and *cylindrical*. However, because he adopts a nonreductive naturalism, one that tolerates (noncircular) appeals to semantic or intentional states, he uses nonconceptual content to individuate concepts. To this end, two distinct kinds of nonconceptual content are utilized, namely, scenarios and protopropositions. The former is a "spatial type," fixed along the lines suggested by Evans, namely, by an origin and axes relative to a perceiver (e.g., left/right, front/behind, and up/down) as well as a set of dimensions (e.g., texture, hue, saturation, brightness, solidity) that fill out the space around the origin. The latter, which is fixed by perceptible individuals and properties or relations, is similar to informational content. While they are primarily used for individuating concepts (by their possession conditions), Peacocke suggests that scenarios and protopropositions also enable us to explain various aspects of experience, including its fineness of grain, its unit-free and analogical character, and the construction of cognitive maps.

Scenarios and protopropositions are nonconceptual because, like informational content, they are fixed independently of anything an individual believes or knows, suggesting that they violate Cognitive Significance, weakly construed, and Reference Determinacy, on any construal. Moreover, like Stalnaker, Peacocke allows for both the second and third renderings of "non." However, it is noteworthy that his rejection of the Autonomy Thesis (at least until recently: see the postscript of essay 16), the view that nonconceptual content can have an explanatory value independently of an entity's possession of concepts, limits the applicability of the second rendering. Although an individual may have a content if she *does not grasp* the concepts involved in its articulation, she must possess at least *some* concepts. According to Peacocke, without conceptual capacities an individual cannot be attributed nonconceptual contents, presumably because their primary explanatory role involves individuating concepts. (See the introduction to section 4 for a more detailed discussion of The Autonomy Thesis.)

While also influenced by Evans, Cussins suggests a different distinction between conceptual and nonconceptual content. Using Cognitive Significance (its strong construal) as a constraint on all contents, he argues that the cognitive significance of indexical and demonstrative thoughts is altered when their contents are specified by descriptions. Since descriptions cannot capture the content of indexical and demonstrative thoughts, an alternative is required, namely, construction-theoretic content. According to Cussins, such contents are specified relative to an individual's disposition to move through her environment as opposed to a static spatial type. (In the postscript, Cussins explicates nonconceptual content more fastidiously in terms of guidance, a realm of mediation, and activity trails—see also essay 16 for an attempt at differentiating Cussins's and Peacocke's notions of nonconceptual content.) Hence, to hear a sound coming from a particular direction involves being disposed to move or orient oneself in a certain way towards the source. In addition to accounting for the content of indexicals and demonstratives, Cussins believes that construction-theoretic content can be used to explain concept acquisition, the experience of pain, the behavior of entities without concepts as well as skills, practices, and everyday activities. In fact, he goes so far as to endorse a global nonconceptualism when he notes that his argument "can be extended from the case of indexical and demonstrative senses [contents] to all senses [contents]."

Unlike Stalnaker and Peacocke, Cussins clearly advocates the third rendering of "non": a content is nonconceptual if, and only if, an individual *need not have* the concepts (descriptions) required to specify it. And like Evans he maintains that construction-theoretic content violates Cognitive Significance, weakly construed, and Reference Determinacy, descriptively construed (though, as is suggested in the postscript, he may deny the applicability of any construal of Reference Determinacy since through nonconceptual content the world is presented [determined?] as a *realm of mediation* rather than a *realm of reference*). Moreover, based on his general approach in "The Connectionist Construction of Concepts," Cussins also presumes that construction-theoretic content violates Compositionality, which is reinforced in the postscript by his claim that it is neither propositional nor about particulars, objects, or properties. The denial of compositionality is significant because it serves to distinguish his notion of nonconceptuality from Evans's. In *Varieties of Reference*, Evans is clearly committed to the idea that demonstrative thought heeds the Generality Constraint, which presupposes the Principle of Compositionality. Furthermore, Evans does not, strictly speaking, maintain that demonstrative content is nonconceptual. His claim is that the perceptual content upon which demonstrative identification is founded is nonconceptual. In this way, different views about demonstratives reveal different views about nonconceptual content.

The papers by Bermúdez and Clark focus on the nature of computational states. Clark maintains that nonconceptual content enables us to explain the distinctive kind of knowledge that certain artifacts, animals, young children, and even mature human beings have. His discussion centers on NETtalk, a first-order connectionist system that transforms text into speech. While there is a sense in which the system "knows," for example, what vowels are, its "knowledge" is conspicuously inflexible. For instance, to cope with an encrypted message in which vowels and consonants are reversed, NETtalk would have to be completely retrained. Unlike a more powerful cognitive system such as a mature human being, it could not make the necessary adjustment by learning the requisite rule (intelligent self de-bugging). Clark believes that the system's inflexibility (also illustrated by its failure to exhibit "creative cognition" and "reasoning by analysis") suggests that its contents are unstructured and in this sense nonconceptual.

The principle presumed to be violated here is Compositionality. As for the rendering of "non," in the case of NETtalk, sandfish, and young children, the second evidently applies, since such entities are said to lack structured thoughts. However, in the case of mature human beings, the third rendering applies. It is allegedly because we have different kinds of computational architectures that some of our contents are nonconceptual. More specifically, Clark suggests that while nonconceptual contents (and the first-order architecture[s] supporting them) cannot account for the cognitive flexibility exhibited by mature human beings, they are nevertheless crucial for explaining how we navigate around the world, a view evidently inspired by Evans and Cussins. Without them our conceptual contents would be *empty*; and conversely, without structured contents our nonconceptual contents would be *blind*, that is, as inflexible as those of NETtalk, sandfish, and young children.

Bermúdez argues that nonconceptual content should be attributed to subpersonal computational states as well as to perceptual experiences. After briefly reviewing different ways of characterizing nonconceptual content and suggesting its explanatory value in developmental psychology, he offers four criteria for attributing content to a state: (1) such a state should serve to explain the behavior of an entity where law-like connections cannot be plotted between its sensory input and behavior; (2) it should admit of cognitive integration; (3) it should be compositional; and (4) it should allow for the possibility of misrepresentation. The need for such criteria is driven by his intuition that ascribing contents to entities without concepts is in some cases warranted (e.g., children and higher animals)—that is, where individuals possess intentionality *originally* or *intrinsically*—and in other cases not (e.g., tree-trunks and thermostats). Since computational subsystems don't have conceptual capacities, he uses the criteria to support the view that subpersonal states genuinely have content and that this content is nonconceptual.

By endorsing the Priority Thesis, which claims that there is an interdependence or, at least, a close connection between having concepts and having a language, Bermúdez seems to be using Reference Determinacy to characterize nonconceptuality. That is, subpersonal states have nonconceptual content because they violate the principle, descriptively construed. (Once again, the weaker construal of Cognitive Significance is also violated.) Because a subsystem *does not* (and probably *cannot*) have the capacity to determine the reference of its computational states, the relevant rendering of "non" is the second. (Note that the distinction between subpersonal and personal suggests that the state is attributed to the subsystem rather than the person. This is significant since, if the computational state were attributed to the person, she presumably would have the capacity to determine the reference of her computational states, suggesting the applicability of the third rendering of "non.")

Chapter 4

What Might Nonconceptual Content Be? (1998)

Robert Stalnaker

I start with a bit of philosophical jargon, first introduced by Gareth Evans, but used since by many others who cite Evans, including Christopher Peacocke, John McDowell, and Michael Tye. My initial question was, what do these philosophers mean by "nonconceptual content," and its contrast, "conceptual content"? What kinds of objects are these different types of content, and how are they used to characterize perception and thought? It is controversial among those who talk of nonconceptual content whether there is such a thing, and whether perceptual states have a kind of content that is different from the kind that characterizes belief states and speech acts. But Evans gives us no direct and explicit characterization of the notion of nonconceptual content that he introduces—at least none that I can find. And it is not clear to me that the different philosophers using this term mean the same thing by it. Without some account of what nonconceptual and conceptual contents might be, it is difficult to have more than a general impression of what this controversy is about.

Some things Evans says suggest that it is mental states, rather than their contents, that are conceptual or nonconceptual, and sometimes he substitutes "nonconceptualized" for nonconceptual, but it is clear that he thinks there are two kinds of content, and not just two kinds of states that content is used to characterize, or two ways in which content might be expressed. "The process of conceptualization or judgement," he says, "takes the subject from one kind of state (with a content of a certain kind, namely nonconceptual content) to his being in another kind of cognitive state (with a content of a different kind, namely, conceptual content)" (Evans 1982, p. 227). John McDowell, on the other hand, argues that the process of judgment does not introduce a new kind of content, but "simply endorses the conceptual content, or some of it, that is already possessed by the experience on which it is grounded" (McDowell 1994b, p. 49) [essay 3, p. 77]. It is the issue behind this dispute that I want to try to get a little clearer about.

Let me confess at the beginning that I will not propose answers to my questions about how these philosophers should be understood. I am puzzled by much

Reprinted with the kind permission of the author and Ridgeview Publishing Company.

of what they say—I have the impression that their arguments are being guided, on both sides, by conceptions of content and its role in the explanation of perception and thought that have underlying presuppositions that I don't share, and don't fully understand. So my strategy will be indirect: rather than trying to ferret out those presuppositions by detailed examination of the texts, I will spell out my own assumptions about representational content, and ask how, given the way I understand this notion, a distinction between conceptual and nonconceptual might be drawn, and what role it might play in the explanation of the relation between perception and thought. I will begin with what I take to be some platitudes about content, assumptions that I would expect to be disputed only by a philosopher who rejected the whole idea of representational or intentional content. After a while, more controversial assumptions may emerge, but I hope we will be able to identify the point at which disagreement begins.

The notion of propositional content begins with the idea that *what is said* in a speech act—the proposition expressed—can be abstracted from two different aspects of the way it is said: first from the means used to express it, second from the force with which it is expressed. The same proposition can be expressed by different sentences of the same or different languages, and the same proposition can be the content of an assertion in one context, and of a supposition, a component of a disjunctive assertion, or a request in other contexts. Furthermore, the contents expressed in speech acts with different force are the same kinds of things as the contents of mental states of different kinds, such as belief, desire, intention, hope, and fear. Just as *what is said* can be separated from how it is said, so *what is thought* can be separated both from the means of mental representation and from the kind of mental state (belief, wish, tacit presupposition, hope, or fear) that the proposition is used to specify. Just as you and I might say the same thing, even though you say it in French and I say it in English, so you and I might believe the same thing even though the systems of mental representation in which the information is encoded in our respective minds is different. And just as I may assert what you merely suppose, so I might believe what you doubt, but hope for. And it seems at least prima facie reasonable to say that when something merely looks to me to be a certain way, even though I don't really believe that it is that way, then there is a perceptual state with a certain content that might have been, but is not the content of any of my beliefs.

So what might these things be—things that are the contents of speech acts and mental states of various kinds? There are many different theories about what propositional content is, but two things seem common to all theories that take content seriously at all: first, a content is an abstract object of some kind (as contrasted, for example, with a sentence token, or a mental representation); second, it is essential to propositional contents that they have truth conditions. Perhaps they *are* truth conditions, perhaps something more fine-grained that allows for the possibility that different propositional contents may have the same truth conditions. Either way, what is assumed is that for any state, act or object with propositional content, one can ask whether or not things are as the state represents things to be, and this is to ask whether the truth conditions of the propositional content are satisfied.

What are truth conditions? Different things might be meant by this expression; here is one: think of the meaning of a sentence as a recipe for determining a truth value as a function of the facts. The recursive semantic structure of the sentence encodes such a procedure. One might identify the recipe with the truth conditions, since it spells out the procedure, or conditions, for determining whether the sentence is true. Here is a contrasting explanation: one might instead identify the truth conditions of a statement simply with the circumstances (the way things must be) for the proposition expressed to be true—the conditions under which the statement is true. Different recipes determined by statements with different constituent structure might end in the same place, no matter what the facts (as, for example, with statements of the forms ~(P ∨ Q) and (~P ∧ ~Q). Such statements will have different truth conditions in one sense, but the same truth conditions in the other. I will make only the weaker assumption that propositional contents have truth conditions in the second sense.

Now there are many kinds of abstract objects that have, or determine, truth conditions in this sense—different candidates for a kind of representational content. Some of them may be appropriately called "conceptual" in some sense; others might appropriately be called "nonconceptual." For example, one might define complex objects, nested ordered sequences that reflect the recursive semantic structure of the sentences with which the structure is associated. The ultimate constituents of such structures might consist wholly of senses or concepts. Maybe *conceptual* content is an object of this kind, though it remains to be said what senses or concepts are. Alternatively, one might take the ultimate constituents of such structures to be individual objects and properties and relations (the referents of names and the properties and relations expressed by the predicates in the relevant sentences). Perhaps this is a kind of *nonconceptual* content. And there might be mixed cases—structures that contain concepts or senses (associated with predicates) and individuals (associated with names).

These different candidates for a kind of content are not independent; there will be correspondences between contents of the different kinds. In some cases there will be straightforward ways of determining a content of one kind as a function of a content of one of the other kinds. In particular, whatever senses are, they determine referents; whatever concepts are, it seems reasonable to say that concepts of the appropriate kind determine properties. (A concept of cat determines, I assume, the property of being a cat.) If this is right, then a structure that is made up of senses or concepts will determine a unique structure of the kind made up of individuals, properties and relations, though the reverse will not be true. So there is a clear sense in which structures made of senses or concepts are more fine-grained than those made of individuals and properties and relations, with the mixed cases falling between the two.

All of the candidates considered so far build into the content a recipe for determining truth conditions. One might instead take the recipe determined by some sentence as part of the means by which content is determined, rather than as essential to the content itself. One might, that is, identify the content with the truth conditions themselves—the possible circumstances that must be realized in order for some expression or thought with that content to be true. This is the most coarse-grained conception of content—the outer limit on a conception of content that meets the minimal conditions that we are requiring that any conception of representational content meet. Any conception of representational content meeting these conditions will determine a unique content of this most coarse-grained kind, so this is a kind of content that everyone should agree can be used to characterize mental and linguistic states, acts, and events that can be said to have representational content of any kind. I will use the label "informational content" for content as truth conditions, propositions as functions from possible circumstances to truth values, or equivalently, as sets of possible situations. I suppose that if this is a kind of content, it is a kind of nonconceptual content, although since it can be used to characterize any kind of representational act or state, its use says nothing one way or another about whether any kind of act or state essentially involves the exercise of conceptual capacities (whatever this might mean).

Thus far I have been talking about the kinds of abstract objects that might be thought to be the representational contents of acts and states that have representational content, but I have said nothing about the states themselves, or about what it is about a cognitive, perceptual, or motivational state, or a speech act or act of judgment in virtue of which it has some particular representational content. Recall that part of the initial motivation for developing a conception of content at all was the idea that content could be abstracted from the force with which it is expressed and from the attitudes that are characterized in terms of content—a conception that might be used to describe states and acts of different kinds, and that was intelligible independently of its use to describe any representational states or acts. But of course the interest of these abstract objects will derive from their use for describing in a revealing way the phenomena they are used to describe, and for bringing out the relationships between different acts and states that are involved in representation. So I turn now to questions about the role of content in characterizing representational events and properties, beginning, again, with some platitudes.

Statements involving sentential complements (for example, statements of the form *x believes that P, it appears to x that P, x asserted that P*), state that a certain relation holds or held between *x* and something denoted by the term *"that P."* Sometimes the problem of intentionality is posed as the problem of how it is possible for a person to be related, as a matter of contingent fact, to the kind of abstract object denoted by a that-clause. The puzzlement is exacerbated by the causal metaphors philosophers often use to describe the ways we are related to propositions: they seem to be things we can get our hands around: we grasp propositions, we gather information, process it, and send it. Content travels in vehicles. Information saturates our thoughts (Evans 1982, p. 122), seeping into them like some kind of spiritual fluid. But the sober reality behind the metaphors need not be so mysterious. To be related to an abstract object is just to have a property that can be determined as a function of such an object, in the way that (to use a now familiar analogy) the property of weighing 75 kilograms can be determined as a function of the number 75. One way to get at the question, what is content? is to ask how whatever it is that is denoted by such sentential complements as "that the cat is on the mat" determines the properties that are ascribed in predicates like "believes that the cat is on the mat."

Consider a simple and straightforward example borrowed from Evans (*ibid.*). I am thinking about something I can see: a black and white cat sleeping on a mat. I see that the cat is sleeping. Perhaps I suspect or speculate that the cat is a favorite of Queen Elizabeth. I entertain the possibility that the cat is ginger, rather than black and white, and judge that it is not (or in Evans' terms, I "grasp [the thought that the cat is ginger] as false"). Various properties are ascribed to me with the help of reference to some kind of abstract object that has truth conditions. Whatever is going on in me when I entertain the possibility that this cat is a favorite of Queen Elizabeth, we can describe it by attributing to me a relation to the proposition *that the cat is a favorite of Queen Elizabeth* (a proposition that is true in possible worlds in which that cat is one of her favorites and false in possible worlds in which it is not). The problem is to say what the world must be like for me to be related in the right kind of way to such an abstract object.

The thought episodes and belief states in such cases are, Evans notes, based on some *information* that the subject receives. "People are," he says, "in short and among other things, gatherers, transmitters and storers of information. These platitudes locate perception, communication, and memory in a system—the informational system—which constitutes the substratum of our cognitive lives" (*ibid.*). Evans says little about what information is, or what informational states are, but here is a simple minded and crude version of a familiar story: one thing contains information about another if there are causal and counterfactual dependencies between the states of one and the states of the other. An object contains information about its environment if the object is in some state that it wouldn't be in if the environment weren't a certain way. x carries the information that P if the object would not be in the state it is in if it were not the case that P. Some objects are sensitive to a range of alternative states of the environment in a way that makes them apt for transmitting or storing detailed information about some aspect of the environment. The pattern of light and dark on the ground on a sunny day, for example, carries information about the shape of the tree since there are systematic counterfactual dependencies between a range of alternative possible shapes of the tree and a corresponding range of alternative patterns on the ground. Obviously, artifacts such as thermometers and cameras are designed to be sensitive to the environment in just this way, and they are naturally described as devices designed to carry information. Equally obviously, animals have evolved a diverse range of systems—perceptual systems as well as internal monitoring systems of various kinds—that carry and use information in this sense. For a philosopher looking for a naturalistic account of intentionality, this conception of information and informational states provides a natural starting point.

Of things that carry information, we can say *what* information they carry. Information itself is something described with that-clauses—the information that a black and white cat is sleeping on a mat, or that *this* black and white cat is sleeping on a mat, or the information that the tree trunk is shaped roughly like a Y, that the temperature is seventeen degrees centigrade. Informational states have content—presumably (at least in some cases) a kind of content that is in some sense nonconceptual, since it would not be reasonable to attribute conceptual capacities to the patterns of light on the ground in virtue of the counterfactual dependencies that make it the case that those patterns have informational content.

Of course things that lack conceptual capacities (such as books) still might carry conceptualized information, and so might be correctly describable in terms of some notion of conceptual content. But whatever conceptual content turns out to be, it seems reasonable to think that for anything that *has* conceptual content, the fact that it does must have its origin in something with conceptual capacities, as the information contained in books has its origin in the thoughts and intentions of the members of the community in which they are written. (*Pace* George Washington, who is alleged to have said that all knowledge has its origin in the knowledge in books.) If the notion of an informational system is, as Evans suggests, to "constitute the substratum of our cognitive lives," and if the notion of information is to contribute to an explanation of the source and nature of the content of full-blooded intentional states—acts of judgment, states of belief—then it is important that our account of what constitutes the carrying of information not presuppose, or be derivative from, states of mind.

Artifacts that are designed to record, display, or store information (fuel gauges, thermometers, cameras, compact disks) are among the best examples of information carrying systems, and are often used to illustrate the strategy for explaining intentionality in terms of systems that function to carry information. Since the design of such things is explained in terms of the intentions of the designers, their information carrying capacities are in a sense dependent on the intentional states of persons. But it would be a mistake to think that the information such artifacts carry is derivative in the same way as is the capacity of a book to carry the information expressed by the sentences written in it. Thermometers and cameras are designed with an information carrying purpose in mind, but facts about the way such devices happened to come by their informational capacities are inessential to the explanation of what it is that constitutes those capacities. A natural thermometer or camera brought into being by some fortuitous process (Swamp-thermometer, or Swamp-camera) would carry the same information in the same way as actual thermometers and cameras. The word-like marks in Swamp-book, on the other hand, don't mean anything, and they don't carry information that has anything to do with what such marks usually mean. I don't know whether Evans is making this mistake when he says "what gives a photograph its content is, of course, something quite different from what gives states of our brain their content. (The former is parasitic on the latter)" (*ibid.*, p. 125, n. 8), but I think this claim is at least misleading in that it ignores the distinction between the inessential way in which the capacities of cameras are parasitic on those of our brains, and the important way that the capacities of books are parasitic on ours, but the capacities of cameras are not.

Information is by definition veridical. According to the simple story I have sketched, *x* cannot carry the information that *P* unless it is true that *P*. If this concept is to provide a basis for an account of representational content, we need to complicate the story, but the strategy for doing so is straightforward. As Fred Dretske has emphasized, even in the simple story, any characterization of the information carried by some object will presuppose a distinction between the facts that form the background conditions (or channel conditions) for the causal structure in virtue of which the object carries information and the facts that constitute the information carried. The correctness of the characterization of the content of the information carried will be relative to such presuppositions. So we say that the thermometer (which is in fact functioning normally, and which registers 17) carries the information that the temperature is 17 degrees centigrade, even though if, contrary to fact, the temperature were 27 degrees, and certain particular anomalous conditions also obtained, the thermometer would still be in the state it is in. The presupposed background conditions must obtain for information to be carried in the strict sense, but one can use the same content ascriptions, and the same distinction, without making the assumption that relevant conditions in fact obtain. One can say, that is, that *x* *indicates* that *P* if it is in a state that *would* carry the information that *P* if the appropriate background conditions obtained. If the conditions do not obtain, then what is indicated may be misinformation rather than information. But the essentials of the story remain the same.

Perceptual systems are paradigm cases of systems apt for receiving information, and statements about perceptual achievements are cases of content attribution that most straightforwardly fit the information theoretic picture. To say that O'Leary sees that the zebra is striped is to say, at least, that O'Leary receives via the visual system, the information that the zebra is striped. In this kind of straightforward perceptual statement there is no question of misinformation or misperception: the zebra must be striped for the statement to be true. Furthermore, if it is true that O'Leary sees that the zebra is striped, he must also come to believe—in fact, to come to *know*—that the zebra is striped. Suppose O'Leary thinks this: "That animal sure looks striped, but who ever heard of a striped horse. It is probably just the way the sunlight is filtering through the trees that makes it look that way." O'Leary is wrong to doubt his senses, let us assume. It really is a striped zebra that he sees; lighting is normal, and things are just as they appear to be. I assume that in such a case it would be wrong to say that O'Leary sees that the zebra is striped, though it might still be right to say in such a case that O'Leary received the information, through the visual system, that the zebra is striped. Despite the fact that O'Leary withholds judgment, it is still true that had the zebra not been striped, it would not have looked the way it does.

In the normal case—the one that is correctly describable by the statement, "O'Leary sees that the zebra is striped"—the information that the zebra is striped is received through the visual system and results in the knowledge that the zebra is striped. A case might be abnormal in at least two independent ways. First, the "information" might be misinformation: to use the terminology suggested above, it might be that the state of the visual system merely *indicates* that the zebra is striped, meaning that it is in a state that, under normal conditions, would constitute receiving the information that the zebra is striped. Second (as in our example), it might be that the information (or misinformation) did not result in belief, and so not in knowledge. O'Leary's case deviates from the norm in the second way, but not in the first. It is also true that in this case, O'Leary falsely believes that it deviates from the normal one in the first way.

To describe what happens in a way that does not exclude either kind of deviation from the normal case, one might say that it looks to O'Leary as if the zebra were striped, or that it appears visually to O'Leary that the zebra is striped. (Though this is not how O'Leary would put it, since he doesn't realize that what appears to him to be striped is a zebra.) But how exactly are such statements about how things appear to be analyzed?

One idea, considered and rejected by Evans, is this: statements about the way things seem should be understood as dispositions to believe, or as something like defeasible or prima facie beliefs. For it to seem to you that P is for you to be in a state that would, except for some intervening factor, result in the belief that P, or perhaps for you to be in a state that produces an inclination to believe that P. More specific seeming or appearing states such as its *looking* to you that P, would, on this strategy, identify a particular source for the inclination: something seems to be so as a result of the way things look. But on this proposal, one would still derive the content of the state from the content of the belief states that it would produce under normal conditions. Evans argues that this gets things backwards. Belief states are sophisticated cognitive states, while "the operations of the informational system are more primitive" (*ibid.*, p. 124). But I think the main problem Evans has with this attempt to explain the content of seeming states is not that the perceptual systems are intrinsically more primitive, but that they are earlier links in an informational chain. The informational content of a state should be explained in terms of the causal source of the state, and not its normal result. Consider the analogy between testimony and the senses, an analogy Evans alludes to and takes seriously (*ibid.*, p. 123, n. 5). The senses are like witnesses who tell us things that we may accept or reject. Just as in the normal case, when it looks to be that P, one comes to know that P, so in the normal case, when one is told that P, one comes to know that P. This implies that to be in the state of having been told that P is to be in a state that would under normal conditions result in the knowledge that P. But it would obviously be absurd to try to explain the content of the witness' testimony in terms of the content of the knowledge state in which it would normally result. Similarly, it gets things backwards to try to explain the way things look in terms of what one would come to believe if one judged that things are as they look.

This seems persuasive, but the way the contents of the components of some informational system are determined, and the way such contents are related to the way things seem, may be more tangled than this analogy suggests. Consider another kind of situation in which information received by the visual system fails to result in knowledge, this time a case where the explanation for the failure is that the subject lacks the conceptual resources to form the relevant belief. Eucalyptus trees, let us suppose, have a quite distinctive look. If the tree in the garden were of any other kind, then things would look differently to O'Leary than they do, so we might say that O'Leary's visual system receives the information that there is a Eucalyptus tree in the garden. But O'Leary doesn't come to know, or believe, that there is a Eucalyptus tree in the garden, since he doesn't have a concept of a Eucalyptus tree (by that name, or any other). While O'Leary's visual system succeeds in discriminating Eucalyptus trees from other kinds, O'Leary himself does not. Now it does not seem to me that this situation is correctly described as a case in which it appears to O'Leary that there is a Eucalyptus tree in the garden. Why not? One might think that it cannot be right that things seem to someone to be a certain way unless the person has the capacity to endorse the appearance—to judge that things really are that way. If this is right, then the knowledge and beliefs that normally result from perceptual states may constrain the content properly attributed to the kinds of states that are ascribed when one says how things look, appear or seem to be.

But whether this is right or not, it is clear that one cannot, in all cases, identify the way things seem, or look, with the information received or delivered by some component of the informational system, some link in a chain of information transmission that in normal cases results in knowledge. It is surely essential to seeming that the way things seem be accessible to consciousness, but this need not be true of information bearing states that are part of a process that normally results in knowledge. Consider a very early stage of the visual processing system such as the retina. Suppose the image of a tree is on our subject's retina: it is in a state that it would normally be in when, and only when, the subject is confronted by a tree (as we may suppose he is). So the subject's retina indicates, and carries the information, that there is a tree before him. But suppose a distortion is introduced very early in the process, so that the subject is under the impression that he is looking at something that bears no resemblance to a tree. There is no sense in which it would be correct to say, in this case, that it seems to him (retinally speaking?) that there is a tree before him. But the retina surely does carry information, and is in a state that has representational content. The retina is part of the informational system that "constitutes the substratum of our cognitive lives." In the normal case when the information on the retina is successfully transmitted up the line, it contributes to determining the content of the subject's states of knowledge and belief, and to the way things appear to be to him. And since I assume that it will be agreed that the retina does not have conceptual capacities, I assume that it is safe to conclude that states of the retina have only nonconceptual content.

Evans regards it as important to identify information-bearing states of perceptual system with states of seeming since he is anxious to avoid the traditional epistemologist's picture according to which the subject receives, through the perceptual systems, sensory data that is "intrinsically without objective content," but which forms the basis for inferences about the world that causes them. "The only events that can conceivably be regarded as data for a conscious, reasoning subject are *seemings*—events, that is, already imbued with (apparent) objective significance" (*ibid.*, p. 123). But information-bearing states of all kinds, even those of things that are too primitive for anything to seem to be some way to them, are imbued with objective significance. This will be true whether one is talking about the rational judgments of an articulate and conceptually sophisticated person, or about the way things look to such a person, or to an animal, or about the image of a tree on a retina, or about that of the moon on the surface of a pond. To attribute informational content to the state of someone or something is to make a claim about a relation between that person or thing and its environment, and so is to make a claim that is in part about the environment—about the kinds of things that are found in the environment, and about the way the states of the person or thing are disposed to reflect the properties of those things. So, for example, if it is true that it appears to O'Leary that the zebra is striped, then there must be a zebra that O'Leary is looking at. The claim that O'Leary's retina indicates that the zebra is striped has the same consequence. Of course O'Leary's visual system might be in an intrinsically indistinguishable state even if there were no zebra present, even if he were seeing nothing, but was hallucinating. In that case it couldn't be true, or even intelligible, to say that it appears to O'Leary that the zebra is striped. We would have to say that it looks to O'Leary like there is a stripped zebra in front of him, and this would be to attribute a different property to him—to make a different claim, one that relates his visual system to a different piece of information—a different informational content.

One might be tempted to think that the *real* content of O'Leary's state of seeming is one that abstracts away from the environmental dependence. The zebra can't be part of the real content of the way things look to O'Leary, since things could look just as they do even if it weren't the zebra that looked that way, or even if nothing looked that way. But it would be a mistake to yield to this temptation, since one cannot eliminate the environmental dependence without getting rid of informational content altogether. (Suppose O'Leary were in an intrinsically similar state in a world in which pigs looked exactly like zebras in fact look, and vice versa. Then it would look to O'Leary like there was a striped pig before him. This counterfactual possibility should not incline us to say that it is compatible with the way things look to O'Leary that there is a striped pig before him.) If one succeeded in purging the content of perceptual states of their environmental dependence, what would be left is sensory data, "intrinsically without objective content." One would be left with the dreaded Myth of the Given.

Ascriptions of informational content are external in that the concepts used to ascribe them are not thereby attributed to the subject. When I make a claim about the informational states of some subject, I use my concepts to describe the way her environment is disposed to affect her, but the concepts I use may or may not be ones that she shares with me. That is why it does not matter very much whether the parts of the informational system to which we attribute content and that we take to be the proximate sources of the information that is the content of our beliefs and knowledge are themselves accessible to introspection—are properly described as states of seeming. We use conceptual resources to refer to the contents of states of seeming, and also of more primitive informational states, but we do not thereby refer to some kind of content that has the concepts we express as constituents. We can give a reasonably clear account of a kind of abstract object that satisfies our conditions for being a kind of representational content, and that is apt for describing both primitive states of informational systems and the states of belief and acts of judgment of sophisticated reasoners.

My concluding question is this: why shouldn't one take the contents of belief and judgment to be the same kind of content as the kind used to characterize the more primitive information carrying states? Let us grant (without looking too hard at what this means) that states of belief and judgment are essentially conceptual—states and acts that require the capacity to deploy concepts, and that manifest the exercise of this capacity. That does not by itself imply that the concepts that subjects deploy and are disposed to deploy when they are in such states or perform such acts are thereby constitutive of the contents that are used to describe the states and acts. Even if both I and the subject to whom I attribute beliefs must be assumed to have conceptual capacities, it might be that my concepts and hers are different—that we cut the world up in somewhat different ways. If your concepts are different from mine, then I would be unable to use my concepts to attribute beliefs to you if in doing so I were saying that you had beliefs with those concepts as constituents. But we might think of concepts as part of the means used to refer to informational contents, in the way we do when we ascribe content to more primitive informational states that do not involve the deployment of concepts at all. In general, we might say, to attribute content is to characterize various kinds of internal states of others by describing how they tend to vary with certain alternative states of the environment (or more generally, the world). We use our own conceptual resources to distinguish the alternative states of the world, but do not thereby imply that the subject uses the same means to distinguish the alternatives. We might say this even about information-bearing states that belong to what I refuse to call the space of reasons, or the realm of spontaneity.

Gareth Evans proposed that we distinguish different kinds of informational states, that are characterized by different kinds of content. John McDowell argued, in his criticism of Evans, that both kinds of states had the same kind of content: content is conceptual all the way down. I am inclined to agree with McDowell that the different kinds of states have the same kind of content, but I am suggesting that it is nonconceptual all the way up.

Chapter 5

Scenarios, Concepts, and Perception (1992)

Christopher Peacocke

1 Scenarios

A perceptual experience represents the world as being a certain way. What is the nature of the content it represents as holding? How is our mastery of observational concepts related to these perceptual contents? In the course of addressing these questions, I will be identifying two kinds of representational content on which we can draw in giving accounts of concepts which have peculiarly close links with perception.

The representational content of experience is a many-splendored thing. This is true not only of the remarkable range of detail in the perceptual content but also of the range of different, and philosophically interesting, types of content that can be possessed by a particular experience. I begin with what is arguably the most fundamental type of representational content. The sense in which this type of content is arguably the most fundamental is that representational properties of other sorts all in various ways presuppose the existence of this first type of content.

I suggest that one basic form of representational content should be individuated by specifying which ways of filling out the space around the perceiver are consistent with the representational content's being correct. The idea is that the content involves a spatial *type*, the type being that under which fall precisely those ways of filling the space around the subject which are consistent with the correctness of the content. On this model, correctness of a content is then a matter of instantiation: the instantiation by the real world around the perceiver of the spatial type which gives the representational content in question.

We can sharpen up this intuitive formulation. There are two steps which we have to take if we are to specify one of these spatial types. The first step is to fix an origin and axes. The origin and axes will not be a specific place and set of directions in the real world. This is precisely because at the moment we are fixing a type which may potentially be instantiated at many different places in the real world. Nevertheless, it is important that the origin and axes be labeled by certain interrelated properties. It is this labeling by interrelated properties which helps to

From *The Contents of Experience*, T. Crane (ed.), pp. 105–135, Cambridge: Cambridge University Press, 1992. Reprinted with the kind permission of the author.

constrain what are instantiations of the spatial type we are determining. Thus, for instance, one kind of origin is given by the property of being the center of the chest of the human body, with the three axes given by the directions back/front, left/right and up/down with respect to that center.

The use of a particular set of labeled axes in giving part of the content of an experience is not a purely notational or conventional matter. The appropriate set of labeled axes captures distinctions in the phenomenology of experience itself. Looking straight ahead at Buckingham Palace is one experience. It is another to look at it with one's face still towards the Palace, but with one's body turned towards a point on the right. In this second case, the Palace is experienced as being off to one side from the direction of straight ahead—even if the view remains exactly the same as in the first case.

To say that bodily parts are mentioned in the labeling of the axes is not to imply that the bodily parts are given to the subject in some visual or other sensory manner. It is not necessary, in experiencing something as standing in certain spatial relations to one's own body, to perceive one's own bodily parts. They may even be anaesthetised. The nature of the way in which bodily parts are given when they are appropriate labels for the axes is actually an issue of considerable interest. For present purposes, though, let us just note that we are committed in using this framework to the existence of some such way in which bodily parts are so given.

In giving the content of tactile experience, we would sometimes have to use as origin something labeled with the property of being the center of the palm of the human hand, with axes defined by relation to parts of the hand. Actually in the specification of the representational content of some human experiences one would need to consider several such systems of origins and axes, and we would need to specify the spatial relations of these systems to one another. There are many other complexities too; but let us keep things simple at this stage.

Having fixed origin and axes, we need to take the second step in determining one of our spatial types, viz. that of specifying a way of filling out the space around the origin.[1] In picking out one of these ways, we need to do at least the following. We need, for each point (strictly one should say point-type) identified by its distance and direction from the origin, to specify whether there is a surface there, and if so what texture, hue, saturation, brightness and temperature it has at that point, together with its degree of solidity. The orientation of the surface must be included. So must much more in the visual case: the direction, intensity, and character of light sources; the rate of change of perceptible properties, including location; indeed it should include second differentials with respect to time where these prove to be perceptible.

There is no requirement at this point that the conceptual apparatus used in specifying a way of filling out the space be an apparatus of concepts used by the perceiver himself. Any apparatus we want to use, however sophisticated, may be employed in fixing the spatial type, however primitive the conceptual resources of the perceiver with whom we are concerned. This applies both to the apparatus used in characterizing distances and directions, and to that employed in characterizing the surfaces, features and the rest. I will return to the significance of this point later.

We are now in a position to say with slightly more precision what one of our spatial types is. It is a way of locating surfaces, features and the rest in relation to such a labeled origin and family of axes. I call such a spatial type a *scenario*.

With this apparatus, we can then say what is required for the correctness of a representational content of the sort with which I am concerned. Consider the volume of the real world around the perceiver at the time of the experience, with an origin and axes in the real world fixed in accordance with the labeling in the scenario. We can call this a *scene*. The content of the experience is correct if this scene falls under the way of locating surfaces and the rest which constitutes the scenario.

It is important to give for experiences a notion of their representational content which is evaluable as correct or as incorrect outright, rather than merely as correct or as incorrect relative to some assignment or other. The point parallels (and indeed is connected with) a familiar point in the philosophy of language. Consider a particular utterance of the indexical sentence "He is witty." A theory should provide a statement of the conditions under which this particular utterance is true outright, rather than merely the conditions under which it is true relative to any given assignment of objects to its indexical elements (Burge 1974). It is the content of the utterance which is assessable outright which concerns particular objects. Similarly, it is the content of a perceptual experience which is assessable outright that concerns particular places. For perceptual experience, I identify such an outright-assessable content with a *positioned scenario*. A positioned scenario consists of a scenario, together with (i) an assignment to the labeled axes and origins of the scenario of real directions and places in the world which fall under the labels, and (ii) an assigned time. For a particular perceptual experience, the real directions and places assigned at (i) are given by the application of the labels to the subject who enjoys the experience—if the origin is labeled as the center of gravity of the body, the real place assigned to it is the center of gravity of the perceiver's body; and so forth.[2] The time assigned at (ii) is the time at which the perceptual experience occurs: perceptual experience has a present-tense content.[3] We can then say that the content given by the positioned scenario is correct if the scene at its assigned place falls under its scenario at the assigned time, when the scenario is positioned there in accordance with the assigned directions.

The requirement that any perceptual experience has a correctness condition imposes restrictions on what other forms of perceptual experience, besides those of human beings, are possible. Suppose it were said that there could exist a being whose perceptions have scenario-involving contents which concern an origin, but do not contain labeled axes. Now a correctness condition for a particular experience occurring at a given time is not fixed until its scenario is positioned in the real world. An origin alone does not suffice for this positioning: there will be many different ways of orienting it around the perceiver's location at the time of the experience. Until one of these orientations has been selected as being the appropriate one, no correctness condition has been determined. Even in the case of spherical organisms, existing in a fluid, whose perceptions are caused by the impact of light all over the surface of their bodies, the scenarios presented by such organisms' experiences must have axes labeled by parts of their bodies. (The parts mentioned in the labeling need not be limbs.) I will return to this labeling later.

I should also emphasize that the positioned scenario is literally meant to be the content itself. It is not a mental representation of the content; nor a specification of a representation; nor a way of thinking of anything. Subpersonal mental representations of different sorts may equally have for their content the same particular component of a scenario. For example, the orientation of a surface at a particular point may be given by specifying its slant and tilt, or equally by specifying components for its representation in gradient space.[4] Mental representations which differ in the way such orientations are represented may nevertheless represent the same scenario as instantiated in their respective subjects' surroundings.

Since we have now touched on the issue of mental representation, it may be helpful for me to comment on the relation between the account being developed here and Marr's $2\frac{1}{2}$-D sketch. There can be much in a positioned scenario which is not in the content of a $2\frac{1}{2}$-D sketch. The $2\frac{1}{2}$-D sketch has only retinocentric coordinates, and does not include illumination conditions. The present material does, though, give a natural framework in which to give the content of a $2\frac{1}{2}$-D sketch, if such mental representations exist.

Is the present account committed at least to the existence of mental representations with roughly the properties of Marr's $2\frac{1}{2}$-D sketches? In Marr's work, such representations are computed after the primal sketch and before any 3-D models are assigned to shapes in the environment. Is the present philosophical treatment committed to the existence of such a temporally intermediate representation? It is not. What matters for the purposes to which this apparatus will be put is that there exist some mental representation at least part of whose content is given by the positioned scenario. It does not matter if the representation also has other, perhaps simultaneously computed, contents. It will matter that certain systematic connections hold between these scenario-involving contents and other contents that the representations may possess. I will be arguing that the identity of certain other contents depends upon the nature of their links with scenario-involving content. But again, this does not require the existence of distinct mental representations with roughly the properties of Marr's $2\frac{1}{2}$-D sketches.

A good theory must elucidate the appropriate correctness conditions for perceptual experiences if it is adequately to distinguish these experiences from states which do not represent to the subject the world as being a certain way. But the importance of elucidating representational content goes far beyond the need to draw that distinction in the right place. By perceiving the world, we frequently learn whether a judgment with a given conceptual content is true or not. This is possible only because a perceptual experience has a correctness condition whose holding may itself exclude, or require, the truth of a conceptual content.

Some conceptual contents are actually individuated in part by their relations to those perceptual experiences which give good reasons for judging those contents. I will give some detailed examples later. But in advance of the details, it should be clear that scenarios are a promising resource for anchoring notions of conceptual content in some level of nonconceptual content. For a scenario is a spatial type, and a positioned scenario is just a spatial type as tied down to a particular location, orientation and time. A spatial type is quite different from a concept. The identity of a concept, as the term is used here, is answerable to Fregean considerations of cognitive significance. A concept is also ultimately individuated by the condition required for a thinker to possess it. A spatial type is not. So a theory of nonconceptual content which employs the notion of a spatial type promises one way in which a hierarchy of families of concepts can be grounded in a noncircular way.

The notion of a positioned scenario I have been employing is one that can give the content of a fully perceptual experience, and can equally give the content of an experience which is hallucinatory. But it would be quite consistent with the apparatus I've introduced to hold that the fully perceptual case has a philosophical primacy, and that nonperceptual cases have to be elucidated by the relations in which they stand to the fully perceptual case. Consider two different scenes, the objects in each of which are distinct, but which are perceived fully veridically, and in the same way. We can regard a scenario as being the type which captures the similarity of two such different perceptual cases. It is then open to us to say that a hallucinatory experience represents the environment as being a scene of such a type, though there is no such scene there. In brief, the scenario account neither exacerbates nor by itself solves epistemological problems.

2 Scenarios: Consequences and Comparisons

There are several desirable consequences of the thesis that the objective content of an experience is given by its positioned scenario.

(a) Writers on the objective content of experience have often remarked that an experience can have a finer-grained content than can be formulated by using concepts possessed by the experiencer. If you are looking at a range of mountains, it may be correct to say that you see some as rounded, some as jagged. But the content of your visual experience in respect of the shape of the mountains is far more specific than that description indicates: The description involving the concepts *round* and *jagged* would cover many different fine-grained contents which your experience could have, contents which are discriminably different from one another.

This fine-grained content is captured in the scenario. Only those ways of filling out the space around you which are consistent with the veridicality of your experience will be included in the scenario. The ways included in the scenario will omit many which equally involve the appropriate mountains being rounded or jagged.

In describing the scenario, of course, we do have to employ concepts. If we are to fix on the scenario uniquely, we will indeed have to use very fine-grained concepts too, to capture the fine-grained content. But it is crucial to observe that the fact that a concept is used in fixing the scenario does not entail that that concept itself is somehow a component of the experience's representational content, nor that the concept must be possessed by the experiencer. The fine-grained concepts have done their work when they have fixed a unique spatial type. We should not confuse the scenario, the spatial type itself, with the infinitely various ways of picking it out. It is the type which is involved in the content of the experience, not descriptions of the type.

Correlatively, we have on this account to recognize the rather indirect way in which descriptions in ordinary language, which are always at least partially conceptualized, help to characterize the way someone is experiencing the world. The ordinary-language characterization of the scenario can be at most partial.

(b)   In some of my own earlier writings, I discussed the senses in which the type of content possessed by perceptual experience is analogue and unit-free (see Peacocke 1986c, Peacocke 1989c). Let us take "analogue" first. To say that the type of content in question is analogue is to make the following point. There are many dimensions—hue, shape, size, direction—such that any value on that dimension may enter the fine-grained content of an experience. In particular, an experience is not restricted in its range of possible content to those points or ranges picked out by concepts—red, square, straight ahead—possessed by the perceiver. This fact is accommodated by attributing a scenario content. It is accommodated for characteristics of points in the environment because any values of a perceptible dimension may be mentioned in the ways which comprise the scenario. The restrictions on the environment determined by the veridicality of the experience need not be formulable using concepts possessed by the subject independently of the occurrence of the experience. With some important qualifications to be given below, nonpunctual properties such as shape in the scenario will be determined by the assignments to points. Again there will be no restrictions resulting from the thinker's repertoire of shape concepts on the shapes he may perceive things as having.

The unit-free nature of spatial perception is illustrated by the fact that when we see a table to have a certain width, we do not see it as having a certain width in inches, say, as opposed to centimeters. This is also explained by the distinction between the ways of characterizing a scenario and the scenario itself. Suppose we prescind here from qualifications about perceptual acuity. Then we can say that one and the same restriction on the distance between the sides of the table, one and the same restriction on the ways in which the space around the perceiver can be filled consistently with the experience being fully veridical, is given by doing these two things: saying that the sides are 39.4 inches apart, and saying that they are 100 centimeters apart.

The same point also holds for directions and the units in which they may be measured.

(c)   The scenario account provides for the possibility of amodal contents of experience, in the sense that it allows for overlapping contents of experiences in different sense modalities. The restrictions on the environment required by the correctness of a visual experience may overlap with the restrictions required by the correctness of a tactile experience. This can be so if the positions, relative to each other, of the origins and axes for the scenarios of the contents of each experience are fixed by the subject's total conscious state. Both a visual experience, and a tactile experience resulting from stretching out your arm at a certain angle, may represent the existence of a surface in front of you at a certain distance. It is because this is so that, at a higher, concept-involving level, the judgment "That surface is red and warm" does not, when one is taking one's experience at face value, rest on any identity belief concerning the surface in question. I will consider amodal conceptual contents further below.

There is a very great deal more to be said on all aspects of this account. But even on this very primitive foundation, two considerations support the claim that an account mentioning scenarios cannot be dispensed with in favor of purely propositional accounts of the representational contents in question. By a "purely propositional" account I mean one which identifies the representational content with a set of propositions (whether built to Frege's, Russell's, or some other specification), where the constituents of these propositions do not involve, directly or indirectly, scenarios.

First, it is hard to see how a purely propositional account can be made plausible without being parasitic on something properly treated by use of scenarios. Suppose you are in a field in the early autumn in England, and see mist in a certain region. Can a theorist specify part of the representational content of your visual experience by means of the proposition, concerning that region, that it has the property of being misty? Consider in particular the Russellian proposition, which has the region itself as a constituent. This proposal seems inadequate for very familiar reasons. Suppose the region in question is to your north. Someone for whom the region is in a north-easterly direction may also see it to be misty, and the same Russellian proposition would be used by this theorist in specifying the content of his experience. But the region is clearly presented in perception in different ways to you and to the other person. Each of you sees it as being in a different direction relative to yourself, and your actions may differ as a result. Any description of the contents of your two experiences which omits this difference is incomplete. If we fill out the propositional theory to include "ways in which regions are perceived," the advocate of the scenario account will understandably say that these "ways" are a prime example of something of which only his account gives an adequate explanation.

To this the purely propositional theorist may reply that the relevant aspect of representational content should be formulated not just as "R is misty," where R is the region in question, but with a conjunction of Russellian propositions: "R is misty and R is located in direction D." Here D is an egocentric direction.

The theorist of scenarios should say that this move is inadequate on either of the two ways of taking it. The two ways of taking it result from two different ways of construing "egocentric." Take first the construal on which seeing something to be in egocentric direction D involves merely seeing it as having a certain direction in relation to object x, where in fact x is the perceiver himself. This reading is too weak to capture what is wanted. This is because one can see something as having a particular direction in relation to an object x which is in fact oneself whilst not realizing that the object to which one sees it as bearing that relation is in fact oneself. Examples of persons seen in mirrors suffice to make the point.

This suggests that the propositional theorist needs rather the stronger construal. On the stronger construal, to see something as having an egocentric spatial property is to see it as standing in a certain relation to oneself, where this involves use of the first-person way of thinking in giving the content of the visual experience. But the second consideration I wish to develop is precisely that purely propositional accounts, unlike the theory of scenarios, make impossible an adequate account of the first-person way of thinking.

We have just seen that the pure propositionalist will have to mention the first-person way of thinking in giving his propositional contents of experience. For the pure propositionalist, propositional contents exhaust the nonconceptual representational content of experience. But this position is incompatible with the conjunction of two other principles which we have reason to accept.

One of these principles is what we can call "Evans' Thesis" (Evans 1982, pp. 223–224). This states that it is partially constitutive of a subject's employing the first-person way of thinking that he is prepared to make, noninferentially, suitable first-person spatial judgments on the basis of his perceptions when these are taken at face value. These will include "I am on a bridge" when he has an experience as of being on a bridge, "I am in front of a building," "There is a dog on my right," and so forth.

The other principle is what I call "the Principle of Dependence," which states that there can be no more to a concept than is determined by a correct account of what it is to possess that concept. If the Principle of Dependence is true, then we can (with many qualifications and refinements) individuate concepts by filling out this schematic form: concept F is that concept C to possess which a thinker must meet condition $A(C)$. Here the concept F must not be mentioned as such within the scope of psychological states ascribed to the thinker. If it is, we will not have individuated the concept without residue in terms of what it is to possess it (see Peacocke 1989a).

In my judgment, the Principle of Dependence is a powerful tool in the theory of thought and in philosophy more generally. But the application of the Principle which is of interest here is to first-person thought. If we accept Evans' Thesis, then the first-person way of thinking will be individuated in part by the rational sensitivity of present-tense spatial judgments containing it to the content of a thinker's perceptual experiences. But according to the propositionalist, these experiences themselves already have a first-person content which is not itself explained directly or indirectly, in terms of scenarios. So the propositionalist will not have given an account of the first person which respects the Principle of Dependence. An account of mastery of a concept is still circular if it adverts to the enjoyment of perceptual states with a content requiring possession of the concept whose possession was to be elucidated.

This problem is not solved for the pure propositionalist merely by saying that he holds that neither experience nor thought is prior in the individuation of the first-person way of thinking (a "no-priority" view). As long as it is agreed that part of the account of mastery of the first-person concept involves a certain distinctive sensitivity of first-person spatial judgments to the deliverances of perceptual experience, there is an obligation to say what that sensitivity is without simply taking possession of the first-person concept for granted. If we accept the Principle of Dependence, an account of grasp of the first-person concept must distinguish it from all other concepts. Certainly the pure propositionalist does not have something individuating if he says that the first person (for a given subject) is that concept m such that his judgments about whether Fm display a certain sensitivity to experiences which represent Fm as being the case. This condition will be met by much else, including demonstrative ways of thinking of places in his immediate surroundings. A natural further condition is one which relates first-person present-tense spatial judgments in a particular way to the scenario content of experience. But if this further condition is correct, the resulting treatment of the content of experience is not a purely propositional theory—it employs scenario content after all.

It should not, of course, be any part of the scenario account to deny that the first person has to be mentioned in fully specifying the representational content of perceptual experience. It should insist on first-person contents, as it should equally insist on the partially conceptual character of the perceptual content when one sees something to be a dog, or a tree. The issue is rather, in the case of the first person, whether or not the theorist can say more about the nature of the first-person content. The scenario account can respect the Principle of Dependence applied to the first person in the following way. The scenario account already says that a fundamental type of representational content is given by a scenario, a spatial type which involves a labeled origin and labeled axes. The rational sensitivity picked out in Evans' Thesis should be understood as a rational sensitivity of first-person present-tense spatial judgments to the spatial relations things are represented in the scenario of the experience as having *to the labeled central bodily origin and axes*. This avoids the circularity, and in an intuitive way. Of course we still owe a philosophical account of what it is for one scenario, with one set of labeled axes and origin rather than another, to be the content of an experience. But once we recognize the level of the scenario, there is nothing to make this problem insoluble.

Devotees of the theory of indexical thought will note that points exactly corresponding to those just made about first-person thought can be made about the perceptual-indexical concept *here*. There would equally be a circularity in the philosophical account of mastery of *here* in its relation to perceptual experience if we were not able to make reference to the labeled origin in an experience's scenario. [See essay 16, postscript.]

Though I have been arguing that scenario content cannot be replaced by pure propositional contents, propositional contents (even of a neo-Russellian kind) can still be important in characterizing further features of perceptual content, once we have the level of scenario content in place. I shall be arguing for just such a view in the next section.

3 A Further Level of Content: and an Application

We have touched on one way in which scenarios can contribute to the individuation of a concept, the first-person concept. I turn now to discuss how some other conceptual contents are individuated in part by their relations to a level of nonconceptual representational content. I will be suggesting that we need to recognize a kind of nonconceptual representational content in addition to the positioned scenario. [See essay 16, postscript.]

How is mastery of such apparently partially perceptual shape concepts as *square, cubic, diamond-shaped* or *cylindrical* related to the nonconceptual content of experience? In the general framework I favor, the task is to say how the various possession conditions for these concepts mention the nonconceptual contents of experiences (see Peacocke 1989a). We can take the concept *square* as the example for discussion. The concept intended is the relatively observational shape concept which can be possessed without the subject's awareness of any geometrical definition. It is also a concept which has, inherently, fuzzy boundaries.

We can enter the issues by considering a natural, simple suggestion about what is necessary for possession of the concept *square*. This simple suggestion is built up using the materials we have developed so far. Suppose a thinker is taking his experiences at face value. Suppose too that in the positioned scenario of his experience, the area of space apparently occupied by a perceived object is square. Then, this simple account suggests, the thinker must find the present-tense demonstrative thought that that object is square to be primitively compelling.

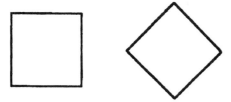

Figure 5.1

This simple account is not circular. It uses the concept *square* in fixing a certain sort of scenario; we emphasized earlier that that does not require the thinker to possess the concept *square*. This simple account can be written out in a way which makes it clearly capable of featuring as part of a longer story which, in the terminology of "What Are Concepts?", is of the *A(C)* form. Indeed it is plausible that any theory of possession of these relatively observational shape concepts will have at some point to exploit this way of avoiding circularity.

The necessary condition proposed by the simple account is, however, not in fact necessary. That it is not necessary is already shown by Mach's example of the square and the diamond (figure 5.1; see Mach 1914, p. 106). A thinker, taking his experiences at face value and possessing this concept *square,* need not find it primitively compelling (without further reflection) that a floor-tile in the diamond orientation is square. But it can still be that in the positioned scenario of his experience, the region of space apparently occupied by the floor-tile is square—as indeed it will be if his experience is veridical.

The case illustrates a first respect in which we need to qualify Evans' pioneering discussion of these issues. He wrote that

> To have the visual experience of four points of light arranged in a square amounts to no more than being in a complex informational state which embodies information about the egocentric location of those lights. (Evans 1975, p. 392)

Four points of light arranged in a regular diamond shape will produce an informational state which embodies information about the egocentric location of those lights. The informational state produced need not be an experience of them as arranged in a square.

Mach's example does not show that scenarios are irrelevant to the difference between the concepts *square* and *regular diamond*. What it does show is that they cannot be used in so simple a fashion; they need to be supplemented with the use of further materials. I doubt that this can be done solely with the materials provided by scenario content. Certainly one should not impose the condition that mastery of the concept *square* is tied in some distinctive way to perception of squares in the orientation of the left-hand square in figure 5.1. It is certainly

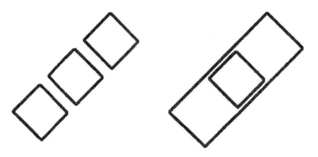

Figure 5.2

possible to see a square at other orientations as a square. Indeed, as Stephen Palmer has emphasized, one can even, naively, see a square at a 45 degree angle as a square, rather than a regular diamond, if the context is right (see figure 5.2, from Palmer 1983, p. 301).

Intuitively, the difference between perceiving something as a square and perceiving it as a (regular) diamond is in part a difference in which symmetries are perceived. When something is perceived as a diamond, the perceived symmetry is a symmetry about the bisector of its angles. When something is perceived as a square, the perceived symmetry is a symmetry about the bisectors of its sides.[5] So intuitively, the simple account should be supplemented by requiring that, for the case it treats, the object apparently occupying the region in question be perceived as symmetrical about the bisectors of its sides. But does perceiving something as symmetrical require the perceiver to possess and make use of the concept *symmetrical*? If so, then what we will have done is simply to explain (this part of) mastery of the concept *square* in terms which require mastery of other concepts. We will not have anchored the difference between the concepts *square* and *diamond* at a level of nonconceptual content. If on the other hand there is a sense in which perceiving something as symmetrical does not require possession of the concept *symmetrical*, what is that sense? And how do we capture the nature of the additional content which distinguishes a case in which we have not merely veridical perception of a symmetrical region, but also have that symmetry perceived? I will sketch one way of answering these two questions.

I suggest that perceptual experience has a second layer of nonconceptual representational content. The contents at this second layer cannot be identified with positioned scenarios, but they are nevertheless distinct too from conceptual contents. These additional contents I call *protopropositions*. These protopropositions are assessable as true or false. A protoproposition contains an individual or individuals, together with a property or relation. When a protoproposition is part of the representational content of an experience, the experience represents the property or relation in the protoproposition as holding of the individual or individuals it also contains. I write of proto*propositions* rather than protothoughts because protopropositions contain objects, properties and relations, rather than concepts thereof. I write of *proto*propositions because they are not, on the present account, determined as part of the content of an experience by being fixed by some conceptual content the experience possesses. The protopropositions which enter the representational content of ordinary human visual experience contain such properties and relations as SQUARE, CURVED, PARALLEL TO, EQUIDISTANT FROM, SAME SHAPE AS, and SYMMETRICAL ABOUT.[6] These properties and relations can be represented as holding of places, lines or regions in the positioned scenario; or of objects perceived as located in such places. There will of course be many equally acceptable set-theoretic ways of building up such propositions.

Because it is properties and relations, rather than concepts thereof, which protopropositions contain, there is no immediate circularity in mentioning this level of representational content in individuating certain conceptual contents. As always, of course, we will want to have a substantive theory of what it is to be in perceptual states with protopropositional contents.

Protopropositional content is not determined by positioned scenario content. Two experiences can have the same positioned scenario content but different protopropositional contents. Many familiar cases can illustrate this. One illustration is given by the case in which one comes to see two shapes in the environment to be the same—one a tilted version of the other, say, even though the single shape in question is quite unfamiliar. The experiences before and after seeing the identity of shape have the same representational content at the level of the positioned scenario. They differ in that the later experience has amongst its protopropositional contents that the two objects are of the same shape. An even more familiar case is given by certain differences in spatial grouping. When you see a two-dimensional array of elements as grouped in columns rather than rows, your experience has the protopropositional content that certain elements, which are in fact vertically arranged, are co-linear. But there need not be any difference in the positioned scenario content between the case in which the array is seen as grouped in columns and that in which it is seen as grouped in rows.[7]

Protopropositional content plays an important role in memory, in recognition, and in the subject's construction of a cognitive map of his world. When a subject perceives some of an object's properties and the relations of some of its parts, his memory of the object and its perceptual type is greatly facilitated. When his perceptual experience has such protopropositional contents, the subject does not have to remember highly detailed scenario contents, with their specifications for each point. There is no need for so much detail, provided he can remember the salient properties and relations in which the object and its parts were perceived to stand. Protopropositional content is equally important to recognition. We may see an object, and thereby acquire an ability to recognize it when we re-encounter it. But the re-encounter will frequently present the object from a different angle, a different distance, and the object's own orientation to its environment may vary too. If there were only a meager protopropositional content in the original perception of the object, immensely complex operations on a highly detailed content would be necessary for perceptual recognition of the object. But with a detailed proto-propositional content, the task is eased. That two lines are straight, that they form a right angle, that an object is symmetrical about one of its axes, can enter the content of two experiences in which the same object is presented at very different angles, distances, or in a different orientation to its surroundings. A correspond-ing point applies to the construction of a cognitive map. The presence of proto-propositional content reduces the demands on the thinker. As he moves, he can register that a certain line is straight, and enter this appropriately in his cognitive map after he has moved away, rather than having to transform one complex scenario content into a corresponding complex content for his map.

The reader will not be surprised to learn that it is this level of protoproposi-tional content which I propose to employ to avert the threatened failure to give an account of the difference between the concepts *square* and *diamond*. When we say that in an experience of something as a square, the symmetry about the bisec-tors of its sides must be perceived, we are noting a restriction at the level of pro-topropositional content. An experience in which something is perceived as a square is one whose nonconceptual representational content contains the proto-proposition that a certain figure is symmetrical about a line, a line which in fact in the positioned scenario of the experience bisects the figure's sides.

The reader may also have been wishing to protest for some time that there is an argument that the components of content I have tried to capture by the pro-perties and relations of protopropositions are after all really conceptual. Consider the predicative component of the demonstrative content, judged on the basis of perception, "That line is straight." Isn't what is judged here of the line the same as the way experience represents the line to be? So if the component of the content judged is conceptual, must not that of the perception be likewise?

My reply is twofold. First, there are many examples which should make us acknowledge that a subject can perceive a property or relation without conceptu-alizing it. The symmetry of an ink-blot shape can be perceived by one who does not have the concept of symmetry. Such a shape does not appear the same to one who does not perceive the symmetry as to one who does. But to perceive the sym-metry, the subject does not have to be capable of exercising the concept *symmetri-cal* in his thoughts, or to be capable of combining it with any singular mode of presentation he possesses. The property SYMMETRICAL features in the proto-propositional content of this subject's experience, without being conceptualized by him. Again, there is a difference between hearing the note middle C and the F# just above it, when sounded simultaneously, as an augmented fourth and hearing it as a diminished fifth. I now follow DeBellis (1995) in describing the dif-ference between the two cases in terms of the relations in which the notes are per-ceived to stand. When they are perceived as an augmented fourth, the F# is perceived as the seventh of the scale with G as tonic, and the C as the fourth thereof. When they are perceived as a diminished fifth, the upper note is perceived as the fourth of the scale with D flat as tonic, and the C as the seventh thereof. There is no question but that the interval can be perceived in either of these ways by someone without even the most rudimentary personal-level knowledge of the classifications of music theory; that is, by someone without the apparatus for conceptualizing the relations he perceives. Finally, as a third case, consider the two most salient ways of perceiving an utterance of the familiar sentence, "Visiting royalty can be boring." It seems to me correct to say of an English hearer of an utterance of this sentence that he hears it under one rather than another of its structural descriptions. What this involves in one of the two cases is the hearer perceiving it as, roughly, the royalty of which the boringness is being predicated, rather than that of a certain kind of visit. When heard this way, the components of the uttered sentence are heard as standing in certain relations to one another. But I doubt that the ordinary speaker-hearer has to have, at the personal level, the apparatus for conceptualizing these syntactico-semantic relations. I doubt that the ordinary speaker-hearer has to be capable of thoughts about these syntactico-semantic relations. The ordinary speaker-hearer either hears the utterance as meaning that it can be boring to visit royalty, or hears the utterance as meaning that when royalty visit, they can be boring. It would not be right to say that talk of one structural description rather than another being perceived is merely projected backwards from the sentence being heard as having one complete meaning rather than another. Consider someone who understands much of English, including the "-ing" suffix applied to verbs, but who does not understand the verb "to bore" as intended in the example. This subject can still hear the sentence under one rather than another of its structural descriptions. The plausible hypothesis, it seems to me, is that far from perception of structural descriptions being projected backwards from perceived meaning, it is rather true that perception of the sentence as structured one way rather than another, or what underlies such perception, positively contributes to the hearer's perception of the sentence as having one meaning rather than another. As in the musical and the spatial cases, the syntactico-semantic relations are perceived but not conceptualized.

The second part of the reply to the imagined objection is concessive, at least to part of the spirit of the objection. There is indeed a conceptual component of the judgment that is intimately related to experiences with protopropositional contents that certain perceived things are straight. But this conceptual content is one which is individuated in part by certain of its relations to such protopropositional contents. As in the first-person case, and certain others to follow, it is not part of the present position that perceptual experiences do not have conceptual contents involving this concept *straight*. They do in general have such a conceptual content. What matters to the present position is that if we are to have a noncircular and individuating account of mastery of this perceptual concept *straight*, that mastery must be related to some feature of experience which does not have to be explained in terms which presuppose possession of the concept. We cannot supply this by relating the mastery to experiences whose positioned scenarios require for their correctness that a certain line be straight: for that can be so without the straight-ness being perceived. Having the property STRAIGHT in the protopropositional content respects that point, without threatening a circular account of mastery. These points, just made for properties and certain concepts of them, also have structural analogues for objects and perceptual-demonstrative modes of presen-tation of them.

A congenitally blind man can possess the perceptual concept *square*, and apply it on the basis of his tactile experience of the world. There is a good case to be made that *square* and other perceptual shape concepts are not modality-specific— are amodal, as I will say. There is a natural criterion for the amodality of a concept within the framework of the A(C) form and possession conditions. A concept is amodal if there is no particular sense modality such that the concept's possession condition mentions the thinker's sensitivity of beliefs containing the concept to experiences in that particular modality. Let us adopt that criterion. It treats amodality as a property of the concept itself, as opposed to a property dependent upon one amongst other means of grasping it. By this criterion, the modified simple account of the concept *square* can itself be a fragment of a possession con-dition for an amodal shape concept. Suppose a possession condition for a concept mentions a sensitivity of certain judgments whose contents contain it to states with scenario-involving contents, or to anything else which can equally be present in more than one sense modality; and suppose too that it does not mention anything else which requires experiences in a particular modality. When these suppositions hold, the concept is amodal. Despite the departure already made from it, this is very much in the spirit of Evans' idea. On the present account, there remains a "single conceptual capacity" which is exercised both in response to visual expe-rience, and in response to tactile experience, when, in response to experiences of each kind, a thinker judges something to be square (see Evans 1975, p. 374).

Given the present criterion for the amodality of a concept, it is a *non sequitur* to deny the amodality of a particular concept F solely on the ground that some par-ticular subject can experience things as F in one modality but not in another. For it may be that experiences in one modality have protopropositional contents which are lacking in that particular subject's experiences in the other modality. So, for example, symmetry and parallelism are not, as we actually are, made salient in the protopropositional content of our tactile experience in nearly so wide a range of cases as they are in visual experience. Since this is so, some shape con-cepts may be applied on the basis of visual experience of an object which are not immediately applied when the object is touched. It does not follow that the con-cepts are modality-specific in the way the concept *red* is. We may rather be able to explain the difference by citing the different properties entering the proto-propositional contents of visual and tactile experiences.

This treatment of perceptual shape concepts is consistent with acknowledging that experiences have conceptual content. In Evans' work, experiences are con-ceived as not having a conceptual content at all.[8] This part of Evans' conception is not obviously obligatory. It is not clear that there is good reason for denying the overwhelmingly plausible view that we see things as trees or hear a sound as that of a car approaching. However, accepting the overwhelmingly plausible view does not seem to give us a new resource to use in building possession conditions for perceptual shape concepts. If we try to make the possession condition for the perceptual concept *square* a matter of a certain sensitivity to experiences with a content containing the concept *square* we will be open to the charge of circularity. This circularity is parallel to that suffered by the propositional theorist we noted earlier, who tries to make possession of the first-person concept a matter of the sensitivity of thoughts containing it to features of experiences which already have first-person contents. Like that theorist, we would be attempting to individuate a concept by reference to something which already takes for granted the thinker's possession of the concept in question, viz. the capacity to have experiences whose contents contain the concept in question.[9]

The moral we should draw is that though experiences do indeed have conceptual contents, a possession condition for a concept should appeal at most only to the nonconceptual contents of the thinker's experiences, amongst which are the positioned scenarios and the protopropositional contents. If this is correct, then Evans' view that experiences have no conceptual contents was not by itself depriving him of any resource that is legitimately usable in the individuation of particular concepts.[10]

While the direction of constitutive explanation has so far been running from experience to concept possession, it is essential to allow too that there is some causal explanation in the opposite direction. Once a thinker has acquired a perceptually-individuated concept, his possession of that concept can causally influence what contents his experiences possess. If this were not so, we would be unable to account for differences which manifestly exist. One such difference, for example, is that between the experience of a perceiver completely unfamiliar with Cyrillic script seeing a sentence in that script, and the experience of one who understands a language written in that script. These two perceivers see the same shapes at the same positions; it may be that the positioned scenario and the protopropositional contents of their respective experiences are identical. The experiences differ in that the second perceiver recognizes the symbols as of particular kinds, and sequences of the symbols as of particular semantic kinds. The question of the nature of this difference, and more generally of what it is, constitutively, for an experience to have a conceptual content, remain as urgent and as open as ever.

Obviously the remarks of this section cannot purport to give a full possession condition for the concept *square*. A full possession condition must elucidate a thinker's ability to judge that an unperceived thing is square. Many intriguing issues arise in the attempt to elucidate that ability. One of them is the nature of a thinker's understanding that imperceptibly small things can be square, and that objects too large to perceive can be so too. Another such question is the relation of this understanding to the ability to judge of an unperceived but perceivable thing that it is square. Pursuing these issues would take us too far away from the other topics I wish to discuss. We can note, though, that the partial possession condition developed so far has a bearing on the answers to these questions. Consider, for instance, a thinker's ability to judge of something unperceived but perceptible that it is square. A theorist might try to explain this as follows. Just as the nonconceptual content of perception is given by a spatial type, so that of a cognitive map is given by a way of assigning objects, properties, relations and so forth in the space itself in which the subject is embedded. So far, this is tempting and plausible. But suppose the theorist goes on to say that to judge that an object at a specified, unperceived location is square is simply for the location in the content-specification of one's map to be assigned something square. That is identical with assigning it something diamond-shaped. But judging that the object there is square is different from judging it to be diamond-shaped. The distinctions between nonconceptual contents discussed above thus infuse our thought about the nonperceptual cases too.

4 Spatial Reasoning and Action

Is nonconceptual representational content autonomous? Is there, or could there be, a creature which is in states with nonconceptual representational contents, even though the creature does not possess any concepts? Some passages in Evans suggest he was tempted by such a claim of autonomy for his nonconceptual contents (1982, pp. 124, 158) [essay 2, p. 52, and see all of section 4].[11] But such a thesis of autonomy is not obligatory.

Even for the most primitive level of scenario content, there are strong arguments against such autonomy. Scenario content is spatial representational content. Specifically spatial content involves more than just a sensitivity to higher-order properties of stimulation patterns. I doubt that we could ever justify the attribution of genuinely spatial content to an organism's states, of a kind going beyond such sensitivity, unless the subject were on occasion to employ states with these contents in identifying places over time. Such an identification might on occasion consist in identifying one's current location with one previously encountered. The possibility of such identification is also involved in the subject's appreciating that the scene currently presented in his perception is something to which his own spatial relations can vary over time.

Identification of places over time requires that states with scenario content contribute to the construction of a cognitive map of the world around the subject. It is, in turn, highly questionable whether we can make sense of the subject engaging in such construction unless he employs at least a rudimentary form of first-person thought, that is, unless he possesses at least some primitive form of first-person concept. If this is correct, scenario content is not autonomous. On the approach I am advocating, then, nonconceptual content is not a level whose nature is completely explicable without reference to conceptual content at all. It is rather a type of content which, though nonconceptual, cannot be explained except in part by reference to its relations to certain primitive conceptual contents. At the most basic level, conceptual and nonconceptual content must be elucidated simultaneously. The most basic elements of the scheme themselves form a local holism.

To identify places over time requires the subject to be able to integrate the representational contents of his successive perceptions into an integrated representation of the world around him, both near and far, past and present. We can label this the ability to engage in spatial reasoning. Some parts of spatial reasoning may be conceptual. Some, though not conceptual, will still be propositional—we earlier emphasized the role of protopropositional contents in building a cognitive map of the environment. But where spatial reasoning involves only scenario content, the reasoning will be neither conceptual nor propositional.

Spatial reasoning involves the subject building up a consistent representation of the world around him and of his location in it. It is worth remarking on what "consistent" means here, given that scenario content is neither conceptual nor propositional. One of the distinctive relations to which spatial reasoning is answerable is the following notion of consistency: that of a given perceptual experience's positioned scenario being consistent with a given cognitive map. What this means is that there are ways of filling out the mapped space around the subject such that both of the following are instantiated: (i) the way of locating features in it required by the cognitive map and (ii) one of the ways of locating things in the world sufficient for the correctness of the positioned scenario.

Whenever we claim that a certain role in reasoning is essential to a particular kind of content, we incur an obligation. The obligation is to elucidate the relation between the content's role in reasoning and its correctness (truth) conditions, or the contribution the content makes to such correctness conditions. This is a natural generalization of the obligation to provide, for any given concept, an account of the way in which what individuates the concept also succeeds in determining (together with the world) a semantic value.[12] Ideally, we would like to have a theory of how a role in spatial reasoning determines the correctness of assigning one positioned scenario content rather than another to an experience. The task of providing this theory is one of the many which lie in intriguing regions visible from the main route of this paper. The task is of course not precisely analogous in detail to that which arises for conceptual contents. For in those cases, the concepts are being individuated by their possession conditions; whereas, I have been emphasizing, a scenario (a spatial type) is not. Nonetheless, the obligation to say what it is for one spatial type rather than another to be involved in the content of an experience still exists, and must be met in part by its detailed role in spatial reasoning.

Genuine spatial reasoning must in turn be capable of explaining the spatial properties of a thinker's actions. The spatial property may just be the minimal property of being carried out at a particular location. The fact that such properties are included leaves room for the possibility of an equally minimal case, touched upon earlier. This is the case of a being which is not capable of initiating changes in its own configuration or location, but whose nonspatial actions (such as changes of color or of the acidity of its surfaces) are controlled by its representation of its own and other things' locations in its cognitive map. Human beings are, though, obviously capable of controlling a much wider range of the spatial properties of their actions, and in the remainder of this section I will consider the role of scenario content in this control. This further role cannot be taken as unconditionally constitutive of having experiences with scenario content, since the minimal case is possible. But the further role is crucial to the content-involving explanation of human action.

To characterize the further role, we must first remind ourselves of the distinctive kind of knowledge a subject has about the position of his limbs and the configuration of his body. As Wittgenstein (1980, §§770–772, 798) and Anscombe (1981) long ago emphasized, this knowledge is not inferred from, or even caused by, sensations. You can know the position of your own arm even when it is anaesthetized, and even when you are not seeing it or feeling it with another limb. What is important for us is that in the content of this distinctive kind of knowledge, the location of a limb is given egocentrically, in relation to the subject's body. It is given in the same kind of way in which a location is given in the positioned scenario of an experience, where the scenario is labeled with bodily axes.[13]

In characterizing the distinctive type of knowledge in this way, I differ in some respects from Brian O'Shaughnessy's penetrating treatment (1980, chap. 10). O'Shaughnessy's insight was that knowledge of the position of our "bodily extremities" is "non-conceptual" and "nonpropositional." But he also says that this knowledge is "entirely practical"; and that its content "is exhaustively manifest in a set of physical acts" (1980, p. 64). It is certainly not true that a person's knowledge of the position of his limbs and body at a given time is exhaustively manifest in actions he actually performs. Much of this knowledge possessed at a given time is not put to use in action at all. Perhaps O'Shaughnessy would say rather that the distinctive knowledge consists in certain dispositions to act. There must be something right about mentioning dispositions to act, and I will return to them soon. But we will not get a proper understanding of the knowledge in question until we acknowledge its content. For it seems clear that the content of the distinctive knowledge has correctness conditions, which may or may not obtain. As a result of drug or neural damage, a subject's belief about the location of his hand may be false. We cannot accommodate this just by saying that a false belief is one which, when manifested in action, does not lead to success. A distinction between the success and the failure of an action depends upon a notion of the content of its generating intentional or subintentional state, a content whose correctness condition may obtain (success) or not (failure). And the content of these (sub)intentional states is of the same kind as the content of one's knowledge when one knows that one of them has succeeded.[14]

It is not surprising, given his views, that O'Shaughnessy says that there is a structural parallel between subintentional states and sensations. If what I have been saying is right, the content of the subintentional state has a correctness condition on the external, objective world. The sensation does not. So there *is* no structural parallel of that sort on my position. Absence of conceptual content does not mean absence of all genuine content.

Now let us return to the further role of scenario content in human action. In supplying a subject with information about the location of things relative to bodily axes, perception supplies that nonconceptual information in a form immediately usable if the subject wants to move his body, or some limb, towards, or from, or to be in some other spatial relation to what he perceives. It is only because the bodily-based scenario-involving contents are common to perception, to our distinctive knowledge of bodily position, and to what is under our immediate (sub)intentional control, that the information in perception is immediately usable in performing actions. When a propositional attitude has a conceptual constituent individuated in part by scenario content it can play an intermediary role between perception and action.

This intermediary role made possible by scenario contents with labeled (bodily) axes explains more fully a connection, which I mentioned in earlier work (1986c, 1989c), between the nonconceptual contents of perception and bodily action. A normal individual, asked to direct the beam of a spotlight in a forest onto a tree 47 degrees to the right of straight ahead, will not, in the sense relevant to action, know where to point the beam. The normal individual does not know which perceptually individuated direction is 47 degrees to the right of straight ahead. He will, though, have no difficulty if the tree in question is marked, so that he can see in which precise direction it lies.

It is helpful here to consider an explicit statement of the subject's practical reasoning in this second case, in which the normal individual has no difficulty in carrying out the task. He forms the intention with this content:

(1) I will move my arm in the direction of that tree.

He also knows from his perceptual experience that

(2) That tree is in the direction d (identified egocentrically, using scenario content).

So he forms the intention with the content

(3) I will move my arm in the direction d.

He can then carry out this intention without further practical reasoning. This description makes it clear that the connections between perception and action rest on two links. The first is the link between the perceptual demonstrative "that tree" and the availability of the perceptually-based knowledge of (2) which contains that demonstrative way of thinking. The second is the link between the egocentric mode of identification of the directions and the subject's "basic" actions. If either of these links does not hold for some other mode of presentation in place of "that tree," such connections between perception and action will not hold, *ceteris paribus*.

Actually even if both these links hold, that is not strictly sufficient for the link between perception and action to hold, because of the phenomenon known as "optic ataxia." A subject with optic ataxia cannot reach accurately for visually presented objects; nor can he orient his hand correctly to fit into a slot which he sees. We should not conclude from such cases that the representations which control bodily movements do not involve scenario content. A better hypothesis is that the representations which control the limbs do use scenario content, but that in the cases of optic ataxia the contents of visual experience are *inaccessible* to the motor control systems. That is, we have two different representations, not two different kinds of content (which would need some kind of "translation" procedure). This is a better hypothesis because subjects with optic ataxia display a "well coordinated, rapid and accurate pattern of movements directed at the body."[15]

There are also unusual cases in which two or more systems of labeled axes are properly used in giving the positioned scenario content of a single experience, but in which the spatial relation between those two systems is not specified in the content of that experience. There are, for instance, certain positions in which, when lying on your back, you can twist your arms up behind your head. A piece of furniture touched with a hand of the twisted arm may be experienced as standing in certain spatial relations to one's hand, fingers and wrist, but not as standing in any particular relation to the rest of one's body. In such a case of fragmentation, there is also fragmentation of the person's systems of knowledge which help to explain bodily actions. The subject will know what to do to move his fingers away from the touched furniture, but not, without further reasoning, how to move them closer to his torso.

Of the many substantive questions which arise in this area, one which seems somewhat more tractable than the rest is this: what gives a subintentional state or trying one nonconceptual content rather than another? One subpart of this question concerns the labeling of axes in a scenario. We need to say something illuminating about this labeling which does not take for granted a partially scenario-like nonconceptual content which already has labeled axes.

I should emphasize that the problem here does not concern merely notational variants of particular axes and coordinate systems. One notational variant of the basic human axes would rotate them by 45 degrees, and adjust coordinates in specifying a scenario in a compensating fashion. That this is a purely notational, insubstantial, matter should be especially clear in the case of scenario content— for it is clear here that the variation is solely in means of specifying one and the same spatial type. The important question is rather this: why are axes labeled in *some* way involving particular bodily parts and limbs appropriate in giving the spatial type which is in turn used in giving the content of a trying, and of other subintentional states? We could encapsulate the point by saying that the question is about frames of reference for spatial types, rather than about coordinate systems.

Here is one possible answer. Let me say that two instructions ("tryings") of a given subject are of the same type if they differ only in the reference of their "now" component. So trying to move one's left hand to a particular position in front of oneself at 9 a.m. and trying to do so at 10 a.m. are instructions of the same type. Now take a given type of instruction with nonconceptual, partially scenario-like content. I suggest that the frame of reference to be used in labeling the axes of its scenario is that frame with respect to which instructions of the given type always have the *same* effect, when characterized in relation to that frame, in all normal spatio-temporal contexts (and when the efferent nervous system is functioning properly). When an instruction is an instruction to move one's hand in a certain relation to one's body, it will have the same effect, described in relation to a bodily frame of reference, whether the thinker is in London or in Edinburgh. It will not have the same effect if the bizarre choice were made of a frame of reference involving longitude and latitude. Nor would it always have the same effect (when the thinker is functioning properly) in any other frame of reference defined by objects with respect to which the subject can move. Nor will descriptions of the effect in terms of muscle changes be the same in all spatio-temporal contexts. For they will depend on the starting point of the hand. This criterion can be called the *constancy* criterion for fixing the frame of reference, and so the labeling, of any axes used in individuating the scenarios for a given subject's subintentional states. The constancy criterion is a small first step towards the formulation of a substantive theory of the nonconceptual content of subintentional states.

5 Conclusion

I have been arguing that we should recognize scenario and protopropositional contents as forms of nonconceptual representational contents. These nonconceptual contents must be mentioned in the possession conditions for perceptual and demonstrative concepts. A proper appreciation of their role allows us to explain the possibility of noncircular possession conditions for these very basic concepts, and to give an account of the relations between perception, action and a subject's representation of his environment.

At several points, I have indicated philosophical issues arising out of the approach of this paper. Before closing, I wish to mention very briefly some of the links between, and open questions about, the types of nonconceptual representational content I have been discussing and issues in the cognitive sciences.

Suppose, with Roger Shepard (1981), we regard the task of the mechanisms of visual perception as that of computing an inverse of the projective mapping from the environment to the retinal image. From this lofty perspective, we would certainly expect representations with positioned scenario and protopropositional contents to be computed (along the way): for it is the real scene, in our sense, which produce the retinal image. In a content-involving psychology, we would expect the early stages of vision to compute and combine various partial specifications of the scene around the perceiver. The several feature maps, and the integration thereof, studied by Anne Treisman and her colleagues (Treisman and Gelade 1980, Treisman and Schmidt 1982) are just such partial specifications. They also begin to suggest mechanisms by which protopropositional content is made explicit in mental representations. If we want the explanatory power that only a content-involving description of a computation can supply, we should use positioned scenarios and protopropositions in describing the mechanisms outlined in that research.

If the treatment in this paper is roughly along the right lines, an important item on an interdisciplinary agenda should be the construction of a theory of the ways in which the various types of representational content proposed here are mentally represented. We should certainly want to know the relation between these types of content and the theory that mental images are interpreted symbol-filled arrays (Tye 1991, pp. 90–102). It is also important to understand the possibilities for the realization of states with scenario content in connectionist systems. We need to consider the following proposal. We might partition the three-dimensional space around the subject into suitably small cells. Each cell could be represented by a "binding" unit which is connected to three other elements. These three other elements each represent the values of the cell on the labeled axes of the scenario. The binding unit can then have connections to other assemblies for the features represented as instantiated at that cell; and so forth. Do problems about binding make this too costly and implausible? A third, closely related, area in which we have interdisciplinary questions is that of the mental models discussed in philosophical terms by Colin McGinn (1989).[16] We have the prospect of further understanding, both of mental representation and potentially of content itself, emerging from future work on this interdisciplinary agenda.[17]

Notes

1. Strictly, in giving the content we should consider a set of such ways of filling out the space. By doing so, we can capture the degree of perceptual acuity; greater acuity corresponds to restriction of the set of ways of filling out the space whose instantiation is consistent with the correctness of the representational content. I shall take this qualification as read for the remainder of this paper.

2. There are several oversimplifications here; I am aiming to capture the spirit of a position.

3. The time at which the mental representation underlying the experience is computed however, may bear a complex relation to the time represented in the content of the experience. See Dennett 1991.

4. For these two ways of representing surface orientation at a point, see Marr 1982, pp. 241–243.

5. "People perceive different geometrical properties of the figure when it is seen as a square rather than as a diamond" (Palmer 1983, p. 293). Palmer's paper contains further material of great relevance to a philosophical theory of these matters.

6. I use upper-case letters for a word to indicate that I am referring to the property or relation to which it refers, rather than to the concept it expresses.

7. The preceding discussion revises the treatment of this case given in Peacocke 1983, without altering the general view required of the relation between sensational and representational properties of experience. For another discussion which treats this case by using propositional contents, see DeBellis 1995. DeBellis develops the use of propositional contents in giving the contents of perceptions of Western music.

8. See Evans 1982 [also see essay 2]; the view is endorsed by Colin McGinn (1989, p. 62).

9. This was a problem which was noted, but far from satisfactorily resolved, in Peacocke 1983.

10. John Campbell has emphasized the philosophical significance of real cases of subjects suffering from visual disorientation—see Campbell 1989. These subjects are able to identify and apparently perceive the shape of objects in their environment, without experiencing them as having any particular (egocentric) location. There is a readable case study in Godwin-Austen 1965. As Campbell says, these cases show another respect in which we need to revise Evans' description, displayed above, of perceiving something as square. For Evans' description apparently leaves no room for the possibility of experiencing something as square without experiencing it as having a particular location. The present account can accommodate the possibility at the level of protopropositional content. Even if an edge e and an edge e' are not localized in the subject's perception, that perception can still have the protopropositional content that e is PARALLEL TO e'. The same applies to protopropositional contents about the relations of SYMMETRY and of BEING AT A RIGHT ANGLE TO such-and-such. But for something to be perceptibly square is to be defined in terms of these notions: and so the possibility is allowed that something is perceived as square, without being localized. This does not mean that scenario content drops out altogether from an account of what it is for an experience to have a protopropositional content containing a given property. It is plausible that a subject must have some ability to use those of his perceptual experiences in which instances of properties are localized to confirm or refute the represented instantiation which occurs without localization. (If this ability has disappeared altogether, and we still want to attribute perceptual identifications without localization, the attribution will be correct because there was once a connection with such abilities.)

11. Evans' position was that a perceptual informational state with a nonconceptual content is an experience only if it serves as input to a *"thinking, concept-applying,* and *reasoning system"* (1982, p. 8—Evans' italics). He regarded this as a "further link" of perceptual informational states with nonconceptual content. He also said of the operation of the informational systems which include the perceptual systems that their operations are more primitive than those involving the "far more sophisticated cognitive state" of belief (p. 124), and speculated that these more primitive operations may be carried out "in some phylogenetically more ancient part of the brain" (p. 158) [essay 2, p. 52].

12. This is the obligation I described in Peacocke (1989a, pp. 6ff.) as that of providing a "Determination Theory," for any given concept's possession condition. There is a detailed attempt to meet the obligation for the logical constants in Peacocke 1987.

13. It is a question worth investigation how the limb is given in this distinctive knowledge. It is certainly not conceptualized descriptively—as a particular finger might be conceptualized as "the fourth finger on my left hand." On the way a particular finger is given in the content of the distinctive knowledge, it is potentially informative that it is the fourth on one's left hand. One supposition worth considering is that it is partially constitutive of the way the finger is given in the distinctive knowledge that the intention (or subintention) to move the finger, thus given, from one place to another is one which, when things are working properly, results in that movement of that finger.

14. It should be emphasized that subintentional states and acts in O'Shaughnessy's sense are not subpersonal in Dennett's sense. The subintentional states are so characterized because their content is not fully conceptualized; but they occur at the personal level.

15. Perenin and Vighetto 1988, p. 661. See also p. 662: "None of the patients showed any significant motor, proprioceptive, visual field or visual space perception disturbances." My thanks to R. McCarthy for this reference.

16. McGinn indexes mental models with truth-evaluable propositions. If these are built up from constituents solely at the level of reference, I would remarshal the arguments of §2 to argue that mental models need a more discriminating assignment of content. If the indexing propositions are at the level of sense, then we need to mention scenario and protopropositional content. The assignment of these nonconceptual contents to mental models is entirely within the spirit of McGinn's views.

17. The views expressed here relate also to other writings. Quine (1969, p. 147, pp. 153–154) emphasizes the need to give some psychological states contents that are neither conceptually nor linguistically individuated. And Lewis takes the contents of someone's visual experiences to be sets of "those possible individuals who, according to the content of his visual experience, he himself might be; they share just those properties he sees himself to have. These will mostly be relational properties: properties of facing such-and-such an arrangement of nearby things" (1983a, p. 30): Lewis certainly does not conceive these sets to be linguistically or conceptually individuated. The relation of my account to Lewis' merits more discussion. Here, I just note two major issues. First, is Lewis right to attribute the same kind of content to perceptions as to other propositional attitudes? Second, while Lewis' apparatus captures every positioned scenario content, it assigns no special status to the labeled axes and origins. I think an experience can only have a correctness condition about (say) a particular direction if it has a labeled origin and axes. (Lewis may of course restrict the contents of perception to take account of these theses.)

Earlier versions of this material were presented in 1988–1989 to an interdisciplinary conference on the mental representation of space at King's College Cambridge, to a seminar at Oxford University and to the International Colloquium on Cognitive Science at San Sebastian/Donostia. I thank John Campbell, Adrian Cussins, Martin Davies and Michael Martin for valuable comments.

Chapter 6

Content, Conceptual Content, and Nonconceptual Content (1990)

Adrian Cussins

Introducing Content

I will begin with a pocket account of the notions of content, conceptual content, and nonconceptual content, before presenting a more careful analysis of them.

Human persons act as they do, and thus often behave as they do, because some aspect of the world is presented to them in some manner. The term "content," as I shall use it, refers in the first instance, to the way in which some aspect of the world is presented to a subject; the way in which an object or property or state of affairs is given in, or presented to, experience or thought. For example, I see the grey, plastic rectangular object in front of me as being a typing board, having the familiar Qwerty structure. I also see it *as being* in front of me, and these facts are responsible for my hands moving in a certain way. Representational states of mine have content in virtue of which they make the world accessible to me, guide my action, and (usually) are presented to me as something which is either correct or incorrect. I shall speak of *a representational state (or vehicle) having content*. It may be that a single representational vehicle carries more than one content, even more than one kind of content.

The theory of content—in terms of which we explain what content is—locates the notion with respect to our notions of experience, thought, and the world. But it is important to see that this is consistent with the notion of content being applied to (though not explained in terms of) states which are not states of an experiencing subject.[1] There are derivative uses of the notion in application to the communicative products of cognition, such as speech, writing, and other sign-systems, or to non-conscious states of persons such as subpersonal information-processing states, but these uses must ultimately be explained in terms of a theory of the primary application of content in cognitive experience.[2]

Conceptual content is content which presents the world to a subject *as* the objective, human world about which one can form true or false judgments. If there are other kinds of content, kinds of *nonconceptual* content, then that will be because

From "The Connectionist Construction of Concepts" in *The Philosophy of Artificial Intelligence*, M. Boden (ed.), pp. 380–400, Oxford: Oxford University Press, 1990. Reprinted with the kind permission of the author. The postscript is published here for the first time.

there are ways in which the world can be presented to a subject of experience which do not make the objective, human world accessible to the subject. It is not unnatural to suppose that there must be nonconceptual forms of content, because this is the kind of thing that we want to say about very young human infants (before the acquisition of the object concept, say), or very senile people, or certain other animals. It is compelling to think of these beings as having experience, yet they are unable to communicate thoughts to us; we are unable to understand—from the inside—how they are responding to the world; we are unable to impose our world on them.

Conceptual content presents the world to a subject as divided up into objects, properties, and situations: the components of truth conditions. For example, my complex conceptual content (thought) that the old city wall is shrouded in mist today presents the world to me as being such that the state of affairs of the old city wall being shrouded in mist obtains today. To understand this content I have to think of the world as consisting of the object, the old city wall, the property of being shrouded in mist, and the former satisfying the latter. The possession of *any* content will involve carving up the world in one way or another. There will be a notion of *nonconceptual* content if experience provides a way of carving up the world which is not a way of carving it up into objects, properties, or situations (i.e. the components of truth conditions).[3]

It is natural to say that the possession of content consists in having a *conception* of the world as being such and such. But the word "conception" is too closely related to "concept" for it to function neutrally as between conceptual and nonconceptual presentations of the world. I shall say[4] that a content *registers* the world as being some way, and so ask, is there a way of registering the world which does not register it into objects, properties, or situations?

Definitions of Conceptual and Nonconceptual Properties

I will begin a more careful analysis of these notions by introducing definitions of conceptual and nonconceptual *properties*, and then show how these definitions can be applied within the theory of content.[5]

> A property is a *conceptual property* if, and only if, it is canonically characterized,[6] relative to a theory, only by means of concepts which are such that an organism *must have* those concepts in order to satisfy the property.

> A property is a *nonconceptual property* if, and only if, it is canonically characterized, relative to a theory, by means of concepts which are such that an organism *need not have* those concepts in order to satisfy the property.

Notice that the difference between these two definitions lies principally in the difference between the italicized "must have" in the first definition, and "need not have" in the second definition.

Consider the property of thinking of someone as a bachelor. A specification of what this property is will use the concepts *male*, *adult*, and *married*. But nothing could satisfy the property unless it possessed[7] these concepts, since nothing would count as thinking of someone as a bachelor, unless he or she was able to think of the person as being male, adult, and unmarried. So the property of thinking of someone as a bachelor (unlike the property of being a bachelor) is a conceptual property.

Or consider the belief property of believing that the Stanford Campus is near here (where I think of the Stanford Campus *as* the Stanford Campus, rather than as the campus of the richest university in the West, and I think of here as here, rather than as 3333 Coyote Hill Road). Given this, nothing could satisfy the property unless it possessed the concept of the Stanford Campus *qua* Stanford Campus. Thus the property is canonically characterized only by means of concepts which an organism must have in order to satisfy the property, and is therefore a conceptual property. Contrast the property of having an active hypothalamus. Such a property is characterized by means of the concept *hypothalamus*, but an organism may satisfy the property without possessing this concept. Therefore the property of having an active hypothalamus is a nonconceptual property.[8]

Formally, the idea is that conceptual content is content which consists of conceptual properties, while nonconceptual content is content which consists of nonconceptual properties. Can we give any substance to this formal idea?

The Application of the Definitions of Conceptual and Nonconceptual Properties within the Theory of Content

In order to show that there is a notion of nonconceptual content we need to show that the definition of nonconceptual properties can be applied within the theory of content. What does this mean?

The definitions of conceptual and nonconceptual properties use the notion of canonical specification, for otherwise every property would be a nonconceptual property, since, trivially, every property—including conceptual properties—can be specified by means of concepts that the subject need not possess. So we need to employ the notion of *canonical* specification. If we are to apply these definitions within the theory of content then the notion of canonicality that we are interested in is the notion of being a canonical specification within the theory of content. Certain specifications of a state or an activity are identified within a theory of content as being canonical when they are specifications generated by the theory in order to capture the distinctive way in which some aspect of the world is given to the subject of the state or activity. So, as brought out by McDowell (1977), "'aphla' refers to aphla" would be canonical, but "'aphla' refers to ateb" would not be, even though both would be true, because aphla is ateb. The notion of being canonical within the theory of content is parallel to the notion of being canonical in the theory of number, where the canonical specification of the number nine is not "the number of planets," but "nine."

The Case of Conceptual Content

The Notion of a Task-Domain. In order to understand how conceptual content works we need the notion of a task-domain for a behavior. *A **task-domain** is a bounded domain of the world which is taken as already registered into a given organization of a set of objects, properties, or situations,*[9] *which contains no privileged point or points of view, and with respect to which the behavior is to be evaluated.*[10]

SHRDLU's blocks micro-world was SHRDLU's task-domain (see Winograd 1973). The notion of a Model in formal semantics, and (often) the notion of a possible world in logic are notions of task-domains. Likewise, the performance of a chess computer is evaluated with respect to a chess task-domain which consists of 64 squares categorized into two types, 32 pieces—each with an ownership property—a legal starting position, three types of legal ending position, and a set of transformations from each legal position to all of the legal continuations from that position. The computer's task-domain excludes, for example, human emotions and plans, lighting conditions, reasons for, and the point of, winning, etc. What this means is that the performance of a chess-playing computer is evaluated with respect to transformations of chess tokens on a 64-square board, but not with respect to its response to human emotions, the lighting conditions, the historical pattern of the game, or "its reasons for winning." Moreover, because the domain is fixed so that certain situations are registered as wins for White, and certain others as wins for Black, the performance of the computer is not assessed with respect to its ability to transfer its knowledge to a different game, chess*, which is identical to chess except that those situations which are wins for White in chess, are wins for Black in chess*, and those situations which are wins for Black in chess are wins for White in chess*.[11]

A task-domain, then, is a conceptualized region of the world which provides the context of evaluation (true/false, win/lose, true-in-a-model/false-in-a-model, adaptive/non-adaptive, successful/unsuccessful, etc.) for the performance of some system. How is the notion of a task-domain connected to the notion of conceptual content?

The Specification of α Content by Concepts of the Task-Domain. Consider again the cognitive occurrence in me that we express in words as, "I am thinking that the Stanford Campus is near here." This is a representational state of mine, and may possess more than one kind of content.[12] What kind of content does the state carry? There is a type of content (let us call it "α content") which is stipulated within the theory of content[13] to be a kind of content that has determinate[14] truth conditions;[15]

that is, whose evaluation as correct imposes a determinate condition on the world. It follows that the linguistic expression, "that the Stanford Campus is near here" cannot fully capture the α content of the representational state, since this requires a fixed interpretation for "near" and "here." (In order for the state to be a state with α content, we need to know what truth condition it imposes on the world. But the words "here" and "near" do not tell us.)

Now suppose that this state occurs as part of a project of mine in which I am planning how best to eat lunch given various parameters and constraints on me: time, money, hunger, distance to eating locations, speed of transport available to me, cost of food at various locations. These parameters and constraints establish a task-domain which fixes an interpretation for the terms "near" and "here": suppose that it follows from the time constraints on me, and my hunger, that I need to be eating within fifteen minutes. Then "near" means: can be reached by a mode of transport available to me within fifteen minutes. Likewise "here" will mean something like: the region between the spot on which I am standing and a line joining the embarkation points for all the modes of transport which are part of my planning domain.

The interpretation of my cognitive occurrence as having α content depends on specifying the content by means of concepts of a task-domain; in this case, the domain of my planning to eat lunch under various constraints and given various parameters. In other words, the provision of determinate truth conditions for my cognitive state, required by the interpretation of it as having α content, entails that the content is canonically specified by means of concepts which reflect the objective structure of the task-domain: its organization into objects, properties, and situations. Since an organism can only grasp an α content if it grasps its truth conditions (or its contribution to the truth conditions of contents containing it), it follows that an organism which grasps such a content must know what the (relevant part of the) t-domain of the content is. But a t-domain (unlike the world) is essentially conceptually structured, so there is no way of knowing what the t-domain of a content is without possessing the concepts in terms of which the t-domain is structured. Hence possession of an α content requires possession of the concepts in terms of which it is canonically specified. It follows that α content is a kind of content which consists of conceptual properties, as defined above. That is, α content is conceptual content.

The process of identification of α content as conceptual content may be mimicked in order to demonstrate a notion of nonconceptual content. We must ask, is there a way to motivate in a similar fashion the application of the definition of nonconceptual properties within the theory of content? In asking this, I am asking whether nonconceptual specifications of states or activities can ever be canonical within the theory of content. Thus I am asking whether nonconceptual specifications of an activity can ever be *required* by a correct theory of content in order to capture the distinctive way in which some aspect of the world is given to the subject of the activity.

We can clarify what is involved in doing this by setting out, as a summary of the above discussion, the different elements that I have used in motivating the definition of conceptual properties within the theory of content:

1. The definition of conceptual *properties* (by stipulation);
2. The claims that there is a constraint within the theory of *content* which requires determinate truth conditions,[16] and that possession of content which satisfies this constraint requires knowledge (grasp) of its truth conditions (these claims are given by the theory of content, and are constitutive of this notion of content);
3. A psychological state expressed linguistically as "thinking[17] that the Stanford Campus is near here," not yet analyzed with respect to the kind of content that it has;
4. The claim, argued in the text, that the interpretation of (3) under (2) requires the notion of a task-domain and the specification of the content of (3) by means of concepts of the task-domain.
5. (4) results in the satisfaction of (1), hence the identification of content which satisfies the constraint in (2) as *conceptual* content.

The notion of a task-domain provides the link between the philosophical notion of α content, and my stipulative definition of conceptual properties; a link which is needed to show that the analysis of a psychological state in terms of α content entails satisfaction of the definition of conceptual properties.

The Case of Nonconceptual Content
I can show the need for nonconceptual content by showing that there are psychological states the full understanding of which requires a notion of content which cannot be analyzed in this way; that is, which must be canonically specified by means of concepts that the subject need not have. The discussion will have to parallel the discussion for the case of conceptual content, so we need a parallel for (1)–(5):

1′. The definition of nonconceptual properties (by stipulation);
2′. Some constitutive conditions on a kind of content, β content, which are provided by the theory of content, but which are different from the conditions in (2).
3′. Some psychological or representational state as yet unanalyzed with respect to the kind of content it has.
4′. An argument for the claim that the interpretation of (3′) under (2′) requires the notion of some domain other than the task-domain and the specification of the content of (3′) by means of concepts of this domain.
5′. A demonstration that (4′) results in satisfaction of (1′), hence the identification of β content as nonconceptual content.

We already have (1′). What about (2′)?

Cognitive Significance. A good theory of content is answerable to various constraints. For example, a good theory of content should be appropriate for use within a content-based scientific psychology, it should have resources to explain how certain contents have determinate truth conditions and a good theory of content should also capture *cognitive significance*, that is, the role that content plays with respect to perception, judgment, and action.

How can the theory of content accommodate cognitive significance? Frege's notion of sense was introduced, in the first instance, to explain how certain identity statements could be informative (Frege 1891). For example, to learn that Hesperus = Hesperus is not to learn anything new, but to learn that Hesperus = Phosphorus may be to learn something of considerable significance, yet Hesperus *is* Phosphorus. It follows that possession of the content expressed here by the word "Phosphorus" cannot consist just in the ability to think of the planet Venus (specified no further than this), because just the same ability is associated with "Hesperus." There is here a motivation for introducing a notion of content (sense) which differs from a purely referential notion of content (reference). There is a content expressed by "Hesperus" which is different from the content expressed by "Phosphorus" because the former content plays a different role from the latter content in a person's judgments of the truth value of contents of the form ". . . = Hesperus." Frege generalized this motivation into a criterion of identity for such contents (senses) (see n. 20). We may generalize it still further to yield a generalized notion of sense which I call "β content," whose identity conditions are fixed, not just by its constitutive connections to judgment, but by its constitutive connections to perception, action, and judgment.[18] Possession of a particular β content requires possession of a contentful state which plays that role in the psychological economy of the subject which is constitutive of the β content.

A major success within recent work in the theory of content has been to show that there are indexical and demonstrative β contents that cannot be canonically specified, in the way appropriate to conceptual content, by means of any description.[19] This has been achieved by showing that were a description—*per impossibile*—to provide canonical specification of the content, in the way appropriate to conceptual content, it would alter the cognitive significance of the content, that is, the character of its constitutive connections to action and judgment. Since cognitive significance is constitutive of β content, it follows that this form of specification cannot canonically capture β contents.

For example, Perry (1979) shows this for the indexical "I" and connections to action, and Peacocke (1986) shows it for demonstrative perceptual contents and connections to perception and judgment. Perry's point is that the conceptual use of any descriptive canonical specification—*the x such that* φx—for the indexical content *I*, will alter the cognitive significance of the thought *I am* Ψ by altering its constitutive connections to action. The reason for this is that it is always possible that one may not realize that I am the x such that φx, so that even if one would act immediately on the basis of judging *I am* Ψ (e.g., *I am spilling sugar all over the supermarket floor*), one might not act on the basis of judging *the x such that* φ*x is* Ψ.

Peacocke contrasts what a person knows when he or she knows the length of a wall in virtue of just having read an estate agent's handout, and what a person knows when he or she knows the length of a wall just in virtue of looking at it. Frege's intuitive criterion of difference[20] for contents can be used to show that although both people know the length of the wall, neither knows what the other knows. Thus suppose that my wife's and my cognitive states were identical except for the fact that I know what the length of the wall is just in virtue of having read the handout, and she knows what the length of the wall is just in virtue of having seen it. But then, thinking of the length of the wall in only that way which is available to each of us, I may be agnostic about the thought *that length is greater than the length of our piano* (because, for example, we don't know how long in feet our piano is), whereas my wife will judge this thought to be true because, simply by looking, she can see that our piano will fit against the wall. Therefore, the perceptual demonstrative β content differs from any descriptively specified conceptual content, and so cannot be canonically specified, in the way appropriate to conceptual contents, by means of any specification such as "the person sees that distance-in-feet $(a,b) = n$" where a and b are the end-points of the wall.

We could treat examples such as Perry's and Peacocke's in a way which was similar to my treatment of thinking that the Stanford Campus is near here—that is conceptually—by means of concepts of the respective task-domains. That would be, in effect, to characterize these indexical contents in a descriptive, conceptual fashion.[21] But Perry's and Peacocke's arguments show that justice cannot be done, in such a way, to the *cognitive significance* of these contents. So we have only to recognize a notion of content for which cognitive significance is essential, to see that there is a kind of content which cannot be canonically specified by means of concepts of the task-domain.

The argument so far shows that there is a very large class of cognitive states (all states which contain indexical or demonstrative elements[22]) which have a kind of content (β content) for which the only canonical conceptual specification is the use of a simple demonstrative or indexical under the conditions of a shared perceptual environment or shared memory experience. Such a specification is evidently useless for the construction-theoretic purposes of a scientific psychology since the only way the theorist can have to understand the nature of the content is either to share the experiential environment of the content, or draw on similar experiential environments available to the theorist in memory experience.[23] (Scientific psychology, here, is psychology which is aiming to solve the problem of embodied cognition, and which therefore is aiming to construct any explanatorily indispensable notion of content out of non-content involving levels of description.[24]) Yet this class of contents is particularly important for psychology, at least because of its direct connections to action and its crucial role in learning.

Is the theoretical psychologist therefore incapable of capturing those contents which are basic to our ability to act in the world and to learn from it?

Only if the psychologist assumes that he or she must work with conceptual content. The problem arises because there is no conceptual structure within the demonstrative or the indexical or the observational content which can be exploited to yield a canonical conceptual specification of the content which would be appropriate for the purposes of a scientific psychology. But this doesn't exclude there being any *nonconceptual* structure within the content. If we can make sense of this notion, then there is here an argument to show that much of the psychological life can only be captured by means of, and should, therefore, only be modeled in terms of, nonconceptual content.

The Notion of a Substrate-Domain.   Abandon, then, the demand that every content must have its theoretical specification given in the way which is constitutive of conceptual content; that is, by means of concepts of the task-domain. What other theoretically adequate method of specification could there be? I introduce below one kind of canonical nonconceptual specification. It is not necessarily the only kind,[25] although I believe that it is the only kind in terms of which we can solve the problem of embodied cognition.

It will help to consider the operation of an autonomous, mobile robot known as "Flakey" which lives at a research institute, SRI, in California (see Reifel 1987). Flakey navigates the corridors of SRI. His task is to move up and down the corridors, avoiding hitting the walls, and to turn into particular doorways.

In order to be able to behave flexibly in a range of task-domains a system must be able to employ representations[26] of features which are special to the domain in which it happens to find itself. For example, if the width of corridors varies in Flakey's environment, then Flakey will need to respond differentially to corridor width. Given the kind of system that Flakey is, this will mean that Flakey will have to represent this variable. The system need only not represent that which does not change throughout the career of the system. So the greater the system's representational capacity, the greater its potential flexibility. Should we suppose, therefore, that the cognitively ideal system would computationally represent—in the traditional AI style—all the facts there are? That although nothing achieves this ideal, the closer one comes to it, the better one's cognitive capacities will be?

To suppose this[27] is to miss an important distinction between two kinds of fact. What I want to show is that computational representation of only one of these kinds of fact is required for the ideal Artificial Intelligence system. Flakey is sometimes imagined to deliver pizza throughout SRI. It might be that only one weight of pizza is allowed through the extensive security system, and that Flakey would therefore be built on the assumption that if something is recognized as a pizza, then the mobile arm needs to exert a certain force to lift it. This would have the effect of "unburdening" the representational capacities of Flakey, with respect to having to work out each time it was about to lift a pizza, how much force was required to lift it (see Barwise 1987). This connection could simply be built into the hardware. However, the folks down at Hewlett Packard, intrigued by Flakey's growing reputation, might want to try him out on delivering pizza for them. They would be sorely disappointed because, unfortunately for Flakey, the security system at HP labs lets all weights of pizza through. Flakey was discovered to be throwing pizza around in a way not likely to impress DARPA.[28]

Indeed, DARPA could reasonably argue that this was a *cognitive* defect of Flakey's. We treat intelligence in an open-ended way: so-and-so may be great at chess, but if he can't learn to play Go, then we think him the less intelligent for it. For Flakey, representation of pizza weight is required for acceptable, let alone ideal, cognition.

But we shouldn't conclude therefore that to be truly intelligent Flakey must represent all the facts there are. For example, it would be surprising if Flakey were to represent the distance between the sonar sensors at its base. This is not only for the reason that this distance is a constant throughout Flakey's career, but, more importantly, because Flakey's own structure is not part of Flakey's task-domain. Flakey never has to manipulate the distance between his sonar sensors; this distance is not something with respect to which Flakey's performance will be evaluated. Rather, it is part of Flakey's substrate of abilities in virtue of which Flakey has those corridor-movement behavioral capacities which he in fact has. This distinction between task-domain ("t-domain") and the domain of the system's substrate of abilities ("s-domain") is essential to understanding what a flexible system is required to represent. To be able to operate flexibly in a range of t-domains a system must be able to represent those features of a t-domain which vary, or may vary, within the range of t-domains. But so long as the s-domain is outside this range, as it usually will be, a flexible system has no need to represent aspects of its s-domain (see Cussins 1987).

My visual capacity may be quite superb and open-ended: I can visually discriminate any kind of object, in an extensive range of conditions of illumination, and distances from me, and so forth. But nobody would suggest that it is a defect of my visual capacity, that I am ignorant of the algorithms employed by my visual information-processing system. With respect to my personal level visual capacity, my subpersonal information-processing capacities are part of the s-domain.[29] Given a division between t-domain and s-domain in a particular case, performance in the task-domain—even fully conceptual performance—does not require the possession of any concepts of the s-domain.

Specifying β Contents by Concepts of the Substrate-Domain.   As we saw, the notion of a t-domain provided the link between a content and the definition of conceptual properties. Can the notion of the s-domain provide a parallel link between β content and the definition of nonconceptual properties? An intelligent agent does not need to have concepts of its s-domain, so if β content can be canonically specified by reference to the objects and properties of the s-domain, we will have motivated a kind of content which is specified by means of concepts that the system or organism need not have.

Consider the following quotation from Evans:

> What is involved in a subject's hearing a sound as coming from such and such a position in space? . . . When we hear a sound as coming from a certain direction, we do not have to *think* or *calculate* which way to turn our heads (say) in order to look for the source of the sound. If we did have to do so, then it ought to be possible for two people to hear a sound as coming from the same direction and yet to be disposed to do quite different things in reacting to the sound, because of differences in their calculations. Since this does not appear to make sense, we must say that having spatially significant perceptual information consists at least partly in being disposed to do various things. (1982, pp. 154–155) [essay 2, p. 50]

When Evans asks, "what is involved in a subject's hearing a sound as coming from such and such a position in space?" he is asking about the nature of the content by which the subject is presented in experience with this aspect of the world. Evidently the content is indexical or demonstrative since, were we to express the content in words, we would say that perception presents the sound as coming from "that location," or "from over there." The conclusion drawn on the basis of Perry's and Peacocke's examples applies: there is no way to canonically specify this content as a conceptual content, if we wish to do theoretical justice to the cognitive significance of the content; in particular its direct connection to action. What Evans adds, is, first, a further reason why this kind of content cannot be captured conceptually (no conceptual content can be necessarily linked to action as directly as certain β contents require), and, secondly, the suggestion that the way to capture the cognitive significance of the content is by reference to a way of moving in the world; the subject's ability to reach out and locate the object, or walk to the source of the sound, which the perceptual experience makes available. At the place in the argument which we have now reached, it is this second idea which is important, because, for Evans' content, a way of moving in the world is part of the s-domain.

Given our usual views about consciousness, the idea here can seem quite strange: it is the idea that certain contents consist in a means of finding one's way in the world (tracking the object, say) being available to the subject in his or her experience, even though it may not be available to the subject conceptually, and, indeed, the subject may be incapable of expressing in words what this way of moving is.[30] My knowledge of where the sound is coming from consists in, say, knowledge of how I would locate the place: knowledge which is exhausted by what is available to me directly—without depending on any concepts—in experience. I may have that knowledge even though I am unable to entertain any thoughts about the way of moving in question; I require no concepts of my ability to find my way in the environment, in order to have an experience whose content consists in presenting to me a way of moving.

It may help to consider one of the most extreme cases of non-conceptual content (see Cussins 1990, §8): the case of pain-experience. We have been taught in the philosophical tradition not to view pain-experience as experience with any *content* at all; its function isn't to represent the world, we are told. But the reason for this is not because pain-experience isn't phenomenologically very similar to the experience of color or shape of objects, but, rather, because we do not view the world as possessing various paining properties. We say that the edge of my desk is colored brown on the basis of a visual experience as of brownness, but we do not say that the edge of my desk has a sharp paining on the basis of a tactile experience of a sharp pain. I give a reason (*ibid.*) as to why this is the case, but for now the point is to think of experience as a spectrum of kinds of experience ranging from pain-experience where we are not remotely inclined to attribute the experienced property to the world, through color-experience where we do attribute the experienced property to the world (but we get into some trouble for doing so—see Cussins 1990, §6), to shape- or motion-experience. Pain-experience is just much less objective[31] than shape-experience. This will show up in the kinds of content that pain-experience can have, as against the kinds of content that shape-experience can have. Pain-experience never has conceptual content, but it doesn't follow that it has no content at all. Pain-experience presents the world as being painful; paining is made available to one in pain-experience. But we don't suppose that we need concepts of pain for this to be the case; we just have to *be* in pain, or to remember being in pain. In a similar way, experience can present a way of moving in the world, even though the subject of the experience has no concepts of ways of moving.

Our kinesthetic sense provides another example. On the basis of kinesthetic experience the subject knows how his body is arranged; how his hands are in relation to each other and to his head, for example. But the person need have no concepts of this spatial arrangement in order to have this knowledge. Rather, the knowledge consists in an experiential sensitivity to, for example, moving one's hands closer together, or bringing one's hands next to one's torso. The capacities one has to rearrange one's body are directly present in kinesthetic experience without having to possess any concepts of the arrangement of a body.

Returning to the example from auditory experience, Evans' idea is that the spatial content of the auditory perception has to be specified in terms of a set of conceptually unmediated abilities to form judgments and to move in the egocentric space[32] around the organism. This is because the content consists in the experiential availability to the subject of a dispositional ability to move. The experiential content of perception is specified in terms of certain fundamental skills which the organism possesses, "the ability to keep track of an object in a visual array, or to follow an instrument in a complex and evolving pattern of sound." These are skills which belong to the subject's s-domain. So, if Evans is right, this class of contents is canonically specified by reference to abilities which are part of the s-domain, and therefore by means of concepts which a subject need not have in order to grasp any member of this class of contents. So the structure of the (conceptually atomic) indexical, demonstrative, and observational contents of experience is the structure of their nonconceptual content. β content is non-conceptual content.

People often misunderstand this as a behavioristic theory, so let me emphasize again that the claim is not, in the first instance, about the characterization of a *subpersonal* perceptual state of the organism (Dennett 1969, pp. 93–94; Dennett 1978, pp. 101–102, 153–154, 219). The aim is to capture how the person's perceptual experience presents the world as being (i.e. a genuine notion of personal level content). The notion of nonconceptual content is a notion which must ultimately be explained in terms of what is available in *experience*. If the content is canonically characterized as a complex disposition of some specified sort, then the claim is that this disposition is directly available to the person in his or her experience, and that the content of the experience consists in this availability. But for a behaviorist, the notion of experience can have no explanatory role.[33]

In summary, then, I have discerned a constraint on content in terms of cognitive significance, rather than in terms of truth conditions; I have suggested in a Fregean spirit that we need to introduce a kind of content which is answerable to this constraint; I have shown that this kind of content cannot be canonically specified in any way which is appropriate to conceptual content, and that it is therefore not a type of conceptual content; we have seen that we need to employ this kind of content to do full justice to any cognitive psychological state with indexical or demonstrative elements (most of our cognitive life); that a plausible suggestion for how to canonically capture the content is by means of concepts of the s-domain; and that since a cognitive creature does not need to have concepts of its s-domain, I have shown that this kind of content satisfies the definition of nonconceptual properties, and is therefore a kind of nonconceptual content.[34] I will call the kind of nonconceptual content which I have introduced, "construction-theoretic content (CTC)," because I go on to show how this kind of content can form the basis for a construction of conceptual capacities (Cussins 1990).

How Widespread is the Phenomenon of Nonconceptual Content?
The content of certain conceptual states has only the structure of their nonconceptual content, and so can only be psychologically analyzed in terms of their nonconceptual structure. There are two levels of analysis of content, conceptual and nonconceptual, and it has been demonstrated that the psychological explanation of a certain portion of our cognitive life can only be given in terms of its nonconceptual structure. It is irresistible to wonder, how widespread is this phenomenon? Could it be that even for those areas of cognition where there is conceptual structure, the correct level of scientific psychological analysis is still in terms of its

nonconceptual structure? *Is the psychological structure of cognition its nonconceptual structure?* I believe that the hypothesis that it is the basis for a connectionist alternative to the Language of Thought Thesis. But this is to run ahead of ourselves.[35]

It will help to consider some other examples. Evans quotes Charles Taylor [1978–1979] as follows:

> Our perceptual field has an orientational structure, a foreground and a background, an up and down. . . . This orientational structure marks our field as essentially that of an embodied agent. It's not just that the field's perspective centres on where I am bodily—this by itself doesn't show that I am essentially agent. But take the up-down directionality of the field. What is it based on? Up and down are not simply related to my body—up is not just where my head is and down where my feet are. For I can be lying down, or bending over, or upside down; and in all these cases "up" in my field is not the direction of my head. Nor are up and down defined by certain paradigm objects in the field, such as the earth or sky: the earth can slope for instance. . . . Rather, up and down are related to how one would move and act in the field. (Evans 1982, p. 156) [essay 2, p. 51]

Taylor is here asking what the significance of our concept *up* consists in. He considers three answers, two of which are: up is where my head is, and, up is where the sky is. But the significance of our notion of up cannot consist in our grasp of the direction of our head or the direction of the sky, because, for example, we can perfectly correctly employ the concept *up* when we are lying down. And so on. Then Taylor offers a third answer, "up and down are related to how one would move and act in the field." This immediately strikes one as a very different sort of answer from the first two answers that Taylor considers. In the first two cases what is being offered is a traditional conceptual analysis; a definition, as we might define "bachelor" to refer to an unmarried adult male. Where it is proper to give a traditional conceptual analysis, a person's understanding of the left-hand side of the definition must consist in the cognitive availability of the conceptual structure which is displayed on the right-hand side. But Taylor's third answer is not a definition; it simply states that our possession of the concept *up* must be analyzed in terms of certain basic, nonconceptual abilities that we possess, such as our ability to move and act in a co-ordinated way. These basic abilities may be characterized by means of technical concepts (such as concepts of the way in which the gravitational force structures our field) which an organism need not possess in order to possess these basic abilities. Taylor has hit upon the analysis of a concept in terms of its nonconceptual content.

Or consider recognitional abilities in those cases (the majority) where recognition does not depend on the recognition of the object as *the x such that φx and ψx* (for any concepts of properties φ and ψ). For example, my ability to recognize my wife's face as Charis' face is not an ability (even a subpersonal ability) to recognize the unique face with certain conceptual features (e.g. Roman nose, distance between eyes being n inches, etc.). When I think a perceptual-demonstrative thought of the form *That is Charis*, my cognitive state is not correctly reconstructable as involving the inference, that is the φ person, the φ person is Charis, so that is Charis. In fact, my ability to recall a person's features (even a person whom I know very well) when not in their presence is extremely limited, but this in no way diminishes my ability to hold a particular person in memory. (In an extreme case, I might not be able to recall a single perceptual feature of my wife, and yet be unrivaled in my ability to think singular thoughts about her.) So it cannot be that the capacity for me to hold someone in memory in the way required for me to have a singular thought about the person consists in my storing some set of conceptual features which, as it so happens, are uniquely satisfied in the world.[36]

What this suggests is that although there will be mental features in our theory of recognition, they won't be features whose analysis depends on a *semantic* account, i.e. a semantic relation between the feature and some objective element of the appropriate ready registered task-domain. Our ability to recognize massively outstrips our ability to recall, and cannot be analyzed in terms of it (see Evans 1982, chap. 8). The suggested alternative is that our ability to recall objective features of the world is dependent on the structure of the nonconceptual content of our recognitional capacities; content specified in terms of basic spatial and temporal tracking and discriminatory skills which are required to find our way around the environment. . . .[37]

Postscript: Experience, Thought, and Activity (2002)

1 A Postscript to C3[38]

The "Connectionist Construction of Concepts" ("C3") was published twelve years ago when the phrase "nonconceptual content" was used only by a small group of mostly Oxonian philosophers. It has become quite popular recently, and on both sides of the Atlantic, although it is still the case that the proper demeanor to be worn by the analytic philosopher on confronting the phrase is an air of perplexity; a concession has been made in agreeing to talk about such a thing. A greater sense of perplexity would be a good thing—too much of the literature around nonconceptual content has been conducted as if we already understand the basic notions used to introduce the idea of nonconceptual content: *content, mode of presentation*, a *way* in which something may be *given*. . . . We could divide the literature into two camps: those who assume that notions introduced for the theory of thought are well understood and, with appropriate modification, these notions can be adapted to characterize nonconceptual content. And a camp which holds that confrontation with the phenomena of nonconceptual content shows that our understanding of these notions is deficient and that we have a whole lot of basic work to do in reconfiguring the theory of content. Do we have a grip on the very idea of content that doesn't already presuppose that all content is built out of concepts? If we try to work with such a general notion of content, what then are *conceptual* contents? Are we entitled to assume that resources introduced in a Fregean and neo-Fregean context (*the intuitive criterion of difference, reference, correctness conditions . . .*) are robust enough to figure unproblematically in a project that many neo-Fregeans (for example, Dummett) think is fundamentally misconceived?

I'd recommend the second camp. It's difficult, but philosophically it is more exciting. It also helps open up a space for conversation between different philosophical traditions. The formal tradition in analytic philosophy has truth as its central concept, whereas concepts of practice and activity are central in the phenomenological tradition. Coming to see how truth and activity can figure as concepts with the same importance in a theory of meaning can only enhance such a conversation.

Don't be put off by funny terms like "s-domain" (or, what it has now become, "realm of mediation")—they"re just devices to help throw open the notion of content; to free it from the presupposition that we begin our investigation of nonconceptual content already understanding the very idea of content. Don't get hung up on the definitions of conceptual and nonconceptual properties; they're only a place to start, and they're only definitions. What matters is what happens to concepts like *reference*, or *object*, or *world*, when we accept that our responsibility is toward a theory of content in which experience, thought, and activity figure equally. Once you come to see that there are very different generic kinds of content, nothing in philosophy ever remains the same.

Another prefatory remark: the phrase "the theory of content" is loaded with all sorts of more-or-less backgrounded exclusions and inclusions. That's too heavy to address here, except this: the "content" of an experience or thought is sometimes distinguished from the "object" of the experience or thought. It is noticed that the same object can be "given" in different ways, or "presented" under different "manners" or "modes." It is then supposed that a specification of the experience or thought should specify two things: which objects (and properties, etc.) it concerns and in what manner those objects are presented. The theory of content properly concerns only the latter; something like a theory of reference is needed for the former. This is a mistake. A theorist of *information* may be entitled to such a separation of tasks; a theorist of information may be entitled to speak of which objects and properties are in question without having to address questions about cognitive access (and an information-processing psychologist may address questions of cognitive access but not objectivity). But a theory of *content* is a theory of cognition—the concepts of content and of knowledge are tied together: distinctions in kinds of content are, essentially, distinctions amongst kinds of knowledge. A theorist of content must not speak of objects of content except through speaking of forms of epistemic access. This is the flip-side of an old but crucial insight of neo-Fregeans: if the reference of an expression is specified carefully it is not a separate task to specify the sense of the expression (the sense will have been shown in the statement of the reference). The right specification of *what* the referent is will also reveal *how* the reference is made; and it is crucial to understanding semantics to see that this is so. Likewise: if you get right the specification of the mode of presentation (the content) then something would have gone wrong if, having done that, the theorist had to go on to specify the reference. A specification of content is a specification of cognitive availability. If the reference was not captured in the correct specification of cognitive access (the epistemic presentation) then the reference is not cognitively accessible, so is not part of the content, and so should not be specified as part of the content specification. If, on the other hand, the reference *is* captured in the specification of cognitive access, then it would be redundant (and misleading) to specify it all over again. Either way, ordered pairs whose first member refers to the "object" of experience or thought, and whose second member refers to a mode or manner of presentation have no place in a theory of content. The right specification of *how* is also a specification of *what* is available in a cognition; and it is crucial to understanding the theory of content to see that this is so. (I exaggerate: this wouldn't be so in an epistemically Cartesian or Lockean theory of content.) It's in this spirit that I float the following idea in this brief essay: that *reference* is not only a semantic notion but also a notion within the theory of content—that reference is a generic kind of content. (And once you see this you will see that it is not the only generic kind of content.)

The point of a theory of content is to reveal cognitive accessibility to the world, and therefore should be given in terms of elements of subjects' access to the world. For example, by means of concepts that the subjects possess. That's how a theory of conceptual content specifies contents. But that a theory of nonconceptual content can make canonical use of concepts that are not possessed by the subjects of content does *not* mean that a theory of nonconceptual content is not in the exclusive business of specifying forms of cognitive access to the world. It does not therefore mean that a theory of nonconceptual content can liberate itself from content specifications in terms of the elements of subjects' access to the world. What it *does* mean is that there are elements of subjects' access to the world *other* than concepts. What are these elements? Well, that's the right question to ask. It is, I think, kind of unfortunate that scenarios and protopropositions [see essay 5] and Stalnakerian propositions [see essay 4] and just about anything else you"ll find in the literature supposedly on nonconceptual content won't help you with this question. So let's go back to the beginning: what are the distinctive ways in which the world is made available when it is not made available conceptually?

2 Two Ways of Knowing about Speed

Many years ago I used to ride a motorcycle around London and I would often exceed the speed limit. One time a policeman stopped me and asked, "Do you know how fast you were traveling?" He didn't mean it to be a difficult question; really just a preamble to his *telling* me how fast I was going. But, lost inside my full-face motorcycle helmet, it dawned on me that this was in fact a difficult philosophical question. On the one hand, I did know, and know very well, how fast I was traveling. I was knowingly making micro-adjustments of my speed all the time in response to changing road conditions. These micro-adjustments weren't simply *behaviors*, the outputs of some unknown causal process. They were, instead, epistemically sensitive adjustments made by me, and for which I was as epistemically responsible as I was for my judgments.

On the other hand, I did *not* know how fast I was traveling in the sense of the question intended by the policeman. I was unable to state my speed, in an epistemically responsible way, as some number of miles per hour. I knew what my speed was, but not as *a* speed. The speed was presented to me as a certain way of wiggling through and around heavy traffic and past the road dividers and traffic bollards of a London street. This kind of knowledge of speed does not entail that I be able to recognize it as the same speed again as I rode down an uncluttered motorway outside the city. In short, the speed was not given to me as a referent, an object, that I could present to the policeman, to myself, to the traffic court, to other drivers, in other driving conditions, objectively, as the very same object, the very same speed in all of these different contexts or perspectives. My knowledge of my speed wasn't structured in that kind of way.

The right way to put this point is this: the speed of my motorcycle was not made available to me as that which would render true certain propositions, and false certain others. The speed was given to me not as a truth-maker—for example, a truth-maker of the proposition that I was exceeding the speed limit—but as an element in a skilled interaction with the world, as a felt rotational pressure in my right hand as it held the throttle grip, a tension in my fingers and foot in contact with brake pedals or levers, a felt vibration of the road and a rush of wind, a visual rush of surfaces, a sense of how the immediate environment would *afford* certain motions and *resist* others; *embodied and environmental knowledge* of what it would take to make adjustments in these felt pressures and sensitivities. This knowledge was a moment-by-moment practical manifestation of my competence as a motorcyclist, and in this respect was wholly unlike knowing that I was traveling at 50 mph, because any incompetent could know *that*, just by reading the dial on the policeman's speed gun. My knowledge was directly and non-inferentially useful for how I rode, and consisted in the knowing capacity to guide my motorcycle riding—again, wholly unlike a speed given to me as an *object*: as the truth-maker, 50 mph, or as what would be presented on the instrument dial of the speed gun.

This latter *objectual* knowledge can be used to guide a motorcyclist, but its links to activity must be established by taking up the objectual knowledge into propositionally structured forms of practical reasoning. I don't need to be a skilled motorcyclist to know that I or someone else is traveling at 50 mph, but instead I require some propositional contexts in order to establish the motorcycling-relative *significance* of the object, 50 mph; for example in the proposition *50 mph exceeds the speed limit of 30 mph*. The motorcycling-relative significance of the object is given by a subject's mastery of the inferential relations amongst propositional contexts for the object, 50 mph. Whereas the significance of the speed as it is available experientially to the motorcyclist who does not look at his speedometer is given via the subject's skilled competence in the activity of getting about by motorcycle. The speed-content has in one case a cognitive significance characteristic of propositional judgment, whereas in the other case it has a cognitive significance characteristic of experience-guided activity.

I have suggested that there is a double dissociation between two ways in which a subject may know about his or her speed. A subject (for example, myself as queried by the policeman) may possess experiential, activity-based knowledge of speed without objectual, propositional knowledge, even though both forms of knowledge are knowledge of the same speed. And a subject (for example, the incompetent motorcyclist who reads off the speed from the instrument dial) may possess propositional knowledge without experiential knowledge.

Not only does possession of one kind of knowledge not entail possession of the other, but there is even a *tension* between the two kinds of knowledge. They are taken up in very different, sometimes competing, cognitive orientations to the world. For example, a motorcyclist's reliance on objectual knowledge ("50 mph") of their speed would be characteristic of a novice. A more competent rider constantly makes assessments of how fast they are traveling, of how fast it is safe to travel in *these* road conditions (as they rush by) *without* looking at the speedometer.

In the case of a novice who has to *infer* the significance-for-motorcycling of their speedometer-given speed, the characteristic functionality of conceptual knowledge interferes with the characteristic functionality of experiential knowledge. The interference can also go in the other direction. The great advantage of experiential content is that its links to action are direct, and do not need to be mediated by time-consuming—and activity-distancing—inferential work; work which may at any point be subject to skeptical challenge. Experiential knowledge of the kind possessed by the skilled motorcyclist may be subject to *resistance*, but not to skeptical challenge.[39] That's its great cognitive virtue, but it also suffers from an equally great cognitive vice: it is situation-specific. If my *only* knowledge of the speed consisted in this particular vehicle and road, specific, hands-on knowledge of speed, then I would have no basis for even understanding what it would be for *others* to ride at this speed, or for me to travel at the *same speed* in a car or a boat. Because of its situation-specificity, this kind of content cannot by itself provide what we have come to regard as the constitutive requirements on *thought* content: generality, objectivity, standardization, transportability of knowledge from one embodied and environmentally specific situation to another. The cognitive virtues of experiential content are in tension with the virtues of thought content because experience's direct connection to action entails the situational specificity of experiential content, and situational specificity is in tension with the generality of thought content.

I want now to ask how this picture of a commonsense distinction between kinds of everyday knowledge might be represented within the theory of content. In a neo-Fregean/neo-Husserlian theory of content, a distinction between kinds of content is a distinction between kinds of modes of presentation (for example, senses) and between kinds of normative conditions (for example, truth and reference). Let's think first about conceptual modes of presentation and conceptual normative conditions.

3 Thoughts Present the World as Truth-Maker. And Their Conceptual Constituents Have Referential/Objectual Structure

Thoughts are those things about which it makes sense to ask, "Is this true or not?" Thus, thoughts include the contents of judgment, but exclude the characteristic contents of paintings, dances, and many experiential states. There are two sides to the constitutive claim that truth is the governing norm for thought content. First, truth is the standard against which a thought is primarily assessed (its normative condition). But second, in judging or entertaining a thought, a subject is conceiving of the world as that which would render the thought true. If truth is the governing norm of thoughts, then a subject who conceives the world through thinking a thought conceives the world in terms of the structure which is necessary to characterize the truth of the thought or its truth-governed relations—inferential relations—to other thoughts. This is conceptual structure. We may say that conceptual content is a way of conceiving the world in terms of the structure necessary to characterize truth; that is, in terms of the conceptual structure of thoughts. (Conceptual modes of presentation have a structure which is fixed by the normative conditions that govern thoughts.)

So, fixing the governing norm for a kind of content not only fixes the normative conditions for contents of this kind, it also fixes the type of mode of presentation of the world which is characteristic of contents of this kind. (1) For thought content the world is *that which would render thoughts true* . But, (2), conceptual structure just is whatever structure is required to specify both the semantic conditions under which a thought is true and the truth-governed relations between thoughts. Therefore, the world is given in thought as having conceptual structure.

What is it for the world to be given as having conceptual structure? Reference to an object is one type of *conceptual* relation because we are forced to appeal to objectual reference in order to capture the rational structure of *truth*, for example in capturing inferential relations amongst propositions. So, if the world is presented to one as that which would render true a thought, then the world may be given as containing a particular object. It is *because* thoughts present the world as the *truth-maker* that thoughts present the world conceptually as consisting of, for example, particular objects: the necessity to refer to particulars arises within the conception of the world as truth-maker.

I shall say that conceptual content presents the world *as a realm (or as realms) of reference*. A realm of reference can include particular objects, properties, relations, events, situations, states of affairs, and so forth, depending on the proper analysis of the structure of truth. A realm of reference is a realm of objects, properties, states of affairs, . . . , with respect to which the *truth* of thoughts is determined.

Conceptual contents, then, are contents that are constitutively governed by the norm of truth, and that present the world as realm of reference. A proper content *specification* should specify both normative conditions and mode of presentation. The *normative conditions* of conceptual contents are specified by specifying truth conditions, or satisfaction conditions. Both truth and satisfaction conditions are specified by referring to the semantic determinants of truth conditions that are elements in the realm of reference. The type of *mode of presentation* that is characteristic of conceptual contents is to present the world as realm of reference. Hence both the normative conditions and the mode of presentation of conceptual contents can be specified by referring to the realm of reference. Reference to the realm of reference does double duty.

I have recommended an explanatory strategy in the theory of content: First we fix a kind of normativity. If there is a kind of content that is governed by this kind of normativity, then we can explain how the world is presented in this content in terms of the structure that is necessary for explaining the norm-governed relations between these norm-governed contents. The abstractness of this formulation is useful because it allows us to ask about kinds of content other than thought content. It shows us what we would have to do, and to explain, if we are to motivate one or another notion of *nonconceptual* content. Thoughts are constitutively governed by the norm of truth and so what is characteristic of thought is content that presents the world as the truth-maker, and therefore as having referential structure. If we are to motivate a distinct kind of content, it will be a kind of content that does not present the world as truth-maker, and which therefore is a kind of content which is not constitutively governed by the norm of truth.

What other kinds of norms can function as the governing norms of contents?

4 Experiences Present the World as Mediator. And Their Nonconceptual Constituents Are Structured as Activity Trails: Forms of Guidance Through Environments of Activity

Central to an account of normativity is *guidance*. In judgment we are guided by truth, and truth is the governing norm for judgment (judgment aims at truth). In understanding a meaning we are guided by the rules that govern the meaning, but these same rules fix the normativity of meaning: the distinction between correct and incorrect applications of a term with that meaning. Artists are guided by beauty, and beauty is the governing norm for art (that by which art is assessed).

Technologists are guided by efficiency and effectiveness, and it is efficiency and effectiveness that distinguishes good from bad technology. (Not that, in any of these cases, we are *exclusively* guided by the governing norms, nor that any of these activities are *exclusively* assessed by their governing norms. Nevertheless, the governing norms play a constitutive role in making these activities what they are: judgment, meaning, art, and technology.) That the functionality, and the general form, of norms is to provide guidance allows us to explore normativity *by* exploring guidance.

A norm may guide us by being both explicit and propositional, but there are many forms of guidance which are neither explicit nor propositional. Social codes are often not explicit and may not be propositional. Let's consider a form of guidance that is so ubiquitous and so *everyday* that we rarely pay any attention to it.

Think of entering an unfamiliar room, and finding one's way from one side of the room to another. A subject is guided here by the positioned solidity of the furniture, as one's body—or one's informational systems—gently bump up against the materialities of the environment. These "bumpings" are forms of guidance, and so they manifest candidate norms, not with the status of the norm of truth but fully normative nonetheless. The material structures of the room are linguistically mute, but they are nevertheless not mute: salient spaces call to us, drawing us towards them or away from them: Go here! Don't go there! (*Like this* [as one moves] is right! *Like that* is wrong![40]) Such mundane norms are situated in the environment, they are changed by the environment and by the flow of activity through it, and they change the environment and its flow of activity.

When I say, "think of entering a room and finding one's way from one side of the room to another," I don't mean that one enter with the *intention* to get to the other side of the room (although one might). I just mean: consider your activity as you enter the room, *whatever* your intentions might be, and whether or not you have any. You might, for example, find the room full of people who are mingling and moving around, and so you fall into step with what you find, and you too mingle and move around. There need be no intention here; you may just be adapting to the activity in the room—going along with it. Now we ask, what is the normativity that nevertheless governs your activity? (What you do is neither random nor unknowing.) The normativity that guides your activity is not given by your intention because even if you have one—and you may not—there is also a structure to your activity which would be the same whatever was your intention. It is this intention-free normativity that I am here calling "mundane normativity": the gentle bumpings of one's body and informational systems; the cognitive affordances and resistances of the environment.

"There is a structure to your activity which would be the same whatever your intention." This structure is the structure of the afforded paths or *trails* through the environment of the room: the activity trajectories that are afforded and which are bounded by regions of increased resistance (the edges of the trail). The pattern of trails fixes a distinction between skilled and unskilled, or competent and incompetent, activity in the environment, whatever one's intention or propositional goal may be in moving through the space. So when you enter the room, let's say without intention, you confront a space that *mediates* whatever you will do in the room. You might not think about any object in the room, but the room mediates your activity as you pass through it. As you move you are not, or need not, be guided by truth, but you are, nevertheless, guided; you are guided by the mundane structure of the activity-space around you. (So here we start to explore mundane normativities by exploring mundane structures of guidance-in-activity.)

The trail-structured environment of the room stands to any intentional task you may wish to carry out in the room somewhat as a tool stands to some construction task: it does not fix the task; it can subserve many different tasks; it is not itself the goal or "object," but carrying out the task depends on it; it *mediates* the task. Just as—when things are functioning well—the tool is not given to the builder as an *object of thought*, so the structured space of the room is not typically an object for subjects in the room (it is not part of the subject's realm of reference). Nevertheless, it, like the tool, is still cognitively accessible: it is accessible not through thought, but through the subject's skilled and knowing competence in getting about. I will say that, in such cases, the environment is given to the subject as a *realm of mediation*.

Presentations of the world as realm of mediation provide for a distinctive kind of world-knowledge. As in the motorcycle example, thought-free—but intensely cognitive—passage through the environment may manifest the subject's personal-level knowledge of *what it is to be a competent agent in an environment like this*. (The knowledge need not be available to the subject under this description, but only as a mediation of activity.) Likewise, passages through the environment may manifest failures in this knowledge: from fine-grained infelicities of movement to collisions, system crashes, or breakdowns. These knowledge failures are disruptions in a competent flow of activity; disruptions that may, or may not, have much to do with false judgment.

Content that is governed by mundane normativity is content that presents the world as an environment that mediates activity in the environment. When the world is given to one as such an environment, the world presents itself as a realm of mediation. (It may or may not also be present as a realm of reference.) Typically, the realm of mediation in an environment is not itself a realm of reference. Suppose my goal is to greet the visitor at the other side of the room. My goal or intention involves a content with truth conditions: I intend to make it true that I greet the visitor. In such a case, there is a *realm of reference* that includes particular objects (the visitor, myself), the relation of one person greeting another and so forth. Whereas the *realm of mediation* consists of the trails that distinguish patterns of afforded activity from patterns of resisted activity, and which guide me—a skilled traverser of rooms—as I cross to the other side. The network of trails is not, typically, part of the realm of reference in the environment because the truth of thoughts such as *I greet the visitor* does not depend semantically on the structure of activity trails. (In a philosophical discourse, trails might form part of a realm of reference. But that is not the usual case.) Thus, contents that present the environment-for-greeting-the-visitor present a single part of the world as a realm of reference *and* as a realm of mediation: two distinct ontological structures, and two distinct modes of access to the world.

Or think again of the motorcyclist's phenomenology: I knew the speed not as a particular object, 50 mph, but as an activity dynamic within a space for motor-cycling. The object, 50 mph, is a referent, and belongs to the realm of reference for thoughts about the motorcycle's speed (it is a truth-maker or breaker for some of these thoughts). But the activity dynamic is not a referent of these thoughts because the truth of thoughts like *I am traveling faster than the speed limit* is not semantically determined by the dynamic forms of my skilled engagement with, and adjustment to, throttle, road surface, and other moving vehicles. A specifi-cation of the truth conditions of the thought does not refer to skilled practice, to felt rotational pressures, or to patterns of resistance. The truth of these thoughts is fixed only by whether the objectual speed that I am traveling at is greater than or less than the legal speed.[41] Therefore the activity dynamic is not part of the realm of reference for the speed-relevant contents. The activity dynamic is not presented as the realm of reference, and therefore is not presented conceptually. Yet it *is* presented in the motorcyclist's experience. It is presented as a mediation of motorcycling activity. Perhaps as theorists we could use sophisticated concepts *of* trails to characterize the structure of the realm of mediation, and that would be to characterize the content nonconceptually in the good old-fashioned sense of a characterization that uses concepts that the subject of the content need not possess.

Mundane normativity is the normativity of activity guidance. In judgment we are guided by truth, but truth is not a *mundane* norm. Why? How are we to char-acterize the distinction between mundane normativity and the "elite" normativ-ity of truth, veridicality, accuracy, and related norms? One way to begin to think about this question goes like this: In judgment, any *guidance* available to the one who judges is responsible to the *norm* of truth. If uncertain about whether to go this way or that in judgment, one must ask oneself: what does truth demand be done? So in the case of judgment, it is the norm of truth which is explanatorily prior to the forms of guidance which govern the practice of judging: the forms of guidance are answerable to the norm of truth. But with mundane normativity it is the other way about. There is structured activity within some domain, and perhaps, as observers, we can track the local guidances—resistances and affor-dances—that characterize the environment of activity. What is the norm here? Even though there are perhaps no intentions involved, there is normativity nonetheless, but our grip on the shape of the normativity comes only through our understanding of the trails of activity. What forms of activity are fitting and so in place, and what forms are "out of place." Which ways of acting flow well, and which stutter? To understand the norms is to follow the trails of activity. The forms of guidance in activity are explanatorily prior to the mundane norms of activity; this is what makes them *mundane* norms.

The structure of a realm of mediation is the structure of the trails through the environment in which activity is mediated. Trails simultaneously guide those who follow them, and in the very act of guidance are themselves shaped. (Unlike elite norms such as truth: truth guides those who follow truth, but truth is not shaped by this act of guidance.) Trails are contingent, historical, embodied, and fully local entities, but they establish normative boundaries: this is right, this is wrong; this lies on the path, this lies off the path; this is where you are and this is where you are going.

Trails can be global, extending to the limits of some space, yet they are built and maintained locally. Trails vary, are responsive to haphazard local configurations, provide choice points and multiple routes, yet make the difference between arriving and being lost. Trails are fully material entities, constituted out of patterns of disturbance within some material medium. Yet trails are also artifacts. (Perhaps trails are the *first* artifacts.) Thus, trails are simultaneously human and nonhuman, or animal and non-animal. People and animals gather on trails, follow trails because of the droppings of other animals, because of the increased likelihood of finding other animals (mates or prey or colleagues), or in order to get to go where they are going only because others have been there. Thus, trails are simultaneously natural and social and historical. Trails are purely physical, yet they also carry content, having a significance that goes beyond the natural laws that govern their embodiment. They represent directions of movement, places to go, places to be, and places where one has come from; yet they are not part of any symbol system. Trails are technologies of reproducibility; for bringing one home again, for getting back to the water hole that has been out of sight for so many months, for keeping activity "on track." This re-producibility or re-presentation is gained in the face of changing and nonconforming environments: because trails flexibly skirt obstacles, and provide work-arounds for the unpredicted, they can provide a robust reliability in returning to the same place again and again.

Trails exist in ontologically distinct kinds of region: forest and savannah certainly, but also social, theoretical, linguistic, biological, psychological, and historical regions. Typically, an environment is ontologically heterogenous: activity through the environment is structured by many of these "factors." What activity trails there are may depend on the varied embodiments of subjects, learned skills, individual and collective dispositions, social taboos, symbolic systems, and practices of their use, the material environment (both built and found), chance encounters, legal restrictions, and historical constraints. But none of these are distinguished as separate "factors" within the trails: the theorist of content is concerned with these matters only as shapings of activity-trails.

Trails within the space of a scientific laboratory, for example, are structured by the social routines of maintaining the cleanliness of pipettes and beakers as much as by the physical space of the laboratory. And they are structured by the skilled routines involved in maintaining the "data-trails" in which test-tube labels are marked, transferred to logs and computer, and transformed into graphs and statistics. Getting around, getting about, getting up, and getting through are the domains of these commonplace trail-norms of everyday, mundane activity.

There is a general distinction, then, between two kinds of guidance: the kind of guidance that is provided by propositional judgment, which is employed, for example, in practical and theoretical reasoning, and more mundane kinds of guidance employed in everyday getting-about. The former is guidance-in-judgment and the latter is guidance-in-activity. If guidance is the general form of normativity, then we should distinguish between norms of judgment and norms of activity.

Remember section 3: to fix, within a theory of content, the modes of present-ation for a range of contents, analyze the structures necessary for characterizing the norm-governed relations between these norm-governed contents. Thus, corre-sponding to the distinction between two kinds of normativity (elite norms of judg-ment and mundane norms of activity) is a distinction between two kinds of mode of presentation of the world: as realm of reference and as realm of mediation. Just as truth norms generate the referential structure of objects and properties, so norms of activity guidance generate the mediational structure of activity trails. The presentational structure of experiential content is the structure of the realm of mediation: the normative boundaries in the space of activity which are given as trails through an environment. Both the norms and the mode of presentation that are characteristic of experience may be specified within the theory of content by referring to the realm of mediation. Reference to the realm of mediation does double duty in the theory of content: as a specification of normative conditions and as a specification of modes of presentation.

When asked the policeman's question, I knew my speed, but not as an object, not as a referent, not as a truth-maker. How then? If we heed the advice of section 3, there is no need for us theorists to be as stumped by this question as I was by the policeman's question: in figuring out what the content is, ask about the kinds of normativity involved; and to figure out this, ask about the kinds of guidance. And, as we saw, the forms of guidance in the motorcycle example were the envi-ronmental resistances and affordances that shaped my constant readjustments of body and motorcycle. As the normativity that governs the practice of judgment provides a way in which the world is made cognitively present to subjects who think and judge, so the normativity that governs mundane activity provides a way in which the world is made present to active subjects of experience. We can say that speeds and distances were presented to me in terms of the structure of activity trails through the roadscape around me. ("But such an activity-trail doesn't separate out speed and distance as *speed* and *distance*." Of course not; *speed* and *distance* are concepts, and activity-trails are nonconceptual structures of the world.)

	CONCEPTUAL CONTENT	NONCONCEPTUAL CONTENT
Norm (Governing Normativity)	Truth (& other elite norms)	Activity Guidance (& Skill / mastery & other mundane norms)
World given as ... (Content specified by reference to ...)	Realm of Reference	Realm of Mediation
Modes of Presentation (Constituent Structure)	Referents: particular objects, properties, etc.	Activity Trails

Figure 6.1
Distinguishing two kinds of content.

The distinction between conceptual and nonconceptual content as the distinction between referential and mediational content is summarized in figure 6.1.

Notes

1. It is even consistent with this to suppose that there were simple kinds of content around in the world, before there were any experiencing subjects.
2. In this context, this is just stipulation. Some people working in non-Fregean semantical traditions, rather than a Dummettian/Strawsonian tradition, will find my use odd, which is why I have begun with this stipulation. I need to have a notion like my notion of content—whatever it is called— because part of the problem of embodied cognition is to explain how there can be certain physical creatures, like us but unlike paramecia, whose response to the world does not consist wholly in their response to physical stimulations of their sensory surfaces, but which rests, in part, on a conception of how the world is.
3. How could there be such a way? Well, this is what I am devoting much of the paper to trying to explain. So far in this section I take myself to have given only a pocket account of the notions of content, conceptual, and nonconceptual. The rest of this section begins on an analysis, and gives

an argument for the existence of nonconceptual content, while in Cussins 1990, §7 I make more precise the notion of a content's presenting the world objectively as consisting of objects, properties, and situations. The claims in this section don't tell us what content is; they are intended just to give an intuitive feel for the notions. Later, we will see that conceptual content is the availability in experience of a task-domain, and nonconceptual content is the availability in experience of substrate-domain abilities.

4. Following, with some differences, the usage in Bennett 1976 and by Brian Smith (1987).

5. NB: these are not yet definitions of two kinds of *content*.

6. Something is canonically characterized (within a theory) if, and only if, it is characterized in terms of the properties which the theory takes to be essential to it. A game of football, for example, is canonically characterized, in the Football Association, in terms of the notions employed in the rules of the game, not in terms of temporal patterns of disruption to the playing field. A *content* is canonically characterized by a specification which reveals the way in which it presents the world. See below.

7. Notice the difference between instantiating or satisfying or falling under a concept, on the one hand, and possessing a concept on the other. I possess the concept *bachelor*, but I don't fall under that concept.

8. Not a *content* property, obviously.

9. The task-domain objects, properties, and situations are presumed to be fully objective in the sense that it is presumed that it is, in principle, possible to explain what it is for them to exist in a way which is independent of any explanation of what it is for organisms to recognize or perceive or act on them. (It will then turn out that the notion of a task-domain is an idealization.) It is important to see that a task-domain is entirely abstracted from any perceiver or subject. There is no point of view in a task-domain, no essentially indexical elements.

10. One might suppose that a task-domain is simply a part of the world. But this is not so, because a task-domain is a part of the world *under a given conceptualization*. Not only does the world permit of many different true conceptualizations, it also permits of registrations which are *not* conceptualizations (I shall argue).

11. For such a game to be playable, it would have to be supplemented with new rules, such as the rule of obligatory capture: if, on a turn, a player can capture an opponent's piece, then he must do so. But this does not alter the point that an intelligent capacity to play a game (unlike a conventional computer's capacity) entails the capacity to be able to play related games, whose task-domains may differ from each other and from that of the original game.

12. We shouldn't assume that because the state has a linguistic expression, that therefore it has only one kind of content: linguistic content isn't a kind of content, only a kind of *expression* of, or vehicle for, content. It turns out that we need more than one kind of content to do justice to our language use. At this stage in the paper, I am trying to be neutral on this point.

13. See, e.g., Dummett 1975 and 1976, Davidson 1967, Evans 1982, chaps. 1–4.

14. Having probabilistic truth conditions is one way to have determinate truth conditions. When Quine argued that the reference of "gavagai" was indeterminate (Quine 1960), he did not mean that it referred with a certain probability to rabbit, and with a certain probability to rabbit-stage, and with a certain probability to connected-rabbit-parts. From my perspective, fuzzy set theory and probabilistic emendations of semantic theories do not offer us a notion of content different from conceptual content. Rather, they provide a way in which a state or item, etc., may have its conceptual content probabilistically. A coin tossed in a task domain may come up heads with probability 0.5. Task-domains are fully determinate, not deterministic.

15. I am not prejudicing the issue of whether there is more than one kind of content. I am noticing a certain constraint within the theory of content and calling "α content" the content which satisfies this constraint. Later, I introduce a different constraint within the theory of content, and call "β content" the content which satisfies this new constraint. This leaves it open that β content may be identical to α content.

16. Or, a determinate contribution to determinate truth conditions. I shan't continue to make this qualification.

17. It has been a philosophical convention since Frege (see Frege 1918a) that *thinking* is a psychological concept, whereas *thought* is a logical or philosophical notion [concept]. *Concept*, like *thought*, is, in the first instance, a logical notion: concepts are thought constituents. So saying "my *thought* that *p*" within the convention, entails that the content of the state is conceptual. Saying, merely, "my *thinking* that *p*" does not entail any consequence about the kind of content that the state has.

    Part of what I am addressing in the paper is the question whether *concept* should, as well as being a logical notion, also be a psychological notion [concept]. Psychology, I am assuming, must employ some notion of content, but I will suggest that the kind of content which is conceptual content has only a logico-philosophical role; psychology requires a different kind of content—nonconceptual content.

18. See, e.g., Peacocke 1986b. Frege added the further condition on sense, that it *determines* reference. This is not, however, a condition on β content. Only certain β contents (those that are senses) determine reference.

19. Of course, the people I cite don't put their conclusions this way!

20. Frege's intuitive criterion of difference: the thought grasped in one cognitive act, *x*, is different from the thought grasped in another cognitive act, *y*, if, and only if, it is possible for some rational person at a time to take incompatible attitudes to them; i.e. accepting (rejecting) one while rejecting (accepting) or being agnostic about the other.

21. See n. 9 above where I say that the notion of a task-domain prescinds from any notion of indexicality. There is no point of view in a task-domain, so if point of view is essential to indexicality, a notion of content for which indexicality is essential cannot be captured by means of concepts of the task-domain.

22. Are there any representational states which don't contain, either explicitly or implicitly, indexical or demonstrative elements? Perhaps *God is good*, because it is part of the essence of God that He is unique. (Just about every definite description contains an implicit indexical reference to, for example, *our* earth.) But does "good" mean "good to us," "good from our point of view, rather than say, the Devil's"?

23. The theorist can *refer* to the mode of presentation in question without *employing* it, but this doesn't help. What is in question is the kind of explanation of the nature of these contents that a scientific psychologist can give or use, if the psychologist is restricted to conceptual kinds of specification, and accepts as the explanatory task the need to construct any psychologically indispensable notion of content. The trouble is that if the specification is canonical, the theorist's capacity to understand the nature of the content in question depends, ineliminably, on his or her having had similar experiences. Thus, conceptual specification of these contents which is both canonical and *theoretically* adequate fails because there are only two ways to conceptually specify such contents: by means of concepts of the task-domain, or by use of the indexical or demonstrative term where the understanding of the use of the term depends on either sharing the experiential environment, or having had similar experiences. Perry's and Peacocke's arguments show that the first method of specification cannot be canonical for β contents, while the ineffable dependence on having had certain sorts of experiences shows that the second method of specification cannot be theoretically adequate. Why this is so is spelt out in detail in Cussins 1992. (Thanks to Christopher Peacocke for pointing out this worry to me.)

24. It may be objected that I am imposing overly strict explanatory demands on a theory of content. I consider this objection in Cussins 1992.

25. For example, Dretske's notion of information (Dretske 1981) would be a notion of nonconceptual content, were it to be a notion of content, because one does not need to possess the concept of information in order to be in information carrying states. (Evidently so, since even trees—for that matter, anything at all—carry information.) The trouble comes when Dretske tries to justify the

notion of information as a notion of content. Peacocke (1989b) [see also essay 5] develops a different notion of nonconceptual content.

26. I don't want to beg the question as to what kind of representational system is sufficient for the possession of concepts, so, in the discussion of systems such as Flakey, I use a general notion of representation, which is neutral with respect to whether its significance (e.g. its semantics) is only extrinsically attributed, or whether its significance (like that of content) is intrinsically available. I consider the conditions for a physical system to have states whose significance is intrinsically available in Cussins 1990, §7.

27. As certain theorists in AI do; see, e.g., Lenat and Feigenbaum 1987.

28. The American defense department funding agency for "advanced research projects."

29. Evidently, what abilities are part of the s-domain will be relative to a particular task-domain. Knowledge of visual information-processing algorithms is not part of many people's task-domain, but it was part of David Marr's. Hence what kind of content some state possesses, will be relative to the kind of evaluation which is appropriate to it: the particular way of dividing up t- and s-domains for the particular case. There may be more than one task-domain for a single state at a time.

30. For that matter, the subject may also be incapable of moving. A way of moving may be available in my experience, even though I am incapable of acting on the basis of it. (The content would still be canonically characterized in terms of its constitutive connections to perception and action.)

31. In the sense of "objective" which I make clear in Cussins 1990, §§7 and 8. Basically, pain-experience is less objective because it is less perspective-independent.

32. For some exposition of this term, see the discussion of the map-maker in Cussins 1990, §9.

33. Not just for a behaviorist, actually. The cognitive revolution may have reinstated the notion of representation, but it hasn't yet reinstated experience (my notion of content). I hope by this article to push us a little way towards doing that.

34. It should be noted that there may be kinds of β content which are not canonically specified by means of concepts of the s-domain, or, more narrowly, by means of concepts of ways of finding one's way in the environment; if so, these will be kinds of content which are not kinds of conceptual content. Their status will depend on how it is proposed to canonically capture them.

35. The argument given here can be extended from the case of indexical and demonstrative senses to all senses.

36. Remember that *conceptual* does not equal *conscious*. Of course recognition of Charis does not depend on matching to consciously stored features; this is not the point I am making. In claiming that the psychological structure of recognition of individuals is its nonconceptual structure, rather than its conceptual structure, I am claiming that a computational model of individual recognition must be suited to transforming representations which have nonconceptual, rather than conceptual, content. Much of this computational transformation of representations will normally, of course, be quite unconscious.

37. This paper is dedicated to the memory of my father, Manny Cussins (1905–1987). I would like to thank for their help with the paper or with the development of its ideas: Dan Brotsky, John Campbell, David Charles, Bill Child, Ron Chrisley, Andy Clark, Michael Dummett, John Haugeland, Dimitri Kullmann, David Levy, Michael Martin, Geoff Nunberg, Gerard O'Brien, Christopher Peacocke, Jeff Schrager, Paul Skokowski, Scott Stornetta, Brian Smith, Susan Stucky, and Debbie Tatar. I have benefitted from talks at Temple University, at the 1988 Society for Philosophy and Psychology Annual Meeting in North Carolina, at the Institute for Research on Learning, at the System Sciences Laboratory at Xerox PARC, at CSLI, Stanford, at David Charles' Oriel Discussion Group, and at a Birkbeck Discussion Group on Connectionism. I am grateful for support from a Junior Research Fellowship at New College, Oxford, a Post-Doctoral Fellowship at CSLI, Stanford, resource support from the System Sciences Laboratory, Xerox PARC, and the remarkable research environment at PARC. And above all to Charis, for her inspiration and confidence.

38. Only about one fifth of C3 is republished here. The material in this "postscript" is also truncated in order to help keep down the length of this collection on nonconceptual content.

39. Irene Appelbaum suggested the following kind of resistance: consider a golfer who is losing to her opponent who asks, "Do you inhale or exhale on your backswing?"

40. Don't be misled by the demonstrative expression! The bearer of the content, here, is the activity; the demonstrative functions to direct our attention towards the activity—it does not itself say what the content is. Suppose one is interested in the content of a dance movement on the stage. In response to a question about what the dance expresses, you say "Look there! *That's* what the dance expresses." That the linguistic demonstrative word often expresses a concept tells us nothing, in this context, about the nature of the content expressed by the dance movement. The demonstrative functions here as a pointer towards the expressive item (which is then allowed to 'speak" for itself), and so nothing can be deduced about the content of the dance from the conceptual content of the demonstrative.

41. The dynamic forms of activity are the referents of some of my philosophical thoughts in writing this paragraph. Entities that are not part of the realm of reference for one class of thoughts may be part of the realm of reference for a different class. The entities are presented conceptually only in the latter class of thoughts. The key to avoiding confusion here is to avoid doing the philosophy of content while riding one's motorcycle!

Chapter 7

Connectionism and Cognitive Flexibility (1994)

Andy Clark

---

1 Introduction

There are skilled performers, and there are creative cognizers. The beaver is a skilled performer, able to build dams of great complexity in ways subtly fitted to the local environment. But it is not (or so I shall argue) a creative cognizer. It cannot alter and amend its dam building behavior in an open-ended number of ways as determined by other (behaviorally distant) aspects of its knowledge. Its dam-building procedure is not an object for its own further cognitive processes. It cannot operate on and amend the procedure at will, despite its plasticity relative to local context. It has flexibility only in a *restricted* domain. By contrast, human cognition (and perhaps the cognition of some higher animals) seems flexible in a much deeper sense. We are able to bring arbitrary elements of our knowledge to bear on many of the tasks we perform. We are not bound in respect of a given task, to any single conceptual space (see, e.g., Boden 1990b). This more profound kind of flexibility is, I believe, the operational core of the notion of creativity, and marks a divide in the natural order: a divide visible both phylogenetically (between species) and ontogenetically (in cycles in individual human development). What follows is thus not so much a paper about creativity as a discussion of what I see as at least part of its operational core. Understanding the computational roots of the development of the flexible use of stored information is in many ways a prerequisite for understanding the possibility of genuinely creative thought and action.

The angle on creativity and flexibility just rehearsed draws heavily on work developed by Annette Karmiloff-Smith under the title of the Representational Redescription Hypothesis (see, e.g., Karmiloff-Smith 1986, 1990, and 1992, and Clark and Karmiloff-Smith 1993 and, for a specific usage in relation to the creativity debate, Boden 1990b). In what follows, my concern is to locate these issues in the framework of a broader discussion which highlights some computational and philosophical implications of such a view. In particular I shall argue that the

From *Artificial Intelligence and Creativity*, T. Dartnall (ed.), pp. 63–79, Dordrecht: Kluwer Academic Publishers, 1994. Reprinted with the kind permission of the author and Kluwer Academic Publishers.

distinctive kind of flexibility just described is not exhibited by a familiar class of connectionist models.

As an exemplar of the familiar class of connectionist systems I have in mind, I shall consider NETtalk (Sejnowski and Rosenberg 1986). NETtalk, I shall argue, is a system which *knows how to negotiate* a certain problem domain. Further, it negotiates that domain in a way which is grounded in the nature of the domain itself. Further still, we, as external theorists, can *analyze* its behavior in a way which displays its lawful relation to a set of conceptual level categories (such as "vowel" and "consonant"). Nonetheless (or so I shall argue) its knowledge is only partially (and somewhat misleadingly) described in these terms. For there is an important sense in which it lacks the idea of a vowel as an abstraction. It is this lack of genuine knowledge of abstract categories which is distinctive of what I shall call *"first-order connectionist systems."*

First-order connectionist systems model what Cussins has called "nonconceptual content" (Cussins 1990) [see essay 6]. Cussins believes that nonconceptual content provides the basis for an alternative model of cognition to that enshrined in Jerry Fodor's language of thought hypothesis. I review Cussins' suggestions, which have the effect of arguing for a deeply *developmental* model of cognition.

If, however, we turn to the developmental literature itself, we encounter complications. For Cussins' picture of nonconceptual content, and my description of first-order connectionist systems, fit neatly into a phase-like picture of cognitive development developed by Annette Karmiloff-Smith. But whereas Cussins sees himself as providing a *global* alternative to language of thought style explanations, it can easily look as if the later phases of the developmental process positively *require* a language of thought. I analyze this clash of intuitions in some detail before recording an open verdict. Much here depends on unresolved technical issues such as: can a connectionist system create and manipulate large numbers of variables without merely implementing a classical system?

Whatever the outcome of that debate, the phase-like model has implications for an analysis of content. I end by arguing that genuinely contentful thought requires a system which has both nonconceptual *and* conceptual knowledge of its world. The nonconceptual knowledge is the epistemological bedrock which puts the system in *contact* with the world its thoughts are meant to concern. The conceptual knowledge is an ultimate effect of a process of redescription which provides for the integration and wider availability of the knowledge embedded in the lower level representations.

2 What NETtalk Knows

NETtalk (Sejnowski and Rosenberg 1986) is one of the most famous and impressive examples of what I shall call a "first-order connectionist system." The model's goal is successfully to negotiate the problem domain of text-to-speech transformations. NETtalk took 7 letter segments of text as input and mapped the target window of that input onto an output which coded for phonemes. (The output was sent to a speech synthesizer which converted it into actual sound.) In common with most interesting connectionist systems (i.e., any ones tackling a seriously complex, non-toy problem) the net had to be trained rather than programmed. One of the major achievements of contemporary connectionism is a small set of powerful automatic learning procedures. In the case of NETtalk, a back-propagation method was used. What this means is that the network begins with a random set of weights on its connections, and is given an input. A supervising system watches its output, which will inevitably be wildly inaccurate at first. The actual output (in this case a coding for phonemes) is compared with the correct output (as determined by the input). Automatic procedures then minutely adjust the connectivity strengths to bring them more into line, i.e., to make it the case that it would do a little better were it given that input again. This is repeated many hundreds of times for many different inputs. After extensive learning, the system could be heard (via the speech synthesizer) to babble half-recognizable words. By the end of the training sequence it was accurate and intelligible. An impressive achievement indeed. But now let us raise the question: what does NETtalk actually know?

Naturally, NETtalk does not in any sense *understand* what it is saying. But that is not the point. Likewise, I might learn roughly how to pronounce Chinese sequences without understanding them. Nonetheless, NETtalk has gone from babble to an output which is lawfully disciplined with respect to its inputs. That strongly suggests that it has learnt *something*. The question is, what?

It is a point of some methodological interest that having an up and running connectionist system (like NETtalk) does not, in and of itself, much advance our understanding of *how* its target domain is being negotiated. This is because the system is trained, not programmed as a result of some detailed task analysis of a traditional nature (for more on this see Clark 1990). So something has to be done to arrive at a picture of what NETtalk knows.

One possibility is to examine the network using a statistical technique known as "cluster analysis." Cluster analysis proceeds by

1. giving the network a selection of inputs;
2. recording the state of the system's hidden unit activations as a response to each input;
3. grouping together the most similar pairs of hidden unit responses;
4. examining the inputs to the pair to try to see what they had in common;
5. repeating the procedure for pairs of pairs and so on.

A cluster analysis of NETtalk, for example, unearthed similarities of hidden unit responses to p's and b's and, proceeding up the hierarchy of pairs of pairings, to all vowels and to all consonants. In some sense, then, NETtalk had learned to respond very similarly to p and b inputs and quite similarly to all vowel inputs. In short, it seemed to have learnt the structure of a classical discrimination tree for the text to phoneme pairing task. This was quite a striking result. The net had learnt to treat a, e, i, o, u as in some respect similar. So it *knows about vowels*. Or does it?

What cannot be doubted is this: that it knows its *way around* in a domain which *we* (external theorists) characterize by abstractions such as vowel and consonant. I shall now argue that there is an important sense in which these abstractions, useful (even essential?) as they are in helping us to see what NETtalk is doing, are not available to NETtalk itself.

It will help to begin with a somewhat simpler example. Rumor has it that one of the big High Street banks has an up and running connectionist network which assesses loan-worthiness. Imagine this is true. The bank, it is said, had over the years, compiled a vast quantity of data concerning who had or had not proven to be a good risk. But the data was disunified; no clear patterns emerged which a human operative could spot and rely on. Ingeniously, the bank decided to use the data to train a first-order connectionist network. The network learnt to assess loan-worthiness with a *significantly higher success rate* than the bank's best human operatives. A classic case of going directly from a very limited understanding to an up and running system.

Suppose we now attempt to analyze the network. What has it learnt? We might find, by doing a cluster analysis, that it has learnt to regard *postal addresses* as a useful constraint and has portioned the space into good addresses and not-so-good ones. For example, it may respond with a similar hidden unit activation vector to all addresses in the west end of London. In a weak sense, then it "knows about" *west end addresses*. That is, it negotiates its problem domain in a way which we might usefully understand by introducing the concept of a west end address as a label in our cluster analysis of its behavior.

Suppose now that the loans network is just a small part of a larger system, and the larger system is capable of real communication. The larger system (call it "bank manager") is asked to advise a leading Australian bank on the matter of loan-worthiness. That is, it is asked for its *theory* of loan worthiness. As things stand, it may well have nothing to say. Much like a human with an automatic skill, it has learnt an effective procedure for negotiating a particular domain (viz., loan-worthiness-in-England-1994). But if that is all it has learnt, it will have no useful theory to transmit. The set of weights on the connections of the loan-assessment network won't do, since these represent a solution only to a very *specific* instance of the problem, i.e., one heavily dependent on such matters as London postal districts.

What the system needs, in order to be able to tell the Australian system anything useful, is some higher-level analysis of the functioning procedure embodied in the loan-assessment network. Such a theory might require concepts such as "good postal addresses" which could be weighted in importance against concepts such as "professional employment," "stable employment record" and so forth. The first-order network could get by without such explicit abstractions since it only needed to respond to concrete inputs using England-specific categories. Not so its international cousin.

But the point about *communication* of a theory is in an important sense merely secondary. The deeper issue concerns the benefits of such higher-level analysis *to the system itself*. Such benefits seem likely to include (a) intelligent self de-bugging, (b) creatively coping with novel situations, (c) reasoning by analysis.

Let's look at each of these in a little more detail.

(a) Intelligent Self de-bugging

Suppose the system starts to go wrong. For concreteness, let's suppose that London re-defines its postal districts so that west end and east end addresses are reversed. A first-order connectionist system would have to completely re-train the whole network in order to cope. But a more powerful system with explicit representations of east and west end addresses (e.g., a *real* bank manager) could cope by adding a rule which states "treat all west end addresses after 1994 as east and vice versa." In short, the possession of abstract categories and appropriate control structures would enable the system to *isolate* the cause of the trouble and take *focused* action to resolve it.

(b) Creative Cognition

Novel situations present a related problem. Suppose a *new* London postal address is introduced (e.g., for the newly developed sector of the Isle of Dogs). The slow response is to train the system on a plethora of cases involving the address. But a faster one is to assimilate the new address to a category ("good addresses") which the system already knows how to deal with. It is not clear how to achieve such focused assimilation of new material in a simple first-order network. Or, to take an even better case, suppose the training data all concerned loan making in a flourishing, buoyant economy. If we then face a partially altered situation such as loan making in a depressed economy, then we would want to preserve much, but not all, of the strategy evolved for the original case (e.g., a steady job would now count for more than before, but a rich family background would count for the same). What we need is to *selectively exploit* the knowledge gained by the original net. But this would pose serious problems, as all the knowledge embodied in the original net is stored in a highly intertwined manner in a single distributed web of weights. This makes the selective exploitation of parts of the knowledge problematic. Yet one of the key tricks of creative cognition, it seems, is precisely to deploy fragments of knowledge originally developed to serve one purpose to serve a new one.

(c) Reasoning by Analysis

This is a little harder to explain. The general idea is that a first-order connectionist system can only reason about its domain by using *actual examples* of values in the domain. For example, the loans network can reason about the loanworthiness of someone with an income of £30,000 a year, an address in West Kensington and regular outgoing commitments of £20,000. But it cannot reason about someone whose income is 10 times her outgoings but who has a "blackballed" address. That is, it cannot reason abstractly about its domain. It can solve problems only in response to specific inputs.

This last point is very powerfully made in Kirsh 1987 in the context of a discussion of the role of *variables* in classical AI. Rampant variable binding, according to Kirsh, is *distinctive* of classical AI and problematic in connectionist AI. As an example he cites classical planning systems. Such systems depict the act of planning as involving imagining the consequences of many actions and assessing the results. Actions are defined very generally so as to provide abstract frameworks into which particular instances fit. It is the presence of variables inside such frameworks which allows the AI researcher to define very general rules and procedures which may be applied in many situations. We reason, it seems, by working (unconsciously) with *many hundreds* of variables and names. In standard AI these relations are stored in a substantial address space in which we keep track of the variable-value relations.

According to Kirsh the value of having variables in a system is two-fold. First, they can act as placeholders for unknowns. In so doing, they permit the system to "solve for X." Kirsh calls this "the power of analysis." Second, they allow us to formulate abstract rules and generalizations which specify relations or constraints which apply to a *class* of entities. Kirsh calls this "the power of abstraction." Thus assuming that our variables range over numbers we may express the general arithmetical property of commutability by stating $a + b = b + a$ (see Kirsh 1987, p. 122). Very complex regularities can be succinctly expressed in this way. Variables may thus help form simplifying descriptions of complex structures in a way which lets us see, of two such structures, that they instantiate the same more fundamental form.

To perform these functions, the variables must be *explicit* in the system. We must be able to operate on the variable (e.g., defining more and more complex structures embedding it) without cashing it as any particular value. And therein, as Kirsh clearly states, lies the problem for PDP systems. For such systems, at their most basic, can contain no *explicit* representations of variables. For they have no fluent capacity to bind and re-bind the same variable to an arbitrary set of values. Instead, they at best manage (by careful crafting of connections) to act *as if* they knew, e.g., that $a + b = b + a$. But in acting as if they knew this they must in fact always work on particular values of a and b given as inputs. They will find, in each *particular* case, that $a + b = b + a$. But they cannot know this by an *analysis* of the explicit constraint $a + b = b + a$. In this sense, such systems are more dependent on specific inputs than classical ones are.

It is easy to find analogues of all these points for NETtalk. Clearly NETtalk has no genuine abstract notion of vowelhood. It lacks the resources to represent such absolutely general ideas as "every *word* contains at least one *vowel.*" In reasoning about vowels it is *necessarily* driven by specific input instances of a, e, i, o or u. It cannot analyze its own performance in terms of a structured competence involving vowels and consonants. It could not isolate its performance with *vowels* as the cause of some specific fault, and focus restorative action on just its vowel-pronouncing abilities. It could not learn how a new letter contributes to pronunciations by being told it is a vowel and inherits many of the abstract properties of vowels. In short, there is a great deal that NETtalk *doesn't know;* much more than we might be led to believe if we took its cluster analysis at face value. (Of course, it is quite possible that an untutored speaker of English is, in fact, in precisely the same state of ignorance of vowelhood as NETtalk. My claim is not that our knowledge of English pronunciation is more extensive than NETtalk's—although this may well be true. Rather, it is that the limits of NETtalk are illustrative of the general limits of first-order connectionist systems, and in *many* problem domains, humans in fact go on to exceed these limits and develop higher-level representations.)

Perhaps I should also point out that none of this is meant to rule out the obvious possibility of extending or amending NETtalk in ways which would begin to remedy these "deficiencies." Simplistically, one might, for example, fix it so that any one of the many activation vectors grouped in the cluster analysis as "vowel" would be sufficient to activate a single input node to a second network. Such a "grandmother-vowel" node would constitute a step along the road to a real representation of vowelhood. Moreover, some connectionists (e.g., Smolensky 1987; Touretzky and Hinton 1985) have begun to develop connectionist-style solutions to the problem of variable-binding on which much of this analysis of first-order networks hangs. These issues, and the potential of "second-order" connectionism, are taken up in Clark and Karmiloff-Smith 1993. Some further complications are mooted in section 5 below.

3 Types of Content

The observations concerning NETtalk (and first-order connectionist systems in general) find an interesting parallel in some recent philosophical work concerning *nonconceptual content.* Consider the property of "thinking of someone as a bachelor." We would specify the property using the concepts "male," "adult," and "unmarried." And no system could count as thinking of someone as a bachelor *unless* it was able to regard him as falling under the concepts "male," "adult," and "unmarried." That makes the property in question ("thinking of someone as a bachelor") a *conceptual* one.

But conceptual content, according to Cussins, is not the *only* kind of content. There are also, he argues, psychological states which "must be canonically specified by means of concepts that the subject need not have." Thus consider the experience of hearing a sound as coming from a certain place. How are we to characterize the content of this experience? It might occur to us to say that they hear the sound *as* coming from the south, say. But this is, in a way, to fail to capture the content. For two people might both hear a sound as coming from the *south* yet turn their heads or move in *different directions* because one thinks that south is *that way* whereas the other does not. The point, then (following Evans 1982) [see essay 2] is that the content is in fact constitutively tied to a way of orienting oneself in the world. To hear a sound as coming from a certain place inescapably involves being disposed to move or orient oneself in a certain way in response. To specify the content in conceptual terms is thus necessarily to fail to capture it, since ties between conceptual contents and actions are contingent whereas what it *is* to be in the nonconceptually contentful state just *is* to be disposed to move and act in certain ways.

In sum, the idea is that some contents properly consist in being able to negotiate a certain domain. As Cussins puts it:

> It is the idea that certain contents consist in a means of finding one's way in the world (tracking the object, say) being available to the subject in his or her experience, even though it may not be available to the subject conceptually, and, indeed, the subject may be incapable of expressing in words what this way of moving is. (Cussins 1990, p. 395) [essay 6, p. 143]

This should recall vividly our discussion of NETtalk in sections 1 and 2, for NETtalk is a nice case of a system which (a) "knows its way around in a certain domain," yet (b) lacks, in an important sense, the concepts we might use (say, in our cluster analysis) to describe *what* it is that it knows.

First-order connectionist networks are thus ideal contenders for systems capable of supporting nonconceptual content (which is not necessarily to say that NETtalk really has states which are contentful, albeit nonconceptually so; rather, one could say that such a network, if certain other unspecified conditions were met, would *then* enjoy such states).

Moreover, the idea of nonconceptual content seems well suited to describing the cognitive states of many animals. Thus consider the sandfish. The sandfish is a lizard (*scincus scincus*) which buries itself in the sand and detects vibrations caused by surface prey. When an insect on the surface is thus located, the sandfish emerges, with fatal accuracy, to take its dinner. The sandfish thus negotiates a domain which we describe using concepts like "insect" and "vibration." But the sandfish need not literally have any such concepts. We can imagine it as a small network capable of partitioning an input space of vibrations in a way which, under cluster analysis, would yield groupings for "insect at bearing X," "insect at bearing Y" and so on, yet lacking any explicit representation of insects and bearing, just as NETtalk was seen to lack any explicit representation of "vowel."

What we then need to understand, according to Cussins, is how from a basis of nonconceptual awareness of the world, a creature can slowly come to satisfy (or more nearly to satisfy) the constraints we impose on the ascription of *conceptual* contents. What constraints are these? If I describe the frog as spotting a fly, what determines whether I have the right to regard this as a specification of a conceptual or nonconceptual content? Cussins offers a rather intricate account. But one of the leading ideas is this: to have a conceptual content requires *more* than a mere causal or informational link to the state of the world implicated in the description of the content. To have (properly) the concept *fly* involves more than being able to find your way around (like the frog) in a fly-infested domain. It involves having a whole web of concepts in which your concept of a fly is embedded. In particular, it involves having your fly-concept at the disposal of any other conceptual abilities you have. This consciously echoes Evans' Generality Constraint (Evans 1982, pp. 100–105) [essay 2, appendix], which insists that to truly possess a concept *a* you must be able to think *a* in all the (semantically sensible) combinations which it could enter into with other concepts you possess. Thus if you can *really* think *Fa*, and *really* think *Gb*, you must (as a matter of stipulation) be able to think *Fb* and *Ga*. But the frog may be able to have the proto-thought "there is a fly over there" and some other types of proto-thought and yet be quite incapable of having any *other* kind of thought about flies. And what this shows, according to the Generality Constraint, is that it lacks the concept of a fly. Thus the content of the frog's experience cannot be a conceptual content "there is a fly over there" and must instead be a nonconceptual content (which doesn't require that it have the concept *fly* at all) which Cussins (1990, p. 423) suggests we might express as "there-is-a-fly-over-there." The hyphenation marks the fact that the content is *unstructured*. Conceptual content, by contrast, is structured content in which each element implicated in the specification of the thought has a separate significance for the creature, and can enter freely into combinations with elements of the creature's other thoughts.

The move from unstructured to structured contents is, as Cussins sees it, a move from perspective-dependent to more objective representations of the world. The frog lacks the general idea of a fly as part of an objective world, capable of being related to that world in a wide variety of ways (e.g., being dead, being alive, being nearby, being faraway, being crunchy and so on). It knows about flies only from a single and limited perspective, that of "spotting and eating." By contrast, a system which met the Generality Constraint with respect to its idea of flies would have to be able to think about flies in a much wider variety of ways. This is seen as constituting a move towards objectivity. The task of psychological explanation, then, will be to display:

> Psycho-computational transformations defined over non-conceptual contents which have the effect of reducing the perspective-dependence of the contents. (Cussins 1990, p. 424)

Connectionism, Cussins argues, may provide an appropriate vehicle for such explanations. The reasons for this are (i) basic connectionist representations are said to be "naturally perspective-dependent" (*ibid.*, pp. 432–433),[1] (ii) nonetheless much work in connectionism is said to be devoted to generating perspective-decreasing representations in the hidden units, (iii) learning is made central in connectionism and this is appropriate for Cussins' essentially developmental explanatory strategy.

Cussins hopes that connectionists will one day provide an account of how connectionist learning algorithms can evolve the powers of the hidden units so as to yield more and more perspective-reducing representations (*ibid.*, p. 435). The end point of such an evolution will be cognizing creatures like us, capable of meeting the Generality Constraint.

In the next section I introduce a model of cognition drawn from some recent work in developmental psychology. This model is, in many respects, committed to exactly the kind of explanatory strategy which Cussins advocates. Yet as we shall see, the question whether the "higher" representations should be viewed as classical or connectionist remains undecided.

4 *Representational Redescription*

In an influential series of publications, Annette Karmiloff-Smith (1979, 1986, 1988, 1990, 1992) has argued for a phase-like picture of human cognitive development. She holds that humans, unlike most other animals, are compelled by endogenous forces to go beyond simple success in a domain and to seek a more abstract representation of the strategies which brought success. As she puts it, we go beyond "behavioral mastery" and *redescribe* our functioning procedures in a series of higher-level languages. This redescription (which may culminate in conscious, verbal access to a higher-level redescription) is a device which enables the organism to get more mileage out of information which, in a certain sense, it *already* possesses, courtesy of the functioning procedure. The core of the proposal is that knowledge which was once merely *implicit* in a system's ability to negotiate some problem domain becomes an object for the system, and hence can be redescribed in various ways. These redescriptions have the effect of making the knowledge available in a format which facilitates interaction with other kinds of knowledge which the organism possesses, as well as making it more easily manipulable in its own right. These twin effects yield the increasingly open-ended flexibility of use characteristic of the creative cognizer.

The parallel with our discussion of NETtalk is immediate. NETtalk (like the sandfish) has a functioning procedure. It has a kind of behavioral mastery in the domain. But it has not gone *beyond* that mastery. Like the sandfish it is locked into phase one of Karmiloff-Smith's picture. The complete picture involves a number of phases, some of which will be detailed later. For now, we need only stress the coarsest detail, viz:

> *Basic mastery*: the system has a means of negotiating the problem domain. But the procedure is heavily dependent on external inputs and, as far as the organism is concerned, is unstructured.

Higher-level redescriptions: the functioning procedure is treated as a new problem domain and is thus (unconsciously) theorized *about* by the organism. This theorizing results in the organism redescribing the procedure underlying its basic mastery in a series of higher-level languages. (Karmiloff-Smith 1986, pp. 102–103)

Karmiloff-Smith has tested the broad lines of the hypothesis in a number of experiments involving very varied problem domains, ranging from knowledge of the article system (Karmiloff-Smith, 1986) to knowledge of physical causality (Karmiloff-Smith 1988). I shall describe a single, illustrative experiment concerning children's drawing. The experiment, detailed in Karmiloff-Smith (1990, 1992), involved children of two age groups, 4–6 and 8–10. They were asked to draw pictures of familiar, much practiced items such as a house or a person, and then to draw deviant versions ("a funny house," "a man no-one has ever seen," "a funny man," etc). The hypothesis was that at first the children would have basic mastery in the drawing domains but would not have developed higher-level redescriptions of this and hence would exhibit limitations in their drawing ability. Children of all ages were able to draw, for instance, a basic house. The interesting data concerns:

a small number of younger children who seemed unable to produce deviant versions of their basic drawings (thus suggesting a pure "basic mastery" style competence).

and more importantly:

the striking differences between the *kinds* of alterations to the basic drawings exhibited by children of different ages (suggesting various different constraints operating at different phases of the redescriptive process).

Figures 1–6 in Dartnall 1994 (pp. 51–56) show some of the structure within the class of successful attempts. The following pattern of types of change were revealed:

(a) shape and size of elements changed
(b) shape of whole changed
(c) deletion of elements
(d) insertion of new elements
(e) position/orientation changed
(f) insertion of cross-category elements.

It turned out that children of all ages (in the successful class) were able to make changes of types (a) to (c), but only children in the older group (8–10) were generally able to make changes of types (d) to (f) (Karmiloff-Smith 1990 and 1992). How is this to be explained?

One hypothesis is that the younger ones simply hadn't *thought* of the more subtle changes. A more interesting hypothesis is that due to the way their knowledge was represented, the younger ones were actually *incapable* of making such changes. To decide between these two, a follow-up experiment was conducted.

In the follow-up experiment eight of the younger subjects who had made only changes of types (a) to (c) were asked to draw two pictures involving the *other* types of change. One picture was to be of a man with two heads (an insertion change) and the other was to be of a house with wings (a cross-category change). All eight rapidly and fluently drew the house with wings, but seven out of the eight made a revealing "error" in the other task. Instead of drawing a man with two heads they drew one body and head, drew a second head and then:

> went on laboriously and very slowly to draw two bodies, two arms and legs on each body, etc., i.e., they used a complete man drawing procedure for each head.

> They had similar difficulties simply copying a model provided by the experimenter and succeed only very laboriously and slowly. By contrast, when other 8–10 year olds interrupted sequential order to insert a new sub-routine for drawing a second head, they continued drawing a single body with the speed of their normal drawing procedure. (Karmiloff-Smith, 1990, p. 15)

The failure of the children to produce fluently a two-headed figure is *prima facie* evidence that it is not simple lack of imagination which underlies the differences between the age groups. But the winged house case then begins to look anomalous. Karmiloff-Smith (1990, 1992) suggests that to explain the data we need to consider the constraints that operate at the first level of representational redescription. At this point, she speculates, the initial procedure responsible for basic mastery in the domain has been redescribed as a "sequentially fixed list," thus as it were inheriting a constraint from the bare "procedural" level. Such redescription is said to enable the child to "introduce variables on size and shape" (p. 17). But the constraint on the sequential order of elements remains. In the case of the man with two heads the child is required to interrupt this sequential order and this is very hard to achieve. By contrast the wings can be added to a completed house drawing sequence and this addition is thus relatively easy.

The conjecture, then, is that our initial expertise is subserved by fast, efficient but somewhat limiting kinds of internal representations, and that trickier situations (requiring the creative re-use of existing resources) may need to be catered for by representations of a different nature.

But what nature? It has been suggested (*contra* Cussins) that only the phase one style representations are plausibly treated as fully *connectionist* representations, and that the ascent to higher-levels of redescription constitutes a progression towards *classical* representational formalisms culminating perhaps in a full-blooded Fodorian language of thought.[2] Such a conjecture is appealing but, I shall argue, somewhat premature. What the Karmiloff-Smith data really supports is just the observation that human expertise involves greater resources than those developed by a first-order connectionist network. But this leaves open several interest-ing possibilities, to which I now turn.

5 A Premature Opposition?

Our observations concerning NETtalk, Cussins' notion of the evolution of increas-ingly perspective-independent representations, and Karmiloff-Smith's picture of organisms going beyond behavioral success, are all united in highlighting the lim-itations of a certain class of connectionist networks. They agree that merely being able to negotiate a cognitive domain is not enough. And they agree that what is missing is, in a sense, *structured* knowledge of the domain-knowledge which takes the form of an articulated (though not necessarily conscious) *theory*. Should such structured knowledge be conceived as involving classical representations? Or could it be connectionism all the way up? The question is premature. For one thing, all the relevant computational data is not yet in. And for another, there is a dimension in the space of possibilities here which both parties seem to have missed. I shall take these points in turn.

First, the computational data. Cussins is inclined to bet on connectionism all the way up, because the standard evolution of weights in the hidden unit layer looks to be "a perspective-reducing construction," i.e., the hidden units learn effi-cient representations which enable them to deal with many different but related inputs (see Cussins 1990, p. 433).

But this alone won't do, for we have already plotted an intrinsic limitation which afflicts this class of connectionist systems: they do not go on to represent explicitly the categories which the hidden units' partitions embody (categories revealed, say, by cluster analysis) and so, in an important sense, don't have any *theory* of their own functioning. This restricts the scope of their problem-solving abilities in ways detailed in section 2 above. So *if* cognition is to be connectionist all the way up, it looks as if we will at least need to consider more than just first-order connectionist systems (for more on this see Clark and Karmiloff-Smith 1993).

Second, we must be aware that the question "Connectionist or classical?" has *two* dimensions. One concerns the question of the *nature of the learning algorithms*. The other concerns the question of *the nature of the representations learnt*. Thus it could be, for example, that it is a connectionist learning strategy (this time tar-geted on an *internal* data source, such as a network with a basic mastery of some domain) which throws up the redescriptions. In such a case it is conceivable that *what* is learnt may be a classical representational formalism even if the *way* it is learnt is recognizably connectionist. One thought, then, is that there could be a connectionist explanation of the learning and development of a classical system of representation—in which case we would need both classical style accounts of content and connectionist accounts of learning. The space of possibilities here is much larger than it first appears (see Clark 1993 for some excursions into this space). We can likewise consider using a *classical* system to seek out a set of representations for input and output which (e.g., by reducing the number of variables needed) makes it possible to train a first-order connectionist network to solve a class of problems. In short, the computational questions are complex and still largely unresolved.

6 Reinterpreting the Generality Constraint

Suppose we accept two central tenets from the preceding discussions:

> 1. That human cognition involves endogenous pressure to go beyond behavioral mastery and to achieve greater flexibility and scope by developing higher-level representational redescriptions (or control structures);
> 2. That it is the ubiquity and depth of this tendency in humans which most crucially distinguishes our cognitive achievements from those of NETtalk or the sandfish.

The question naturally arises: just how should we conceive the philosophical significance of these claims? There are at least two options here. There is what I shall call the "*conservative* option," which is to see tenet 1 as just a sketch of the mechanisms by which we happen to satisfy the demands made on genuine thought by Evans' Generality Constraint. And there is what I shall call the "*radical* option," which is to regard the process of representational redescription as *itself* being conceptually necessary for genuine thought, and the Generality Constraint as offering just a rough and ready *test* for whether or not it has taken place to a sufficient degree. I shall attempt an argument for the radical option.

It is a powerful intuition that there is a philosophically significant difference between, say, my *belief* that there is a fly in front of me and a frog's awareness of the same kind of fact. The frog can register the information that a fly is in front of it *without* possessing the concepts *fly* or *in front*. But I cannot be properly said to believe that there is a fly in front of me if I lack the general concepts *fly*, *in front* and *me*. I can only have these general concepts if I can think many *other* thoughts involving flies. In fact I must be able to think that the fly is P where P is any other semantically compatible concept I genuinely possess, such as *made of plastic*, *in Australia*, etc. Such, in essence, is Evans' Generality Constraint (Evans 1982; Cussins 1990; Davies 1990) [essays 2 and 6]. In Cussins' terminology, the frog has experiences with nonconceptual content (which he represents as the belief there-is-a-fly-in-front-of-me) whereas my belief state has conceptual content. (It is structured, and the elements of the structure are available for use in a wider variety of ways.) This idea of the elements of the structure being available for wider use provides the link to Karmiloff-Smith's work on representational redescription. For the point of redescription is precisely to *liberate* and allow us to make better use of, the knowledge that, in some sense, is *already* present (in unliberated form) in the phase one representations.

But suppose we concentrate for a moment on the pure demand made by the Generality Constraint. It is just this. That an organism, if it can *really* think that *a* is *F*, and that *b* is *G*, *must* (on pain of not really having those structured thoughts at all) be able to think that *b* is *F* and *a* is *G*. If we try to cash this out (say as a working, cognitive ethologist) we must demand that an animal, if it is to behave in ways which warrant the ascription of the *conceptual* contents "*b* is *F*" and "*b* is *G*," must show itself able to behave in ways which would warrant the ascription of the contents "*a* is *F*" and "*b* is *G*." But—and this is the crunch—an animal might *pass* such behavioral tests by means of an internal look-up tree which *happens* to have a line for *a* is *F*, a line for *b* is *G*, a line for *a* is *G* and a line for *b* is *F*. However, this way of meeting the constraint surely violates the *spirit* of the requirement. For this animal does *not* have a structured grasp of "*a* is *F*." It is not some *elements* of its thought that *a* is *F* which reappear in its thought that *b* is *F*. Instead, it has a closed set of *unstructured* abilities (to think *a*-is-*F*, to think *b*-is-*F*, etc.) which *mimic* a structured ability. It is for this reason that I now think we ought to perform the radical inversion of the standard idea.[3] Let us treat meeting the Generality Constraint (as cashed in behavioral requirements at least) as a *fallible sign* of what we are really (conceptually, philosophically) demanding—which is that the system have *structured internal representations*. In short, the real demand is that the being must genuinely (as a matter of its internal organization) have gone beyond unstructured behavioral mastery and generated representations which divide up and label elements of the phase one representation.

In construing the Generality Constraint as a constraint on internal organization, I do not (contrast, e.g., Davies 1990) wish to commit myself unequivocally to a classicist vision of the representational redescriptions. We can construe the Generality Constraint as a requirement on internal organization, without opting for either classicism or connectionism. What our picture *does* require is a move away from pure first-order connectionist systems. It requires a multi-level architecture with fast, efficient, domain-specific phase one representations and redescriptions of these allowing for more flexible and integrated uses. The redescriptions without doubt constitute some form of *abstraction* from the phase one details. It will be convenient to have a short term for such representations. So let us—*without* begging the classicist/connectionist question—call these "*symbols*." And let us call the phase one representations, "*subsymbols*." The final point I want to notice may now be put like this. The satisfaction of Generality is achieved by means of the *symbolic* levels of representation. But the *content* of those representations depends crucially on the *subsymbolic* procedures which they redescribe. For it is the *subsymbolic* procedures which put the organism in touch with its world (perhaps through the kind of learning that is characteristic of first-order connectionist models). It is the *subsymbolic* representations which enable the organism to *know its way around* the domain. The higher-level redescriptions are valueless if they are cast adrift from this basic mastery.

The Generality Constraint is thus satisfied by internal representations whose content is parasitic on that of the less-abstract phase one representations. We might say:

> *Subsymbolic* know-how without *symbolic* redescription is *blind* (inflexible, animal); *symbolic* redescription without *subsymbolic* know-how is *empty* (lacks content).

7 Conclusions: An Unblushing Ecumenicism

NETtalk, we saw, is a system in touch with its domain. It has learnt to negotiate its way around a world which we, as external theorists, would describe using abstractions such as "vowel" and "consonant." Indeed, NETtalk itself encodes information about these very features as evidenced in the partitionings of the hidden unit space revealed by cluster analysis. Nonetheless, NETtalk is in many ways a rigid and inflexible system. It cannot exploit its knowledge about vowels in the service of any novel but related task (e.g., counting the number of vowels in a sentence). Instead, its knowledge about vowels is totally geared to the particular shape of a single task (text-to-phoneme mapping). This task-specificity of the knowledge representation stands in stark contrast with the abilities of the more creative cognizer. For the creative cognizer can deal with novel task demands in part by drawing directly on bodies of knowledge originally acquired in the service of other goals. To do this, a system must somehow come to separate out the basic acquired knowledge from the original conditions of its use. This is the crucial further step which human children, but not first-order connectionist networks, go on to take. Although in the first instance constrained to deploy their acquired knowledge in a single manner (like NETtalk), children go on to progressively loosen the bonds which tie their knowledge to a specific use. The reason, Karmiloff-Smith suggests, is that humans, but not NETtalk or the sandfish, are subject to powerful, endogenous pressure to go beyond behavioral mastery and to theorize about their phase one representations. Such (unconscious) theorizing yields a sequence of increasingly abstract redescriptions of the phase one knowledge. These redescriptions power the ever-increasing integration of knowledge across domains which is the ideal to which we aspire.

Conceptual content (content which satisfies the Generality Constraint) and creative cognition thus go hand in hand. Both require a mixture of integrative, flexibility-inducing high-level abstractions *and* the tightly coupled task-specific competencies which both ground and maintain our contact with the world which our thoughts concern. To understand the bridge between these twin abilities is to understand the operational core of creative thought.[4]

Notes

1. The now-canonical example of this perspective or context-dependence is the distributed connectionist representation of "coffee." "Coffee" (the conceptual level construct) has no unique, recurrent, syntactic isomorph in a distributed network. Instead, we expect different coffee-signifying vectors according to the surrounding context. Coffee from the cup and drinking perspective has one representation. Coffee from the jar and buying perspective has another. For a full account see Smolensky 1988.

2. This was Karmiloff-Smith's original view, as presented in a talk to the Annual Meeting of the British Psychological Society, Sussex University, 1987. Her current view is, however, much more ecumenical. See Clark and Karmiloff-Smith 1993.

3. I have been known to champion the weaker (conservative) option—see, e.g., Clark 1991. I now suspect that this is a mistake.

4. Some of the material in this paper is drawn from Clark 1993. Thanks to The MIT Press for permission to reproduce it here. A fuller account of the work discussed in section 5 appears in Clark and Karmiloff-Smith 1993.

Chapter 8

Nonconceptual Content: From Perceptual Experience to Subpersonal Computational States (1995)

José Luis Bermúdez

How distinctive are the cognitive processes, such as beliefs, desires, hopes and fears, which constitutively involve the possession of concepts? Recent work in philosophy, psychology and cognitive science has suggested that there might be various types of cognitive state that possess content although they do not require possession of the concepts needed to specify that content. If there are indeed states with this sort of *nonconceptual content*, then this suggests that the concept-involving states which have long been thought to be the only means by which cognition can take place are not really so distinctive after all. The familiar propositional attitudes and the cognitive processes defined over them might just be part of a larger set of cognitive processes which have representational content in virtue of features which do not make constitutive reference to concept possession.

This paper pursues this thought by considering two different domains of cognition to which the notion of nonconceptual content seems applicable. The first domain is that of perceptual experience, while the second is provided by the subpersonal computational states posited by information processing accounts of how we interact with the world. The paper has two central claims. The first thesis is that states with nonconceptual content do exist in both these domains. According to the second thesis, what makes it appropriate to describe such states as contentful is their satisfying certain basic conditions deriving from a general account of the nature of representation-driven behavior that is neutral between conceptual and nonconceptual content. This general account is intended to be an account of content in the abstract, which fits the conceptual case but does not make it a matter of definition that conceptual content is the only form of content. What emerges from considering the notion of content in this way is the existence of important structural commonalities between states with conceptual content and the different classes of states with nonconceptual content.

In the first section I explain and discuss the distinction between conceptual and nonconceptual content, starting from the thought that a theory of nonconceptual content is required to capture the phenomenology of perceptual experience. This

From *Mind and Language*, vol. 10, no. 4 (1995), pp. 333–369. Reprinted with the kind permission of the author and Blackwell Publishers.

section also defends the thesis that a creature can be in states with nonconceptual content without possessing any concepts at all. Section 2 develops these points further by discussing the general notions of content and representation, putting forward four conditions which states with content will have to meet. These conditions neither build in a requirement of concept possession, nor do they rule such a requirement out. In the third section it is argued that all these four conditions are met by the subpersonal computational states of the visual processing system.

1 Conceptual and Nonconceptual Content

In understanding the distinction between conceptual and nonconceptual content it is best to start with the content of perceptual experience, since this is the domain of application in which the distinction is most securely entrenched. The example of perceptual experience will provide us with a formal characterization of nonconceptual content, as well as an opportunity to discuss the important question of how being in states with nonconceptual content is related to the possession of conceptual capacities.

1.1 The Nonconceptual Content of Perceptual Experience

It is a dominant view among philosophers that the ways in which a creature can represent the world are determined by its conceptual capacities. This is associated with a widespread rejection of the traditional empiricist distinction between sensation and belief. Recently, though, the existence of mental states with nonconceptual representational content has been discussed among philosophers of mind (Evans 1982; Peacocke 1992b) [see essays 2 and 5].[1] The general thought is that it is theoretically legitimate to refer to mental states which represent the world but which do not require the bearer of those mental states to possess the concepts required to specify the way in which they represent the world. These are states with nonconceptual content. A nonconceptual content can be attributed to a creature without thereby attributing to that creature mastery of the concepts required to specify that content.

Perhaps the central impetus for legitimating a notion of nonconceptual content has come from the study of perceptual experience. Like traditional theories that see sensations as ineliminable components of perceptual experience, theorists have been attracted to nonconceptual content by the thought that the richness and grain of perceptual experience is not constrained by the concepts a perceiver might or might not possess. What distinguishes the theory of nonconceptual content, however, from theories of the sensational component of perceptual experience is that nonconceptual content is representational. If a given perceptual experience has a nonconceptual content that φ, this means that the experience represents the world as being φ. Conceptual and nonconceptual contents are distinguished not by whether they are representational, but according to how they represent. They are distinguished according to whether in specifying how they represent the environment we need to restrict ourselves to concepts possessed by the perceiver. This is in stark contrast to the traditional distinction between sensation and belief, according to which the sensational component has no role to play in explaining how the experience represents the world as being.

Nonetheless, there is an element of the traditional empiricist distinction that has bearing on the motivations for introducing the notion of nonconceptual content, deriving from the belief-independence of perceptual experience. In the normal course of things, perceivers tend to believe that the world is the way they perceive it to be. But there are times when belief and perception come apart. Optical illusions are a case in point. Knowing that one is witnessing an optical illusion does not make the illusion go away. In cases like this it makes sense to distinguish between perception and (perceptual) belief, and to identify a non-doxastic (non-belief) component in perceptual experience. But once such a distinction is made it becomes pressing to explain how the doxastic and non-doxastic elements of perceptual experience are related, and it is very natural to think that they are fundamentally different in kind. Perceptual experience has a richness, texture and fineness of grain that beliefs do not and cannot have. According to traditional empiricism, of course, this is because perceptual experience has a non-doxastic element understood in terms of sensations or impressions. But, as optical illusions make clear, the relevant distinction is between ways in which the world is represented. What makes an optical illusion illusory is the fact that it represents the world as being a way which it either is not or cannot be. What are at stake are two forms of content—not just a belief based upon sensations or impressions which are not themselves representational.

Suppose we combine the two ideas, first, that perceptual experience has a non-doxastic component that is nonetheless representational, and second, that the nondoxastic component of perception is richer and finer grained in a way that the doxastic component is often unable to capture. How are we to capture the difference between doxastic and nondoxastic representational content that this opens up? We can begin by noting that the contents of perceptual beliefs are limited by the conceptual resources of the believer. Given, though, that the crucial difference between doxastic and nondoxastic representation is one of range and richness, it seems natural to try to capture this difference by suggesting that this limitation does not apply in the case of nondoxastic representational content. And this leads us, of course, directly to the idea that perceptual experience has nonconceptual content.

This notion of nonconceptual perceptual content can be put to work in explaining what it is to possess certain concepts (Peacocke 1992b). The general thought here is that, in the case of a large and probably foundational class of concepts, an adequate explanation of what it is for a subject to possess a given concept will have to contain a clause stipulating how that subject responds when enjoying experiences with an appropriate content. There is an obvious danger of circularity, however, if the content in question is conceptual. This danger of circularity makes the notion of nonconceptual content appealing, because one promising way of overcoming it is to specify the conditions for concept possession so as to require responding in appropriate ways (say, by applying the concept in question) when enjoying experiences with the appropriate nonconceptual content.

1.2 Defining the Nonconceptual Content of Perceptual Experience

There are two different levels at which a characterization of nonconceptual content needs to be given. First, there is the formal level specifying the difference between conceptual and nonconceptual content. What are the general features that distinguish a conceptual content from a nonconceptual content? Second, there is the level at which a substantive theory of nonconceptual content is given.

An influential and helpful account at the formal level is to be found in Cussins 1990 [see essay 6]. The account starts from a distinction between conceptual and nonconceptual properties. Conceptual properties are those canonically characterized by means of concepts that a creature must possess for that property to be applicable to it, while nonconceptual properties are those canonically characterized in terms of concepts which a creature need not possess for the property to apply. Acquisition of the relevant concepts will not transform a nonconceptual property into a conceptual property, because what makes a property nonconceptual is only that possession of the relevant concepts is not necessary. Conceptual content is then defined as content specified in terms of conceptual properties, and nonconceptual content as content which can be specified in terms of nonconceptual properties.

It has been objected to this general account that it is unnecessary to give a general characterization in terms of conceptual properties (Peacocke 1994b, p. 423) [essay 16, p. 312]. Since the definition of a conceptual content presupposes an account of what concepts are, Peacocke suggests defining a conceptual content directly as a content that is composed of concepts. One worry that might be entertained with regard to this proposal is that it forecloses unnecessarily on the possibility of contents being conceptual without being composed of concepts. Contents understood in Russellian terms are not composed of concepts, but this need not prevent them from being conceptual. The machinery of conceptual properties is a good way to capture what might make such contents conceptual.

This is only a formal definition, however. It gives us a way of distinguishing conceptual from nonconceptual contents, but does not address the substantive question of how nonconceptual content is actually specified. Cussins' own answer to the substantive question is based on practical abilities. He offers an account on which nonconceptual content is specified in terms of "basic spatial and temporal tracking and discriminatory skills which are required to find our way around the environment" (1990, p. 400) [essay 6, p. 147]. It is, however, perfectly possible to accept his formal account without accepting his substantive account. There are competing accounts in the field, particularly that offered by Peacocke.

Peacocke develops an account of the content of perceptual experience based on the idea that a given perceptual content should be specified in terms of all the ways in which space could be filled out around the perceiver that are consistent with that content being a correct representation of the environment. In specifying such a content we need to start by organizing the space around the perceiver. This is done by specifying origins and corresponding axes based on the perceiver's body. There will be a range of such origins and they will vary according to the modality in question. Once we have selected a particular origin and defined a set of axes in terms of them we can identify points (or rather: point-types) in terms of those axes. Then we characterize each point-type in terms of whether or not there is a surface there, and if so what the texture, hue, orientation, solidity, etc., of that surface are. This spatial type Peacocke terms a *scenario*. Assigning to the origin and axes real places and directions in the world, as well as a time, yields a *positioned scenario*. A positioned scenario is correct if, and only if, the volume of perceptually discriminable space around the perceiver at a specified time instantiates the spatial type specified by the scenario.

This is not the place to decide between these two rival accounts of the nonconceptual content of perceptual experience. It is important to note, however, that if (as will be argued below in section 3) the formal notion of nonconceptual content has application in domains other than perceptual experience, there is no reason to think that such domains will require the same substantive theory of nonconceptual content as perceptual experience. (In fact, as will be suggested in section 3.3 below, a teleological theory of content may well be more applicable in the domain of subpersonal computational states.)

1.3 Nonconceptual Content and the Autonomy Thesis: The Example of Infant Cognition

Theories which agree on the significance of nonconceptual content for understanding perceptual experience nonetheless differ in their commitment to what, following Peacocke (1992b, p. 90) [essay 5, pp. 124–125], we can term the Autonomy Thesis:

> *The Autonomy Thesis*: It is possible for a creature to be in states with nonconceptual content, even though that creature possesses no concepts at all.

There is a considerable amount at stake here. Theories of nonconceptual content offer promising ways of dealing with problems in several areas of scientific psychology. It seems, from work both in animal learning theory and developmental psychology, that a form of intentional explanation is required to account for the behavior of creatures which it is not appropriate to describe as concept-using. Such explanations clearly require the ascription of states with nonconceptual contents. But this is only possible if the Autonomy Thesis is accepted.

The principal argument that I know against the Autonomy Thesis has been offered by Peacocke (1992b, p. 90) [essay 5, pp. 124–125] who argues that states with scenario content are available only to creatures who have acquired at least a rudimentary conception of the objective world. I have discussed this argument elsewhere (Bermúdez 1994—but see Peacocke 1994b) [see essays 15 and 16] and will not pursue it further here. What I will do instead is sketch out some reasons emerging from recent work in developmental psychology that compel the adoption of autonomous nonconceptual content as a theoretical tool.

Developmental psychology has long been concerned with the question: At what stage, in early childhood or infancy, is it appropriate to ascribe a grasp that objects exist even when not being perceived? On the traditional view, derived ultimately from Piaget, object permanence does not appear until relatively late in development, towards the end of the sensorimotor period. Much recent work in developmental psychology, however, has attacked the view that object permanence develops so late (see Spelke 1990 and Spelke and van de Walle 1993 for overviews). There is strong experimental evidence that infants have the capacity from a very young age to parse the array of visual stimulation into spatially extended and bounded objects which behave according to certain basic principles of physical reasoning.

It will be helpful for the following briefly to outline the conclusions that Spelke draws from her own experiments, and those of other workers in the field. She suggests (Spelke and van de Walle 1993) that young infants are capable of organizing the perceived array into bodies that obey two basic principles. According to the *principle of cohesion*, only connected surfaces lie on a single object, while according to the *principle of contact* only surfaces that are in contact can move together. These perceptual principles are closely related to the principles that Spelke thinks govern infant reasoning about the behavior of objects. Here she identifies both a *principle of continuity* (an object moves on a unique connected path) and a *principle of contact* (only objects in contact can move together). She claims that the deployment of these principles allows infants to trace object identity over successive encounters and grasp the persistence of obscured objects, as well as to form expectations about how a temporarily obscured moving object will continue to move and where it will come to rest.

Suppose we accept that object permanence does in fact appear much earlier than Piaget thought. This raises the following two questions. First, is this capacity one which should be reflected in accounts of the content of the perceptual experience of young infants? Second, how is this capacity related to mastery of the concept of an object, as well as to mastery of the other concepts involved in a rudimentary conception of an objective world?

An affirmative answer to the first question is compelling. The whole point of the experimental evidence is that what young infants perceive is not a "blooming, buzzing confusion" of sensations, but rather a world composed of determinate and bounded objects behaving in reasonably fixed and determinate manners.

And if that is how they perceive the world then it is clear that it must feature in an account of their perceptual experiences. Moving on, then, to the second question, anyone who does not accept the Autonomy Thesis is committed to holding that the infants in question will have to possess the basic conceptual abilities required to support a rudimentary conception of an objective world. Whatever detailed account is favored of what it is to conceive the world as objective, it will clearly have to include the following: mastery of the concept of a place, mastery of some form of the first-person concept, mastery of the connectedness of space, and mastery of the concept of an object. These conceptual abilities are at the core of any account of what it is to apprehend the objectivity of the world, however rudimentary.

If we do not want to prejudge the issue for or against the Autonomy Thesis, we will need to consider whether there are in fact independent reasons for ascribing these basic forms of conceptual mastery to young infants. Let us focus on mastery of the concept of an object, since we are discussing object permanence. Does the experimental evidence supporting early grasp of object permanence also support ascriptions of mastery of the concept of an object? Is there any difference between the phenomena that developmental psychologists label "object permanence" and anything properly describable as mastery of the concept of an object?

Whatever detailed theory of concept possession is accepted, it will have to reflect the close connection between possessing a concept and carrying out certain forms of inference. Mastery of a concept is tied up with grasp of its inferential role, where a concept's inferential role can be understood in terms of its contribution to the inferential powers of propositions in which it features. It is interesting, then, that there does seem to be an analogue for this in the infant behavior. It is clear that the notion of solidity or impenetrability is essential to the concept of an object, so that if something is an object it follows that it will be solid and hence that nothing can pass through it. So, we may take the following as a very basic example of the type of inference licensed by possession of the concept of an object:

$$\frac{\text{X is an object}}{\text{Nothing will pass through X}}$$

Let us turn, then, to Baillargeon's well-known drawbridge experiments (Baillargeon 1987). Baillargeon habituated her infants to a screen rotating 180 degrees on a table. She then placed an object behind the screen, so that it was completely occluded by the time the screen had been raised 60 degrees. She was interested in whether infants would distinguish between trials on which the screen stopped when it reached the place occupied by the object, and trials on which the screen continued rotating all the way (hence apparently passing through the object). The infants looked longer during the second type of trial, indicating their surprise and hence that they found it a novel type of event.

At one level, it seems possible to describe what is going on in the drawbridge and similar experiments in terms of a primitive application of the inference pattern connecting objects with solidity and impenetrability. This seems a natural way of understanding the idea that the infants are engaged in a form of physical reasoning. In which case, it would be plausible to ascribe mastery of the concept of an object to infants who demonstrated the appropriate dishabituation behavior in a range of contexts sufficiently wide to indicate that they had grasped several such inference patterns. On such a view, the basic elements of the concept are in place very early on in life. What happens subsequently in development is their refinement and incorporation into a body of knowledge about the physical, mechanical and dynamical properties of objects.

This view, however, blurs some very important distinctions. The fact that young infants are surprised when certain expectations they have are thwarted does not mean that they have drawn inferences from the fact that something seems to be an example of an object. This is so for (at least) two reasons. The first is that there do not seem to be any grounds for describing the infants as apprehending that something is an instance of the category "object." Identifying something as an object is something that one does for *reasons*. An individual identifies something as an object if he knows what the criteria for objecthood are, and can recognize that they are by and large satisfied. The subject is making a judgment which can be justified or unjustified, rational or irrational. It does not seem, however, that anything like this is going on in the infant behavior under consideration. The fact that infants are capable of parsing their visual array into bounded segments that (more or less) correspond to objects does not warrant the thought that there are reasons for this that can be evaluated according to the standards appropriate for ascriptions of justified belief. Of course, there are reasons why such parsing abilities are in place, but they are of a different type and to be judged by different standards. It might, for example, be explicable purely at the level of early visual processing. This point can be appreciated by considering what the appropriate response would be to an infant who shows surprise when an object passes through something which, although bounded, is not an object (say, a shadow). It would be totally inappropriate to describe such an infant as making an unjustified judgment. It is not the infant's standards of rational assessment that are at fault (he hasn't got any). The problem is that his visual processing is not sufficiently discriminating within the general category of bounded segments.

The second problem follows on from this. If a subject justifiably thinks that something exemplifies the concept of an object, then this licenses him in drawing certain inferences. But, whatever drawing an inference means, it must mean more than having certain expectations which manifest themselves only in the presence or absence of surprise. Drawing inferences requires grasping general rules of inference and recognizing that their application is appropriate in a given situation. The paradigm cases of inference are conscious, reflective acts, and there seem no reasons for thinking that there is anything like this, or even approaching it, going on in dishabituation behavior. Of course, many of the inferences which mature concept-users make are unconscious and unreflective, but they are exercises of capacities which could be made conscious and reflective. But what would count as genuine inferences in infancy?[2] Piaget's (1954) well-known discussions of searching behavior provide good examples of cases both where inference is obviously absent and where it is obviously present. Consider the A, not-B error (the Stage IV error). An object which an 8-month-old infant has successfully found at place A is moved in full view of the infant and hidden at place B. Instead of searching at B the infant searches again at A. It would clearly be inappropriate to describe this behavior in terms of the infant making any inferences about the object still being where it was first found. Consider on the other hand, however, cases of "transitive inferences" in 12-month-olds, where A is hidden behind B and B is hidden behind C. Here the infant does in fact search at the right place—and it seems right to describe this as the result of an inference about where A is to be found. It seems to me that there is nothing in the dishabituation experiments comparable to this sort of transitive inference.[3]

For both these reasons, then, it is compelling to deny that the phenomena which developmental psychologists interpret in terms of object permanence can be a sign of mastery of the concept of an object. Maintaining the Autonomy Thesis is the only way in which we can reconcile this with the earlier thought that young infants' capacities to register object permanence should feature in an account of the content of their perceptual experience. Denying the Autonomy Thesis leaves one with the choice between either ascribing to the infants mastery of certain basic objective concepts, or denying that the infants have experience with representational content and that this content has a role to play in explaining their behavior. Neither of these possibilities is plausible. The first has already been discussed, while the second seems to be vitiated by the existence of counterfactuals like the following: "if the infants had perceived an array of unstructured visual sense data rather than bounded segments, they would not have shown surprise when an apparently continuous surface comes apart." The infants in dishabituation experiments show surprise because they see things a certain way, and it is natural to describe the way they see things by saying that they parse the visual array in a way that maps (more or less) the boundaries between objects, even though they have no conceptual grasp either of what those objects are, or of what an object in general is.

1.4 Extending the Notion of Nonconceptual Content
Many theorists have felt that there is an extremely close connection between mastery of concepts and mastery of a language. There is, of course, a spectrum of different ways in which this connection can be expressed. On the strongest and simplest view of the matter, mastery of a concept is exhausted by the capacity properly to manipulate certain terms of a language. An example of a weaker view would be that certain linguistic abilities are essential criteria of conceptual

mastery. The following thesis, however, does seem to be common to all the views on this spectrum.

> *The Priority Thesis*: Conceptual abilities are not available to nonlinguistic creatures.

Those who espouse the Priority Thesis have often recognized that there seem to be rather difficult borderline cases, like those discussed in the preceding section. One standard strategy for dealing with these has been to retain the Priority Thesis while allowing the existence of proto-concepts which are available to non-linguistic creatures. But this is an inherently unstable position, however, when held in conjunction with the view that the capacity for representation and thought in general is dependent upon concept possession. If proto-thoughts really are representational, then it follows on this view that they cannot be available to non-linguistic creatures.

The Autonomy Thesis is significant because it allows this problem to be side-stepped. If the Autonomy Thesis is held in conjunction with the Priority Thesis, then the constitutive connection between concept possession and language mastery can be affirmed, while at the same time leaving open the possibility of non-linguistic representational states. What is needed is the recognition that conceptual content is neither the only form of content, nor a necessary condition of other forms of content. Conceptual mastery is closely tied to language mastery, but the existence of states with nonconceptual representational content can be independent of either of these.

This is, of course, an alternative to the traditional post-Fregean view that the analysis of thought has to be undertaken through the analysis of language. But it raises two important questions. Although these two questions seem distinct there is an important connection between them that will become clear and that will occupy the remainder of this paper.

The first question arises out of the adoption of the Autonomy Thesis. If, as has been suggested, non-concept-using and non-linguistic creatures can be in perceptual states with nonconceptual content, then an account needs to be given of the conditions under which such content can be ascribed. It is clear that not all non-concept-using creatures who are perceptually sensitive to their environ-ment can appropriately be described as being in perceptual states with represen-tational content, but a principled account is needed of this distinction. Moreover, the plausibility of such a general account rests upon its applicability to concep-tual content. What is needed is an account of the distinguishing marks of contentful states that prescinds from the distinction between conceptual and non-conceptual states.

The second issue is a more general one. Showing that the notion of noncon-ceptual content is required for a proper understanding of perceptual experience immediately raises the question of whether perceptual experience is the only domain for which we need such a notion. Are there other areas of cognition to which we can apply a notion of representational content that is divorced from concept possession?

One highly plausible suggestion that could be made in answer to this second question is that the information processing systems studied by psychologists and cognitive scientists also require a notion of nonconceptual content. On this view, any adequate account of the subpersonal mechanisms integral to explaining how we interact with the world will have to incorporate the idea that the states of those mechanisms have nonconceptual representational content. It will be useful to consider this general thesis through the example of Marr's (1982) account of the visual processing system, both because it is one of the most developed information processing accounts available and because it is reasonably familiar to the philosophical community.

Marr's (1982) theory of visual processing describes the stages by which variations in illumination are parsed to yield an image of objects in space in terms of a series of representations, termed "sketches," each of which is the product of a limited series of specialized processes, dedicated to discriminating distinct features of the available information. The 2½-D *sketch*, for example, is claimed to provide a representation of the depth and orientation of visible surfaces from the vantage point of the viewer. Many have thought it appropriate to speak of content when describing such forms of computation, simply because the result of those computations seems to be a representation of the scene perceived. But how are we to evaluate this proposal to extend the notion of nonconceptual content from perceptual states to subpersonal computational states? It may seem *prima facie* that the two domains of cognition are too disparate to have any interesting commonalities.

It is at this point that the two questions raised in this section intersect. Let us suppose that we have a satisfactory answer to the first question. Such an answer will take the form of a statement of the conditions under which an attribution of representational content is appropriate. But this will then provide the key to determining whether the notion of nonconceptual representational content can plausibly be extended beyond perceptual experience. Once we know what these conditions are then we will be in a position to evaluate the suggestion that subpersonal computational states can be content-bearing states. In the next section of this paper I offer four such conditions. The final section then considers whether these conditions are satisfied by the subpersonal computational states of the visual processing system, as understood by Marr.

2 Content, Correctness Conditions and Representation

On many philosophical construals, content is whatever is specified in a "that" clause when attributing a propositional attitude. In attributing belief, desire, fear, or any other propositional attitude to an individual we do three things: identify a particular person; attribute a particular attitude to that person; and specify the proposition to which that attitude is held. Specifying the proposition to which an attitude is held is equivalent to giving the content of that attitude—i.e., what it is that is believed, desired or feared.[4]

If this familiar conception of propositional content is deemed the only appropriate one, then it seems natural to resist the suggestion that there might be forms of content that are nonconceptual in the sense discussed in section 1.2, because propositional attitudes are paradigmatically conceptual. To make any progress, then, we need an account of what it is for a state to have content that will not rule out the notion of nonconceptual content as a matter of definition. A promising start is provided by Peacocke's (1992b) suggestion that a state has content if, and only if, it has a correctness condition. On Peacocke's view (the *minimal account of content possession*), a state presents the world as being in a certain way if, and only if, there is a condition or set of conditions under which it does so correctly, and the content of the state is given in terms of what it would be for it to present the world correctly. This certainly leaves open the possibility of nonconceptual content, but does it say all that needs to be said about content at the level at which it is pitched?[5]

Suppose we distinguish two different tasks which a general account of content possession might be called upon to perform. The first (*constitutive*) task would be to give an account of what the content of a given state is, on the assumption that such a state has content. The second (*criterial*) task would be to explain how one might tell whether a state has content at all. The minimal account certainly fulfils the constitutive task, but it is not clear that it satisfies the criterial task. Correctness conditions are conditions of some state of affairs being represented correctly. So, before we can determine whether a state has a correctness condition, we must determine whether it is a representational state.

Consider, for example, how the minimal account would deal with the question of whether carrying information betokens the presence of content. As standardly construed (Dretske 1981), a state of affairs carries information about another state of affairs if, and only if, there is nomological covariance between the respective types of which they are tokens [see also essay 4]. Familiar examples are the rings of a tree which carry information about the age of the tree and fossils which carry information about the bone structure of extinct animals.

In both the cases discussed it would seem that a correctness condition can be provided, such as "the rings on the tree correctly indicate the age of the tree if, and only if, the number of rings = the number of years the tree has been in existence." But would these be *genuine* correctness conditions? Many would think not. They might argue as follows. No state could count as a representational state unless it was possible for it to *misrepresent* the environment. But it is the law-like connection between, for example, the number of rings and the number of years that makes it plausible to speak of the former carrying information about the latter, and what makes it a law-like connection is the fact that the number of rings and the number of years invariably coincide.[6] Such invariable coincidence, however, clearly rules out the possibility of misrepresentation.[7]

In cases like these, then, the minimal account is not sufficient to settle the question of whether we are dealing with genuine content or not. We need to supplement it with an account of representation—of what it is for a creature to be representing the environment. As is required by the argument in section 1.3 rejecting the Autonomy Thesis, this account will have to identify the conditions which must be satisfied for nonconceptual content to be ascribed to non-concept-using creatures. On the other hand, such an account should also be able to explain what is going on in ascriptions of conceptual content. Conceptual and nonconceptual content are both forms of content because there is a single notion of representation applicable to both of them. What is needed is an account of the general conditions under which it makes theoretical sense to hold that creatures are representing the environment.

What is at stake here, of course, is the appropriateness of distinct types of explanation. Theorists have traditionally distinguished between two different categories of explanation of behavior-mechanistic explanations and intentional explanations (Taylor 1964). Intentional explanations have several distinguishing characteristics. First, they are *teleological*. That is, they explain an organism's behavior in terms of the purposes and desires which that behavior is intended to satisfy. Second, they have to be intentional. Intentional explanations cannot be eliminated in favor of non-intentional explanations. Third, intentional explanations appeal to desires and purposes in conjunction with representational states. Simply specifying a desire that an organism could satisfy by performing a particular action cannot provide a satisfactory explanation. Two different types of representation need to be involved—perceptual representations of the environment and representations of how performing that action can satisfy the desire in question.

Explanations of behavior, particularly when dealing with the cognitive abilities of non-linguistic creatures, quite rightly operate with a principle of parsimony. Appeals to representational states should be made only where it is theoretically unavoidable, where there is no simpler mechanistic explanation of the behavior (preface to Fodor 1987, *pace*). This raises the question, of course, of quite how "behavior" is being understood here. It is natural to ask whether what is at stake is behavior narrowly construed in terms of independently characterizable bodily movements, or behavior broadly construed in terms of bodily movements related in certain ways to the environment. This is a complicated question, and I state my position without argument. It seems to me that the distinction between narrow and broad construals of behavior maps cleanly onto the distinction between mechanistic and intentional explanations of behavior. Mechanistic explanations of behavior are appropriate when, and only when, the behavior to be explained can be specified in terms of non-relational bodily movements. Intentional explanations, in contrast, go hand in hand with relationally characterized bodily movements. So, to return to the issue of parsimony, this provides a further way of conceptualizing the difference between behavior that needs to be explained through representational states and behavior that does not. The latter but not the former can be satisfactorily characterized non-relationally.[8]

As a first step towards building on this, consider the thesis that representational states are intermediaries between sensory input and behavioral output which are (theoretically) required to explain how behavioral output emerges on the basis of sensory input. We can identify situations, such as the operation of primitive evolutionarily hard-wired connections, in which the connections between sensory input and behavioral output are such that they do not demand the attribution of representational states. Consider a creature genetically programmed to respond in a certain way to a certain stimulus, say, to move away from the perceived direction of a particular stimulus. One can explain why it made such a movement in any particular situation without saying that it was representing the distal cause of the stimulus. Registering the relevant stimulus causes the appropriate response, and this can be fully understood, explained and predicted without any appeal to an intermediary between stimulus and response. By the same token, the movement can be satisfactorily described in bodily terms. It does not have to be described relationally, as a movement away from whatever the distal cause happens to be.

So, situations in which the connection between sensory input and behavioral output are invariant in this way are not ones in which we need to bring in representational states. This does not just rule out primitive and hard-wired forms of reflex behavior. Consider the classic situation of hungry rats for whom the sound of a tone regularly precedes the delivery of food to a magazine. Suppose (as is in fact the case) that after exposure to this setup the rats acquire an approach response, so that they approach the magazine during the sound of the tone. There seem to be two ways of describing this behavior. The first, and perhaps the most intuitively appealing, would be to describe the situation in representational terms. This would involve two different representations—a representation of the goal (the food) and a representation of the instrumental contingency between approaching the magazine and attaining the goal. The goal is taken to be intrinsically motivating, and what drives the approach response is a comprehension that the response will lead to the goal. Alternatively, a completely non-representational account might be given, appealing simply to law-like connections, built up through associative conditioning, between the rat hearing the sound and his approaching the magazine.

How could we decide between these two options? One way of doing so discussed in the psychological literature (Holland 1979; Dickinson 1980) would be to employ an omission schedule. The operative idea here is that, if the rat's response (approaching the magazine) is really determined by a representation of the instrumental contingency between approaching the magazine and gaining the food, then one would expect the response not to occur when this instrumental contingency ceases to hold. In fact, one would particularly expect the approach response not to occur when it actually results in the non-achievement of the goal. Accordingly, the experimental paradigm for omission schedules is one in which food is omitted if rats approach the magazine during the sound of the tone. What emerges in such situations is that rats acquire the approach response even though this response is directly in conflict with their interests. Although what they should do to gain food is stay away from the magazine, they approach it.

There are two comments to be made here. The first is that the persistence of the original behavior militates strongly against the idea that the rat's behavior is driven by a representation of the instrumental contingency between performing the action and attaining the goal—since it continues to perform the action even when the goal is not attained. The second is that the invariance of the behavior is an integral part of its being explicable solely in terms of law-like connections between stimulus and response which are built up by associative conditioning.

This is closely connected with the earlier point about the importance of the connection between representation and misrepresentation. The reason that tropistic and classically conditioned behavior can be explained without reference to representational perceptual states is, as already stressed, that the response is invariant, if the creature in question registers the relevant stimulus. What this means, of course, is that the behavior can be explained by the way things are in the immediate environment. There is, therefore, no need to appeal to how things are taken to be (or: how they are represented as being). The need to appeal to how things are taken to be comes in only when the law-governed correlation between stimulus and response breaks down. This can come about either when the response occurs in the absence of the stimulus, or when the stimulus occurs and is registered without the response following. In the first of these cases one might say that there is a representation of the stimulus and that that is what generates the response, and in the second case one might say that even though the stimulus is there it is not represented in a way that would bring about the appropriate response. Both of these are different types of misrepresentation, and the existence or possibility of misrepresentation is a good criterion for the necessity of bringing in representational perceptual states.

Jerry Fodor has made some interesting suggestions about how the possibility of misrepresentation might be explained by the lack of a law-like correlation between stimulus and response (Fodor 1986, pp. 14–16). Explaining why there should be an invariant connection between stimulus and response requires postulating the existence of *transducers* (devices that transfer sensory stimuli into physical output that is in a suitable form to interact with the motor system). We need transducers to explain how an organism can pick up stimuli at all, and when there is an invariant connection between stimulus and response we need to postulate the existence of transducers that are sensitive to specific properties (what are often known as *dedicated* transducers). The existence and operation of these dedicated transducers, hooked up in the appropriate ways to the motor system, is all that we need to explain the invariant behavior in question. Now, in the case of intentional behavior which does not involve a law-like connection between stimulus and response, it is clear that we are not dealing with dedicated transducers. Creatures who are behaving intentionally are of course sensitive to particular properties of the stimulus, but these are not properties which can be detected by dedicated transducers. So how are they detected? One answer is that their presence is inferred from the presence of properties which can be picked up by transducers. The need for such a process of inference, however, brings with it the possibility of error, because it is inductive not deductive inference that is at stake. Hence the possibility of misrepresentation.

This connects with another strand in the notion of representation. When we appeal to representational states to explain behavior we rarely, if ever, appeal to single states operating in isolation. The behavior of organisms which are suitably flexible and plastic in their responses to the environment tends to be the result of complex interactions between internal states. As Robert van Gulick notes (1990, pp. 113–114): "Any adequate specification of the role which a given state or structure plays with respect to the system's behavior will have to be in terms of the partial contributions which that state makes to the determinations of behavior in conjunction with a wide variety of internal state combinations." There are several reasons for this. First, interaction between internal states is one possible way of explaining why there do not exist law-like correlations between input and output. It is a familiar point from the philosophy of perception that the same state of affairs can be perceptually represented in different ways determined by the influence of varying beliefs governing what one expects to see, or to what one has just seen.

A second general reason for this interactive complexity is that representational states alone are not sufficient to explain behavior unless they are related to something that will actually trigger certain behavior, hunger perhaps, or the need for shelter or to reproduce. Representations considered in isolation are behaviorally inert. It seems right to draw a general distinction between representational states and motivational states and claim that in situations in which it is appropriate to appeal to representational states in explaining behavior a theorist will also be compelled to appeal to motivational states. And, of course, it is not just the conjunction of representational states and motivational states that is relevant, but their interaction.

Third, representational states have to interact with other representational states. Organisms respond flexibly and plastically to their environments partly in virtue of the fact that their representational states respond flexibly and plastically to each other, most obviously through the influence of stored representations on present representations. The possibility of learning and adaptation depends upon past representations contributing to the determination of present responses, and hence interacting with them. Moreover, representing a particular feature of the environment does not have effects on behavior just when a creature is confronted by that very feature. It can also be effective when the creature is confronted by something that is relevantly similar to the represented feature, or when the feature is absent and there is nothing relevantly similar in the environment (as when a creature determines to leave its shelter because it cannot detect either a predator or anything predator-like in the vicinity).

Two separate constraints follow from this. First, there must be pathways enabling a given representational state to connect up with other states, both representational and motivational. There must be *cognitive integration* of the relevant states. This point is most familiar in the context of propositional attitudes. Part of what it is, for example, to have a belief is that it should be open to modification from newer, incompatible beliefs, or that it should in appropriate cases hook up with desires to bring about actions, or with fears to prevent action.

Second, part of what is involved in the integration of representational states is that a creature representing the environment should be capable of registering when the environment is relevantly similar over time. The simplest example would be when the represented current environment is identical in all respects to the represented previous environment. But the appropriate sort of flexibility requires being able to register that in certain respects there is a match in the environment as represented, although in other respects there is no such match, picking out what is common and what is different so that a suitable response can be determined by integrating the relevant match with previous experience and current motivational states.

This means that representational states must be structured so that they can be decomposed into their constituent elements which can then be recombined with the constituent elements of other representational states. Suppose, for example, that a creature represents its environment as containing food in an exposed place with a predator within striking distance. Assuming its ensuing behavior is not to be driven either by the association "food-eat" or by the association "predator-flee," the creature will need to evaluate whether it can reach the food without the predator noticing; whether the food is worth the risk; whether having gained the food it can then escape to safety, etc. All this requires being able to distinguish the various elements in the original representation and to integrate them with comparable elements in other representational states.

This requirement of compositional structure is at the core of one important recent discussion of the ascription conditions of conceptual content. Evans (1982) [see essay 2, appendix] understands thoughts as essentially structured, composed of distinct conceptual abilities which are constitutively recombinable in indefinitely many distinct thoughts. The idea of concepts as the essentially recombinable constituents of thought is familiar enough not to require further discussion, falling naturally as it does out of the parallelism widely assumed to hold between conceptual thought and language. What is perhaps less clear is how this requirement of structure is met by the nonconceptual perceptual states discussed in section 1. What can count as the recombinable elements of a perceptual state? It seems to me that the key here is the thought that nonconceptual perceptual experience nonetheless involves parsing the perceived array into distinct elements. In the case of vision (as discussed in the context of infants in section 1.3) this involves the ability to parse the array of visual stimulation into spatially extended bodies whose behavior maps approximately onto the behavior of bodies. Placing this parsing ability in the context of perceptual recognitional abilities that allow such spatially extended bodies to be reidentified in subsequent experiences makes the structure of nonconceptual perceptual experiences much clearer.

It should not be thought, though, that a requirement of compositionality at the level of content has to impose a strong requirement of compositionality at the level of vehicle. Fodor and Pylyshyn (1988) have famously suggested that when this compositionality requirement is properly understood it entails that the Computational Theory of Cognition (CTC) provides the only viable cognitive architecture. They argue that the main alternative to CTC, the Parallel Distributed Processing (PDP) paradigm, is faced with either being a mere implementation of CTC (if it does satisfy the compositionality requirement) or failing to provide an adequate account of cognition. The debate that this challenge has raised is enormous and this is not the place to discuss it in any detail. There are two brief points that do have to be made, however. First, it does seem to me that Fodor and Pylyshyn's challenge cannot be defused by the sort of instrumentalist moves made in Clark 1989. At a minimal level the compositionality requirement entails that representational states have constituents that are causally efficacious, because the only alternative is to make constituent structure epiphenomenal. The vehicle of content does have to be structured. On the other hand, however, and this is the second point, it is far from obvious that this minimal level of structure *ipso facto* counts as an implementation of CTC. Smolensky (1991) has argued that there is an important class of PDP representations (which he terms *tensor product* representations) which are compositionally structured in a way that approximates rather than implements a CTC architecture (see also Horgan and Tienson 1992). If he is right about this, then this would provide good reasons for thinking that the compositionality requirement that flows from the nature of intentional explanation is neutral with regard to cognitive architecture.[9]

The discussion in this section suggests the following four criteria that need to be satisfied before given states can properly be described as representational states.

> (1) They should serve to explain behavior in situations where the connections between sensory input and behavioral output cannot be plotted in a law-like manner.
> (2) They should admit of cognitive integration.
> (3) They should be compositionally structured in such a way that their elements can be constituents of other representational states.
> (4) They should permit the possibility of misrepresentation.

As has emerged during the discussion of these four marks of content, they are all satisfied paradigmatically by the conceptual contents that are the objects of folk psychological propositional attitudes. But, on the other hand, it does not follow from them that conceptual propositional content is the only genuine form of content. This gives us a way of determining the issue of nonconceptual content. When confronted with states that are candidates for the ascription of nonconceptual content, we can ask whether these states satisfy the four conditions of content and thus qualify as representational states. If the four conditions are satisfied, then this will show that the states in question are contentful in virtue of features which are common to the conceptual contents of folk psychology.

3 Subpersonal Computational States As Content-Involving

This section applies the four criteria just isolated to the question raised in section 1.4, whether the notion of nonconceptual content can properly be extended to subpersonal computational states, particularly those postulated by Marr's theory of visual information processing.

3.1 Subpersonal Explanation of Behavior

The initial requirement upon states with content was that they should have a role to play in the explanation of behavior in situations where the connections between sensory inputs and behavioral output cannot be plotted in a law-like manner. Do subpersonal computational states play such a role?

A necessary preliminary here is to clarify what is at stake in the distinction between personal and subpersonal levels. Dennett first introduced the distinction as a distinction between levels of explanation (1969, pp. 90–96). At the subpersonal level, explanation is mechanical and physiological, with brain events and neural networks playing a central role.[10] At the personal level, however, mental phenomena and purposive actions are explained through categories which are properly descriptive of personal activities, as opposed to the activities of brain centers. There are different ways of glossing this broad contrast. On one view, what distinguishes the states implicated in personal-level explanations is that they are properly attributable to persons. Subpersonal states, in contrast, cannot be properly attributed to persons, but only to subsystems or modules whose operations are to be understood in a fundamentally different manner from the operations of persons. There are problems, however, with trying to make a firm distinction between persons and parts of persons in this way. The principal difficulty comes in clarifying what is meant by "properly attributable." Either personal level states have further features in virtue of which they are properly attributable to persons rather than parts of persons, or they do not. If they do not then the distinction is doomed. But if they do have such further features then it makes more sense to state the distinction in terms of these further features. It seems to me that the strongest way of stating the distinction is through the constraints governing explanation at the two levels. On this view the crucial point is that constraints of rationality, charity and coherence constitutively involved in understanding the behavior of persons are deemed not to be operative at the subpersonal level.

While accepting that there is a story to be told about how the vocabulary of the personal level is linked with events at the subpersonal level, Dennett and all those who place weight on the distinction insist that it would be a category mistake to hope for a single explanation combining results from the two domains of enquiry. This distinction is compatible with the idea that subpersonal computational states have an important role in the explanation of human behavior. But is it the sort of role that would qualify them as representational states?

It might seem compelling that subpersonal computational states could not possibly satisfy the first criterion for the following three interconnected reasons. First, if subpersonal explanation is causal and mechanical then it can only be concerned with establishing law-like connections between sensory input and behavioral output, which might seem to rule out the possibility of representational states at the subpersonal level. This fits rather well with the familiar suggestions that folk psychological explanations at the personal level are not law-governed in the sense that they do not fall under nontrivial empirical general laws, and that this is so because folk psychology is reason-based rather than causal. These three ideas suggest that representational states will only have a role to play in the sort of folk psychological explanations that could be given at the personal level.[11]

A theorist persuaded by these three points might well go on to argue for a straightforward mapping between the respective domains of conceptual content and personal-level explanation. There are two thoughts here. The first is that content-involving explanation takes place only at the personal level, while the second is that such explanation involves only conceptual contents. This equation seems doubly questionable. As emerged from the discussion in section 1, perceptual states can have nonconceptual content, although they are paradigmatically personal-level states. So, even if it is held that contentful states exist only at the personal level it fails to follow that conceptual content is the only type of content. Moreover, it is worth pointing out that there are theories at the subpersonal level which do seem to entail the existence of subpersonal states qualifying as conceptual according to the definition in section 1.2. Theories which explain linguistic understanding through subpersonal mechanisms sensitive to the semantic properties of words make constitutive reference to concepts at least some of which have to be possessed by the speaker (Peacocke 1992b, p. 181). If such theories are well founded then conceptual content will have to be attributed at the subpersonal level. Nonetheless, theorists firmly committed to deploying the distinction between personal and subpersonal levels in the manner described in the previous paragraph will most probably dispute such theories of tacit linguistic knowledge. To make progress here we need a less controversial line of attack. I propose to set aside the question of whether conceptual contents are appropriate at the subpersonal level. It seems clear, in any case, that the vast majority of subpersonal states which are candidates for being content-involving will have nonconceptual content, due to the recondite nature of the concepts required to specify them (like the concept of a zero crossing, for example). So the central issue is whether the conditions for the ascription of nonconceptual content are met at the subpersonal level.

Something often neglected by those who appeal to the distinction between personal and subpersonal levels is that it was originally formulated in the context of a thorough-going instrumentalism. In *Content and Consciousness* Dennett maintained that the vocabulary of personal-level explanation was non-referential, and that all that ultimately exists is what is appealed to in explanations at the subpersonal level. Instrumentalism (the view that the conceptual framework of folk psychology is just a convenient tool for imposing order on observable behavior, rather than a description of genuinely existing entities) goes naturally with such a view. Behavior is generated mechanistically, and the terms of personal-level folk psychology enter the picture only when behavior is rationalized from the intentional stance.

This certainly makes sense of the sharp distinction between levels, but it rules out content-bearing representational states having a genuine and indispensable explanatory role to play. Can one have the distinction between levels without this unacceptable consequence? This would require an account allowing personal-level representational states to play a role in the generation of behavior, and hence allowing them to be causally efficacious. Suppose, then, that personal-level representational states are causally efficacious. This leaves the distinction between levels untouched, but it does threaten the claim that the forms of explanation at the two levels are radically different, since at both levels we have causes and causal laws.[12]

The collapse of the distinction could be avoided via a Davidsonian strategy (1984), which accepts that reasons are causes but construes their causal basis so as to rule out the possibility of causal laws at the personal level. His position is that all personal-level events are identical with subpersonal events, and that it is *qua* subpersonal events that personal-level events cause behavior. Thus he claims that personal-level events are causally efficacious, but denies that there are causal laws governing personal-level events. The causal laws hold at the subpersonal level, regulating the same events under a different description. Unfortunately, this strategy runs into familiar difficulties (Robinson 1982, pp. 8–13; Lennon 1990, pp. 49–55). The causal efficacy of personal-level events requires not just that they have a causal role to play *under some description*. It requires, *pace* Davidson, that they play a causal role under their personal-level description, on pain of rendering the personal-level facts epiphenomenal. This requires the existence of causal laws formulable at the personal level.

If personal-level events are to be genuinely explanatory, then there must be personal-level causal laws. Of course, the antecedent can always be denied, and some sort of instrumentalism, epiphenomenalism or, more radically, elimina-tivism adopted, but any theorist who thinks that states with content really do exist will have to accept that they are causally efficacious, with all that that entails. In which case, even if a distinction between personal and subpersonal levels of explanation is maintained, it seems clear that the *type* of explanation will be fun-damentally similar in both cases.

But what about the normative constraints governing the attribution of per-sonal-level contents (constraints of intelligibility and charity, for example). It seems open to an objector to argue, first, that such constraints have a constitutive role in meaningful attributions of states with content and, second, that these con-straints are not met at the subpersonal level. Certainly, constraints of intelligibil-ity cannot play the same role in the ascription of subpersonal states as they play at the personal level. But, as has been stressed before, the question is not whether personal and subpersonal states are the same, but whether they are sufficiently similar in structure and operation. And it does seem that there are parallel con-straints operating at the level of subpersonal attributions. A good example is Peacocke's "Overarching Constraint" (1994a, p. 312):

> Correct ascriptions of content to subpersonal states are answerable to facts about the relational (environmental) properties of the events they explain, and to counterfactuals about the relational properties of the events they would explain in various counterfactual circumstances.

The Overarching Constraint places requirements on the ascription of subpersonal states that parallel those normative requirements operative at the personal level. As Peacocke himself suggests, this is a very plausible subpersonal equivalent for the overarching personal-level constraint of making the subject of the attributions intelligible.

None of this actually *shows* that we do need to appeal to subpersonal repre-sentational states in the explanation of behavior, but that is hardly a matter to be settled *a priori*. The best reasons for thinking that subpersonal representational states are essential theoretical tools are explanations of behavior that make indis-pensable use of such states, and the best place to look for these is in cognitive science in general, and the theory of visual processing in particular. Provided that there is not a fundamental confusion in the whole idea of subpersonal represen-tational states (and we have already dismissed some grounds for thinking that there might be, and will go on to consider more), then it seems reasonable to follow the best theory available.

There are those, however, who dispute what they would see as an abdication of responsibility. John McDowell has recently (1994a) argued that although it is useful for cognitive scientists to ascribe content to computational states, this is a form of "as-if" content, parasitic on the genuine content which can only be ascribed to persons.[13] For McDowell, subpersonal explanation is concerned only with the "enabling conditions" of personal-level content. It involves neither an alternative form of content, nor the basic material from which to develop a constitutive account of personal-level content (McDowell 1994a, p. 198):

> A subpersonal or "subpersonal" informational system is a physical mechanism, connected to its surroundings by transducers that convert physical impacts from outside into events of the sort that the system can work on, and perhaps by transducers that convert the system's end-products into physical interventions in the exterior. The system knows nothing about even the character of the immediate physical impacts on the input transducers, or the immediate physical interventions in the exterior that result from its operations by way of the output transducers, let alone about the nature and layout of the distal environment. The operations of the system are determined by structures exemplified in the initial contributions of the transducers, and in intermediate events and states in the system, which have no meaning for the system. In short, in Dennett's own memorable and exactly right phrase, the system is a syntactic engine, not a semantic engine. The same goes for its parts.

One interesting feature of McDowell's position is that it brings out very clearly what the alternative is to allowing representational states at the subpersonal level. On such a view what cognitive scientists tend to consider as information-processing systems really are just syntactic systems—a set of formal operations defined over syntactic objects.

This suggests that an appeal to the explanatory practice of cognitive scientists will not be legitimate if there is a good and workable syntactic theory that will do all the explanatory work without postulating representational states at the subpersonal level. The most familiar line of thought here is the syntactic theory of the mind developed by Stich (1983). Stich's theory is explicitly designed to be content-free, because he thinks that when psychological explanation admits references to the contents of mental states it is then limited by the interests and conceptual resources of the theorist. There are, he claims, interesting and important cognitive regularities (involving, for example, brain-damaged subjects, or animals) that cannot be captured within a content-based psychology, but can be described syntactically.

Stich's theory as it stands is not really a suitable way of pressing a distinction between subpersonal computational states and genuinely content-bearing propositional attitudes, because his concern is to eliminate content from *all* areas of psychological explanation. If we want to use the syntactic theory to press a distinction between computation and thought we need something weaker. One plausible candidate here would be a dual component theory of the form that Frances Egan (1992) thinks best describes Marr's theory of vision. The first part of such a theory is an independent and free-standing syntactic explanation of events at the subpersonal level. Such an explanation does not advert to any semantic features of those events. It treats cognitive processes as sets of formal operations defined over symbol structures, where a symbol is understood as being individuated by a *realization function* mapping equivalence classes of physical features onto computable symbolic features. Such a free-standing syntactic explanation is not itself intentional, but it does have intentional interpretations, and specifying an intended interpretation is the second task of the dual component theory. Here the theory appeals to an *interpretation function* specifying an isomorphism between the computable symbolic features given by the realization function and features of the represented domain.

A dual component theory along these lines is the most plausible way of fleshing out the idea that the explanation of events at the subpersonal level is syntactic, or, as McDowell puts it, that the brain is a syntactic engine. Of course, there is a sense in which it falls short of providing a purely syntactic theory, because it allows that states at the subpersonal level can indeed have content. The point, however, is that such states do not have content essentially. Insofar as cognitive processes are individuated computationally, the same state can have different contents depending on how it is embedded both within the organism and within the environment. Moreover, the fact that the content of a particular subpersonal state is to be understood in terms of a model given by the relevant interpretation function opens the door to a range of unintended interpretations which multiply the range of possible contents. The key issue here, of course, is one of individuation. According to the dual component theorist, subpersonal states are individuated without reference to their distal contents. It is this feature of its taxonomy that makes it a syntactic theory.

The key question, then, is whether there is a good and workable theory with a syntactic taxonomy that can perform all the explanatory work required, in a way that obviates the need to appeal to subpersonal states with representational content. It seems to me that there are three good reasons for thinking that there can be no such theory.

The first problem with the dual component theory has been brought out by Peacocke (see Peacocke 1993 and 1994a). Consider the following passage from Egan, where she contrasts her account of content in terms of models with an alternative account (Egan 1992, p. 457):

> According to the alternative proposal, when a system produces an early representation R1, as part of a process that culminates in the production of a later representation R2, *R1's having the content it does explains the production of R2.* The alternative view, in my opinion, misplaces the explanatory contribution of content in computational accounts of cognitive capacities. Computational processes are blind to the semantic properties of the structures over which they are defined . . . But the fact that the system produces structures that are appropriately interpretable explains how a system that computes the hypothesized function could subserve the cognitive task that it does, where the task is typically described intentionally.

The crucial claim here is that an explanation of the syntactic properties of a given computational state can provide an adequate explanation of the semantic properties of that state, even though the original explanation is itself purely syntactic. It is envisaged that a given state S1 produces a later state S2. Both S1 and S2 are syntactic states—essentially so. Associated with each of them under the intended interpretation is a content which it has nonessentially, so that S1 has content R1 and S2 has content R2. According to Egan, an adequate explanation of the existence of a state with content R2 will be provided once we have:

(1) An explanation of how S1 causes S2;
(2) An explanation of how S2 has content R2 which will take the form of a specification of the environmental circumstances of S2.

But there is a serious objection to this (Peacocke 1994a, pp. 323–326). Insofar as R2 is a content it has certain relational properties (such as being a registering of a certain object as a predator, for example). Consequently, an adequate explanation of the existence of a state with content R2 will have to explain why it has those relational properties, and this in turn requires that the explanation support appropriate counterfactuals (perhaps that if a different predator had been nearby then that predator would have been registered). The problem, of course, is that these counterfactuals will not be among the counterfactuals supported by the syntactic explanation of how S1 causes S2. Syntactic explanations do not generally support content-involving counterfactuals, and to that extent the explanatory model under consideration fails to provide a genuine explanation of the existence of a state with content R2.

This creates a dilemma for the defender of the program of syntactic explanation. If the conjunction of (1) and (2) above fails to support the relevant relational counterfactuals, then it fails to provide an adequate explanation of the existence of a computational state with content R2. If, on the other hand, the explanatory model is supplemented in such a way that the content-involving counterfactuals are sustained and explained, then it is unclear why the explanatory model can be described as syntactic and insensitive to semantic features of the relevant states.

Of course, this line of argument is effective only against those who hold the dual component version of the syntactic theory of mind. It will obviously fail to be effective both against those who deny, like Stich, that psychology needs to advert to content-involving states at all, and against those instrumentalists who deny that appeal to content-involving states has any more than a predictive and instrumental function. There are, however, further considerations here which do seem to militate against these more extreme positions. These are problems that arise for the central claim of any version of syntacticism, namely, the claim that it is possible to individuate computational states without any reference to their semantic features.

We can begin with an analogy from the more familiar project of the radical interpretation of a completely unknown language. No radical interpreter could formulate hypotheses about the syntax of a completely unfamiliar language without at the same time forming hypotheses about its semantics. How one takes the words to fit together depends on what one takes the words to mean. The question of which syntactic category a word falls into, and hence the possibilities that it has for being combined with other words according to syntactic rules, is determined by semantic considerations. To take a very basic example, one has to determine at the very least that a word is a referring expression before deciding that it falls into the category of nouns, and hence can be qualified by adjectives, etc. It would be absurd in talking about natural languages to hold that a word is individuated by its syntactic features, if syntactic features are taken to include membership of appropriate lexical categories and the consequent rules indicating what combinations of words it can enter.

Of course, if syntactic features are construed in brute physical terms (as a combination of strokes on a page, for example, or as a particular sequence of sounds) then it might be plausible to individuate words by their syntactic features. But this will hardly help us to understand why particular words occur at particular times. To understand that we need to understand the semantic properties of these brute physical features—not least as a way into understanding their syntactic properties in the broad sense discussed above.

This rough analogy brings out a rather fundamental equivocation at work here between two different ways in which we can understand syntactic properties. On the one hand, they can be understood in brute physical terms, while on the other they can be understood in functional terms. Depending on which sense is employed the notion of syntax seems appropriate for different tasks. If syntax is understood in physical terms, then it can seem relatively straightforward to individuate syntactic items. If, on the other hand, one understands syntax in functional terms (as dictating permissible operations and combinations, for example) then it seems possible to understand why one syntactic item follows another in purely syntactic terms, by appealing to the relevant operations and rules of combination. Putting these two points together, then, it can seem compelling that a wholly syntactic account is available—one that will explain in wholly syntactic terms why one syntactically individuated event follows another. But this is a mistake, because there is a crucial problem left open. How does one move from a particular combination of physical properties to a particular syntactic functional role? It is only if this can be done without adverting to semantic features that the wholly syntactic account will be forthcoming.

Bearing this in mind, let us return to the view that cognitive processes are formal operations defined over symbol structures. According to Egan (1992, p. 445):

> To describe something as a symbol is to imply that it is semantically interpretable, but (and this is the important point) its type identity as a symbol is independent of any particular semantic interpretation it might have.

Symbols are just functionally characterised objects whose individuation conditions are specified by a realization function f_R which maps equivalence classes of physical features of a system to what we might call "symbolic" features. Formal operations are just those which are differentially sensitive to the aspects of symbolic expressions that under the realization function f_R are specified as symbolic features.

Here Egan helps herself to the existence of precisely those functions in question. She assumes that it is unproblematic to move from brute physical features to functional syntactic role. There are good reasons for thinking that this is not at all unproblematic. These reasons stem from the need to isolate all and only the relevant physical features (Sterelny 1990, pp. 102–103). For example, it is a familiar point that among the various potentially salient physical events going on in the early visual processing subsystem at a given moment there will be many that do not have a genuine causal role to play (because they are just noise). These need to be distinguished from the events that are genuinely causally relevant. By the same token, it is likely that any given computational state will have certain properties that are a result of its physical realization, rather than its functional role. Again, these are not functionally relevant. When Egan and other supporters of the syntactic approach refer to a realization function f_R they are assuming that both of these operations can be carried out syntactically. It seems clear, however, that they cannot. It is implausible in the extreme that noise and other functionally irrelevant features can be discriminated in brute physical terms. And there is no point in appealing to functional role, because that presupposes precisely the operations in question. It is compelling to conclude that if we are to be able to move from brute physical features to functional role we will only be able to do so by adverting to semantic properties of the states concerned.

Marr's theory corroborates this point. He distinguishes three different levels at which visual processing can be analyzed: the *computational level*, dealing with the general constraints posed by the information-processing task; the *representational level*, dealing with the representational format of the appropriate input and output, together with the algorithms governing the transformation of input into output; and the *implementational level*, dealing with the physical realization of the representations and algorithms. The suggestions he offers at the representational and implementational levels are motivated by the discussions of constraint and function formulated at the computational level. This is relevant because considering vision at the computational level involves viewing the organism as a semantic engine, and considering which features of the environment the organism needs to model. The constraints that emerge from this govern the lower-level explanations, as is clear in Marr's account of the earliest stage in visual processing, the transformation from image to primal sketch. A crucial part of the function of vision is to recover information about the reflectance, distance and orientation of visible surfaces. This computational requirement generates the following subordinate requirement upon the representational primitives in the primal sketch; namely, that they should be the sort of things to which one can assign values of orientation, size, position and brightness. And this takes Marr towards his candidate representational primitives, and in particular to the idea that zero-crossings (registers of sudden changes in light intensity) are fundamental.[14]

The natural conclusion is that cognitive scientists find attributions of content at the subpersonal level so indispensable precisely because of these difficulties in the syntactic theory that is the only conceivable alternative. And that should be enough to warrant the conclusion that there is nothing in the distinction between personal and subpersonal levels of explanation to rule out explanatory appeals to subpersonal states with content and so it seems sensible to shift the onus of responsibility onto the practice of cognitive science. Of course, if a purely syntactic theory in the strong sense ever emerges then appeal to such states will be nugatory. But that does not seem very likely.

3.2 The Cognitive Integration and Structure of Subpersonal Computational States

Stich claims that subpersonal computational states (which he terms subdoxastic states) "are largely inferentially isolated from the large body of inferentially integrated beliefs to which a subject has access" (1969, p. 507). He explains (*ibid.*, pp. 507–508):

> If we think in terms of a cognitive simulation model, the view I am urging is that beliefs form a continuously accessible, inferentially integrated subsystem. Subdoxastic states occur in a variety of separate special purpose cognitive subsystems. And even when the subdoxastic states within a specialized subsystem generate one another via a process of inference, their inferential interactions with the integrated body of accessible beliefs is severely limited. . . . suppose that, for some putative rule *r*, you have come to believe that if *r* then Chomsky is seriously mistaken. Suppose further that, as it happens, *r* is in fact among the rules stored by your language processing mechanism. That belief along with the subdoxastic state will not lead to the belief that Chomsky is seriously mistaken.

There are really two points here which need to be separated out. The first is the (relatively) uncontroversial one that subpersonal computational states are not inferentially/cognitively integrated with propositional attitudes. The second depends upon a strong version of the modularity principle, and claims that each subpersonal information state falls into one of a set of dedicated cognitive modules which do not communicate with each other, and hence that subpersonal computational states are not cognitively integrated with each other.

The fact that subpersonal computational states are not cognitively integrated with propositional attitudes tells us only that subpersonal computational states are not propositional attitudes. This we knew already. The real question is whether something approaching the cognitive role generated by the cognitive integration of propositional attitudes is applicable in the case of subpersonal computational states.

Suppose it is granted that subpersonal computational states exist in dedicated and informationally encapsulated cognitive subsystems. This cannot mean that no processes of inference go on at all within those modules. Input into a cognitive subsystem could not be transformed into a radically dissimilar output without conceding the existence of cognitive relations between subpersonal computational states. But is this rich enough to allow for integration with stored representations, or with motivational states?

Let us begin with stored representations. Modular accounts of visual processing are based upon the principle that as much specialized processing as possible must be done before any such integration can take place. This approach is underwritten by the thought that only thus would the relevant computations be manageable. But stored representations are not completely irrelevant. The point is that the interaction with stored representation is pushed back until a relatively late stage in visual processing, rather than completely banished, as it would be on most construals of J. J. Gibson's theory of perception. Indeed, Marr saw one of the crucial elements of his approach to visual processing as the insight (in spired by work on patients with parietal lesions) that ". . . vision alone can deliver an internal description of the shape of a viewed object, even when the object was not recognised in the conventional sense of understanding its use and purpose" (1982, p. 35). The implication of this, of course, is that the visual system must have a far greater *recognitional* capacity than it is accorded in many traditional theories, and hence that stored representations have a greater role to play than often thought.

As Marr himself points out (1982, p. 326), the requirement that an organism be able to act effectively in its environment requires that it be able to recognize objects by their shape, and this depends both upon the construction of a three-dimensional representation from the information originally available in the image, and the matching of such a three-dimensional representation with a range of stored representations. He goes on to comment that ". . . the recognition process itself involves a mixture of straightforward derivation of shape information from the image and the deployment of gradually more detailed stored 3-D models during the process of recognition-derivation. Thus critical ingredients of this process are a collection of stored shape descriptions and various indexes for the collection that allow a newly derived description to be associated with an appropriate stored description" (*ibid.*, pp. 325–326). Among the indexes which he proposes for the collection of stored representations are: the *specificity index*, which classifies stored shape representations hierarchically in terms of their degree of detail; the *adjunct index* which classifies 3-D models according to the shape, relative sizes and orientations of their relative components; and the *parent index*, which indicates how overall shape might be recovered from components of that shape (*ibid.*, pp. 320–321). These access paths seem rich enough to justify talk of cognitive integration of current representations with stored representations within the visual processing system.

Moving on, then, to the question of integration with motivational states, the first point to make is that this seems in principle to be compatible with the modular approach to cognitive functioning which underlies theories like Marr's. Of course, the actual theory of visual processing does not contain any reference to motivational states. They have no part to play there. But, just as the outputs of the various subsystems of the visual processing system are integrated with each other in the later stages of visual processing, so too are the outputs of the visual processing system integrated with the outputs of other processing systems, amongst which are motivational states. Information processing models of the mind are hierarchical, and the further up the hierarchy one goes the greater are the possibilities of integration. The usual metaphor for this is spatial, with informational encapsulation at the edges and increasing integration as the center is approached (which is why the metaphor suggests, but does not imply, that there is some sort of supermodule in control at the very center).

To see how this sort of cognitive integration between the outputs of different modular subsystems might work in practice we need to recall the earlier point that the cognitive integration of content-involving states goes hand in hand with their possessing a structure permitting their various elements to be distinguished and recombined with comparable elements in different representational states. Cognitive integration requires structure, and there seem to be two principal criteria for the presence of structured representational states. First, they must be built up out of components which can be recombined to generate new representational states. Second, the process governing transitions between representational states must be sensitive to their composite structure.

Marr's theory is an account of a series of transformations effected upon an initial image to yield a representation of the three-dimensional shape and spatial arrangements of objects that is independent of the direction from which those objects are viewed (i.e., within an object-centered rather than viewer-centered coordinate frame). The initial image is provided by the arrays of image intensity values detected by the photoreceptors (pixels) in the retina. Now, each transformation in the progression from image to 3-D sketch is effected by algorithms defined over representational primitives. In the case of the primal sketch, for example, those representational primitives are oriented edges, points of discontinuity in their orientations, bars (pairs of parallel edges), the terminations of edges, and blobs (doubly terminated bars). These representational primitives are themselves arrived at by selective and grouping processes operating on the more basic representational primitives of intensity values and then on the zero-crossings. Similarly, the 2½-D sketch, which registers the orientation and depth of visible surfaces, is generated by algorithmic processes operating upon the representational primitives of the primal sketch. It has its own representational primitives (discontinuities in depth and surface orientation, for example) which provide the raw material for the algorithms that generate the 3-D sketch.

This provides an initial way of supporting the idea that subpersonal and computational states are structured. It could be suggested, for example, that the relevant representational primitives are the recombinable elements of structured representational states. The sketches, whether raw primal, primal, or $2\frac{1}{2}$-D, are not atomistic. They have a structure in virtue of the way in which they are built up by grouping and selection processes from lower-order representational primitives. And, moreover, the transitions between them take place precisely in virtue of their being structured in this way. In this sense, then, the second criterion for structure is satisfied, because transitions between representational states are sensitive to their composite structure.

Nonetheless, the need for structure was not just to explain the cognitive integration of representational states with each other. Structure was also important for the cognitive integration of representational states with motivational states. Can this be accommodated? This is not an easy question to answer. Although we have, thanks to Marr and other workers in the field, a good understanding of what is involved in visual processing itself, there is little understanding of what happens to the representational states generated by the visual system when they interact with other subsystems. Something that is worth pointing out, however, is the empirical evidence in favor of a common-coding account of visuo-motor control (see Prinz 1990 and Brewer 1993 for philosophical discussion).

The issue here is how information about the spatial properties of objects (i.e., their distance and orientation relative to the viewer/agent, as well as their internal spatial properties) is coded respectively by the visual and motor systems. On one view, the *separate-coding* approach, afferent visual information and efferent motor information/commands are recorded and extracted in fundamentally different codes, creating obvious problems about how they can be translated into each other. An alternative is a *common-coding* approach, according to which spatial information is identified and discriminated in the same way whether it is afferent or efferent. There is good experimental evidence from choice reaction-time tasks in favor of a *common-coding* account, and if a common-coding account is correct, then there will be important communalities of structure between visual representations and motor commands, and the way in which visual representations generate motor commands will presumably be sensitive to those communalities of structure. This gives us a further level of cognitive integration. Moreover, if there is a single code for visual and motor information then it seems plausible that such a common code also applies to motivational states, so that a motivational state to go to a particular place would involve spatial information about that place being coded in the same way as it is coded when the place is seen, and as it is in the motor command to go there. If this is right, then this offers the possibility of a very rich connection between the structure of subpersonal representational states and their cognitive integration.

3.3 Correctness Conditions and the Possibility of Misrepresentation

In section 1.2 the distinction was drawn between formal and substantive theories of nonconceptual content. The only substantive theories of nonconceptual content so far discussed have been the rival theories of Cussins and Peacocke, both developed as accounts of the nonconceptual content of perceptual experience. It is not clear how either of them can be applied to the case of subpersonal computational states. But a substantive theory of nonconceptual content is required if it is to be shown that subpersonal computational states satisfy the fourth condition on contentful states, namely the possibility of misrepresentation.

Fortunately, subpersonal information states lend themselves to a teleological theory of content (Millikan 1984; Papineau 1987; McGinn 1989). The key notion here is the proper function of, for example, the mechanisms underlying a particular stage in visual information processing (construed normatively in terms of what those mechanisms *should* do, and usually underwritten by evolutionary considerations). Proper functions are *relational*, where this means that they are defined in relation to features of the environment. According to teleological theories, content can be specified in terms of relational proper function. So, for example, the content of a state in early visual processing might be specified in terms of the edges in the perceived environment that that stage has evolved to identify.

This permits correctness conditions to be defined in terms of relational proper function. Given the particular features that a processing mechanism has been "designed" or "selected" to detect, it is functioning correctly when it responds appropriately to the presence of those features, and incorrectly when it responds in their absence (for example, to a sudden contrast in light intensity not due to the presence of an edge). Correctness conditions are fixed with reference to evolutionary design and past performance. Of course, there is a sense in which on this account correctness conditions are fixed by (previous) correct functioning, but on any given occasion the correctness or incorrectness will be independent of the correctness conditions, and vice versa.

This is not to say, however, that specifying correctness conditions for the computational states of the visual processing system will be at all easy.[15] Brief mention of a point discussed by Burge (1986) and by Segal (1989) will make the point. On Marr's account, it is possible when the outputs of the zero-crossing filters are conjoined to derive a representation with the content *edge* As he points out, though, justification is required for attributing this particular content (Marr 1982, p. 68):

> The reason for this is that the term *edge* has a partly physical meaning—it makes us think of a real physical boundary, for example—and all we have discussed so far are the zero values of a set of roughly band-pass second derivative filters.

How are we to get from zero values to representations of edges? Are we entitled to do so at all, or should we instead think that the representational primitive really refers to the output of the zero-crossing filters (as Segal 1989, p. 291 suggests)? Clearly, everything here hinges upon how the relational proper function is characterized, and this will be no easy task.[16]

The important point, though, is that teleologically specified correctness conditions allow for the possibility of misrepresentation, because there is no guarantee that the various stages of processing will invariably and only respond to the particular features to which they have been designed to respond.

4 Conclusions

This paper began with the general thought that the concept-involving states of folk psychology might not exhaust the class of contentful representational states. Perhaps, it was suggested, the propositional attitudes and processes defined over them are just part of a larger group of content-bearing cognitive states which are not defined in a way that makes constitutive reference to concept possession. This general proposal has now been substantiated in several ways. First, it has been shown that the notion of nonconceptual content is applicable both to perceptual experience and to the subpersonal computational states of information processing systems. Second, the plausibility of the Autonomy Thesis shows that the applicability of nonconceptual content can be independent of concept possession. Third, the discussion of the marks of content in section 3 provides good reasons for thinking that states with nonconceptual content are content-involving states in virtue of their satisfying conditions imposed by a univocal account of content equally applicable to the conceptual contents of folk psychology.

This has potentially rather wide-ranging implications. A firm belief in the distinctiveness of conceptual content is what underwrites much if not most philosophical resistance to the thought that it might be possible to give a subpersonal computational account of personal-level states. If I am right that concept-involving contents are not so distinctive, but rather form part of the broader class of contentful representational states, then this removes one important barrier to the project of giving a satisfactory psychological account of human cognitive activity.[17]

Notes

1. The original impetus came from Evans 1982 [see essay 2]. It is important to note, though, that Evans' understanding of nonconceptual content is distinctive. He holds that it applies to perceptual information states, which do not become conscious perceptual experiences until they are engaged with a concept-applying and reasoning system (*ibid.*, pp. 226–227).
2. I am grateful to Jim Russell for pressing me here.
3. It is worth mentioning in this context that, although developmental psychologists seem to find unproblematic the conclusion that infants show surprise in the drawbridge experiments because

it is *impossible* for the screen to pass through the object, this is at best questionable. On the inferential interpretation, the surprise would be due to the infant's identifying an object and inferring from its knowledge of how objects behave that what it sees is impossible. But why say this, rather than that the infants show surprise simply because there are no precedents for what they see? Certainly, more argument is needed than simply pointing out that what the infants see really is impossible.

4. By propositional content I mean the content of propositional attitudes, not any content that can be specified propositionally.

5. The minimal account is an account of what it is in general for a state to have content. This is a different level of theorizing from specific theories of content. A possible worlds account of content is an example of such a specific theory, as is Peacocke's own theory of scenario content. The general theory explains what the specific theories have in common.

6. The importance of exceptionless connection for the theory of information is stressed in Dretske 1981, chap. 3. He gives several arguments for refusing to accept conditional probabilities of less than 1. The most important are the following. First, that doing otherwise would admit the possibility that a signal could carry the information that s is G and the information that s is F, but not the information that s is G and F (because the probability of s being F and G might be below the acceptable value of conditional probability). Second, that the flow of information is transitive and that this transitivity would be lost if the value of conditional probability were less than one.

7. It is this that led Dretske substantially to modify the theory proposed in Dretske 1981. See Dretske 1990 and Dretske 1992, chap. 3.

8. This will be returned to in section 3.1.

9. The core of Smolensky's proposal is that compositional structure can be captured within a network if the network represents particular "fillers" (e.g., a noun) occupying particular roles (e.g., the role of a grammatical object). But there are other ways in which researchers in PDP have suggested that the compositionality requirement might be satisfied without collapsing into CTC. Ramsey 1992, for example, describes a class of connectionist networks in which the different syntactic roles of particular atomic units are encoded via slightly different patterns of activation. These different patterns of activation legitimate different types of molecular combination.

10. I am restricting myself to Dennett's original presentation of the distinction here. Although in later writings he treats subpersonal states as having information content (e.g., Dennett 1987b, p. 63), it is the contrast between the mechanical and the intentional that has been most influential in subsequent discussion.

11. This is not to say that the distinction is completely secure. I have voiced some relevant worries in Bermúdez 1995a and 1995b.

12. A sustained and convincing working out of the thought that reason-based explanation is a form of causal explanation is found in Lennon 1990.

13. I discuss McDowell's position in more detail in Bermúdez 1995a.

14. Burge 1986 provides a more sustained development of his point. Dissenting views will be found in Segal 1989 and in the paper by Egan already discussed.

15. Jerry Fodor has expressed a general scepticism about the possibility of specifying correctness conditions for teleological theories in Fodor 1987, chap. 4. I agree with Millikan 1991, however, that his arguments are not effective against all versions of "teleosemantics."

16. Burge himself offers a causal theory of content, according to which the distal cause or causes of a representation are necessary determinants of content. On causal theories it will be more difficult to identify a particular point on the causal chain (say, the physical boundary rather than the zero-crossing filter) as the relevant cause and hence the content. The advantage of the teleological theory is that it offers a framework for such discrimination.

17. I am very grateful for comments from Paul Noordhof and four referees for *Mind and Language*. Work on this paper was made possible by the award of a British Academy Post-Doctoral Research Fellowship.

Part III

The Nature of Experience

Philosophers of mind appeal to nonconceptual content in explanations of a number of experiential phenomena including fineness of grain, situation-dependence, qualitative states, visual illusion, and emotion.

In the opening essay, Kelly intercedes in a debate between McDowell and Peacocke on the fine-grained character of perceptual experience. While sympathetic to the view that perceptions have nonconceptual content, he contends that Peacocke centers on the wrong phenomenon. Rather than fineness of grain, Kelly suggests focusing on situation-dependence, the dependency of perceived properties on (1) the *context* in which they're perceived, as illustrated by perceptual constancy, and (2) the *objects* they're perceived to be properties of, as suggested by Merleau-Ponty's claim that "the blue of the carpet would not be the same blue were it not a woolly blue." While McDowell's appeal to demonstratives may enable the conceptualist to account for fineness of grain, Kelly argues that it cannot explain situation-dependence. In fact, not even a conjunction of demonstratives is likely to capture situation-dependence since there are an indefinite number of contextual features involved in perception.

In considering the limitations of concepts, Kelly believes that an individual's linguistic resources (including demonstratives) cannot determine what she perceives, for example, they cannot fix the semantic value of her perceptual experience. In this way, perceptual content allegedly violates the Principle of Reference Determinacy, descriptively construed. Moreover, an inability to determine the indefinite number of contextual features of perceived properties is allegedly the result of a limited mental capacity. However, it isn't apparent whether this limitation concerns concept possession or application. Hence, it isn't clear whether Kelly's notion of nonconceptuality is based on the second or third rendering of "non."

Crane's argument for nonconceptuality is based on the Waterfall Illusion. In the illusion, which is generated by fixing one's attention for a time on a waterfall and then by turning to a stationary object, the object in question appears to be simultaneously moving in the direction opposite to the waterfall and, yet, not moving. An orthodox conceptualist might try to explain away this apparent contradiction by positing different concepts of motion; for instance, while the object appears to be moving intrinsically, extrinsically, that is, relative to the objects around it, it appears stationary. However, Crane argues that such an explanation is unsatisfactory because it fails to account for the distinctly paradoxical character of the experience. Instead, he claims that the content of the experience should be considered contradictory and, in this way, nonconceptual.

Crane believes that perceptual content violates the strong construal of Cognitive Significance. For when applied to perception, the principle states that

> F and G are different concepts, if an individual could have a perception about an object, a, with the content a is F and a is not-G,

from which it follows that a perceptual content could not be contradictory, not at least if it is conceptual. But an experience of the Waterfall Illusion, Crane contends, violates the principle because the perceiver sees an object simultaneously moving and not moving, a perception that Fa and not-Fa. While it is not apparent that the argument shows that all perceptual content is nonconceptual, Crane seems committed to the third rendering of "non." After all, an individual may experience the illusion even if she possesses the requisite concept of motion, suggesting that the concept in this case is not being exercised on the perceptual content. And this, once again, is suggested by the intuition that there is a rift between the faculties of perception (receptivity) and cognition (spontaneity), one we should explain in terms of the kind of intentional currency with which each faculty trades.

In "Perception, Concepts and Memory," Martin presents us with a scenario involving an individual, Mary, who remembers playing a board game with a pair of irregular dice. One of the dice, which is eight-faced, has three colored spots, and the other, which is twelve-faced, has four colored spots. Although she has not played or even seen the game since childhood, since she acquired the concepts *octahedron* and *dodecahedron*, she realizes one day that the die with the four colored spots was a dodecahedron. But how could Mary come to believe that the die with four colored spots is a dodecahedron when she couldn't form a belief about (let alone a recognition of) shapes with more than six sides at the time she played the game? Martin's solution is to regard the content of Mary's adulthood memory, like that of her childhood perception upon which it is based, as nonconceptual. Consequently, her belief, which is assumed to have conceptual content, is based on mental states with nonconceptual content.

The notion of nonconceptuality Martin draws on is based on three principles. In assuming that beliefs have conceptual content, and by insisting that Mary's memory and childhood perception are belief-independent and that, as a child, she is unable to discriminate the relevant dice (in the required way), he suggests that the contents of these experiences violate both the weak construal of Cognitive Significance and the recognitional construal of Reference Determinacy. However, Martin also claims that concepts play an integral role in explaining why someone possesses or lacks certain thoughts or beliefs. An individual's failure to form a belief based on an experience can be regarded as a failure to draw the necessary inference, which may result from the fact that the content of her experience lacks structure. In this way, as a child, Mary is unable to form the belief that the die with four colored spots is a dodecahedron because the content of her experience violates Compositionality. As for "non," Martin seems to have both the second and third renderings in mind. The content of Mary's childhood perception allegedly exemplifies the second rendering since she didn't possess *dodecahedron* then. Yet, since she grasps the concept as an adult, her dormant memory is *non-*conceptual because of her failure to exercise the relevant concepts on it. And this, we might suppose, has something to do with the insularity of the faculty of memory.

Like McDowell, Hamlyn staunchly defends the doctrine of conceptualism, against not only Evans but Crane, Martin, and others. Nonconceptualists, he insists, make unsupported claims about perception and its relationship to causal structure and belief. For example, he agrees that an information processing model can provide us with a sophisticated account of the causal mechanisms underlying perception, but he rejects Evans's assumption that so-called "information states" provide the *individual* with information. The relevant sense of "information," he contends, is structural rather than intentional and should be distinguished from personal-level states that serve to explain the actions of individuals rather than the operations of subsystems. In fact, the charge might just as well be leveled against Bermúdez and Clark. One might contend that in blurring the distinction between the personal and the subpersonal, both Bermúdez and Clark have helped themselves to the intentional sense of "information" when, in fact, they have a right only to its structural sense. (Specifically, one might deny both Bermúdez's claim that subpersonal states explain an individual's behavior (his first criterion for content) and Clark's claim that connectionist states explain an individual's ability to navigate around the world; instead, one might suggest that only the subpersonal causal mechanisms of the subsystems rather than the actions of the person are thereby accounted for.) (See McDowell 1994 and Gunther 1995 for an elaboration of this position.)

Against Crane, Hamlyn argues that nothing about a concept, F, implies that something cannot look, seem, or appear F and *not-F*. In effect, he denies that the strong construal of Cognitive Significance applies to perceptual content, although he doesn't explain why, especially since the principle, as I have suggested, seems to be motivated by Charity. Against Martin, he maintains that his argument at best shows that perceptual experience isn't always entirely determined by the concepts an individual has, which is not to say that nonconceptual content has an explanatory role. Instead, how we see or hear things is, according to Hamlyn, also determined by qualitative features of experience including sensations, attention, and sensory consciousness, features that he assumes do not have content. In fact, he claims that the belief-independence of perception, as indicated by visual illusions and even our ability to react to sound, reveal the effect that such non-intentional features have on perception. Such phenomena, Hamlyn insists, do not show that the content of perception is anything but conceptual, and they certainly don't establish that nonconceptual content has a genuine explanatory role to play in intentional psychology.

While many nonconceptualists focus on various aspects of perceptual experience, Tye argues that the contents of pains are nonconceptual, a view alluded to though not developed by Cussins in essay 6. According to Tye, pains are token sensory experiences that, like afterimages, are representational. Hence, to experience a pain in one's leg is to represent that something in one's leg is damaged. This is not to say that an individual must have the resources to conceptualize (describe, categorize, etc.) what her pain represents, for instance, the tissue damage in her leg. In fact, she need not be able to conceptualize the relevant phenomenological character of the pain, which Tye also believes is a component of a pain's intentionality. Although pains are representational, this doesn't imply that their computational architecture is sentential as a proponent of the language of thought thesis might claim. Rather, based on the topographic organization of the somatosensory cortex, Tye suggests that their architecture is map-like and therefore noncompositional.

Based on his account, the intentional contents of pains violate several Fregean principles. His rejection of a language of thought thesis, for example, may (though need not) imply that their contents violate Compositionality. Moreover, in maintaining that one need not believe or correctly apply the term "pain," Tye suggests that they violate both the weak construal of Cognitive Significance and the descriptive construal of Reference Determinacy. For if an experience of pain represents that tissue is damaged in one's leg, one can have the experience without having a belief or being able to formulate (or correctly apply) a description about the relevant tissue damage. His endorsement of the third rendering of "non" is suggested by his claim that pains or their phenomenal character *can* be experienced without an individual's possession of the requisite concepts, which is to say that pain contents are nonconceptual irrespective of whether an individual has the requisite belief or description. What might account for this inability to conceptually integrate pain contents? Tye suggests that it may be because pains and beliefs (or descriptions) have different computational architectures. (For an alternative account that regards pains as not only intentional but conceptual, see McDowell 1989.)

The final paper in the section, entitled "Emotion and Force," outlines an account of the emotions that accommodates both their intentionality and uniqueness as mental causes. Where the latter is often identified as phenomenological, evaluative, or perspectival, Gunther focuses on the apparent failure of the emotions to exhibit full logical complexity. This failure, he contends, is due to the kind of intentionality emotions have, namely, one where force is an indissoluble aspect of emotional content. From this, he claims, four consequences follow, namely, (1) that emotions cannot be reduced to cognitive and/or motivational states, (2) that their violation of Force Independence requires the development of an independent theory of meaning/content based on propriety rather than truth, (3) that this violation also indicates the need for the partial desegregation of psychology and semantics, and (4) that emotional content presents a compelling paradigm for nonconceptuality, one that avoids controversial ontological and epistemological agendas.

Emotional content, according to Gunther, is nonconceptual because it violates the Principle of Force Independence. Whether it violates other Fregean principles, for example, Compositionality, isn't explored in the paper. As for the rendering of "non," it may initially seem as if the third is advocated. Experiencing an emotion, one might suppose, reflects a failure or inability to exercise the relevant conceptual capacity, which in this case involves a capacity to separate content and force. But this is misleading since it suggests that the emotional attitude (force) can in principle be distinguished from its content, from that intentional element which it shares with other mental states (and which might thereby be represented conceptually). Gunther's claim, however, is stronger than that. An emotion is essentially what it is in virtue of the indissolubility of its content and force. For this reason, the first rendering of "non" is perhaps more applicable: emotional content is nonconceptual because it *cannot* in principle be represented conceptually, which is just to say that it cannot be shared with states whose contents can be distinguished and separated from their force.

Chapter 9

The Nonconceptual Content of Perceptual Experience: Situation Dependence and Fineness of Grain (2001)

Sean Kelly

1. Recently, Christopher Peacocke published an article defending the idea that the content of perceptual experience is nonconceptual (Peacocke 1998, pp. 381–388). Peacocke defends this claim against John McDowell's attack on nonconceptual content in chapter 3 of *Mind and World* [essay 3]. The debate between Peacocke and McDowell focuses on one of the ways (there are others) in which perceptual content is often said to be different in kind from the content of our (conceptual) linguistic utterances or thoughts: namely, perceptual content is often said to be "finer grained" than the concepts in terms of which we report our perceptual experiences. I am myself sympathetic to the idea that perceptual content is nonconceptual, and I am therefore, in a general way, sympathetic to the project in which Peacocke is engaged. I believe, however, that the defense he offers of nonconceptual content is weaker than it should be. This weakness stems, in my view, from the fact that the fine-grainedness of perceptual experience is not as relevant to its nonconceptual structure as a certain kind of situation dependence is. In this paper I will first suggest a number of ways in which Peacocke's arguments fail to make the case for the nonconceptual structure of perceptual content. My criticism of Peacocke's argument is different, I believe, from the criticism that McDowell proposes in his response to Peacocke's paper, though I will not attempt to compare our views here (see McDowell 1998, esp. pp. 414–419). Having shown that Peacocke's arguments do not succeed, I will go on in §3 to describe two features of perceptual experience—the dependence of a perceived object on the perceptual context in which it is perceived and the dependence of a perceived property on the object it is perceived to be a property of—which, I believe, are more likely than fineness of grain to be relevant to the claim that perceptual content is nonconceptual.

Before I get started on my criticism of Peacocke's argument, let me first give a general idea of the contours of the debate between him and McDowell (as I understand it). The question at issue, to begin with, is whether perceptual experience is more finely grained than the concepts we have to describe it. For the standard

From *Philosophy and Phenomenological Research*, vol. 62, no. 3 (2001), pp. 601–608. Reprinted with the kind permission of the author and *Philosophy and Phenomenological Research*.

example of this, think of the various shades of color we can discriminate percep-tually but for which we have no general color concept. Insofar as our perceptual discriminations are more finely grained than our general color concepts—we can discriminate more colors than we have color concepts for—one might be tempted to claim that perceptual experience is nonconceptual: the general color concepts seem to be insufficient to characterize adequately the content of the experience.

Once we understand this basic idea, then roughly speaking, the debate between Peacocke and McDowell goes like this: McDowell claims that even if perceptual content is not articulable in terms of general concepts, it is articulable in terms of demonstrative concepts, concepts like *that shade*; Gareth Evans, he notes, the orig-inal proponent of nonconceptual content, failed to consider this possibility. Once we allow for the possibility of demonstrative concepts, according to McDowell, the need for a nonconceptual perceptual content is no longer pressing: demon-strative concepts can do the job of characterizing the content of our perceptual states.

Peacocke counters by claiming that demonstrative concepts aren't up to the task. I'll explore this claim more carefully in §2, but the general idea is that perceptual content, according to Peacocke, is inadequately characterized both by general concepts, like the color concept *mauve*, and by demonstrative concepts, like *that shade*: it cuts more finely than the one (general concepts), but less finely than the other (demonstrative concepts). The result, Peacocke argues, is that per-ceptual content is not conceptual even if we allow for McDowell's trick of using demonstrative concepts.

The details of the debate will become clearer, I hope, as this paper proceeds. For the moment what is important to remember is that McDowell introduces the following idea into the debate: a demonstrative concept may be able to be used to characterize the content of a given perceptual experience. Now, I'll turn to Peacocke's treatment of the situation.

2. Peacocke distinguishes between three levels of description that are applicable to a subject perceiving the shape of an object (or generally, some visible property F of an object). Roughly, these levels are:

(i) the shape itself,
(ii) the shape as perceived in experience (or, as we might say, the "perceived shape"),
(iii) the shape as demonstratively conceptualized (as, for instance, in the utterance "that shape" or "that square").

The goal of the nonconceptualist, according to Peacocke, is to show that levels (ii) and (iii) come apart. (We can agree that this is at least a necessary condition for the success of the nonconceptualist position.) McDowell, on the other hand, as a conceptualist about perceptual content, wants to explain level (ii) in terms of level (iii). The argument comes over whether this is possible.

In order to show that it is not possible to explain perceived properties in terms of demonstrative concepts, Peacocke first tries to show that demonstrative concepts are too fine-grained:

> I think McDowell is right when he complains that Evans, for all his important contributions, overlooked demonstrative concepts. But it seems to me that these demonstrative concepts slice *too* finely to capture the ways of level (ii). Consider *that shade, that red, that scarlet*. These are all different conceptual contents. It seems to me quite implausible that just one of these, and not the others, features in the representational content of the experience of a shade of red. (1998, p. 382)

I don't think this is a very strong argument. The crux of the argument seems to reside in the claim that many different demonstrative concepts must feature in the representational content of a single experience. It is "quite implausible," as Peacocke says, that this should fail to be the case. But I'm not convinced. Here's why.

It is true, of course, that "that shade," "that red," and "that scarlet" express different concepts, and it is also true that they could all pick out the same color swatch. If that color swatch *is* both colored and red and scarlet, then naturally all those demonstrative concepts will pick it out. But what the demonstrative concepts pick out in this case is the property itself, as described at level (i). To claim further that they all pick out the same *perceived* property, as described in level (ii), seems to me to require independent justification. After all, at least on the face of it, the fact that the color of my scarf is accurately describable as a shade and as a shade of red and as a shade of scarlet doesn't indicate that my experience of it as a shade is the same as my experience of it as a shade of red and my experience of it as a shade of scarlet. Indeed, it seems plausible to think that if I'm grouping it with a variety of different red things I may experience its color differently than if I'm grouping it with a variety of different scarlet things. And in fact, if I'm grouping it with a variety of different red things then it's at least conceivable that the demonstrative concept *that red* will get the experience right, but the demonstrative concept *that scarlet* won't. If that's right, then demonstrative concepts don't slice too finely at all. They slice just about right.

Now, I'm not sure how seriously to take this criticism of Peacocke. At least it seems to require a response if the nonconceptualist wants to stick with his strategy of showing that demonstrative concepts are too fine-grained to account for perceptual experience, and I don't see that Peacocke has one. Since I don't think this strategy does much to help the nonconceptualist anyway, I'm tempted to leave the issue to one side. But Peacocke pursues the problem one stage further, so let me just say this extra bit.

Suppose it could be more convincingly argued, *pace* the criticism above, that demonstrative concepts are too fine-grained to account for the content of perceptual experience. Still, it seems that the conceptualist has available to him either of two moves. In the first place, he could accept the option Peacocke offers him of taking "the most specific concept in the repertoire of the perceiver to capture the fine-grained content"(*ibid.*) of the experience. Peacocke thinks this won't work because of the intuition he has that the experience of the color of, for instance, a scarlet scarf is exactly the same for the person whose conceptual repertoire includes *scarlet* as it is for the person whose repertoire stops with *red*. As Peacocke says, "[T]here is a single shade . . . that they both experience, and in the same ways" (*ibid.*). But is this intuition enough?

Peacocke leaves the intuition undefended, and it seems at least *prima facie* plausible to deny it. For instance, we might reasonably imagine that the painter or the interior decorator, with her mastery of the various color minutiae, just sees things differently than I do with my limited array of color concepts. To defend this idea we might say that part of what she sees is that this scarlet scarf looks like color chip r-235, but not like r-110; and this could mean, if we chose the color chips properly, that she saw it as scarlet, but not as a more canonical shade of red. If for me there is no distinction between the experience of these two shades, while for her there is, then surely the content of my experience is different from the content of hers. Therefore, if this account of color perception is right, then although there is a single shade that we both experience, we nevertheless experience that single shade differently. And furthermore this difference seems to be attributable to our different conceptual repertoires.

Now, I don't think this account of color perception is ultimately defensible, for reasons I'll explain in §3. But the reasons I bring to bear against it there have nothing to do with the intuitions that motivate Peacocke's view. So I don't see that Peacocke has a decent response to this line of argument, at least not on the basis of the account he develops in the article I'm considering. So much for the first conceptualist line of response.

The other option for the conceptualist is also suggested by something Peacocke says. The conceptualist could simply accept Peacocke's intuition that the experience stays the same no matter what fine-grained concepts I have, and explain the content of the perception in terms of the "medium-grained" demonstrative concept *that shade*. If it is true, as Peacocke says, that "there is a single shade . . . that [the variously adept observers] experience, and in the same ways" (*ibid.*), then the demonstrative concept *that shade* should properly pick out the right perceived shade, and hence get the content of the experience right. Peacocke's description of the claim makes this unavoidable, since once he identifies the content of the experience in terms of the single perceived shade, pointing to it with the phrase "that shade" seems a perfectly reasonable way to pick it out. The way Peacocke gets around this explanation in his example is by stipulating that neither of the observers has the general concept *shade*. In the example in question Peacocke wants to focus on:

the fine-grained representational content of experience of two people, *neither of whom has the general concept, shade,* but one of whom has the concept *scarlet,* and the other of whom has only *red* but not *scarlet* . . . (*ibid.,* my italics)

But this seems to me unfair. If you have the specific concept *red,* then you must know that it refers to some feature of the object, and what is that feature if not its color or shade? So it seems to me that if McDowell is going to accept Peacocke's intuition that the possession of fine-grained concepts doesn't change experience, then it is still open to him to explain perceptual content in terms of demonstrative concepts of the medium-grained sort—concepts like *that shade, that shape,* and so on. Again, I will argue in §3 that this rejoinder does not work, but I remain unconvinced that Peacocke's stance against it is satisfying.

3. It looks to me, then, that the argument that demonstrative concepts are too fine-grained to account for experience is not a very convincing one. But in a way that's all by the by, since I don't think that it was getting at the important phenomenon anyway. I think that the important point about the perception of properties is twofold: first, that properties are not, as presented in experience, independent of the context in which they are perceived, and second, that they are not, as presented in experience, independent of the object they are perceived to be a property of. I suspect that Peacocke has believed in these two types of dependencies at various points in his career, though I'm not sure he's ever advocated both simultaneously. I think he should, and I also think that if he does, he will have the resources necessary to block the possible responses I considered just now on McDowell's behalf. So let me say a bit about the dependencies.

The first kind of dependency—the dependency of a perceived property on the context in which it is perceived—is admirably illustrated by the phenomenon of perceptual constancy. In the case of color this is the phenomenon whereby I experience an object to be the same color in various lighting conditions even though these conditions change the way I experience the color. For instance, I see the color of my entire office wall to be white, and indeed the same shade of white, even when some parts of the wall are better lit than others. At the same time, however, my experience of the poorly lit section is not the same as my experience of the well-lit section: one looks better lit than the other. Peacocke uses this phenomenon to great effect in chapter 1 of *Sense and Content*[1] in order to argue that perceptual experience has an essential sensory component, the component that characterizes "what-it's-like-to-have-the-experience." The French phenomenologist Maurice Merleau-Ponty, on the other hand, uses this phenomenon to argue, among other things, that perceptual experience has an essential informational component, the component that tells something about the features of the object being experienced (see Merleau-Ponty 1962, part 2, chap. 3).

Properly understood, both of these are important aspects of the phenomenon of perception. It may be, however, that they are not properly understood as sensory and informational components of experience. Indeed, I suspect that

Peacocke now thinks the conclusion he then reached in considering these phenomena—the conclusion that there is an ineliminable sensory component to perceptual experience—is a faulty one. I suspect this because the argument for that claim depended upon the premise that representational content is always conceptual, and of course he doesn't believe that anymore. But even if the conclusion is faulty, the phenomenon it was meant to explain is still an important one to consider. And it's especially important in this context because I think that, rightly considered, the phenomenon of constancy shows why medium-grained demonstrative concepts can't completely capture the content of perception. Let me try to say why.

On my view the phenomenon of perceptual constancy shows us something crucial about the context dependence of perceptual experience. In particular, it shows us that the complete and accurate account of my perceptual experience of the color of an object must contain some reference to the lighting context in which that color is perceived. Without a reference to the context we won't have the resources necessary to explain the change in experience that occurs when the lighting context is varied. If it is right, as all perceptual psychologists agree, that this change is not a change in color (hence the name "color constancy"), then no color concept, not even a demonstrative one, could completely describe the content of a color experience. So even if McDowell were to try to explain perception in terms of the medium-grained concepts mentioned above, such an explanation would be inadequate because the phrase "that color" is unable to distinguish between that color as presented in the sun and that same color as presented in the shade. Because the relevant difference is not a difference in color, no color term could make such a distinction. Since such a distinction is clearly made in experience— the color looks different in the sun than in the shade—the demonstrative concept is inadequate to account for the experience.

The second kind of dependency—the dependency of a perceived property on the object it's perceived to be a property of—is shown by Peacocke's example of the height of the window and the height of the arch (see Peacocke 1989c), and also by Merleau-Ponty's equivalent claim[2] that "the blue of the carpet would not be the same blue were it not a woolly blue." The basic idea is that when I perceive a property like height or color, what I see is not some independently determinable property that any other object could share; rather what I see is a dependent aspect of the object I'm seeing now. The dependency of the perceived property on the object is so complete that even if I see the color of the carpet to be the same as the color of some other object—a shiny steel ball, for instance—I can always rationally wonder whether they are in fact the same color. I can, of course, satisfy myself that they are the same color by measuring the wavelength of the light they reflect, just as I can satisfy myself that the window and the arch are the same height by measuring them with a tape measure. But this doesn't tell me anything about the content of the original perceptual experience, since it's on the basis of the new, measuring experience that I come to believe in the equivalence.

Now, if it's really true that this second type of dependency obtains, then it seems to block the possibility of the initial conceptualist line of thought. Remember that this is the line of thought according to which we accept the claim that the most specific concept in the repertoire of the perceiver captures her perceptual experience, while denying Peacocke's intuition that perceptual experience doesn't vary with conceptual sophistication. The justification for this denial is found in the *prima facie* plausible claim that the painter sees the scarlet scarf in terms of its resemblance to a certain color chip, not some other. But if a perceived color isn't describable independently of its object, then it must be false that the painter's perception of color is explicable in terms of resemblance to an objective measure. After all, the color chip r-235 presents an independently specifiable property that any object could have, while the scarlet of the scarf is not presented in perception as a color identifiable independently of the scarf. The point is much like that made above concerning context. A demonstrative concept like *that scarlet* can only pick out one scarlet among others. But the difference between the experience of the scarlet scarf and the experience of the scarlet steel ball is *ex hypothesi* not due to a difference of color (this shade of scarlet versus that shade of scarlet), but rather is due to a difference in the object that manifests that color. No color term alone could make that distinction.

If these two observations about perception are right, then demonstrative concepts are too coarse-grained, not too fine-grained, to capture perceptual content. Concepts, even demonstrative ones, pick out situation independent features, but the perceptual experience of a property is always dependent upon the two aspects of the situation I mentioned above—context and object. It is still open to the conceptualist to argue that perceptual content is explicable in terms of the conjunction of a variety of demonstrative concepts—one that picks out the property, one that picks out the object that manifests that property, and then a large set of demonstrative concepts that picks out the relevant features of the context in which the property is being perceived. But it seems as though this last set will present a sticking point, since there could be an indefinitely large number of relevant contextual features, and which features of the context are relevant will change from situation to situation. This seems to me a more likely reason that perceptual content is nonconceptual—because it's situation dependent, and situations aren't specifiable in conceptual terms.

Notes

1. I don't think Peacocke actually groups his examples under the heading of perceptual constancy, but the examples he considers—the color of a wall in different lighting contexts, the size of a tree at different distances, and the loudness of a car engine when far away or close—are obvious examples of that phenomenon.
2. I see these examples as equivalent, both pointing to the second dependency. But it may be that Peacocke is making a different point when he uses the example in Peacocke 1989c.

Chapter 10

The Waterfall Illusion (1988)

Tim Crane

If you stare for a period of time at a scene which contains movement in one direction, and then turn your attention to an object in a scene which contains no movement, this object will appear to move in the opposite direction to that of the original movement. The effect can be easily achieved by attaching a piece of paper with a spiral drawn on it to the spinning turntable of a record player, and then turning the turntable off while continuing to look at the spiral (see Frisby 1979, pp. 100–101 for a detailed description of how to bring this about). But the illusion of movement can also occur when looking at a waterfall, for instance, and turning one's attention away from the waterfall to a stationary object such as a stone; hence its name—the "Waterfall Illusion."

The effect is quite striking, and not difficult to achieve. But the above description is not quite right. For although the stationary object *does* appear to move, it does not appear to move relative to the background of the scene. That is, there is a clear sense in which it also *appears to stay still* (see Blakemore 1973, p. 36). There is a distinct appearance of lack of motion as well as motion. Understandably enough, many find this aspect of the illusion quite extraordinary; John Frisby writes that

> although the after-effect gives a very clear illusion of movement, the apparently moving features nevertheless seem to stay still! That is, we are still aware of features remaining in their "proper" locations even though they are seen as moving. What we see is logically impossible! (Frisby 1979, p. 101)

Presumably what Frisby thinks is logically impossible is that something could be both moving and not moving at the same time; and this claim must be correct. I will argue that this aspect of the Waterfall Illusion poses a problem for a familiar claim about perception: the claim that the content of perceptual experience is composed of *concepts*.

Of course, what one makes of such cases as the Waterfall Illusion partly depends on one's methodology. One could dismiss such cases as uninteresting exceptions, to be dealt with once the truth about normal perceptual functioning

From *Analysis*, vol. 48 (1988), pp. 142–147. Reprinted with the kind permission of the author.

has been found. Perhaps this is the right way to treat illusions. But my own sympathies lie with Helmholtz:

> The study of what are called illusions of the sense is, however, a very prominent part of the psychology of the senses; for it is just those cases which are not in accordance with reality which are particularly instructive for discovering the laws of those processes by which normal perception originates. (noted in Coren and Girgus 1978, p. 9)

On this view of the significance of illusions, the study of illusions could be compared to pathology: one studies the body's abnormal functioning in order to understand normal functioning. Or—closer to home—it could be compared to Russell's idea that one uses logical puzzles (about, e.g., non-referring singular terms) to test the adequacy of a logical theory (see Russell 1905, p. 47). I shall adopt Helmholtz's advice, and see what we can learn about perception from the Waterfall Illusion.

The problem is: what is the content of such a visual experience? Note that the problem concerns the *content* of the experience, not the *attitude*. We are familiar (from discussions of phenomena such as the Müller-Lyer Illusion) with the fact that illusions can occur even when the victim of the illusion knows the truth about what he is seeing. And there is an extensive discussion of whether this fact can be accounted for by a theory which claims that perception is a sort of belief. (Armstrong 1969 argues that it can, Jackson 1977 and Fodor 1983 argue that it cannot.) I cannot enter this debate here, and I do not need to; for *whatever* the fate of the idea that perceptions are beliefs, there is still a problem about characterizing the *content* of an experience like the Waterfall Illusion. In fact, it seems to me to be implausible that the victim of the illusion, knowledgeable or not, would judge the stationary object to be moving—though he might judge that he is drunk (a similar effect can be had by playing the child's game of spinning oneself around and then trying to stay still). But this is not directly relevant to the present point; we are concerned in this paper with contents, not attitudes.

The crucial difference between the Müller-Lyer Illusion and the Waterfall Illusion is this. The Müller-Lyer Illusion presents a conflict between *two* intentional states: the state of believing that the lines are the same length, and the state of the lines *looking to be* different lengths (I leave open the question as to whether this is a "suppressed inclination to believe" as the belief theory of perception holds). The Waterfall Illusion, however, presents a contradiction in the *one* content of one attitude. The viewed object seems to be both moving and not moving at the same time. This is the natural way to describe how things seem; unlike the Müller-Lyer Illusion, the content of the *experience itself* is contradictory.

Now if the content of this experience is indeed contradictory, then a significant problem arises for those who claim that the contents of experiences are individuated according to certain familiar principles. We may call these principles "Fregean" because of their origin in Frege's Theory of Sense and Reference. Frege introduced a criterion of difference for senses which distinguished senses as the *cognitive value* of expressions; for example, the criterion of difference for the senses of sentences may be expressed as follows:

> (I) For any thinker A, and any sentences S and S', if A understands S and S' and accepts S as true while not accepting S', then S and S' have different senses.

(I) allows subjects to take different attitudes to sentences with the same truth-conditions; the notion of sense is introduced to explain this possibility. So (I) is meant to individuate the senses of sentences (their *contents*) finely enough to rule out the unnecessary ascription of contradictory beliefs to rational subjects. *De re* considerations aside, we do not want to credit Ralph with the belief that Ortcutt is and is not a spy. So (I) is invoked to explain why it is that Ralph does not have contradictory beliefs in this situation, and therefore how identity statements can be informative. The principle is thus meant to provide a test for the cognitive significance of senses; it does not tell us what this is, but it tells us when it is distinct.

Clearly, similar principles apply to the constituents of contents: the senses of singular terms and predicates. If we call the sense of a predicate a *concept* (departing, of course, from Frege's own use of that term) we can introduce a criterion of difference for concepts inspired by (I):

> (II) F and G are different concepts if it is possible for a subject to rationally judge, of an object a, that a is F and that a is not-G.

Like (I), this principle allows the possibility that a rational subject can apply incompatible concepts to the same object, by taking these concepts to differ in cognitive significance.

One writer who has urged that we individuate contents and their constituents in this way is Christopher Peacocke (see, e.g., Peacocke 1984, p. 365). Now Peacocke has also suggested that we use these principles in individuating the contents of perceptual experience (see Peacocke 1983; but for an important reconsideration not related to the problem discussed in this paper see Peacocke 1986c, pp. 9–11) [see also essay 5]. In *Sense and Content* he claims that

> it is a conceptual truth that no one can have an experience with a given representational content unless he possesses the concepts from which that content is built up. (1983, p. 19)

If the concepts which build up the representational content of an experience are individuated along the lines of principle (II), then we arrive at a further principle:

> (III) F and G are different perceptual concepts if it is possible for a subject to have (at the same time) an experience with the content that a is F and an experience with the content a is not-G.

It follows from this that one cannot have an experience with contradictory representational content. This thought seems to have struck Edward Craig, who writes (in defense of his claim that experience "belongs to the category of judgment") that one cannot see a Necker Cube looking one way, and then imagine it looking *at the same time* the other way (see Craig 1976, p. 13).

But, as we have seen, the Waterfall Illusion is precisely a case where a scene looks as if it is both one way and another (incompatible) way at the same time. Craig's point is no doubt true of the Necker Cube (and indeed, of most normal perception). But the Waterfall Illusion is a vivid counterexample to a generalization of the point. For what it suggests is that a subject can be ascribed an experience with a contradictory content. But if principle (III) is central to the individuation of perceptual concepts (as it seems to be) then the Waterfall Illusion is, surprisingly, a counterexample to the thesis that concepts are involved in the content of perceptual experience. For the subject can see that the stone (for example) is moving and that it is not moving. But this contravenes (III), since we know that there is only one concept being exercised: *moving*.

It seems to me, then, that this illusion presents a problem for those views (such as Peacocke's [1983] or Craig's [1976]) which treat the content of perception as conceptual. The argument is not decisive—there are various ways in which one could resist it. One response would be to deny that the two contradictory halves of the content are *really* simultaneous (so that the situation is rather like a very rapid switching between the two "aspects" of the Necker Cube). But this response seems, in the face of the phenomenology, unduly stipulative.

Another response would be to insist that the two halves of the content are not really contradictory, because the concepts involved in each half are distinct. But how plausible is this response? If the concepts in the two halves of the content are not the same, it is hard to see precisely why the illusion presents this apparent contradiction. Indeed, it is difficult to say exactly what the two distinct concepts *are*; perhaps in the case of looking at a waterfall and then a stone, they might be *intrinsically moving* (whatever this may mean) and *not moving relative to other objects*. But in the case of looking at the stationary turntable, the concept *not moving relative to other objects* cannot be the appropriate one, for the position of the spiral on the turntable relative to other objects is *irrelevant* to the production of the illusion. (The turntable itself could be moving through space, and the illusion would still occur.) The problem for the defender of concepts in perception is to say exactly which concepts are being exercised here, without denying that there is a conflict in how the perceived scene seems to be.

Finally, one might dispense with principles (II) and (III) and try to find some other constraint on the identity of concepts. This would surely be an excessively severe reaction. I suggest that we should leave the Fregean constraints where they belong—with the "higher" cognitive faculties of judgment, belief and thought, those faculties which are governed by the "Constitutive Ideal of Rationality" (Davidson 1982, p. 223). Perhaps the fact that perceptual contradictions can occur (however rarely) in the minds of otherwise rational subjects suggests that perceptions are not subject to all of the principles which govern the operations of the higher faculties; perception is, perhaps, a "sub-rational" process. And this may seem to be supported by Fodor's view that the operations of the perceptual system are "informationally encapsulated"; that is, the informational content of perceptual states cannot be affected by the contents of states in "central mind" (Fodor 1983, pp. 64–86). Of course, Fodor's theory of the "modularity" of visual perception does not on its own explain how there can be perceptual contradictions. But it does suggest an explanation of why perception may not be a wholly rational process, and thus why it is peculiarly vulnerable to phenomena like the Waterfall Illusion.[1]

Note

1. Many thanks to Jeremy Butterfield, Hugh Mellor and the editor for useful comments.

Chapter 11

Perception, Concepts, and Memory (1992)

Michael Martin

An intentional theory of perception claims that perceptual states have an intentional content that represents the world as being some way.[1] This is to see experiences as akin to propositional attitudes such as beliefs: believing that there is a glass on the table is being in a state with an intentional content. To claim that an experience has an intentional content is not necessarily to identify experiences with beliefs or to attempt to reduce them to the acquisition of beliefs;[2] after all, one does not always believe things to be the way that they appear. Denying that experience is the same kind of attitude as belief does still allow one to suppose that the two kinds of mental state are nevertheless both attitudes to the same kind of content. The question I wish to raise here is whether that supposition is correct.

How far can one push this analogy between belief content and appearances? We think of beliefs as conceptual states, the possession of a belief resting on one's capacities to think about objects and properties. Could experiences be conceptual states in this way: the appearance of things being restricted by one's conceptual capacities?

I shall argue that the answer to this question is negative. An important part of the role of perception in one's mental economy is its commerce with belief, but perceptions also give rise to memories. The latter connection reveals that perceptual experiences have a richer phenomenological character than one's conceptual resources need allow.

The argument divides into five sections. The first part formulates the claim that appearances are conceptual. In the second, the connection between perception and memory is introduced in relation to the question of whether one can fail to notice how things appear to one; and in the third, the argument is extended to refute the conceptualist position. The fourth and fifth sections then review the consequences of this conclusion and the alternatives to the conceptualist claim.

From the *Philosophical Review*, vol. 101, no. 4 (1992), pp. 745–764. Reprinted with the kind permission of the author and the *Philosophical Review*.

I

It is common to talk of beliefs as being conceptual. This involves a commitment to the idea that the objects of belief, their contents, have a significant structure and that this structure relates to the various abilities that a thinker brings to bear in having the belief.

Much of the utility of talking about concepts arises from the explanations one may give of why a thinker might possess or lack a certain thought or belief despite what else she knows. The proposition that Leo is *a* lion entails that Leo is an animal, so the proposition that Leo is a lion is logically equivalent to the proposition that Leo is both a lion and an animal. Assuming that it is *a posteriori* that one is a lion only if one is an animal, someone could believe that Leo was a lion without thereby believing that Leo was both a lion and an animal. An account of belief therefore needs to make a distinction between these two beliefs. If we see the contents of beliefs as structured, we can distinguish between logically equivalent propositions as distinct objects of belief. Distinguishing between the two beliefs, we may explain why a thinker believes the former without believing the latter, by noting that she does not believe that Leo is an animal. Now she may lack this belief without lacking the concept of an animal—she might just believe that lions are a Disney creation rather than animals, but still believe that her pet cat is an animal. On the other hand, a possible explanation of her failure to believe that Leo is an animal is that she lacks the concept of an animal. This is a distinct explanation from that of simply saying that she lacks the belief that Leo is an animal. One's conceptual abilities are exercised in the thinking of more than one thought, just as there are aspects of the content of a particular thought that may be part of the content of another. One's concept of an animal will figure not only in the thought that Leo is an animal, but also in the thought that Mint Sauce is an animal, that Archimedes is an animal, and that the animals in London Zoo are to become homeless.

Taking beliefs to be conceptual is to see them as arising out of such a web of conceptual abilities, reflected in the particular thoughts and beliefs one has. Concepts are acquired through training and encounters with features of the world that one may come to recognize and so learn to apply again in different circumstances. The ascription of a concept to someone thereby implies a certain generality in the range of thoughts available to them.[3] Where one lacks a conceptual ability, one thereby lacks a thought involving it. One's intentional states are conceptual states where one can be in a state with that content only if one has the concepts required to think or believe that content.

Applying this to the case of experience, we arrive at the following claim. The content of an experience will be conceptual where it meets this condition:

> (C) It appears to S as if $p \rightarrow S$ possesses those concepts necessary for believing that p.

Experience is conceptual in the way that belief is, if (C) holds for all p propositions such that it can appear to one as if p.[4]

For ease of exposition, in the discussion that follows I shall assume that all talk of appearances is talk of the intentional content of experience, ignoring issues about nonintentional qualities. That is, one should understand the following discussion as first being directed against someone who not only thinks that all intentional content is conceptual, but who also accepts a purely intentional theory of experience: a proponent of such a theory claims that all aspects of conscious experience are to be explained in terms of its possession of an intentional content.[5] The argument of the next two sections will show that if intentional content is purely conceptual this claim must be false. The last section then turns to the question of whether those aspects of experience that make it false should all be thought of as nonintentional qualities of experience.

II

The first stage of the argument is to look at the relation between experiencing things to be a certain way and attending to or noticing that they are that way. One simple line of thought is that one can fail to notice how things appear to one. Failing to notice something can be an explanation of why one doesn't have a particular belief. Combining these two thoughts leads to the conclusion that one can have a certain experience that doesn't lead to the belief that things are so precisely because one fails to notice how things appear.

Just such considerations were exploited by Fred Dretske in his arguments for a notion of "nonepistemic" seeing. Dretske suggested that we would not wish to say that someone who had not noticed a cuff link in a drawer when they looked had not seen it, even though they failed to acquire the belief that the cuff link was there or the belief that they had seen it (Dretske 1969, p. 18).

This view will be opposed by anyone who thinks that something can be genuinely experienced only if it impinges on one's beliefs. The crudest such view would be one that claimed that experiencing the world is just coming to believe that it is so. This can't be correct given the incidence of disbelief in perception, but that alone doesn't tell against the thought that experience must have some effect on one's beliefs. If an experience does not lead to the acquisition of a belief that p, then at least it leads to the belief that it appears to one as if p. On such a view, a failure to notice some aspect of the scene in front of one has the consequence that one does not experience it.

Is there any reason to accept one of these views over the other? The one, call it the belief-independent view of experience, equates experience with the noticeable, the other, call it the belief-impinging view, only with what is actually noticed. Dretske offers an argument against the latter, when he writes:

> we say [that someone must have seen something] when we are convinced
> that, despite what the person *thought* he saw, or whether he thought he saw

> anything at all, the physical and physiological conditions were such that the
> object must have looked some way to him. (*ibid.*)

That is, he claims that the physical conditions of perception offer us at least defeasible reason to suppose that someone must have seen how things were. Whether
or not someone has noticed something doesn't affect what those conditions are,
and hence they can provide independent evidence for the claim that things can
be experienced a certain way even when not noticed to be that way.

But these considerations don't get one very far. The opposing view can simply
respond that physical and physiological conditions provide warrant for determining how things appear only on the assumption that the perceiver really is
noticing how things are (see Pitson 1984, pp. 121–129). At best they determine
what can be experienced, but not what is experienced. To settle this dispute, evidence is needed that derives from within the realm of the mental itself. Any appeal
to experience or to belief by either side will just beg the question: the one side will
say we have evidence that experience is a certain way despite the lack of belief;
the other will say lack of belief is evidence of lack of experience. However, I
suggest that there is mental and experiential evidence in favor of the former
position. Consider the following extension of Dretske's example.

Suppose that someone, Archie, is looking for a cuff link. He looks in a drawer
but fails to notice it and continues searching the room. Eventually he gives up and
leaves for dinner. On the way to dinner, he agitatedly thinks back to his search of
the room. Having a relatively good visual memory, he recalls how things looked
as he searched. Suddenly he realizes that the cuff link was in the drawer but that
he had failed to notice it.

When Archie looked in the drawer he did not acquire the belief that the
cuff link was there. Had he done so then, barring some explanation in terms of
suppressed belief, he would not have continued his search. At some later time, on
the way to dinner, he comes to acquire the belief that the cuff link was in the
drawer. This revision of his beliefs at a later time resulted from his memory
recall of the scene. What he recalled was how things were as he searched. One's
memory experiences typically derive from one's past perceptions, so the memory
experience is evidence of how things looked to Archie when he carried out his
search. Since Archie recalled that the cuff link was in the drawer, we have
evidence that it then looked to him as if the cuff link was in the drawer. This
supports the original view: that one can experience something as a certain way
even if it does not impinge on one's beliefs, precisely because one fails to notice
how things appear.

This argument depends on some such principle as this: If, when recalling past
events, it now appears as if it then was the case that *p*, then it then appeared as if
it was the case that *p*. Why should one accept such a principle? The short answer
is that it derives from two marks of our concept of memory: memories are sources

of information about the past; they are also derivative sources of information, dependent for any authority they have on past perception.

The story of Archie revolves around memory experience, a certain kind of episodic memory state. Such states are associated only with direct and not with factual memory, memories that one has only where one has previously observed or witnessed the scene recalled.[6] Memory experiences are states with an experiential or phenomenological character, in which in some sense how things are recalled to be is akin to how they would once have been perceived. For instance, I may recall what someone looks like and my memory will be of their facial appearance. One can also recall sounds and emotions in this way, and, perhaps most strongly, tastes and smells.

This kind of experiential recall is closely associated with past perception, hence the link with direct memory. How one recalls things to have been may be associated solely with one past perception: as when one recalls what a crash looked like on the motorway. It can also be associated with an indefinite number of past perceptions, as in the case of recalling the look of an old friend.

It would be mistaken to think that this kind of memory can be explained simply as a matter of having mental images. For mental images can play a role in factual memory just as well as they can in direct memory. I might, for instance, employ a mental image of a map of the kings and queens of England as a mnemonic aid to remembering (factually) their dates. This image need not trace back to any past perception of such a map, and its role in the recall need be no more than as an additional aid: if the map seems funny then I suspect I am not recalling the dates aright. Here the image does not constitute the remembering but is some corollary to it. Memory experience is not like that; the phenomenal element of such remembering is not merely coincidental with the direct memory of the past incident but actually constitutes it.[7]

One's current perceptions have a coercive influence on one's beliefs. At least when one notices how things appear, one is liable straight off to believe without any reflection that things are so. Examples of disbelief in perception can't show that experience lacks this coercive force, but only that it can be resisted by dint of reason. Memory episodes can likewise have a certain authority over one's beliefs. When one recalls a past scene, one is liable to take it that that is how things were. But our memories are not sources of information about the world independent of our perceptions. Rather, they inherit whatever authority they have from being the traces of past perceptions of how things were. A memory will be authoritative with respect to some past scene because how things appear traces back to how things were once perceived, and from that they derive a coercive force.

The fact that perceptual experiences have a coercive force reflects the fact that our default attitude to them is that they are veridical rather than illusory; that, if it appears to one as if p, then that is (defeasible) evidence that p. One's perceptual experiences are not evidentially inert. We might also introduce talk of memory experience as being more or less faithful to past perception.[8] Where memory experience is faithful, it should carry over the coercive force of past perception. Memory experiences in general have this coercive authority whether or not they are actually faithful, and this suggests that our default attitude to them is that they are faithful unless shown otherwise. That is tantamount to the principle that if it now appears that it once was the case that p, it then appeared as if it was the case that p. One's memory experiences are not, then, evidentially inert with respect to past perceptions.

The nature of memory experience itself supports the principle that current memory experiences can give us reason to think that past perceptual experiences were a certain way. This is just what is appealed to in the Archie case. But note that this is at best defeasible evidence. It can be defeated by specific facts about a particular case. After all, memory is a notorious deceiver. Memories of past events are often colored by later beliefs and false imaginings. In such cases the memory is not faithful to past perception and is no guide to how things did look. The example offered is not so detailed that it can rule out all such explanations.

One must be careful about the way in which to appeal to the case of later recall. The case can never be specified in such detail that one can rule out explanations of it that will defeat the claim that that was how Archie had perceived things to be. But that is not necessarily what is required. The story as told offers no positive reason to think that the evidence is defeated. The cuff link was in a position to have been seen. The memory experience was veridical apropos the scene: the cuff link was where it was recalled to be. Archie has no other source of information for the location of the cuff link, nor any beliefs liable to color his recall. A plausible explanation of the veridicality of the memory experience, then, is its faithfulness to the past experience. There are ways of developing the story in further detail so as to reveal details that defeat this explanation and the evidential tie between memory and perception. But in employing the example one need not deny this. All that is needed is the fact that nothing in our general conception of the links between perception, memory, and belief need rule out the example as it is told. Independent of a commitment to experience being belief-impinging, why should one think that there must be such defeating facts in this case?

Perceptions not only have an effect on beliefs, they also lead to traces in memory. The tie between memory and perception is reflected in the authority that memory experience can have about the past, an authority that can lead to the revision of beliefs. Memory experience can then be a source of evidence about how things were experienced independently of what the subject then believed. Someone who claims that this can't be so must then be committed to revising our conception of the constitutive ties between perception and memory. A simple commitment to the belief-impinging view of experience surely provides no rationale for this. The belief-independent view prevails. Experience can on occasion be inert with respect to belief—one can simply fail to notice how things are experienced.

III

Much the same considerations tell against the conceptualist claim. A conceptualist claims that the content of one's experience must be constrained by what concepts one then has; to oppose conceptualism is to deny this. How can one motivate the thought that one's experience has a certain content, independent of considerations about whether the perceiver does have the concepts in question? An extension of the Archie example offers to do just that.

Later memory experience is evidence of the content of perceptual experience, because it is a re-presentation of how things once appeared. Since a memory experience occurs at a different time from the original perception, what the content of the memory experience is can be determined independently of which concepts the subject had at the time of perceiving. If the memory experience can have a content that exceeds the conceptual resources of the subject at the time of perception, we have reason to think the conceptualist is applying an arbitrary restriction on the content of experience.

Consider this example. Suppose Mary is a keen board-games player, and often plays a game involving unusual dice. One such game involves the use of a twelve-faced die and an eight-faced die. Now suppose that Mary's grasp of elementary geometry is rather poor and she does not like counting past five. She tends to treat alike all regular shapes more complex than a cube, for example, those having more faces than six. Although she uses both the dodecahedral die and the octahedral one, she does not think of them as distinguished in this way; they are both just many-faced. What matters to her about them is just the different distributions of colored spots on the faces: the one has four kinds of spot, the other three.

Mary does not have the concept of the dodecahedron. Although she discerns a difference between the twelve-faced die and the eight-faced one in the context of the game, the difference she focuses on concerns color spots and shape; both dice are just many-shaped to her. As things stand, she would treat any many-shaped die as being of the same type as the dodecahedral one if it had the same number of color spots on its faces, and would not take any other object that was dodecahedral to have anything significantly in common with the dodecahedral die other than being many-shaped, a quality it would also share with the octahedral one. Hence she employs no concept that picks out all and only dodecahedra: here we have an example of someone who fails to have a concept that she might otherwise apply to observed shapes.

There is no difficulty in supposing that Mary can acquire the concept of a dodecahedron, nor that in acquiring the concept she can come to apply it to objects of a distinctive visual appearance: a regular dodecahedron has twelve faces each with five sides.[9] Now imagine that Mary has acquired the concept but not yet gone back to playing her game. She happens to think back to the last time she played the game and recalls her best move, which involved throwing one of the dice. She suddenly realizes that the die she then threw was in fact a dodecahedron. Her current memory experience is of her once throwing a twelve-faced die. As a result of it she comes to believe that she has played a game using such a die. If the memory experience is faithful to her past perception, its content, as reflected in this belief, matches that of her past perception. So it then looked to her as if she threw a twelve-faced die. At that time Mary did not have the concept of something's being twelve-faced. Nevertheless there is reason to suppose that that is how things appeared to her, unless there are defeating reasons to oppose it.

Now it cannot be denied that one's later conceptual sophistication often does alter one's memories. Perhaps one's memories of early childhood concerning parental rows might become colored by one's later knowledge of what divorce is. In a subtler way, one's acquired recognitional capacities can lead to a constitutive change in the way things appear, and that can bear back on earlier memories. But the possibility of this is not what is at issue here; rather the question is whether this simply must be so in Mary's case. As with the Archie example there seems no *a priori* reason to suppose that this must be so, other than a commitment to the conceptualist claim.

The judgment that she threw a twelve-faced die is an appropriate response to her memory experience, just as it would be to a current perception. With no reason to rule out the faithfulness of the memory experience, we have reason to suppose that the judgment that she threw a twelve-faced die would have been appropriate to her past perception. This is so, despite the fact that she did not then have the conceptual resources to make the judgment. The Mary example gives us a case in which (C) does not hold for all the ways in which things appear to her. The conceptualist view of experience therefore seems wrong: it involves an arbitrary restriction on the ways things can be experienced.

The conceptualist will wish to deny that the restrictions placed on the content of experience are arbitrary. What reasons can be given for applying such restrictions? One suggestion is made by Christopher Peacocke, who argues:

> [I]t is the nature of representational content that it cannot be built up from concepts unless the subject of the experience himself has those concepts: the representational content is the way the experience presents the world as being, and it can hardly present the world as being that way if the subject is incapable of appreciating what that way is. (Peacocke 1983, p. 7)

How do these considerations support the conceptualist claim? The thought appears to be this: if we ascribe one content to a subject's experience rather than another, then we must think that there is a significant difference between the experience having the one content rather than the other. What can the difference amount to? Peacocke suggests that the difference must reside in what the subject can appreciate as being the case. On the assumption that appreciating that something is so is a conceptual state on a level with believing that it is so, the conceptualist claim will be established.

But the argument assumes that the difference between possible contents of an experience must be appreciable by the subject at the time of having the experience. Why assume that? The differences between an experience being of a dodecahedron and being of an octahedron is not something that Mary can appreciate when she first plays the game, but it is something that she can come to appreciate and does do so. So the rejection of the conceptualist claim does not leave one unable to show that a difference in content is a significant difference for a subject.[10]

The conceptualist may push the point further. The concepts we are interested in must be ones applicable to how things appear to one, so they will principally be, or involve, recognitional capacities. If one lacks a recognitional capacity, one will not be able to discriminate between the presence or absence of a certain feature in a perceived scene. If a feature is to figure in the content of one's experience, then one must suppose it to have a distinctive appearance. Yet, if a subject cannot tell whether or not that feature is present in a scene, then it cannot have a distinctive appearance for her. Therefore it cannot figure in the content of her experience.

The argument assumes that a feature's having a distinctive appearance is sufficient for one to have a capacity for recognizing its presence or absence. Why should one assume that? Surely there is a significant distinction between two potentialities: that one's experience makes it possible for one to acquire a recognitional capacity; that one's experience makes it possible for one to exercise that capacity and recognize whether a feature is present. Once one grants that someone can experience things to be a certain way without noticing that they are so, one should be sensitive to the differences between these two things. For if someone has never noticed whether a feature is present in her experience, however distinctive its appearance, there is no reason to suppose that she does actually possess a recognitional capacity for it. But it does nevertheless give us sufficient grounds for supposing that the feature has a distinctive appearance and that this would be reflected in the perceiver's recognitional capacities were that feature brought to her notice.

There seems to be reason to collapse the distinction between experience making possible the capacity and making possible its exercise only where one assumes the belief-impinging view of experience. On that view the content of one's experience is restricted to what one notices. Were one to fail to notice the distinctive appearance of some feature in the scene it would thereby follow that it did not figure in the content of one's experience. Therefore if noticing the feature were sufficient for having the recognitional capacity, having the capacity would be a necessary condition of the feature being in the content of one's experience. Indeed the belief-impinging view of experience will also require not only that one have the capacity but that one actually exercise it if one experiences the feature. As concluded in the last section, to adopt the belief-impinging view of experience is to accept an arbitrary restriction on how things can appear to one: it is to restrict them to what one notices rather than what one could notice. Without this restriction, the above distinction arises, and the argument fails.

Note that the role of noticing or failing to notice here need not turn on any carelessness or lack of heed on the part of the perceiver. It is often remarked that the content of experience is replete. There can be an indefinite range of discriminable differences between the things that make themselves apparent to us. The complete range of such differences is too vast for one to cognitively appreciate at any one time. So one won't have recognitional capacities for all of the different ways in which things are discriminable. Think for instance of all the possible distinctions to be drawn among the shades of color between red and orange, any of which we could draw, but do not. This suggests that one just couldn't have recognitional capacities for all of the features of the world that have distinctive appearances, but that is not to deny that for each of the features that have a distinctive appearance one could have a recognitional capacity.

It is sometimes said that the repleteness of experience is no threat to the conceptualist position. Even if there are a multitude of subtle gradations between shades of color and between perceptible types of shape, a perceiver can always fix on the shade or shape perceived with a demonstrative thought, "It is *that* shade/shape" [see essays 3 and 9]. However, this point does not establish the conceptualist claim. It has not been denied that if a perceiver does attend to her experiences she can acquire a concept for something that has a distinctive appearance. What is at issue is whether she must already have that recognitional capacity to have the experience, and the kind of case in question does not bear on that, since it is precisely a case in which the perceiver does direct her attention and notice what is salient about the feature experienced.

In the first section I argued that it is natural to think of experience as being independent of belief, to the extent that how things appear is not restricted to what one notices at a time. The consequence of this is that a distinction arises between the question of whether some feature of a scene has a distinctive appearance and whether the perceiver notices the distinctive way that feature appears to her to be. Nevertheless, the distinctive appearance of a feature may be evidenced by the perceiver's later coming to notice that that was how things were, when attending to what she can recall. There is then no reason to think that how things appear must be constrained by what concepts the perceiver has.

IV

What does the rejection of the conceptualist position show about the nature of experience? The argument has turned on making a distinction between a subject's powers of reasoning and her perceptual capacities for discrimination. The contents of one's beliefs are necessarily restricted by the conceptual abilities one has, reflected in how one can reason; it is in that way that we mark differences between contents of belief. What can be perceptually apparent to a perceiver is not limited solely to what she can reason about.

This line of argument should be clearly separated from another line of attack on conceptualism. It is sometimes objected to conceptualism that nonhuman animals and human infants can perceive in much the same way that adult humans do, although they do not possess concepts or have genuine beliefs. A theory of perception should capture what is common between sapient and sentient experience; since the merely sentient have no concepts, the common element cannot be conceptual. For those of us who have concepts, there will be a distinction between our experiences, shared with the merely sentient, and our reasoning states that are conceptual. For the merely sentient there are simply the nonconceptual states that have to stand in for whatever approximates rational activity in them (see Evans 1982, chap. 5). [See also essay 3, pp. 87–88.]

In contrast to this, the argument offered here depends on making no assumption as to whether the nonrational have the same experiences as us. But there is a more significant point to be made as well. The argument offered against conceptualism in the previous section stressed, not the contrast between the rational and the nonrational, but rather, a contrast between those mental states that are employed in reasoning and those that are not. A parallel distinction can be applied at least to some creatures who are nonrational and possess no concepts. So even for them one should draw a distinction between how things appear to them and how they respond to them.

This will be true for creatures who can engage in some form of proto-practical reasoning that reflects classifications of how their environment is organized and for whom it is possible to modify the classifications they employ. Suppose we have a creature that lives in an environment with three types of foodstuff: cubes, dodecahedra, and octahedra. Cubes are sweet as well as nutritious, but there is no salient difference for the creature between the other two types. In getting about in its environment it is in the interest of the creature to plot where foodstuffs grow, and to mark the difference between cubes and the other types of food; cubes may be significant not only as being sweet but also as being useful to stand on. We might think of the creature as having a map of its environs that highlights where cubes are, and that highlights where dodecahedra and octahedra are, but without making any distinction between the latter two.

Suppose that the dodecahedra ferment and produce a pleasant intoxicating effect. The creature might discover this and hence develop an interest in finding out where dodecahedra, as opposed to octahedra, grow in its habitat. In as far as its map of the distribution of foodstuffs is concerned, it does not have the resources to discover this. Up until now there has been no interesting distinction to be drawn between dodecahedra and octahedra. This is not to say, though, that there isn't a perceptual difference between them, one that the creature can now come to exploit, both through perception and memory, as it develops a new map of its world.

Such a creature is certainly quite sophisticated in being able to modify its behavior in this way to its habitat. But that sophistication does not require anything amounting to full-blown reason (with a capital "R," so to speak) or language use. The distinction to be drawn between experience and cognizing can't simply be marked as one between verbal and subverbal states of mind, or between conceptual and nonconceptual.

Concepts and, more broadly, cognition are associated with how one reacts to the world, what use one makes of the distinctions in the world in order to achieve one's ends. Perception and experience, by contrast, are a matter of the world making itself apparent to us. The limits of experience are a matter of how sensitive we are to the world, and not what we pay heed to in reasoning about it. How things appear to one can't simply be a matter of what thoughts one has (see Dretske 1981, chap. 6) [essay 1].

V

The conclusion of the above is that how things appear to a perceiver need not solely be a matter of what conceptual content, if any, her experience possesses. If one accepts the conclusion, two avenues are open to account for the nonconceptual aspects of experience: either one accepts that there is a distinction to be drawn between a mental state having an intentional content and that content being conceptual, or one accounts for all nonconceptual elements of experience as being nonintentional, that is, as subjective qualities of the experience.

The former option might at first sight look not to be an option at all. If one identifies what it is for the mind to be directed onto the world, to have states with an intentional content, with the possession and exercise of concepts, then it will simply be contradictory to suppose that there are intentional contents that do not involve the exercise of such concepts. But the notion of a concept is also tied to a thinker's powers of reasoning and the range of thoughts with which she can reason. There is no immediately obvious link between having states that represent the world as being some way and having the ability to reason about the world being that way. This suggests that there is indeed room for a notion of intentional content that doesn't have consequences for a thinker's reasoning.

However, to establish definitely that there is any such nonconceptual intentional content, one would need a general account of intentionality. Until that is provided one may rightly remain skeptical of the first option. What I shall argue here, though, is that there is even more reason to be dissatisfied with the latter path.

To adopt such an approach is to suppose that the relevant element of Mary's experience, which I have so far picked out as its looking to her as if there is a dodecahedron in front of her, and which is in common between her original perception and later recall, is not an intentional content of the experience, but rather a qualitative aspect of the experience itself and not a matter of how the physical world is represented. On this view it is only appropriate to pick out this feature of her experience by reference to dodecahedra, because an experience having this feature is normally caused by the presence of such shapes in Mary's environment.

Since this feature of her experience is not intentional, but solely qualitative, there is no problem of explaining how it can be a feature of experience without Mary having the requisite concepts.

The problem with this approach is that it can offer us no satisfactory account of what Mary's experience is like for her. Describing it as being as of a dodecahedron does not simply pick out its typical cause, but is also normally intended to describe its introspectible character, that it is of how the physical world appears to be and not just how Mary's own mental state is. Contrast this example of visual perception with a certain kind of bodily sensation. Nettles produce a very distinctive kind of pain, nettle-stings. From an early age one may learn to recognize on having such a pain that one has had contact with a nettle. Nettle-stings are experiences that are normally caused by nettles, and that normally lead to the belief that nettles are present. Yet such pains appear to lack the kind of phenomenological character that an experience of a dodecahedron has. The claim that perceptual experiences are intentional states is an attempt to explain this phenomenological feature of perceptual experiences, the way in which they appear to introspection to be as of features of the objective world in contrast to a nettle-sting.

A response to this objection would be to claim that it is true of Mary's experience that it has the kind of objective phenomenological character lacked by nettle-stings only after she acquires the concept of a dodecahedron. It cannot then be argued that the common element of Mary's experience prior to acquiring the concept and consequent on it is an intentional content. But this response must assume that Mary's acquisition of the concept of a dodecahedron must alter the phenomenological character of her experience, so that in having the memory recall she can no longer faithfully recapture how things once looked to her. While it is true that concepts can alter how one experiences things, there seems to be no argument that they must do so. Certainly one's concept of a nettle does not appear to make a nettle-sting acquire the objective character of being of a nettle. So the intuition remains that it is the objective feature of Mary's experience that is in common between the earlier perception and the later memory, and not just some subjective element.

The conclusion remains that one cannot satisfactorily account for how things appear to a perceiver solely in terms of conceptual content, that content that figures in one's reasoning. The thoughts that one can reason with are restricted to those for which one has a conceptual ability; how things can appear to one is restricted rather by one's sensitivity to the world. Reflecting on the connections between perception and memory reveals that these two things need not coincide. One might react to this by explaining other elements in terms of nonintentional qualities of experience; but that would fail to accommodate all of the intuitions that support the attribution of an intentional content to experiences. What one cannot do is suppose that those intuitions can be satisfied solely by appeal to a conceptual intentional content.[11]

Notes

1. See, for instance, Armstrong 1968, chap. 10; Pitcher 1971; Dretske 1981, chap. 6 [essay 1]; Peacocke 1983, chap. 1; Searle 1981, chap. 2; Harman 1990.
2. Both Armstrong and Pitcher (see n. 1) suggest such reductions.
3. This is, in effect, what Gareth Evans calls "The Generality Constraint" (1982, pp. 100–105) [essay 2, appendix].
4. In *Sense and Content*, Peacocke adopts a conceptualist view of the intentional content of experience, although he also allows for nonintentional qualities of experience, which he calls "sensational properties." In more recent work—for instance, Peacocke 1989c [see also essay 5]—Peacocke recants his earlier conceptualism.
5. Harman (1990) defends a purely intentional theory of perception.
6. For the distinction between direct and factual memory see Malcolm (1963), who talks of "personal" instead of direct memory, and refers to what I have called memory experience as perceptual memory; see also Shoemaker 1984, and Martin and Deutscher 1966.
7. See Malcolm 1963, pp. 208, 217–219. But Malcolm appears to adopt the view that memory experience is simply direct memory plus mental imagery; there could surely be direct memory that was accompanied by imagery without thereby being memory experience in the sense discussed here.
8. Being faithful to a past perception should not be confused with being veridical. A memory can be faithful without being veridical, or veridical without being faithful, where the past perception was itself illusory.
9. Why not say that Mary has some other, nongeometrical concept of a dodecahedron? There is no reason to suppose that she thinks about the twelve-faced dice in terms of their distinctive shape at all, she thinks of them merely as the dice in the game with a certain number of spots. Surely Mary has some shape concepts when she plays the game: she can recognize the difference between an edge and a face, even if she has no words for them. Can't one adequately describe how the scene appears in these terms, without employing the concept of a dodecahedron at all? That must surely be so, but it is not enough to defend (C). The concept of a dodecahedron is still applicable to how she remembers things as being, and so to how things appeared before she had the concept. Although we can describe the difference between how things appear to her when there is a dodecahedron present and how they appear when there is some other complex shape with the same kind of spots in front of her, Mary could not then appreciate the difference between the two situations. There has been a development in her conceptual resources when she comes to appreciate that, but it is nevertheless applicable to earlier experience. Furthermore, one will not always be able to find simple concepts possessed by a thinker that will adequately describe appearances: in the case of some subtle distinctions of shade, the subject will have no concept of that difference before noticing it; so one would not be able to specify appearances finely enough without appealing to the concept in question. (The need to develop these points was pressed on me by an anonymous referee.)
10. There is an additional reason to be suspicious of the claim. Two shades of red may be indistinguishable from each other while one may be distinguishable from a third. At the time of having an experience of one or the other, the subject may not be able to appreciate the difference between them; she would be able to do so only if she also had an experience of the third. On pain of paradox, we cannot insist that the two experiences are not only indistinguishable but have the same content, since the content cannot both be identical with and different from the content of an experience of the third shade.
11. This paper was originally read to the Wolfson Philosophy Society and a seminar in Cambridge. I am grateful to both audiences for comments, and in particular to David Owens, Howard Robinson, Paul Snowdon, Tim Williamson, and the anonymous referees of *The Philosophical Review* for their comments on earlier drafts.

Chapter 12

Perception, Sensation, and Nonconceptual Content (1994)

D. W. Hamlyn

The problems inherent in the relations which exist between perception and the causal processes which underlie it have beset philosophers almost since the beginning of the subject. The earliest philosophical theories of perception seem to have been purely causal, although the conceptions of the causal processes involved do not always seem to have been ours. Empedocles and the Greek Atomists, for example, seem to have thought not that objects simply bring about effects in sense-organs, but that there is some form of interaction between objects and sense-organs, with the result that in vision, for example, what is seen is, so to speak, out there. This, however, may be the result of the realization, first, that what is seen is indeed out there, and second, that how one sees objects is not always as those objects actually are. However that may be, the concentration on simple causal processes has the effect of assimilating perception to sensation. The same is true of the rather more refined account offered by Aristotle, when he says that in perception something, almost certainly the sense-organ, receives the form of the object without receiving its matter. If that is interpreted as a physical/physiological theory, it is more or less intelligible in the case of at least some of the senses, to the extent that it claims that the sense-organ in question takes on some of the properties of the object which stimulates it. It does not go far, however, as an account of perception itself, as an account of what perception involves, beyond the immediate physiological processes. (It says nothing, of course, about what happens physiologically beyond the sense-organ, but that is not what I have in mind.) In consequence, there have been attempts, from Aquinas onwards, to interpret Aristotle as putting forward an account which is more than physiological, as maintaining that the sense-faculty takes on the form of the object. But that seems to me unintelligible, unless it is merely shorthand for some more complicated story.

Representational theories of perception, introduced by Descartes, in effect put consideration of the details of the causal processes involved on one side (although Descartes himself, in his *Dioptric*, I, employed the example of the use of a stick by a blind man to show how movements are transmitted to the brain without

From the *Philosophical Quarterly*, vol. 44, no. 175 (1994), pp. 139–153. Reprinted with the kind permission of the author and Blackwell Publishers.

producing any representations *there*, as distinct from in the mind). There are causal relations, on this view, between objects and our body, including the brain, but as far as the mind is concerned the immediate objects of perception are mental representations. This set off various, impossible, theories of perception which seek to show how our knowledge of physical objects can be derived from what is knowledge of representations alone, with in one case at least, that of Hume, the conclusion that no such account can be given. Despite that, more recent theories of perception based on sense-data are in the same tradition.

But sensations construed as sense-data or perceptual representations seem to die hard, in spite of Thomas Reid's response to Hume, which involved a clear distinction between sensation and perception, according to which sensations have no object other than themselves, while perceptions have physical things as their object and involve also concepts of those things and beliefs about them. A contemporary fashion among philosophers of perception seems, by contrast, to be to maintain that belief or judgment is distinct from perception and that perceptual content either is or can be nonconceptual. Gareth Evans, who was one of the earliest writers along these lines says "When a person perceives something, he receives (or, better, gathers) information about the world. . . . People are, in short and among other things, gatherers, transmitters and storers of information. These platitudes locate perception, communication, and memory in a system—the informational system—which constitutes the substratum of our lives" (1982, p. 122; also see *ibid.* 5.2, 6.3 [essay 2, pp. 48–60], 7.4). He goes on to say that a traditional epistemologist would have recast these platitudes in terms of the concepts of *sensation* and *belief,* and continues with some comments on the difficulties, indeed impossibilities, inherent in the traditional view. The primitive notion is, he says, that of "being in an informational state with such-and-such content" and this is belief independent and nonconceptual. Belief or judgment about objects, when it comes, however, does not arise from any consideration of that informational state, as beliefs in physical objects were, on the traditional view, supposed to arise from consideration of sense-data (*ibid.*, p. 226).

Nevertheless, what emerges from this is a dichotomy between informational states and judgment, the first of which is nonconceptual, while the second of course depends on and involves concepts. It is not entirely clear whether Evans thinks that perceptual content is always nonconceptual, but other philosophers have said as much.[1] What seems to be agreed by all is that reference to nonconceptual content is required in an account of perception. Why? And why is there this sharp dichotomy between perception as involving an informational state and judgment or belief. These two questions in fact come together.

Tim Crane has put forward some special arguments for the thesis that perceptual content is nonconceptual, arising from a consideration of certain unusual experiences (see Crane 1988) [essay 10], including what is called the "Waterfall Illusion," in which the after-image of a waterfall when projected on to a stationary object produces the contradictory appearances of something moving and yet remaining still. (There are other examples of such illusions, not mentioned by Crane, including some produced by the rotating trapezoid devised by Adelbert Ames Jr. and one demonstrated by Richard Gregory of something appearing to pass through an apparently solid object, which thereby appears both solid and transparent.[2]) The argument seems to be that in the case of ordinary conceptual content, there cannot be contradictory instances of such content. Nothing, however, about the concept F implies that something cannot look, seem or appear both F and not-F. The same considerations apply to contraries: something cannot be both red and green all over, but that does not prevent something looking green and looking red all over at the same time. Looking F and looking not-F are not contradictories, and looking red and looking green are not contraries. The fact, therefore, that certain illusions involve contradictory or contrary appearances does not entail that the content of the perceptions in question is not a matter of the concepts applied in those perceptions.

Another argument for a similar conclusion is provided by M. G. F. Martin in his paper "Perception, Concepts and Memory" [essay 11], in which he argues that sometimes it may be right to say of people that it appeared to them that such-and-such, when they lacked the conceptual apparatus necessary for conceiving of the such-and-such. Memory sometimes tells us that we saw something which we were not attending to at the time. Similarly, he argues, memory may tell us that it appeared to us as if p when we lacked at the time the concepts necessary for belief that p, if we have subsequently acquired those concepts. The situation is thus supposed to be like remembering we saw something which we were not aware of seeing at the time because of lack of attention; memory, it is suggested, preserves a trace of the original perception, with which it therefore has a connection. The claim, therefore, is that, whether or not we saw something as F, we could still have discriminated that something, even if not as F, and the later increase in conceptual sophistication might then lead us to judge that we did, in that discrimination, see it as F. Personally, I am inclined to the view that such a judgment should be regarded as valid only, as it were, by courtesy. Even so, the argument sustains at best the conclusion that perceptual experience is not always totally determined by what concepts one has. That conclusion does not seem to be open to dispute for other reasons to which I shall come, but it is in any case unclear what the argument shows about the precise nature in general of perceptual content. There is also involved, it should be noted, the assumption that the proper place for concepts is in the context of belief, and that is one of the main points at issue.

I mention such special arguments which seek to show that the content of perception cannot, or at least cannot always, be conceptual, to get them out of the way. A more important question that remains is what nonconceptual content can be. Rather than getting involved in the intricacies of the analysis of that term, however, it might be better to go back to the analogous idea of an informational state, as invoked by Evans. The trouble, however, is that the term "information" involves certain ambiguities. When Evans introduces the notion of information

(1982, p. 122) he refers to the psychologist J. J. Gibson, who based his theory of perception on the idea of information. Gibson, however, made clear, in spite of claims to the contrary by, e.g., Fred Dretske[3] that he was invoking something like the ordinary notion of information, which he characterized as "information about," as opposed to information considered as structure. What Evans goes on to say makes clear that he has in mind the technical sense of "information" used by cognitive scientists with computational theories of information-processing in mind, according to which, to give a commonly used example and one explicitly invoked by Crane, the rings in a tree's trunk give information about its age simply because there is a law-like connection between the two factors. That information is indeed a function of the tree-trunk's structure.

When our sense-organs are stimulated, the stimulation similarly has structure in that sense, and this would provide information about the source of the stimulation in the way that the rings on a tree-trunk provide information about its age, via a theory about tree growth, to a suitable interpreter. For there is obviously a law-like connection between the structure of the stimulation and its effects on the sense-organs. But we who perceive are not the interpreters in question, since when we perceive we normally have no concern with what is going on in our sense-organs. Evans is right in saying that the state of our sense-organs, considered as an informational state, is not what enters into any beliefs about the world that result from perception and is not that to which we apply concepts in the process. Hence the information processing that takes place, if any does take place, must not be at the personal level, and may conceivably be assimilated to what takes place when a computer processes information fed into it. I put the matter in that somewhat cagey way because, although it is the current orthodoxy that that is how it is, it does not have to be like that; it depends on whether the brain does in fact work in a computational way.

However that may be, if, given this sense of information, the stimulation of our sense-organs produces an informational state—i.e., a state capable of providing information to a suitable processor—the content of that information, if we must speak like that, is not a matter of any concepts possessed by the processor. Just as, to use Gibson's way of putting it, the information in question amounts to structure, so does the content of that information. If the theory is correct that such information is processed in our perceptual systems by mechanisms which work on computational principles, then that theory will provide a much more complicated and perhaps more adequate account of the causal processes which make perception possible than was once available. No doubt any computational processes involved will themselves be extremely complex, as the theory of perception produced by David Marr (the current favorite in the literature) indicates (Marr 1982). Indeed, Crane invokes that complexity as a reason for rejecting the idea that the perceiver applies concepts to informational states in order that they may have conceptual content—but there is every reason to reject such an idea anyway. In perception concepts are applied to objects, and, in my view, perception always involves concepts. Perception is concept-dependent, and what concepts we have may affect how things look to us.

It does not do so always, however. To give the most notorious or well-known example, in the Müller-Lyer Illusion the lines with arrow-heads on them are likely to look of different length whatever we think about them (which is not to say that we cannot bring it about by considering them in certain ways that they look the same). Those who espouse the idea of perception involving nonconceptual content are likely to appeal to such examples, and they indeed do so, in order to make the point that perception is or can be independent of beliefs. But that is not to say that they are completely independent of concepts, unless some additional argument can be supplied to show that the having of concepts is restricted to beliefs, and that, of course, is the very point at issue. When I say that the lines in the Müller-Lyer Illusion are likely to look of different length whatever we think of them, therefore, I do not mean that they will look of different length if we have no concept of length, if we have no understanding at all of what length is.

It may be objected that, nevertheless, the representations that anyone has when looking at the two lines will be different, and that that is a function of whatever processes take place when the information derived from the situation is processed. That presupposes that it is right to speak of representations in this context; all that is clear is that the patterns of retinal excitation produced by looking at the two lines complete with their arrowheads will be different, and that that has something to do with the illusion. A more traditional way of putting something like the point is to say that illusions like the Müller-Lyer Illusion are purely sensory; they are a product solely of whatever takes place in the sense-organs and subsequent sensory apparatus. The question then arises, however, how one knows this, and it has to be noted that Richard Gregory, for one, has suggested that the prevalence of the illusion has to do with the fact that our environment is one in which corners (the arrow-heads if seen as representations, in the ordinary sense, of three-dimensional objects) are the order of the day (Gregory 1966, chap. 9). (Illusions of this kind are said to be less prevalent among people who live in round huts or houses!) One way to try to settle the issue is to try to see what happens when the influence of experience is minimal, so that there is as much as possible a simple reaction to the environment which is not affected by beliefs or ways of thinking about things. Piaget and his associates, who carried out a welter of experiments with young children on phenomena of this kind, came up with results to the effect that the illusion is at its most extreme in children of the very earliest age that makes investigation with them possible (Piaget 1969; see Hamlyn 1990). He concluded that sensory mechanisms are naturally distorting and only intelligence enables us to overcome that.

Even if such a view, extreme as it is if put in those terms, were true, it would show nothing about any representations which we have when using our senses, and which are independent of any concepts which we have. If one waives objections to the whole idea of representations as constituents of the perceptual process (objections which are, to my mind, considerable [see Hamlyn 1990, chap. 3]), then I take it that what is presupposed is that, when we perceive the world, there is presented to the senses a structured array (what Peacocke has recently, for example in "Scenarios, Concepts and Perception" [essay 5], his contribution to the book edited by Crane mentioned above, called a *scenario*). It is inferred by those who wish to speak of representations that we have a representation of this, independent of concepts, and that its structure affects the form that such a representation takes. One consideration which is taken as favoring this idea (see, e.g., Evans 1982, pp. 154–155) [essay 2, pp. 49–50] is something which I referred to above—that there can be simple reactions to features of the environment, especially spatial features. One can react to sounds, for example, turning to their supposed point of origin, without having to work out where they are coming from, and without having any general conception of the spatial setup. Some such reactions do not appear to be learnt. A reaction of this kind, it has to be said, does not necessarily amount to a perception of the location of a sound, any more than a scratching reaction to an itch in some part of one's body amounts to a perception of that part of one's body. If the reaction were a form of behavior, possibly intentional, that would be another matter; for in that case the behavior would take place in the light of a perception, in the light of where one feels the itch to be. But a bare reaction may be more like a reflex, and reflex reactions take place without any perception of what produces them.

Could the possibility of a bare reaction, however, justify one in speaking of a representation of a spatial layout, even if not one which is mediated by concepts, by a concept of space or a concept of a form of spatial arrangement? What is presented to the senses is structured, certainly, and our sense-organs admit of a structured form of stimulation. Equally the bodily sensations that we have form part of a structure, in a way that has seemed to some to justify speaking of a body-image. Something similar may apply to forms of perception of other kinds. At all events, it is not the case that the perception of spatial or quasi-spatial arrangements is a product of a temporally serial succession of unstructured or atomic perceptions, as has sometimes been suggested in the history of the subject. But none of this is an issue unless and until it really is perception that one is talking about. It is conceivable that an organism might have the structured sensations which I mentioned just now, and react to some element in that structure in the way that a dog reacts to an itch or turns its head in the direction of a sound, without this amounting to perception. If that is the case, there are no grounds for saying that what occurs constitutes a representation of the situation in the organism's environment, let alone a representation which is independent of concepts.

The most that we are justified in believing is that the process of the stimulation of our sense organs is structured in a way that could lead us to say that any information-processing system that exists in our nervous system would be provided with sufficient information thereby to function in relation to the spatial and other characteristics of the world. But that, as I said earlier, is simply a more complex and, no doubt, more adequate account of the causal processes involved than was once available. This leaves unanswered several questions about how all this contributes to the total perceptual experience. What, for example, is it for the situation before our eyes to look such-and-such to us? It is not the case that something's looking *F* to us is for us to believe that it is *F*, as the example of the Müller-Lyer Illusion showed. Moreover, even if it were the case that we are inclined to believe, in that illusion, that the lines are of different length (and I doubt if we are always so inclined), or even if it is the case that we should so believe did we not know that the lines are in fact of the same length, such inclinations to believe and such possible beliefs need explanations. The most obvious explanation is that we are so inclined or would so believe because that is how the lines look.

The question that now arises, then, is what it is for something to look *F*, or, to put the matter in terms of what I believe is, in one sense of the words, its converse, what it is for us to see something as *F*. I say "in one sense of the words," because much has been written about what Wittgenstein had to say about seeing an aspect, in terms of which seeing something as such-and-such involves the imagination.[4] I am not at present considering these imaginative kinds of seeing-as, important though they are for a full account of perception and its various possibilities.[5] I am concerned simply with such things as seeing the grass as green, when indeed it is green and there is no call for any special attitude to it. As I said earlier, one could not see it as green if one had no understanding of what it is for things to be green, and there are interesting questions about the role of experience in relation to that understanding and about the differences in this case from what is involved in seeing whatever it is as *grass*. That is to say that there are interesting questions about the kinds of concepts that may be involved in seeing-as and their relation to experience. It is clear that the concept of grass is less intimately related to visual experience than is the concept of green (see Hamlyn 1969; see also Hamlyn 1971, pp. 180ff. and Peacocke 1983, chaps. 1 and 2). There are also interesting questions about how far from experience a concept may be and yet it be appropriate to say that one is seeing something in its terms. Can one, as Aristotle said one might, see something as sweet? Surely yes, although the phenomenon requires an explanation. Can one see something as composed of a myriad of moving molecules? Perhaps, but the perception would be a very refined one, depending on complex and detailed knowledge of physics, which would have to be related to experience. Other cases would raise similar issues.

What is clear, however, is that, as I said earlier, one's experience of seeing something *may* be considerably affected by what conceptual understanding one brings to the experience. Alan Millar, who has contributed much of interest to discussion of matters in this area (see Millar 1985–1986, 1991a and 1991b), has put forward what he calls the "Detachability Thesis," to the effect that the phenomenal character of an experience is detachable from its conceptual content. Thus, to use his example, if you are running your hand over the wool side of a sheepskin rug, the tactile experience might be of the same type whether or not you had the concepts of, say, smoothness and silkiness, and thus whether or not your experience had the content provided by those concepts. This is to say, in other words, that there is a character of a perceptual experience, its phenomenal character, which is independent of the concepts which are brought to bear, even if there is also a sense in which the total experience may be transformed by the bringing to bear of those concepts. Is Millar's thesis true? I do not think that it is, not at any rate if expressed in his terms.

In "Concepts, Experience and Inference" (p. 496), Millar says that "the Detachability Thesis meshes happily with a certain picture of the relation between cognition and perception," according to which "the phenomenal character of our sensory experience is determined by the interaction of incoming stimuli with our various sensory systems." He claims that the thesis is compatible both with the fact that "the character of our experience depends a great deal on what we do" and with the fact that past experience may affect, causally and not through conceptual capacities, present experience (matters on which, as I have tried to make clear in my *In and Out of the Black Box*, there is much more to be said). Then he says, "The role of conceptual capacities in perception is to extract information from experiences in a form in which it can be stored and retrieved and fed into our thinking. It is not to form the experiences themselves." How is this to be squared with the fact that a new realization, a new way of thinking, a new application of a concept, can totally transform a perceptual experience? The experience derived from running one's hand over the wool side of a sheepskin rug might be totally transformed by the realization that that is what it is, and if one had no concepts of smoothness and silkiness what on earth would the experience be like? It might be replied that we have here an equivocation over the term "experience." Certainly the term is an ambiguous one in all sorts of ways, but the question at issue now is whether there is any place for the term at all when concepts are excluded. This is the same as the question whether there actually is anything to be called the *phenomenal character* of a perceptual experience, in the sense which Millar has in mind.

I have myself pointed out on several occasions in the past (see, e.g., 1983, pp. 25ff., 63ff., and 1990, pp. 85ff.) that in the case of an instance of tactile perception, such as the one that Millar seems to have in mind, it is possible and reasonable to distinguish between the having of certain sensations in our finger-tips and the perception of the so-called tactile properties of the object felt. There can indeed be a vacillation between the two, depending on the direction of our attention. It would be entirely reasonable to assert that the sensations, the sensational experiences if you will, remain the same whatever concepts of tactile properties one has and applies in the course of a tactile experience. The sensations are in that sense detachable from the concepts which determine the content of the perceptual experience. But that is not Millar's version of the detachability thesis, and his version is influenced, I suggest, at any rate in part, by the wish to preserve something of the view that perception involves states the content of which is nonconceptual, states which have what Millar himself calls "informational content" as opposed to "conceptual content." As I have tried to make clear, I do not wish to deny that there is a sense of "information," the one involved in information-processing theory, the one that Gibson called "structure," in which it is reasonable to say that in perception the sense organs receive information. But in that sense of "information" what happens has no necessary connection with experience, whereas, by contrast, sensations have much to do with the perceptual experience and give it the character it has. (In discussing these issues in the past I have spoken of the sensations "coloring" the total perceptual experience, but that is of course no more than a metaphor, and whether it is a helpful metaphor I leave it to others to decide.)

Another point is that it is quite wrong to say, as Millar does, in a sentence that I quoted earlier, that it is the role of conceptual capacities in perception "to extract information from experiences in a form in which it can be stored and retrieved and fed into our thinking." First, this implicitly gives credence to the acceptance of a dichotomy between informational states (which is what the experiences must come to on this view) and thinking or belief, a dichotomy which I noted earlier as espoused by other philosophers in this area. Another straw in the wind here is Millar's willingness to accept the idea of representational content, and to define it in terms of the idea that the content of an experience is that p if and only if in response to the experience "the subject would believe that p in the absence of countervailing considerations" (1991a, p. 495). (Compare the idea that what it is in the Müller-Lyer Illusion for the lines to look of different length is that we should believe them to be of different length, did we not know that they are in fact of the same length—were there not countervailing considerations.) But the exercise of concepts in perception is not, or not just, a matter of abstracting information from experiences which can then affect our beliefs. Perception itself, without reference to beliefs, involves concept-use.

Second, that concept-use involves the application of concepts to the objects of perception, not to experiences. There is of course a sense of "abstracting information from experiences" in which the phrase might be used to describe a form of more or less self-conscious consideration of the experiences which we are having (where by "experiences" I do not mean sensations, but the total perceptual experience which already involves concept-use). Such a consideration is certainly one way in which our conceptual capacities may be exercised; it might have, for example, an aesthetic point. But that is not the most straightforward and ordinary way in which concept-use has a place in perception. In the ordinary way our consciousness is directed on to an object (involving what commonly accepted but perhaps misleading jargon calls "intentionality"). Concepts give that consciousness a focus by bringing the objects within a form of understanding, without which their status as objects would be formal only, and without content. But the total perceptual experience must involve more than that, since there are forms of concept-mediated consciousness of objects which are not cases of perception;

thinking of something would be a case in point. One additional factor is the occurrence of sensations, which make the consciousness sensory and give it the sensory character of which I have already spoken.

There are other things too which might be mentioned in this context. One is that the form of consciousness which contributes to the total perceptual experience, along with concepts and sensations, involves what one might call, to use another metaphor, a point of view. In the case of vision that is scarcely a metaphor, but there is something like it in the case of other senses too. On occasion, reports (perhaps quite bogus reports, but no matter) have been given of people who, it is said, are able to tell the color of an object by passing their hands over it. Of course, certain things might suggest that the discriminative powers involved depended on inferences. On being asked to describe the experiences involved the people in question might give an account which indicates that their hands were sensitive to certain properties of objects, say their temperature, which had, at any rate in these cases, some correlation with color. But suppose that it was not like that, suppose that the description offered was one which genuinely involved looks, not the appearances which go with some other actual or hypothetical sensory modality. Would not the description have to be concerned with looks which are such that they are as if derived from eyes in one's hands? Without necessarily going so far as to say that such people had eyes in their hands, it would surely be the case that the looks of the objects would be ones which are derived from a sense organ in the position of the hands. The looks would be *from* there. The complexities of that "point of view," given our capacity for moving our hands relative to the rest of the body, would be extreme. But that is how it is already with respect to touch, except that, touch being a contact sense, the field of tactile perception is much more limited than is the case with vision, so that the total information available by its means is correspondingly less. Perceptual access to such information is, however, always relative to what is in the case of vision literally a point of view and what is in the case of the other senses analogous to that. Moreover, that point of view is alterable by us to one extent or another, so that the information available to us through it depends on us, and is not simply a matter of what is presented to the sense organs.

Given all this, let us return to the question with which I opened, about the relation of perception to the causal processes which underlie it. I have emphasized that the story about information processing and the setting up of informational states simply makes possible a more sophisticated account of the causal processes which perception involves than was once available. To hold that these processes are computational is to make vast assumptions (although the validity of those assumptions is an empirical matter), but it is undeniable that they lead to the setting up of informational states in the sense that, as it is sometimes put, they constitute codes for a suitable interpreter, because of law-like connections that exist between the states and the stimulation that the environment provides. However, that interpreter is not us. The only interpreting we do in this connection is of what we see of the world, not of states set up in parts of our bodies. It is in fact not just chance that the word "information" appears both in the claim that perception provides us with information about the world and in the claim that the processes involved have to do with the processing of information; for, if I am right, the second use of "information" is parasitic on the first (see Hamlyn 1990, pp. 32–33). So the processes in question are simply some of those which enable us to derive information about the world by perception. Moreover, more is required than causal processes of this kind. Purely causal theories of perception, of which the information-processing theory is an instance, founded on several grounds, including the facts, mentioned already implicitly, that perception depends on what we *do* in relation to the world and that we have *to learn* to perceive things as such-and-suches, which is to say that we have to learn what concepts are relevant and how things that we perceive fall under them.

The question still remains what the relation is between the causal processes involved and the details of the perceptual experience. One obvious answer to that question is that they simply explain them causally and, to follow the general line taken by John Searle in his recent book *The Rediscovery of the Mind*, biologically. If one were really to follow Searle in this respect, the conclusion to draw is that there is no more to be said. Is that so? Yes and no. Yes, in that when one has spelled out the causal processes there is nothing more *of that kind* to mention. No, in that nothing in the story about information processing will enable us to understand completely why perceptual experience takes the form that it does. One aspect of that, the most general one, has to do with problems about the body-mind relation, problems, if they are that, about what there is in bodily processes which can produce states of consciousness. That they do so is clear, and some would hold that that is all there is to it, but there remains the question of what intelligible relation can be thought to link states of such radically different kinds. However, that is not, arguably, a point about the form that experience takes, but one about the nature of experience itself, in the most general sense.

Another aspect of the issue, the one with which I have been primarily concerned, is more relevant in that respect. This has to do with the gap that exists between a causal story, of whatever degree of sophistication, and the story about what it is to perceive things as such-and-suches. That latter story, which is, in part at least, one about concept-use, is not the whole story about perceptual experience, since the facts about sensation and sensory consciousness have to be reckoned with as well, and these facts, as we have seen, sometimes affect how things appear to us, irrespective of what concepts we have. Moreover, there are other factors, such as attention, imagination, and aspects of our agency, which affect how and whether we see things. But concept-use is essential to our epistemic commerce with the world, and this is understandable, since, whatever else concepts are, in having the concept of X we know something of what it is for something to be X. Concept-use may not be essential to every reaction that we make to the world, but, to the extent that perception provides us with knowledge of the world, as it clearly does, perception depends on concepts. Moreover, while to see something as X is not necessarily to know that that thing is X, for the perception may be illusory, we could not see it as X unless we knew something about what being an X amounts to. On the other hand, while knowledge provides the context in which all concept-use is to be understood, and affects perception in the different ways in which perception involves knowledge, belief has no special claim to be the place for concept-use. Those who think otherwise on this last point, as do those who insist on a dichotomy between perception and belief, reserving concepts for the latter, fail to take account of the richness of our experience.

Notes

1. See Davies 1991, p. 462 and Crane 1992. Christopher Peacocke has, in various publications since his *Sense and Content*, given increasing support to the thesis.
2. For Ames' rotating trapezoid, see my *The Psychology of Perception*, p. 103, and Kent Dallet, "Transactional and Probabilistic Functionalism," pp. 387–397, esp. pp. 390ff. The example demonstrated by Richard Gregory involves a three-dimensional construction of an "impossible object," the Penrose triangle, which has a gap in it so that it looks solid from a "critical position," but enables another object to appear to pass through it when it is in fact passed through the gap. For an illustration of the construction see *Handbook of Perception*, p. 265.
3. Dretske 1981, pp. 255–256 [see also essay 1, p. 39, n. 7]. See, against this, my *In and Out of the Black Box*, p. 72 and notes 5 and 6 there, with a reference to an earlier writing of mine on Gibson's use of the concept of information.
4. See what Wittgenstein 1951, p. 200, about seeing a triangle as standing on its base or hanging from its apex, as a mountain, as a wedge, and so on.
5. I ignore here the fact that Kant and, following him, Strawson have seen imagination as having a place in all applications of concepts to particulars in perception. See Kant on the doctrine of the schematism and P. F. Strawson, "Imagination and Perception."

Chapter 13

A Representational Theory of Pains and Their Phenomenal Character (1997)

Michael Tye

The fundamental assumption of cognitive psychology is that the mind is a *representational system* which mediates between sensory inputs and behavioral outputs. The primary task for the cognitive psychologist is one of explaining how the various cognitive capacities operate by reference to the structure of the salient parts of this representational system. The explanations offered are both functional and decompositional: they decompose the relevant capacities into their basic representational components and show how those components function together to produce the capacities. Theories are evaluated by how well they account for the behavior observed in psychological experiments and, at the lowest level, by how well they fit with knowledge gleaned from neurophysiology about the physical bases of the capacities.

Philosophers have usually assumed that pain cannot lie within the domain of cognitive psychology. Pains, it has been supposed, are not like images or memories or visual percepts: they have no representational content. So, there can be no explanation of the desired sort. To understand the various facets of pain, we need to look elsewhere, perhaps to the realm of neurophysiology. Cognitive psychology cannot help us. This, I now believe, is a mistake: pains *do* have representational content. So, the view that pain is not a proper object of study for cognitive psychology is not well founded.

My discussion begins with an old objection to the token identity theory in connection with after-images, and a modem response to it which has become widely accepted. This response, I maintain, is unsatisfactory, as it stands. But, with one key revision, it is, I believe, defensible, and it has ramifications for our understanding of pain. In particular, it points to the conclusion that pains have representational content, as does at least one other facet of our everyday conception of pain. In the third section of the paper, I consider the question of what sorts of representations pains are most plausibly taken to be. Are they sentences in an inner language, like beliefs and desires, on the usual computational conception of the

From *The Nature of Consciousness*, N. Block, O. Flanagan, and G. Guzeleve (eds.), pp. 329–340, Cambridge, MA: The MIT Press, 1997. Reprinted with the kind permission of the author and The MIT Press. An earlier version of the paper was published in *Philosophical Perspectives*, vol. 9, J. Tomberlin (ed.) (Northridge, CA: Ridgeview Publishing).

latter states? Or are they representations of a different sort? I suggest that a sententential approach is difficult to reconcile with some of the neuropsychological data on pain, and I make an alternative proposal. Pains, I propose, are representations of the same general sort as mental images: they are arrays to which descriptive labels are appended. So, pain, I urge, is a proper object of study of cognitive psychology. In the final section, I take up some questions concerning the phenomenal character of pain.

I

In the 1950s J. J. C. Smart (1959) raised the following objection to the identity theory for sensations: After-images are sometimes yellowy-orange; brain processes cannot be yellowy-orange. So after-images are not brain processes. The reply that Smart himself made to the objection was to deny that after-images exist, there really being, in Smart's view, only experiences of *having* after-images, which are not themselves yellowy-orange.

Another less radical response is available on behalf of the identity theory. It is on this response that I wish to focus here. Why not say that in predicating color words of images we are not attributing to them the very same properties that we attribute to external objects via our use of color language. So, after-images are not literally green or blue in the way that grass or the sky have one or the other of these features. Now it is no longer obviously true that brain processes cannot be yellowy-orange in the relevant sense.

The obvious problem that this response faces is that of explaining how it is that color vocabulary is applied at all to after-images, given that they do not really have the appropriate colors. One solution proposed by Ned Block is to say that color words are used elliptically for expressions like "real-blue-representing . . . real-green-representing" and so on, in connection with images generally (Block 1983, esp. p. 518). In my view, this solution has a number of important virtues.[1] For one thing, brain processes can certainly represent colors. So, the identity theory is no longer threatened. For another, as Block has noted (Block 1983, pp. 516–517), terms like "loud" and "high-pitched" are standardly applied directly to oscilloscope readings used in connection with the graphical representations of sounds. In this context, these terms evidently do not name real sounds made by the readings. One possibility, then, is that they pick out representational properties such as loud-representing and high-pitched-representing. If this is so, then there already exists an established usage of terms that conforms to the one alleged to obtain in the case of color terms and after-images.

There is a serious difficulty, however. Mental images are not literally square any more than they are literally blue. So, extending the above proposal to shape, we get that a blue, square after-image is simply an after-image that is square-representing and also blue-representing. But intuitively this seems too weak. Surely, a blue, square image cannot represent different things as blue *and* square.

Unfortunately, nothing in the above proposal rules this out. "Blue", then, in application to after-images, does not mean "blue-representing." Likewise "square."

This difficulty is not peculiar to images. Precisely the same problem can be raised in connection with oscilloscope readings. The way out, I suggest, is to appreciate that there is nothing elliptical about the meanings of terms like "blue" or "loud" in the above contexts. Instead it is the contexts themselves that need further examination. Let me explain.

The contexts "Hopes for an F" and "Hallucinates a G" are typically intensional. Thus, I can hope for eternal life and hallucinate a pink elephant, even though there are no such things. Similarly, I can hope for eternal life without hoping for eternal boredom, even if in reality the two are the same. It seems evident that the terms substituting for F and G in these contexts retain their usual meanings. The above peculiarities are due to the fact that hoping and hallucinating are representational states, and to the special character of representation itself.

Now precisely the same peculiarities are present in the case of the context "an F image," where F is a color or shape term. Thus, in a world in which nothing is really triangular, I can still have a triangular image. Also, if I have a red image, intuitively it does not follow that I have an image the color of most fire engines even given that most fire engines are red. The explanation, I suggest, is straightforward: an F image is an image that *represents that something is F.*[2]

Likewise, an F, G image is an image *which represents that something is* both F and G. My suggestion, then, is that there is nothing elliptical or peculiar about the meanings of the terms "F" and "G" in the context "An F, G image." Rather the context itself is an intensional one, having a logical structure which reflects the representational character of images generally.

It may still be wondered why we say that the image itself is F and G, for example, blue and square. This is, I suggest, part of a much broader usage. Frequently when we talk of representations, both mental and non-mental, within science and in ordinary life, we save breath by speaking as if the representations themselves have the properties of the things they represent. In such cases, in saying of a representation that it is F, what we mean is that it represents that something is F. So, when it is said of some given oscilloscope reading that it is loud and high-pitched, what is being claimed is that loud and high-pitched are features that the reading represents some sound as having. "Loud" and "high-pitched" mean what they normally do here. The context itself is intensional.

The above proposal solves the problem of the blue, square image. Here the image represents that something is both blue and square, not merely that something is blue *and* that something is square.[3]

The claim that after-images are representational, I might add, does not entail or presuppose that creatures cannot have after-images unless they also have the appropriate concepts (at least as "concept" is frequently understood). Having the concept F requires, on some accounts, having the ability to use the linguistic term "F" correctly. On other accounts, concept possession requires the ability to represent in thought and belief that something falls under the concept. But after-images, like other perceptual sensations, are not themselves thoughts or beliefs; and they certainly do not demand a public language, They are, if you like, non-doxastic or nonconceptual representations.

The broad picture I have here very briefly is this. Processes operating upon prox-imal stimuli generate certain sorts of visual representations via mechanical pro-cedures. Categorizations of various sorts occur along the way. Visual sensations are representations that form the outputs of this early modular processing, and stand ready to produce conceptual responses via the action of higher-level cogni-tive processing of one sort or another. So, visual sensations feed into the concep-tual system, without themselves being a part of that system.

In admitting that after-images are nonconceptual representations, I am not thereby granting that they do not really have *intentional* content, that they are rep-resentations of a nonintentional sort. In my view, intentionality does not require concepts. As I use the term "intentionality," the key features are representation (and hence the possibility of *mis*representation) along with the possibility of substitution failures in the associated linguistic contexts. These features, I have argued, are present in the case of after-images. So, after-images are intentional. Those philosophers who want to insist that there cannot be full-blooded inten-tionality without concepts (or that intentionality is restricted to the central exec-utive) are entitled to their use of the term. But any disagreement here is, I suggest, purely verbal. Nothing of substance hangs upon which usage is adopted.

We are now ready to turn to the case of pain.

II

It is often supposed that terms applied to pain that also apply to physical objects do not have their ordinary meanings. Ned Block, who takes this view, says the following:

> There is some reason to think that there is a systematic difference in meaning between certain predicates applied to physical objects and the same predi-cates applied to mental particulars. Consider a nonimagery example: the predicate ____ in ____. This predicate appears in each premise and the con-clusion of this argument:
>
> The pain is in my fingertip.
>
> The fingertip is in my mouth.
>
> Therefore, the pain is in my mouth.
>
> This argument is valid for the "in" of spatial enclosure. . . . since "in" in this sense is transitive. But suppose that the two premises are true in their *ordi-nary* meanings. . . . The conclusion obviously does not follow, so we must

conclude that "in" is not used in the spatial enclosure sense in all three state-ments. It certainly seems plausible that "in" as applied in locating pains differs in meaning systematically from the standard spatial enclosure sense. (Block 1983, p. 517)

This seems to me quite wrong. There is no more reason to adopt the strange position that "in" does not mean spatial enclosure in connection with pain than there is to say that "orange" in connection with images has a special meaning. With the collapse of the latter view, the former becomes unstable. And the infer-ence Block cites does *not* establish his claim. To see this, consider the following inference:

> I want to be in City Hall
> City Hall is in a ghetto
> Therefore, I want to be in a ghetto.

The term "in" has the same meaning in both premises and the conclusion. But the argument is invalid: I might want to be in City Hall to listen to a particular speech, say, without thereby wanting to be in a ghetto. The same is true, I suggest, in the case of Block's example, and the explanation is the same. In both the first premise and the conclusion, the term "in" appears in an intensional context. Just as when we say that an image is blue, we are saying that it represents that something is blue, so when we say that a pain is in my fingertip, we are saying that it repre-sents that something is in my fingertip.

It is perhaps worth noting here that the invalidity of the inference involving pain has nothing to do with the fact that mouths are cavities of a certain sort, and hence items whose ontological status might itself be questioned. If I have a pain in my fingertip, and I slit open a small portion of my leg, into which I then thrust my finger, still it does not follow that I have a pain in my leg. Suppose, for example, that my leg has been anesthetized. In this case, I feel a pain in my finger, but not in my leg.

Nor does it help to say that what the inference failure really shows is that pains themselves are ontologically suspect. For even if it were true that there are no pains, only people who are pained, still this gives us no account of why the infer-ence fails. After all, if "in" means inside, and I am pained in my fingertip, then I am also pained in my mouth, assuming my fingertip is in my mouth.

That there is a hidden intensionality in statements of pain location is confirmed by our talk of pains in phantom limbs. We allow it to be true on occasion that people are subject to pains in limbs that no longer exist. How can this be? Answer: You can have a pain in your left leg even though you have no left leg, just as you can search for the Fountain of Youth. Again the context is intensional: specifically, you have a pain that represents that something is in your left leg.[4]

Of course, there is some temptation to say that if you do not have a left leg, then you cannot really have a pain in it. But that is no problem for my proposal.

For there is a *de re* reading of the context, namely that to have a pain in your left leg is for your left leg to be such that you have a pain in *it*. Now a left leg is required.

But does not a pain in the leg represent more than just that something is in the leg? To answer this question, it is necessary to make some more general remarks about pain. To have a pain is to feel a pain, and to feel a pain is to experience pain. Thus, if I have a pain, I undergo a token experience of a certain sort. This token experience is, I suggest, the particular pain I have.

The identification of pains with token experiences explains why no one else could feel the *particular* pain I am feeling, and moreover why pains are necessarily owned by *someone* or other. Token experiences are events (in the broad sense, which includes token states), and, in general, events are individuated in part via the objects which undergo them. So, laughs cannot exist unowned, and neither can screams. Likewise, killings, births, and explosions. In each of these cases, there must be a subject for the event: a killer, a creature that is born, an object that explodes. Moreover, the subject is essentially related to the event. No one else can die my death or laugh my laugh, although, of course, someone else can certainly undergo qualitatively very similar deaths or laughs.

Now pain experiences, if they are anywhere, are in the head. But in the case of a pain in the leg, what the pain experience tracks, when everything is functioning normally, is tissue damage in the leg. So, a pain in the leg, I suggest, is a token sensory experience which represents that something in the leg is damaged.[5]

So far I have said nothing directly about the painfulness of pains. How is this feature of pains to be accounted for within the above proposal? To begin with, it should be noted that we often speak of bodily damage as painful. When it is said that a cut in a finger or a bum or a bruise is painful or hurts, what is meant is (roughly) that it is *causing* a feeling, namely the very feeling the person is undergoing, and that this feeling elicits an immediate dislike for itself together with anxiety about, or concern for, the state of the bodily region where the disturbance feels located.

Of course, pains do not themselves normally cause feelings that cause dislike: they *are* such feelings, at least in typical cases. So, pains are not painful in the above sense. Still, they are painful in a slightly weaker sense: they typically elicit the *cognitive* reactions described above.[6] Moreover, when we introspect our pains we are aware of their sensory contents as painful. This is why if I have a pain in my leg I am intuitively aware of something in my leg as painful (and not in my head, which is where, in my view, the experience itself is). My pain represents damage in my leg, and I then cognitively classify that damage as painful (via the application of the concept *painful* in introspection).

So, in normal circumstances, a person who has a pain in a leg and who reports that something in her leg is painful is not under any sort of illusion. But a man who reports to his doctor that he has a pain in his left arm is in a different situation, if it is discovered that the real cause of his pain lies in his heart. Such a man has a pain in his left arm—he undergoes a sensory experience that represents to him damage there—but there really is nothing wrong *in his left arm*. What is painful is a disturbance happening in his heart.

There is one objection worth mentioning here. Perhaps it will be said that a person who experiences a pain in a certain bodily part need not be aware *that* there is such-and-such tissue damage inside the relevant part. Such a proposal is too complicated to fit the phenomenology of pain experiences (or many such experiences).

This objection is not compelling. Pains, in my view, are *sensory* representations of tissue damage. To feel a pain, one need not have the resources to conceptualize what the pain represents (see note 6). One need not be able to say or think that such-and-such tissue damage is occurring. Still, the content of the pertinent sensory representation is what gives the pain its phenomenal character.

In my view, the intentionalist treatment I have proposed can be extended to pains of more specific sorts. A twinge of pain is a pain that represents a mild, brief disturbance. A throbbing pain is one that represents a rapidly pulsing disturbance. Aches represent disorders that occur *inside* the body, rather than on the surface. These disorders are represented as having volume, as gradually beginning and ending, as increasing in severity and then slowly fading away (see Armstrong 1962). The volumes so represented are not represented as precise or sharply bounded. This is why aches do not feel to have precise locations, unlike pricking pains, for example. A stabbing pain is one that represents sudden damage over a particular well-defined bodily region. This region is represented as having volume (rather than being two-dimensional), as being the shape of something sharp-edged and pointed (like that of a dagger).[7] In the case of a pricking pain, the relevant damage is represented as having a sudden beginning and ending on the surface or just below, and as covering a very tiny area. A racking pain is one that represents that the damage involves the stretching of internal body parts (e.g., muscles).

In each of these cases, the subject of the pain undergoes a sensory representation of a certain sort of bodily disturbance. The disturbances vary with the pains. Consider, for example, a pricking pain in the leg. Here, it seems phenomenologically undeniable that pricking is experienced *as* a feature tokened within the leg, and not as an intrinsic feature of the experience itself. What is experienced as being pricked is a part of the surface of the leg. This is nicely accounted for by the above proposal. It should also be noted that since pricking pains do not represent pins, my account does not have the implausible consequence that creatures who live in worlds without pins cannot have pricking sensations or that in these worlds creatures undergoing such sensations are misrepresenting what is going on in them.

Pains, I conclude, like after-images, have representational content. Unlike images, however, they have bodily locations (in the representational sense I have elucidated).[8] So, although pains, in my view, are really constituted by physical processes in the head, it is also true to say that they can occur anywhere in the body.[9]

III

The language of thought hypothesis is an empirical hypothesis about how the representational contents of mental states are, in fact, encoded in the head. It is not an *a priori* philosophical analysis. So, it is not intended to cover the contents of mental states of all actual and possible creatures. In its most general form, it concerns the coding of *all* actual mental contents. The basic thesis, stemming from the computer model of mind, is that such contents are encoded in symbol-structures in an inner language.

In the case of the so-called propositional attitudes—that is, those mental states like belief and desire whose contents are standardly expressed in "that" clauses—it has typically been supposed that the relevant symbol-structures are sentences (Fodor 1975, 1978). The apparent need to acknowledge inner sentences in an account of the propositional attitudes (hereafter the PAs) derives from several different sources.

To begin with, the PAs are systematic: there are intrinsic connections between certain thoughts. Consider, for example, the thought that the boy is chasing the dog and the thought that the dog is chasing the boy. Anyone who has the capacity to think the former thought also has the capacity to think the latter and vice versa. Secondly, the PAs are productive: we have the capacity, it seems, to think indefinitely many thoughts and to think thoughts we have never thought before. The PAs are also fine-grained: I can think that you know something important without thinking that you justifiably and truly believe something important, even if the correct analysis of "know" is "justifiably and truly believe." Finally, the PAs have truth-values: my belief that the English pound is worth less than two years ago in dollars is either true or false.

Facts exactly parallel to these obtain in the case of sentences in public languages. According to adherents to the language of thought hypothesis, these parallels are best explained by supposing that the PAs themselves have a sentence-like structure.[10]

What sorts of representations, then, are pains? Are they too inner sentences? It may be tempting to suppose that if they have representational content, as I have urged, and if the language of thought hypothesis is true, then they *must* be sentences. This would be much too quick, however. For a commitment to an inner language within which cognition occurs is not a commitment to sentences in each and every case of mental representation. After all, computers—symbol manipulators, par excellence—operate on all sorts of symbol structures (e.g., lists, sentences, arrays); and, to mention one example, there are well-known theories of mental imagery which fall within the computational approach, but which reject the thesis that images are sentences.[11] Moreover, it is certainly not obvious that the language of thought hypothesis in its unrestricted form is true. Perhaps some mental representations are not coded in our heads in linguistic symbols at all.

A simple appeal to the general language of thought hypothesis does not justify the claim that pains are sentences. Do the considerations adduced above in connection with the PAs support the sententialist view of pains? It might be held that, to some extent, they do. There are some systematic connections between pains: the capacity to feel a burning pain in the leg and (at the same or another time) a stinging pain in the arm seem connected to the capacity to feel a stinging pain in the leg and a burning pain in the arm. Moreover, if pains are representations, then they can misrepresent.[12] So, there is a sense in which some pains may be characterized as false: what they represent is not, in fact, the case.

It must be admitted that these considerations are not very compelling, however. Systematic connections between pains are limited and can easily be accounted for on a model of pains as maps, for example. And the possibility of misrepresentation does not *require* that pains be true or false, any more than the fact that maps or paintings are sometimes inaccurate requires that they be true or false.

Are there any pieces of evidence which count against a sententialist view of pain? It seems to me that there are. We know that in visual perception, the retinal image is reconstructed in the visual cortex so that in a quite literal sense adjacent parts of the cortex represent adjacent parts of the retinal image. There is, then, an orderly topographic projection of the retinal image onto the brain. This has been established from experiments in which a recording electrode is placed inside the visual cortex. Greater neural activity is picked up by the electrode when light is shone onto a particular spot on the retina. Moving the electrode a little results in the continued registration of greater activity only if light is directed onto an adjacent part of the retina.

Topographic organization of this sort is also found in the somatosensory cortex. There is, for example, an orderly topographic representation of the surface of the human body that is dedicated to touch. Here adjacent regions of the body surface are projected onto adjacent regions of the cortex. Enhanced activity in one of the relevant cortical regions represents that the region of body surface projected onto it is being touched. Some relatively small portions of the body, for example, the hands and face, provide input to more neurons than do some relatively large portions, for example, the trunk. This is why, when two separate points on the face are touched, the shortest distance between the points at which both can be felt is much less than the shortest distance when points are on the trunk are touched.

There are further representations of the human body in the somatosensory cortex that are similarly structured. It has been established that the experience of pain is associated with activity in this cortex.[13] Now the fact that the somatosensory cortex is topographically organized and that it is the primary locus of pain raises doubts about the sentential view of pain. For sentences do not have the requisite map-like representational structure.[14]

My suggestion, then, is that pains themselves are topographic or map-like representations. More specifically, I hold that pains are patterns of active cells occurring in topographically structured three-dimensional arrays to which descriptive labels are attached. This proposal may be unpacked as follows.

For each pain, there is an array made up of cells corresponding to irregularly sized portions of the body, with adjacent cells representing adjacent body regions.[15] Each cell, when active, may be conceived of as representing that something painful is occurring at the corresponding body region. The irregularity of the grain in the array is partly responsible, I suggest, for variations in our experience of pain when the same degree of damage occurs in different bodily regions of the same size (e.g., the face versus the torso).

Since the cells within the pain array itself are individually concerned only with arbitrary body regions, there is no representation in the array of natural body parts. Segmentation of the body regions into such parts occurs via inspection processes that examine patterns of active cells in the array, and assess them, on the basis of their location, as pains in arms, legs, and so forth. It is here that descriptive labels that represent the relevant body parts are appended to the array. I speculate that further labels are introduced for global features of the represented damage via further routines that mechanically work over the array and extract at least *some* of the relevant information from its contents. For example, in the case of a stabbing pain, we may suppose that there is a sudden pattern of activity in the array, beginning at a part of the array representing a narrow region of body surface and extending in the proper temporal sequence to cells representing adjacent deeper internal regions (so that a roughly dagger-shaped volume is marked out). The relevant computational routines process this activity and assign an appropriate descriptive term.[16] In the case of a stinging pain, we may suppose that certain cells in the array representing contiguous regions of body surface along a narrow band are strongly activated, more or less simultaneously, for a brief period of time. This activity generates a computational response, and the relevant term again affixed. Whether these suppositions are along the right lines is a matter for investigation by cognitive psychology.

This crude model is, of course, very sketchy indeed. What it gives us, I suggest, is an alternative way of thinking about pains as representations, one which seems to me more promising than the purely sentential view. Pains, I believe, represent in something like the way that maps represent that contain additional descriptive information for salient items ("treasure buried here," "highest mountain on island"). In this respect, they are very like mental images, as I conceive them.

There is strong evidence that images and visual percepts share a medium which has been called "the visual buffer." This medium is functional in character: it consists of a large number of cells, each of which is dedicated to representing, when filled, a tiny patch of surface at a particular location in the visual field. For visual percepts and after-images, the visual buffer is filled, in normal cases, by processes that operate on information contained in the light striking the eyes. For mental images (other than after-images), the visual buffer is filled by generational processes that act on information stored in long-term memory about the appearances of objects and their spatial structure.

Images and percepts, I have argued elsewhere, are interpreted symbol-filled patterns of cells in the visual buffer. The symbols within each cell represent at least some of the following local features: presence of a patch of surface, orientation of the surface, color, texture, and so on. Interpretations are affixed to the patterns of filled cells in the form of descriptions that provide a more specific content, for example, whether the imaged object is a circle or a square, or, in more complex cases, a duck or a rabbit. I have elaborated this view in detail in another work (Tye 1991). So, I shall not pursue it here. I conjecture that bodily sensations generally, perceptual experiences, and imagistic experiences all have their contents encoded in arrays of the sort I have described.

I should perhaps emphasize here a point I made earlier in connection with after-images. On my view, although the processes responsible for filling the arrays in both bodily and perceptual sensation do not essentially require belief or thought, they certainly involve categorization. Consider, for example, the sorts of categorization that go on in very early vision, for example, the detection of edges and the computation of distance away categorizations that are relevant to how the visual buffer is filled. These categorizations are automatic. They do not demand that the creature have beliefs or thoughts about the properties of visual stimuli that are represented in such categorizations. Much the same is true, I maintain, in the case of bodily sensations. So nothing in the proposed account entails that a very small child or an animal could not feel pain. Their relative conceptual impoverishment does not preclude them from undergoing processing and representations of the sort necessary to fill some portion of the appropriate array.

What about the descriptive labels that are appended to the arrays? Is thought or belief involved here? Again I am inclined to suppose that in at least *some* cases, the further categorizations that take place here do so without the essential involvement of concepts (understood as involving a public language or thought). Consider, for example, the case of simple shapes in perceptual experience. Nothing looks square to me, unless the appropriate processes have operated upon the filled cells in the visual buffer and categorized them as representing a square shape.[17] But it is not necessary that I think (or believe) of the object I am seeing that it is square. Indeed, I need not have any thought (or belief) at all about the real or apparent features of the seen object.

Perhaps it will now be said that it is not clear how the model I have outlined accommodates the well-established fact that pain is susceptible to top-down influences. For example, in one experiment, joggers were found to run faster in a lovely wooded area than on a track. Apparently, they experienced less pain in their arms and legs while viewing the trees and flowers, and as a result, ran at a quicker pace (Pennebaker and Lightner 1980). There is also the interesting case of some

Scottish terriers raised in restricted environments. Upon being released, Melzack tells us, they behaved as follows:

> They were so frisky and rambunctious that inevitably someone would accidentally step on their tails. But we didn't hear a squeak from them. In their excitement, they would also bang their heads with a resounding smack on the building's low water pipes and just walk away. I was curious, and lit a match to see how they would respond to the flame. They kept sticking their noses in it, and though they would back off as if from a funny smell, they did not react as if hurt. (Quoted in Warga 1987)

Anxiety, by contrast, increases the experience of pain, as, for example, when one compares a present injury with some past one.

These facts about pain are no threat to the proposal I have made. They may be explained by supposing that the pain receptor pathway in the spinal column leading to the somatosensory cortex has a gate in it that is controlled by input from the higher brain centers (the gate control theory) (Melzack and Wall 1965). When this gate is partly closed, less information gets through and the feeling of pain diminishes. As it opens further, more information is enabled to pass. Anxiety, excitement, joy, concentration, and other higher-level activities affect the orientation of the gate. So, the fact that the experience of pain is, *in the above sense,* cognitively penetrable presents no real difficulty for my proposal.

Still, there is one very important feature of pain on which I have as yet made only a couple of passing comments: its phenomenal character. In what does the phenomenal character of pain consist? What is the relationship of phenomenal character to representational content?

These are questions I shall address in the final section. My concern so far has been simply to establish the thesis that pains have representational content and to make plausible my contention that pains, like images, are a proper object of study for cognitive psychology. Whether pains have phenomenal features that cannot be representationally or intentionally grounded is a further issue (just as in the case of mental images).

IV

It is usually held that pains have intrinsic, introspectively accessible properties that are wholly nonintentional and that are *solely* responsible for their phenomenal character. Such properties are often called qualia, although the term is sometimes used in a broader way to refer to subjective or phenomenal features, however they are analyzed or understood. As a general view about the phenomenal character of pain, this view seems to me clearly mistaken.

Consider the following case. As I write, I have a backache. There is something it is like for me to be the subject of this backache. What it is like to be the subject of this backache is, of course, the same as what it is like to be the subject of this backache. But what it is like to be the subject of this backache is not the same as what it is like to be me, even though I am the subject of this backache. Why not?

The answer, I suggest, is that the "what it is like" context is intensional. Coreferential expressions cannot always be safely substituted without change of truth-value. What creates the intensional context is the intentional nature of phenomenal character or "feel." The specific phenomenal character of a state—what it is like to undergo it—is none other than the state's intentional content, or more accurately, in my view, an aspect of that content.

Consider again the above case of a backache. The qualities I experience (and strongly dislike) are experienced as features instantiated in some region of my back and not as intrinsic features of my experience. Since it could be the case that there really is nothing wrong with my back, the qualities need not be actual features of my back. Rather they are features my experience *represents* as being tokened in my back (e.g., the feature of being such-and-such a sort of disturbance). Moreover, these features are not intrinsic properties of my experience that I mistakenly project onto part of my body. There is no general error embedded in pain experiences.

Now the phenomenal character of my pain intuitively is something that is given to me via introspection of *what* I experience in having that pain. But what I experience is what my experience represents. So, phenomenal character is representational.

Perhaps it will be denied that the qualities I experience when I have a backache are apparently located in my back. But this is certainly what introspection strongly suggests. When I turn my gaze inwards and try to focus my attention on *intrinsic* features of my pain experience in such a case, features the experience has in itself apart from what it represents, I do not seem to come across any. I always seem to end up attending to what I am experiencing *in my back*. Careful introspection reveals only further aspects of *that*, further aspects of my experience's representational or intentional content. The experience itself is transparent.[18] Why? The answer, I suggest, is that my experience has no *introspectible* features that distinguish it from other experiences over and above those implicated in its content. So, the specific phenomenal character of my experience—itself something that is introspectibly accessible—is identical with, or contained within, its overall intentional content.

Still, if the distinctive phenomenal character of pains is an aspect of their intentional content, just which aspect is this? What is phenomenal content? This is a complex question which I take up fully in my book (Tye 1995). In this chapter, I can make only some very schematic remarks.

In my view, phenomenal content is abstract, nonconceptual, intentional content that is poised for use by the cognitive centers. The claim that contents relevant to phenomenal character of pains (and other sensory experiences) must be *poised* is to be understood as requiring that these contents attach to the output representations of the relevant sensory module(s) and stand ready and in position to make a direct impact on the belief/desire system.[19]

This view entails that no belief could have phenomenal character. A content is classified as phenomenal only if it is nonconceptual and poised. Beliefs are not nonconceptual; and they are not appropriately poised. They lie within the conceptual arena, rather than providing inputs to it. Beliefs are not sensory representations at all (although on given occasions they may certainly be accompanied by such representations).

The claim that the contents relevant to phenomenal character must be *abstract* is to be understood as demanding that no concrete objects enter into these contents. The reason for this requirement is straightforward. Whether or not you have a left leg, you can feel a pain in your left leg; and in both cases, the phenomenal character of your experience can be exactly the same. So, the existence of that particular leg is not required for the given phenomenal character. What matters rather is the conjunction of general features or properties the experience represents. The experience nonconceptually represents that there are such-and-such co-instantiated locational and nonlocational features, and thereby it acquires its phenomenal character.

The claim that the contents relevant to phenomenal character must be *nonconceptual* is to be understood as saying that the general features entering into these contents need not be ones for which their subjects possess matching concepts. I have already made some remarks pertinent to this requirement.

Exactly which features represented by pains are elements of their phenomenal contents? There is no *a priori* answer. Empirical research is necessary. The relevant features will be the ones represented by the output representations of the sensory module for pain. We might call features that are so represented in connection with the outputs of the various sensory modules *"observational features."* Since the receptors associated with the modules and the processing that goes on within them vary, features that are observational for one module need not be observational for another.[20] What gets outputted obviously depends upon what gets inputted, and how the module operates. In my view, it is the representation of a certain class of observational features by our pain experiences, and the role that they play, which gives pains their phenomenal character.

Many questions remain here, of course, not the least of which concern the supervenience of phenomenal character upon what is in the head, and the issue of absent qualia (Tye 1995). But I hope that I have said enough to show that a wholly representational approach to pains is a promising one.[21]

Notes

1. These virtues led me to accept the proposal until very recently. See Tye 1991.
2. There is, I might add, a possible *de re* reading of this context as follows: F-ness is such that an F image represents that something has *it*. Now, from "I have a red image" and "Red is the color of most fire engines . . . I have an image the color of most fire engines" *may* be inferred.

3. I might add that, in my view, a necessary condition of any image representing that something is both F and G is that it represent that something is F. So, if I have an F, G image, I must have an F image. The argument for the premise here is straightforward: In having a blue, square image, I experience blue as a feature of something or other, a feature co-instantiated with square. What I experience, in part, is that something is blue. So, my image, in part, represents that something is blue.

4. Phantom limb pain shows that pains do not essentially involve relations between persons and parts of their bodies. This seems to me a decisive objection to the relational view presented in Aune 1967, p. 130.

5. In my view, the representation of damage here is nonconceptual. So, I can certainly see that my leg is damaged without feeling any pain there. In the case of seeing-that, my state involves a belief about damage (and hence the exercise of concepts).

6. According to pain researchers, people who have been given prefrontal lobotomies, or certain other treatments, often report that they feel pain but that they do not mind it or that it does not really bother them (see Melzack 1961 and 1973). These reports, even if taken at face value, are compatible with the proposal in the text. For clearly such cases are abnormal.

7. I do not mean to suggest here that one cannot have a stabbing pain unless one has the concept of a dagger. Pains, to repeat, are nonconceptual sensory representations.

8. I deny that so-called psychological pains, for example, pains of regret or embarrassment, are really pains. I think it plausible to hold that such states are labeled "pains" because, like (normal) pains, people are aversive to them. But this usage of "pain" is, I suggest, metaphorical or analogical. This is not to deny, of course, that real pains may have psychological causes. Embarrassment may certainly *cause* burning facial pain (see Stephens and Graham 1987, p. 413).

9. The constitution relation is weaker than the relation of identity. *A* can be constituted by *B* even though *A* and *B* differ in some of their modal properties (Tye 1992).

10. For a detailed development of the above points concerning systematicity and productivity, see Fodor and Pylyshyn 1988.

11. One such theory is Stephen Kosslyn's Pictorialism (Kosslyn 1980).

12. Cases of misrepresentation are not rare. Pains in the upper left arm are often due to disturbances in the heart.

13. This is not to deny that other neural regions also play a role in some pain experiences. In particular there are pain pathways which terminate in both the posterior parietal cortex and the superior frontal cortex.

14. For a discussion of the representational differences between sentences, pictures, and maps, see Tye 1991.

15. The characteristics of arrays are examined further in Tye 1991.

16. It need not be assumed that the proper temporal sequence referred to in the last sentence of the text *necessarily* corresponds to the real-world temporal sequence. The fact that the inspection routines treat the activity in one cell C as representing a later bodily disturbance than the activity in another cell C does not necessitate an implementation via an arrangement in which C is active after C. For some illuminating comments on the representation of time which can be brought to bear upon this point, see Dennett 1991, chap. 6.

17. For one possible sketch of these processes, see Marr 1982.

18. Transparency has been discussed by a number of philosophers. See, for example, Harman 1990.

19. This is developed further in Tye 1995 and 1996. For a discussion of some differences between Block's conception of what it is for a state to be poised and my own, see Tye 1996.

20. Moreover, in classifying a feature as observational, I am not supposing that it has that status for all possible species of creatures. Observationality, in my view, is relative to creatures with a certain sort of sensory equipment. Thus, some features that are observational for us might not be for other possible creatures (and vice versa).

21. I would like to thank Ned Block, Gabriel Segal, and especially Sydney Shoemaker for helpful comments.

Chapter 14

Emotion and Force (2003)

York H. Gunther

Any satisfactory model of the emotions must at once recognize their place within intentional psychology and acknowledge their uniqueness as mental causes. In the first half of the century, the James-Lange model had considerable influence on reinforcing the idea that emotions are non-intentional (see Lange 1885 and James 1890). The uniqueness of emotions was therefore acknowledged at the price of denying them a place within intentional psychology proper. More recently, cognitive reductionists (including identity theorists) like Robert Solomon and Joel Marks recognize that emotions are intentional but, by reducing them to judgments, beliefs, desires, and so on, fail to capture their distinctiveness as mental causes (see Solomon 1976 and Marks 1982). In other words, their place within intentional psychology is acknowledged at the price of denying them their uniqueness.

Anti-reductionists are committed to the idea that emotions are both intentional and unique. Their uniqueness, however, is rarely, if ever, traced to the intentionality of emotion itself. An anti-reductionist is more likely to single out a phenomenological, perspectival, or evaluative feature that, as purportedly distinctive of emotional experience (attitudes, states), precludes the reduction of emotions to cognitive and/or motivational states (see Perkins 1962, de Sousa 1987, Helm 1994, respectively).

My aim is to sketch an alternative that explains the unique character of emotion in terms of the kind of intentional content it has. The primary support for the view is based on the failure of emotions to exhibit full logical complexity, which suggests their violation of the Principle of Force Independence. From this, I outline four implications. First, the reduction of emotions to cognitive and/or motivational states is implausible given the former's violation of the principle. Second, an account of emotional content requires the development of an independent theory of meaning based on propriety rather than truth. Third, the violation of Force Independence recommends the partial desegregation of psychology and semantics. And finally, emotions present us with a compelling paradigm for nonconceptual content, one that side-steps controversial assumptions associated with other paradigms.

1 Force Independence

Let me begin by clarifying what Force Independence is. Effectively, to heed the principle is to acknowledge a distinction and separation of content and force. In language this involves distinguishing between *what* a sentence or utterance says and the *way* it's said. If, as is widely assumed, content is individuated independently of force, the same content might be expressed by sentences with different moods, for example, indicative, optative, imperative, or interrogative, or by utterances with different uses: to make an assertion or wish, to issue an order, or to ask a question (see, e.g., Stenius 1967 and Dummett 1973, p. 307). Similarly, if we assume that the content of an intentional state or event is individuated independently of its mental force, the same content might be presented through belief, desire, doubt, hope, and so forth (see, e.g., Searle 1983, pp. 5ff; see also essay 4, p. 96). Hence just as I may assert that Gertrude Stein studied psychology at Radcliffe and you may ask me whether she studied psychology there, I may believe that she did and you may doubt it.

Of course, some deny that sentences in the indicative and interrogative moods have the same content, for instance, "Gertrude studied psychology" and "Did Gertrude study psychology?" The content of the latter has been regarded as a set of true or possible answers that includes the aforementioned indicative sentence (see, e.g., Karttunen 1977 and Hamblin 1973). But even such views draw on the force/content distinction implicitly since they presume that there is a principled connection between the contents of an indicative and the corresponding interrogative. For what makes an indicative a true or possible answer to an interrogative is its content. In other words, it is this principled connection between (if not sameness of) the contents of indicatives and interrogatives that enables interlocutors to understand one another. Without at least assuming a principled connection, it would be difficult to explain how a verbal exchange such as "Did Gertrude study psychology?"—"Gertrude studied psychology" could constitute communication.

In modern philosophy, Frege is among the earliest proponents of the distinction and separation of content and force.[1] In *Begriffschrift*, for example, he schematizes force with the vertical stroke and indicates content by what follows the horizontal stroke (Frege 1879, p. 53). And later in "Thought," he explains

> An interrogative sentence and an assertoric one contain the same thought, but the assertoric sentence contains something else as well, namely assertion. The interrogative sentence contains something more too, namely a request. Therefore two things must be distinguished in an assertoric sentence: the content, which it has in common with the corresponding propositional question; and assertion. (Frege 1918a, p. 329; see also Frege 1918b, p. 348, and Frege 1979, p. 177)

While Frege acknowledged the distinction and separation, some maintain he was wrong to deny that it applies across the board (see, e.g., Dummett 1991, p. 114). For example, in the case of commands and wishes, he admits that they have content [*Sinn*] but denies that their contents are shared by or correspond with those of assertions and questions. This led Frege to place commands and wishes on the same level as thoughts and, in essence, to regard them as different kinds of content, namely, as contents that have force as an indissoluble aspect (see Frege 1892, p. 161, and 1918a, p. 329).

With the developments of speech act theory through the writing of R. M. Hare, J. L. Austin, and John Searle, the Principle of Force Independence was extended to all contentful discourse (Hare 1952, Austin 1962, and Searle 1979). Their systematic classifications of illocutionary force reveal different ways in which the same or corresponding contents can be used in language. And as issues involving content have shifted in the analytic tradition from the linguistic to the mental, it has become commonplace to extend the distinction and separation to all intentional states.[2]

Besides its role in explaining communication, the force/content distinction has another advantage. Frege pointed out that Force Independence is needed to account for how an assertoric content can be entertained or made conditional (see Frege 1892, p. 165 and Frege 1979, pp. 185ff and pp. 198ff). For example, if an utterance's assertoric force were an indissoluble aspect of its content (sense), then whenever the utterance appeared in the antecedent of a conditional, it would have to be *asserted* rather than *entertained*. But this is clearly not the case. While one may assert "Gertrude studied psychology," one can also entertain the content expressed by the assertion: "If Gertrude studied psychology, William was her teacher." Similarly, to believe that if Gertrude is in Paris, she'll miss class, doesn't require believing that Gertrude is in Paris. In each of these cases, the force relates to the whole rather than the parts, thereby allowing the conditional structure to be exhibited.

What is true of conditionals is also true of other logically complex sentences (utterances) and intentional states (events). Without heeding Force Independence, the linguistic and mental would fail to exhibit a genuine disjunctive or negative structure. For example, to believe that Gertrude will live in Paris or move back to Allegheny, doesn't presuppose believing either disjunct. The mental force (belief) in this case ranges over both disjuncts, suggesting its separability from the logically basic contents (disjuncts). Or consider the following routine exchange: "Has Gertrude skipped class again?"—"No, she hasn't (skipped class again)." For the interlocutors to understand one another (on a literal level), we must not only assume that the basic contents of the question and response correspond to one another (or are the same) but that the interlocutor's response constitutes a negative answer to the question. In other words, even an exchange as mundane as this presupposes both the correspondence (sameness) and the logical complexity of contents. And as I have been urging, both features depend upon distinguishing and separating content from force.

The question I want to consider is, does all language and thought heed Force Independence as many believe? While Frege may have wrongly supposed that wishes and commands violate it, I contend that he was right in principle to deny that all sentences and intentional states heed it. My own case in support of this centers on the emotions.

2 The Logical Character of Emotion

The violation of Force Independence by the emotions is suggested by their failure to exhibit full logical complexity. To show this, I turn to the apparent failure of expressive utterances to exhibit full logical complexity. The tack evidently assumes that the logical structure of sentences (utterances) mirrors the logical structure of intentional states (events), or as Dummett puts it "that a philosophical account of thought can be attained through a philosophical account of language" (Dummett 1994, pp. 4ff). This is not an uncommon assumption in analytic philosophy—in fact, it is arguably at the heart of the so-called "Linguistic Turn." However, since it specifically concerns expressives and emotions, let me say a word about them.

The relationship between expressives and emotions parallels the relationship between assertions and beliefs. One cannot (sincerely) assert that p and indicate that (at the time of the assertion) one does not believe that p. A sincere assertion presupposes that one has the corresponding belief (see Searle 1983, p. 9). Moreover, while it presupposes the belief, this does not imply that the assertion is *about* the belief. For example, the assertion "William was Gertrude's teacher" is not about the belief that William was Gertrude's teacher. Rather, it is about what the belief is about, namely, that William was Gertrude's teacher, which is just to say that the assertion and corresponding belief have the same content. If this were not the case, one would merely be able to assert *that* one believes that such-and-such rather than assert *that* such-and-such.

Similarly, a sincere expressive utterance presupposes that the requisite emotion is experienced by the individual at the time of the utterance. Hence, thanking William (sincerely) for being your teacher presupposes experiencing gratitude for him being your teacher (at the time of the utterance); apologizing for breaking the window presupposes experiencing regret for breaking the window; and deploring someone's actions presupposes experiencing disgust at or disapproval of those actions. Moreover, just as in the case of assertions, expressives are not *about* the emotions they presuppose. Rather, their contents are the same as those of emotions. It is for this reason that expressives can reveal something about the logical structure of emotional content.

Consider, for example, the following utterances:

Thank you for letting me enroll in your class.
I apologize for coming late.

What is noteworthy is that neither expressive can be made disjunctive or conditional. One cannot thank someone for letting you take their class *or* giving you a passing grade. I cannot apologize that if I come late, I will make a quiet entrance. Such cases are grammatically unsound and reflect one way that counterexamples can be misbegotten.

Of course, in claiming that emotional content resists full logical complexity, I am not claiming that utterances about emotions cannot be logically complex. The following cases illustrate this clearly enough:

> I will not take your class or thank you for letting me enroll.
> If I'm late, I will apologize.

But while grammatically sound, such utterances don't constitute counterexamples since they aren't expressives. The first is a disjunctive assertion whose second disjunct makes a claim about a certain course of action, presumably in anticipation of the gratitude the speaker would experience if she were allowed to enroll in the class; the second is a conditional assertion whose consequent specifies a possible course of action, namely, an apology, in anticipation of the regret she would experience if she arrived late.

However, one might wonder whether emotional ascriptions couldn't tell us something about emotional content. While not expressives, they are about emotions and thus might be taken to reveal something about their logical structure. Moreover, there seem to be cases where emotional ascriptions are grammatically sound and exhibit a conditional or disjunctive structure:

> Gertrude is happy that if she works hard, she will impress William.
> William is sorry that Gertrude either failed or withdrew from the course.

Although initially plausible, these alleged counterexamples are also misbegotten. For unlike expressive utterances, emotional ascriptions don't have the same content as emotional states; they are, after all, *about* emotions. As such, they aren't reliable indicators of the logical structure of emotion. For example, neither ascription presupposes that the individual is experiencing the relevant emotion. Rather than experience happiness at the time of the first ascription, the interpreter is supposing that if she works hard, Gertrude will be happy that she impresses William. Similarly, it isn't that William experiences regret at the time of the second ascription; rather, the interpreter supposes that if Gertrude fails or withdraws from the course, he will feel regret about her doing so. In both cases, it seems to be a disposition to experience an emotion (happiness or regret) that is being ascribed, *not* the emotion itself.[3]

This is not to say, however, that there are no utterances that are grammatically sound, express emotion *and* exhibit an apparent conditional structure. For example:

> If Gertrude has skipped class again, damn her, she'll fail the course!

Like utterances whose point it is to thank, apologize, and so on, when used sincerely, this utterance requires that the speaker experience the requisite emotion, which in this case may be irritation, frustration, or perhaps anger. Since there's no question that the utterance is grammatical, it may be regarded as an instance of an expressive that exhibits conditional structure.

But looks are deceiving. What is conspicuous about the utterance is that its conditional structure isn't genuine. If it were, the speaker should be able to *entertain* rather than *experience* the antecedent. But this isn't the case. The utterance requires that the speaker is *already* irritated (frustrated, angry), which seems puzzling given that the expletive appears only in the antecedent. By contrast, if the utterance represented a fact independently of emotion, then the content of the basic assertion could be entertained in a way consistent with conditionals. For example, in the conditional assertion, "If William is Gertrude's teacher, Gertrude will pass the course," the speaker need not *believe* the content *William is Gertrude's teacher*. The antecedent in this case is entertained rather than asserted (believed, experienced) (see Williams 1973, pp. 210–212).

Something similar is true of negation. If an interlocutor sincerely asks William, "Has Gertrude skipped class again, damn her?!" and William replies, "No, she hasn't skipped class again, damn her!" one of several things might be going on. William may have grown irritated at repeatedly being asked the same question. He may be sarcastically quoting his interlocutor's own words, perhaps poking fun at his inappropriate expression of anger. What is implausible, however, is that William's reply constitutes a negative answer to his interlocutor's question. In fact, the utterance does not even seem to be addressing the question. Matters would, of course, be different if William's interlocutor had asked him a question that didn't express emotion. In such a case, a sincere negative response could constitute a negative answer.

Why, it may be asked, do such utterances appear to be logically complex when they're not? One explanation is that they're performing double duty. In fact, this is generally true when an expressive is logically complex. Take the examples just considered:

> If Gertrude has skipped class again, damn her, she'll fail the course!
> No, she hasn't skipped class again, damn her!

Both utterances are functioning as expressive and directive, an utterance whose point it is to get the hearer to do something (see Searle 1979, pp. 13–14). In the first case, the conditional is plausibly a stern reminder or a threat, perhaps serving as an indirect way of bringing Gertrude (and those in earshot) into compliance with a strict attendance policy. In the second case, William's negative answer is a way of getting the speaker to stop asking the same question, whether because his interlocutor is annoyingly repeating it or because he finds his interlocutor's expression of anger inappropriate. However, in both cases the emotional content being expressed is logically basic: in the first it is an irritation about repeatedly being asked the same question and in the second it is an anger that Gertrude has skipped class again.

Obviously, I can't review every instance involving an utterance that seems logically complex and related to the expression of emotion. I submit, however, that each falls into one of three categories: it is either (a) grammatically unsound, (b) not an expressive, or (c) not genuinely (conditionally, disjunctively, etc.) complex, as in the case of utterances that perform double duty. If this is right, and if indeed there are no instances of expressive utterances that exhibit conditional, disjunctive, or genuine negative structure, then I believe there is good reason to suppose that emotions violate Force Independence.

Of course, as I've presented it, my argument isn't demonstrative in form. It is conceivable, after all, that the comprehensive failure of expressive utterances to exhibit full logical complexity results from something other than a violation of Force Independence. However, as I'm unaware of a viable alternative, my argument seems at the very least to be an inference to the best explanation.

3 Some Implications

From the principle's violation, four notable consequences follow. The first concerns the irreducibility of emotion. If force is an indissoluble aspect of emotional content, then reductionists seem to face an additional obstacle. It isn't just that the phenomenological, perspectival, or evaluative character of emotions precludes their reduction to cognitive and/or motivational states, but their unique logical character does as well. For the reductionist is now faced with the task of accounting for intentional states whose contents violate Force Independence in terms of those whose contents presumably do not. But any account that (in its *explanans*) appealed exclusively to intentional states whose contents heed the principle would be inadequate since it wouldn't explain the unique logical character of emotion, namely, their failure to exhibit full logical complexity.

Of course in response to this, the reductionist might suggest that certain intentional states—motivational states, say—have contents that also violate Force Independence. As such, she might cite these motivational states in her *explanans* in hopes of accounting for the logical character of emotion. Yet, while this would be a step forward, it would not be sufficient. For in addition to establishing that the contents of these motivational states violate Force Independence, she would have to ensure that an individual's possession of the requisite motivational state (perhaps in concert with other intentional states) is sufficient for that individual's experience of the relevant emotion. But, not only would every occurrence of the emotion have to be accompanied by that motivational state, the logical complexity of the motivational state would in each instance have to be the same as the logical complexity of the emotion. While I admit the issue requires further scrutiny, I don't consider the reductionist's prospects to be very promising.

The second consequence concerns the need for an independent theory of emotional content. In the philosophy of mind and language, it is widely believed that a comprehensive theory of meaning (content) can be based on the semantics of indicative sentences, whether formulated in terms of truth or assertability conditions (though I'll focus on the former) (see, e.g., Davidson 1967, Lewis 1983b, Dummett 1973, Montague 1974, Evans and McDowell 1976). Since such theories are meant to be comprehensive, they are meant to account for the meanings of all sentences (and presumably also intentional states), whether they have truth conditions or not. But this raises an obvious question: how could a truth theory specify (individuate) the contents of sentences like optatives and imperatives, or intentional states like desires and hopes, which are governed, respectively, by fulfilment, compliance, satisfaction, and realization conditions?

The answer is that the type of normative conditions a sentence or intentional state has is linked to its force. And as such, a comprehensive theory of meaning presupposes a theory of force that enables one to map the contents of sentences or intentional states that don't have truth conditions—optatives, imperatives, desires, and hopes—onto the contents of ones that do—indicatives and perhaps beliefs.[4] Such mappings, of course, are justifiable only if truth conditional and non–truth conditional sentences and intentional states have the same or corresponding contents. But this presupposes that all (contentful) language and thought heeds Force Independence (see, e.g., Stenius 1967, Dummett 1975, 1976, Davidson 1979, Searle 1983, and Stalnaker [essay 4]). Without the assumption, the very idea of a comprehensive theory of meaning is put into jeopardy. In addition to a truth theory, which would be used to specify the contents of indicatives and beliefs, a fulfillment conditional theory would be needed for optatives, a compliance conditional theory for imperatives, a satisfaction conditional theory for desires, a realization conditional theory for hopes, and so on.

The violation of Force Independence by the emotions and the fact that they are governed by propriety rather than truth suggests a problem for the truth conditional approach to meaning/content. Because they cannot be individuated independently of their force, emotional contents cannot be mapped onto the contents of indicatives or beliefs and, therefore, a truth theory cannot be used to specify them. And as such, we need an independent theory of emotional content based on propriety. I will not venture to offer such a theory here (though, see Gunther under review for an initial attempt).

The third consequence bears on the relationship between psychology and philosophy or, more specifically, psychology and semantics. Since Kant, the disciplines have in various ways been sharply distinguished. Where psychology embraces a methodology characteristic of the empirical sciences, philosophy, including semantics, adopts the method of conceptual analysis. Moreover, they also differ with respect to their focus: where psychology investigates computational (formal) structure and the nature and role of mental states (representings, attitudes, force), semantics investigates logical structure and the nature and role of intentionality (represent*ed*s, reference, content). While there are differing explanations for how this division of labor came about, its justification seems tied to the Principle of Force Independence. For by assuming that intentional content can be individuated independently of mental force, a study of content is not obliged to appeal to the methodology(ies) or focus(es) of psychology.

The violation of Force Independence by the emotions compels us to reconsider this division of labor. For once we acknowledge that emotions blur the distinction and separation of content and force, their study can no longer be relegated to the domain of semantics and philosophy alone. In short, the principle's violation requires the partial desegregation of psychology and semantics. Perhaps more than any other investigation of the mind, the study of emotion demands that philosophers and psychologists work together, not merely out of academic respect or some interdisciplinary fad, but because the nature of emotion itself calls for it. Just what such a psychological semantics (or semantic psychology) should look like is difficult to say. But, if emotions are to be properly understood, its development will most certainly be required.

The final consequence concerns nonconceptual content. Nonconceptualists generally attempt to show that conceptual content alone is inadequate to account for various psychological phenomena such as animal cognition, visual illusion, motor intentionality (know how), cognitive development, perceptual fineness of grain, and so forth. To explain such phenomena, they contend that individuals must be ascribed intentional contents that, in one way or another, don't depend on the possession of conceptual contents. While the prospect of a different kind of intentionality is intriguing, the assumptions guiding most contemporary non-conceptualists are not. The problem is that the motivation for positing noncon-ceptuality is all too often rooted in empiricist dogma: nonconceptual content is presumed to provide the necessary epistemic grounding and/or ontological reduction for conceptual contents. Andy Clark, for instance, offers a particularly stark summation of his allegiance to empiricism:

> genuinely contentful thought requires a system with *both* nonconceptual *and* conceptual knowledge of its world. The nonconceptual knowledge is the epistemological bedrock which puts the system in *contact* with the world its thoughts are meant to concern. The conceptual knowledge is an ultimate effect of a process of redescription which provides for the integration and wider availability of the knowledge embedded in the lower level representations. (1994, p. 64 [essay 7, p. 166])

But, of course, to suppose that such a grounding or reduction is needed, let alone possible, is contentious. And it's, therefore, no wonder that the very idea of nonconceptual content is looked upon with great suspicion (see essays 3 and 12).

The argument for the uniqueness of emotions I've outlined suggests an alternative paradigm. While a violation of Force Independence explains the failure of emotions to exhibit full logical complexity, nothing about emotional content implies that it is epistemologically or ontologically more primitive than conceptual (i.e., force-independent) content. On the contrary, emotional experiences frequently presuppose the possession of higher cognitive states (e.g., beliefs) that have conceptual content. And it seems likely that other experiences, including those described by religious psychologists and philosophers of art, may also be understood within this paradigm. Although more deserves to be said, this much is already clear: when based on a violation of Force Independence, nonconceptual content is free of empiricist dogma.

Acknowledgments

For suggestions and comments on earlier drafts, I am indebted to Kent Bach, Akeel Bilgrami, Bryson Brown, José Bermúdez, Anthony Everett, Lance Hickey, Ron McIntrye, Philip Pettit, Tom Poggler, and Crispin Wright.

Notes

1. It is arguably Brentano himself who not only re-introduced the concept of intentionality into modern philosophy but recognized a distinction between intentional objects (contents) and mental phenomena (force types) (Brentano 1874).
2. It is noteworthy that the principle was applied to the mental by many in the continental tradition quite early. In addition to Brentano, Husserl differentiated matter (content) from quality (force), suggesting that mental acts differing in quality might share the same matter (1901, V, §§20–22). For an overview of the various approaches in this period to these and related issues, see Follesdal 1982, Smith and McIntrye 1982, Dummett 1994, and Kusch 1995.
3. The disposition/experience distinction parallels the habit/act distinction. As Vendler points out (1972, p. 10), "I smoke" doesn't imply "I am smoking" since it's consistent to say "I smoke but I am not smoking now." The same is true for dispositions. To say "Gertrude is happy that if she works hard, she will impress William" doesn't imply "Gertrude is experiencing happiness."

    There are other kinds of cases where conditional emotional ascriptions don't indicate an emotional content that's conditional in form. For example, "William fears that if he goes into the water, he will be attacked by a shark." In this case, while it is plausible that William may indeed experience fear, his fear is a fear of being attacked by a shark. The antecedent of the conditional in this case (viz. if he goes into the water) is tracking not a disposition but the activity of William's imagination. That is, William is imagining himself going into the water, which elicits his fear of being attacked by a shark. In short, this is not a case of a logically complex emotional content either. And generally speaking, these observations should lead us to conclude that emotional ascriptions are not reliable indicators of emotional content.
4. Mark Platts refers to these mappings as the "monistic transformational component" of a theory of force (Platts 1980, p. 3).

Part IV

The Autonomy Thesis

The papers of the last section deal with the question of autonomy: can nonconceptual content be used exclusively to explain the actions of individuals who possess concepts, or can it be used also to explain the behavior of entities that lack conceptual capacities? Of course, only nonconceptualists will consider the question relevant, and of them only those who accept the explanatory value of concepts, namely, content dualists as opposed to global nonconceptualists, would even consider denying the Autonomy Thesis.

In *Varieties of Reference*, Evans comes down in support of the thesis:

> I do not think we can properly understand the mechanism whereby we [as concept-possessors] gain information from others unless we realize that it is already operative at a stage of human intellectual development that pre-dates the applicability of the more sophisticated notion [of information, viz. conceptual content]. (Evans 1982, p. 124; see also p. 158) (essay 2, p. 52)

But it is not merely human infants and children to whom nonconceptual content might be legitimately attributed. If the Autonomy Thesis were correct, the behavior of nonhuman animals and, for that matter, the operations of subpersonal systems and artifacts could also be explained by attributing contents that violate one of Frege's principles.

In part four of "Scenarios, Concepts, and Perception" (essay 5), Peacocke presents a densely formulated argument against autonomy. The argument runs roughly as follows:

(1) Scenario content is spatial content.
(2) Attributing spatial content to an entity is justified only in cases where that entity can identify places over time.
(3) Identifying places over time involves re-identifying places.
(4) Re-identifying places depends on a capacity to identify one's current location with a location previously encountered.
(5) Such re-identification involves constructing an integrated spatial map of one's environment over time.

(6) Neither (4) nor (5) would be possible unless an entity possessed at least a primitive first-person concept.

(7) Therefore, nonconceptual content cannot be autonomous.

While the premises deserve further clarification (see essay 15), it's plausible to suppose that many forms of nonconceptuality are spatial, in other words, are contents that involve locating spatiotemporal particulars. Consequently, if sound, the argument limits the explanatory role of nonconceptual content, preventing its use, for example, by developmental and animal psychologists as well as by many cognitive scientists and researchers in AI.

Bermúdez takes issue with this explanatory circumscription. To begin with, he argues that Peacocke's conditions on scenario content are so strong that they effectively transform scenario content into conceptual content. As he sees it, the problem is that the conditions require that an individual must possess at least one of the concepts used in specifying a scenario, which, according to Bermúdez, suggests that its content is actually conceptual. Furthermore, he claims that phylogenetic explanations of concept acquisition depend upon attributing nonconceptual content to individuals without concepts. In other words, if the Autonomy Thesis were false, a developmental psychologist would have no way of accounting for how children learn concepts, something children unquestionably do. (In fact, without the thesis, it would be difficult to see how scenario contents themselves could be acquired.) The solution, Bermúdez believes, is to preserve the Autonomy Thesis and to develop a model of primitive self-consciousness that doesn't require an individual's possession of a first-person concept as suggested by premise 6. (See Bermúdez 1995c and 1998 for an attempt at developing such a model.)

In "Nonconceptual Content: Kinds, Rationales and Relations," Peacocke defends his rejection of autonomy. In response to Bermúdez's first criticism, he claims that, from the premise that an individual must possess at least one of the concepts used in specifying a scenario, it does not follow that its content is conceptual. A scenario content, he explains, is a spatial type that should be distinguished from any descriptions (concepts) used to pick it out. The distinction, according to Peacocke, is partially motivated by the fact that scenarios can capture the fine-grained character of experience whereas conceptual contents (descriptions) cannot. Of course, as McDowell and Kelly illustrate, this claim is open to dispute. Nevertheless, Peacocke might side-step these criticisms by appealing outright to the third rendering of "non." In this case, even if concepts could determine the fine-grained character of experience, he could claim that they are nevertheless not exercised on scenario contents and thereby not transformed into conceptual contents. But, such a defense would naturally raise questions about whether different kinds of contents should serve to demarcate the boundary between perception and cognition and whether scenarios really have an explanatory role in intentional psychology, issues addressed by McDowell and Hamlyn.

Although his argument is meant to deny the autonomy of scenario content specifically, and spatial content generally, Peacocke insists that it doesn't deny the autonomy of other forms of nonconceptuality such as Cussins's. In this way, construction-theoretic content can legitimately be attributed to entities without concepts and used in explanations of concept acquisition. To support this claim, Peacocke attempts to distinguish construction-theoretic content from scenario content by claiming that the former isn't spatial. In being pre-objective or egocentric, construction-theoretic contents allegedly "do not really have correctness conditions . . . that concern the objective, spatial world." However, it is not apparent that the pre-objectivity of construction-theoretic contents implies that they do not have correctness conditions or that the constraints proposed by Peacocke do not apply to them as well. Peacocke concludes by arguing that scenario contents cannot be reduced to construction-theoretic contents and that the latter can only offer a partial explanation of the acquisition of the former since it leaves us with "the problem of emergence of conscious states."

In the postscript, Peacocke cites two reasons for renouncing his earlier rejection of the Autonomy Thesis. First, he agrees with Bermúdez that there may be forms of self-consciousness (first-person notions, e.g., like *Ich*) that don't presuppose the possession of a corresponding concept. And second, while self-consciousness (whether conceptual or not) may serve to keep track of changing spatial relations—which is allegedly required for the possession of objective spatial contents—having a content like *hier*, whose possession doesn't involve any form of self-consciousness, can do the same. According to Peacocke, neither *hier* nor *Ich* are conceptual because, intuitively, as the description of certain computational systems suggests, an organism without any concepts could have (egocentric) representational contents containing them. Moreover, *hier* and *Ich* seem to violate Recombinability (and thus Compositionality) and can be employed by creatures lacking the ability for critical assessment (judgment), suggesting the violation of Cognitive Significance, weakly construed.

In conclusion, Peacocke suggests that the characterizations of the conceptual upon which he and others draw may be intertwined. This seems to be an issue, which, along with the kind(s) of relationship(s) different forms of nonconceptual content bear to one another and to conceptual content, is worth further exploration.

Chapter 15

Peacocke's Argument against the Autonomy of Nonconceptual Representational Content (1994)

José Luis Bermúdez

The idea that there might be mental states with nonconceptual representational content is receiving an increasing amount of discussion among philosophers of mind, and it is potentially of considerable theoretical importance to psychologists. This paper considers an argument that has been put forward by Christopher Peacocke against the suggestion that nonconceptual content is autonomous—that is, against the possibility of a creature being in states with nonconceptual representational content although not possessing any concepts at all. Peacocke's argument, if sound, would circumscribe the theoretical uses to which the notion of nonconceptual representational content could be put.

The paper is divided into five sections. In the first section I outline some of the motivations that philosophers and psychologists might have for endorsing a notion of autonomous nonconceptual representational content. In the second section I give a more specific characterization of the notion, together with a sketch of the specific form of nonconceptual content that Peacocke puts forward. In the third, Peacocke's argument against the autonomy of nonconceptual content is presented. In the fourth section it is argued that Peacocke's argument effectively destroys the distinction between conceptual and nonconceptual content, while the last section considers two possible responses that a defender of Peacocke's position might make.

1 Theoretical Uses for the Notion of Nonconceptual Representational Content

The general idea underlying the notion of nonconceptual representational content is that it is theoretically legitimate to refer to mental states that represent the world but that do not require the bearer of those mental states to possess the concepts required to specify the way in which they represent the world. Alternatively put, a particular content is taken to be a nonconceptual content if, and only if, it can be attributed to a creature without thereby attributing to that creature mastery of the concepts required to specify that content.[1]

From *Mind and Language*, vol. 9 (1994), pp. 402–418. Reprinted with the kind permission of the author and Blackwell Publishers.

One very general motivation for introducing a notion of nonconceptual content is the thought that in many cases an adequate description of the content of experience will be more detailed and fine-grained than it could possibly be if given only in terms of concepts possessed by the experiencing subject (Peacocke, 1992b, chap. 3) [essay 5]. There seem good grounds, for example, for describing a perceiver as seeing something as magenta-colored, without that requiring that he possess the concept of magenta. He can perceive the particular color even though he has no conceptual grip on it. The same applies to shape. Many would hold that it is legitimate to describe someone as seeing a chiliagon or a rhombus, even though he has no conceptual understanding of what a chiliagon or a rhombus might be. The suggestion is even more pertinent in the case of the modalities for which very few people have a developed descriptive vocabulary, such as taste and smell. Here it seems clear that restricting the characterization of experience to concepts actually possessed by a perceiver will often succeed only in picking out a range of possible perceptual experiences, rather than fixing uniquely on the particular perceptual experience in question.

Another very general reflection on the nature of perceptual experience that might make the notion of nonconceptual content seem tempting is that it offers a way of accommodating the insight that the nature of perceptual experience is partly determined by the concepts brought to bear in that experience without falling into the extremes of perceptual relativism. So, even if one holds that two observers with different conceptual abilities in the same situation (say, a young child and an ecclesiatic confronting a religious painting) will have relevantly different perceptual experiences, one can do justice to the intuition that at a basic level they both represent the world in similar ways by placing the similarities at the level of nonconceptual content and the divergences at the level of conceptual content.[2] By the same token, the notion of nonconceptual content also allows one to capture any continuity one might think there is in the way the world is represented in experience before and after the acquisition of a concept.

Perhaps the most obvious advantage of the notion of nonconceptual content is the promise it offers for explaining what it is to possess concepts and to be in states with conceptual content. It is important to distinguish, however, between two broad forms that such an explanation might take. The first form is what one might term a *developmental explanation* of conceptual content. In such an explanation the acquisition of the capacity for being in states with conceptual content is explained in terms of a developmental progression over time from being in states possessing nonconceptual content. On this sort of view, nonconceptual content comes first and conceptual content emerges from it. Cussins (1990) [see essay 6] gives an account of conceptual content along these lines, suggesting that the gradual development of a conception of objectivity should be understood in terms of the progressive construction of concepts from a basis of structured nonconceptual content—what he describes as "the transition from a preobjective stage where no concepts are possessed to an objective concept-exercising stage" (p. 409). The possibility of a developmental explanation of conceptual content has obvious relevance to developmental psychologists studying the ontogeny of concept development, as well as to evolutionary biologists considering the phylogeny of conceptual abilities.

A different way in which conceptual content can be grounded in nonconceptual contents is offered by Christopher Peacocke in various writings (most comprehensively in Peacocke 1992b). He suggests that what it is to possess a particular concept (i.e. an *explanation of the possession conditions* for that concept) can in certain fundamental cases be explained in terms of more primitive representational contents, which are egocentric and nonconceptual. The general idea is that the possession conditions of some basic concepts involve the subject's being willing to apply the concept when in a perceptual state with the appropriate nonconceptual content. Using the notion of nonconceptual content in this way allows noncircular characterization of the possession conditions for the relevant concept, because the subject's possession of the concept is not mentioned in specifying the content of the appropriate perceptual experience.

These two proposed forms of explanation involve differing degrees of commitment to what we can, following Peacocke (1992b, p. 90) [essay 5, p. 124], term the Autonomy Thesis (AT):

> *The Autonomy Thesis (AT)* It is possible for a creature to be in states with nonconceptual content, even though that creature possesses no concepts at all.

A philosopher who holds that the notion of nonconceptual content can provide a developmental explanation of conceptual content is likely to be sympathetic to AT, to the extent that his project is one of explaining how a creature possessing only states with nonconceptual content can develop into a fully-fledged concept-user.[3] A philosopher committed only to possession conditions explanation, however, does not have to accept AT (although there is no requirement to deny it). He can, for example, maintain that the nonconceptual content of experience will yield a noncircular account of possession conditions for certain primitive concepts, even if AT is denied. What makes this possible is, of course, that nonconceptual content is defined as content that does not require mastery of any of the concepts required to specify it—it is not defined as content that requires mastery of no concepts whatsoever. Indeed, one can be in a state with nonconceptual content despite possessing the relevant concepts. The point is that being in such a state is not dependent on possession of the concepts required to specify it.

On the other hand, however, if AT is rejected, then it will be *ipso facto* impossible to give at least one type of developmental explanation of conceptual content in terms of nonconceptual content—namely, the type of developmental explanation that involves explaining how a creature in states with only nonconceptual content, such as for example a newborn human infant, can develop into a fully-fledged concept-user. By the same token, it will also rule out an account of the phylogenetic development of conceptual content of the sort required by any account of conceptual content that sees it as appearing at a far later state of evolution than nonconceptual content.

In addition to this, moreover, it should be clear that rejecting AT rules out a further potential theoretical use for the notion of nonconceptual content. Some philosophers and psychologists have been struck by the thought that a primitive form of intentional explanation is required to account for the behavior of creatures one might not want to describe as concept-using, and obviously any form of intentional explanation requires attributing to such a creature representations of its environment. One area in which this emerges is animal learning theory (see, for example, Dickinson, 1988, where it is argued that certain cases of instrumental conditioning in rats support an intentional interpretation; see also Premack 1988), but it also seems highly relevant to the study of infant cognition. The suggestion that there are experiential states that represent the world but that do not implicate mastery of the concepts required to specify them is potentially very important here. Clearly, however, it can only be of theoretical use if AT is accepted.

2 Peacocke's Scenario Content as a Form of Nonconceptual Content

In giving a more detailed characterization of nonconceptual content it is useful to start from Cussins' (1990) [see essay 6] discussion. He begins with a distinction between conceptual and nonconceptual properties. A property is a conceptual property if, and only if, it is canonically characterized, relative to a theory, by means of concepts which are such that a creature must have those concepts in order to instantiate the property. As Cussins points out, properties are characterized relative to a theory, and by "canonical characterization relative to a theory" he means characterization in terms of properties that that theory takes to be essential to it. The notion of a nonconceptual property follows easily. A property is nonconceptual if, and only if, it is canonically characterized, relative to a theory, by means of concepts that a creature need not have in order to instantiate the property. The "need not have" is important here. Even if the creature acquires the relevant concepts, that will not transform the property into a conceptual property. The specification of a nonconceptual property requires only that possession of the relevant concepts is not necessary.

The difference between conceptual and nonconceptual properties is straightforward. Consider the two different properties of (a) having a central nervous system, and (b) understanding the functioning of the central nervous system. Clearly, the first is instantiated by innumerable creatures that lack the concept *central nervous system*. Equally clearly, it is hard to see how a creature could be ascribed the second unless it had the concepts of *understanding*, *functioning*, and *central nervous system*. Much depends, however, on the theory relative to which the property is being canonically characterized. There are certain theories on which possession of those concepts would be sufficient—perhaps "naive biology" would be an example here. On the other hand, there are other theories (physiology, for example) on which possession of those concepts would be necessary, but far from sufficient.

Once the distinction between conceptual and nonconceptual properties is granted, it is only a short move to Cussins' distinction between conceptual and nonconceptual content. Conceptual content is "content that consists of conceptual properties," and by the same token, nonconceptual content is "content that consists of nonconceptual properties." In both cases the properties are being canonically characterized relative to the theory of content. This is how Cussins fleshes out the basic idea that nonconceptual content is content that can be ascribed to a creature without thereby ascribing to it possession of the concepts involved in specifying that content.[4]

So, a particular content is nonconceptual if, and only if, it can be specified wholly in terms of nonconceptual properties, where a nonconceptual property is a property that can be canonically characterized relative to a theory by means of concepts none of which need to be possessed by a creature satisfying that property.

With the general notion of nonconceptual content sharpened up we can move on to a specific proposal that has been put forward for understanding the nonconceptual content of perceptual experience. Christopher Peacocke's conception of scenario content explains the nonconceptual representational content of an experience in terms of a spatial type (1989b, pp. 8–9) [see also essay 5, pp. 107–109]:

> The idea is that specifying the content of a perceptual experience involves saying what ways of filling out a space around the origin with surfaces, solids, textures, light and so forth, are consistent with the correctness or veridicality of the experience. Such contents are not built from propositions, concepts, senses, or continuant material objects.

Such spatial types are specified in terms of a labeled origin and axis egocentrically centered on the perceiver. Within the framework yielded by the origin and axis, specifying how space is "filled out" is done in terms of points (pp. 9–10).

> We need, for each point (strictly one should say point-type) identified by its distance and direction from the origin, to specify whether there is a surface there, and if so what texture, hue, saturation, brightness, and temperature it has at that point, together with its degree of resistance to touch. The orientation of the surface must be included.

The conceptual resources with which such a specification of the spatial type is carried out are not, of course, attributed to the perceiver, and this is what makes it an account of nonconceptual content. The account is completed as follows. This spatial type, which Peacocke terms a *scenario*, yields the nonconceptual content of the experience when its axes and origins have been assigned places and directions in the real world, and a time has been allocated.[5] This content is correct if, and only if, the volume of the real world around the perceiver, specified according to the same constraints as the scenario, instantiates the type specified by the scenario.

The specific use to which Peacocke puts his notion of scenario content is in specifying the possession conditions of concepts. Such a specification takes two parts. The first part of the specification for a particular concept yields the constraint that the subject be in a perceptual state with the appropriate scenario content, and that he be willing to apply the concept when in that state. The second part is a version of the Generality Constraint first suggested by Evans (1982, §4.3) [essay 2, appendix]—namely, that the subject be capable of a generalized concept application. Broadly speaking, the thought is that if a creature is properly to be credited with the thought *a is F*, then that creature must be capable both of thinking *a is G* for any property of being *G* of which he has a conception, and of thinking *b is F* for any object *b* of which he has a conception.

3 Peacocke's Argument against AT

From the description in the previous section it should be clear that Peacocke is committed neither to accepting nor denying AT. Nonetheless he does deny it, in favor of the claim that "conceptual and nonconceptual content must be elucidated simultaneously. The most basic elements of the scheme form a local holism" (1992, p. 91) [essay 5, p. 125]. I will take the liberty of schematizing his argument, which is presented in a very condensed form (1992; p. 90) [essay 5, pp. 124–125]:

> (1) Scenario content is genuine spatial representational content.
> (2) The attribution of genuine spatial representational content to a creature is only justified if that creature is capable of identifying places over time.
> (3) Identifying places over time involves reidentifying places.
> (4) Reidentifying places requires the capacity to identify one's current location with a location previously encountered.
> (5) Reidentifying places in this way involves building up an integrated spatial representation of the environment over time.
> (6) Neither (4) nor (5) would be possible unless the subject possesses at least a primitive form of the first-person concept.
> (7) Therefore, nonconceptual content cannot be autonomous.

Several of the stages in this argument seem relatively unproblematic. (1) can be provisionally accepted, although it would be helpful to have a clearer sense of what is to count as spatial representational content, given the claim in (2). (3) is a familiar claim, associated in particular with Strawson (1959). However, (4) and (5) could do with further discussion.

It is important to realize that (4) is making a substantive claim, rather than just explaining what it is to be capable of reidentifying places. Peacocke is claiming that genuine spatial content rests on a particular type of place reidentification, and, conversely, that there are capacities that some theorists might describe as capacities for place reidentification but that a creature could have without it being appropriate to attribute genuine spatial content to that creature. As he stresses, "spatial content involves more than just a sensitivity to higher-order properties of stimulation patterns" (1992, p. 90) [essay 5, p. 124], and the type of place reidentification implicated in genuine spatial content is precisely one that cannot be explained in terms of such sensitivity. Of course, this all depends upon how sensitivity to higher-order stimulation patterns is understood, but a plausible suggestion here would be that behaving in a way that merely reflects such a sensitivity is behaving in a way that could be explained in terms of stimulus-response (S-R) theory. (4) should be read as claiming that there is more to the sort of place reidentification implicated in genuinely spatial content than a minimal capacity to find one's way back to a given place, because an SR account could be given of such a minimal capacity (as it often is in accounts of the spatial abilities of animals). Place reidentification requires the exercise of certain cognitive as well as navigational abilities. It involves something like a conscious registering of particular locations as locations that have been previously encountered.

It is because so much is built into the idea of place reidentification that Peacocke claims in (5) that an integrated representation of the environment over time is also involved. An argument from *Sense and Content* (Peacocke 1983) can shed light here. In *Sense and Content* his argument against genuine spatial content being attributable to a creature whose behavior is explainable in S-R terms is that, however complicated and apparently purposeful S-R behavioral response might be, allowing genuine content to be ascribed on the basis of those responses would be to admit the possibility that a creature might bear propositional attitudes to just one place in their environment, while not bearing propositional attitudes to any others (1983, p. 65). This Peacocke holds to be unintelligible because places are essentially related to other places and place identification is a holistic phenomenon. Genuine spatial content involves a grasp of the connectedness of space and that is why it involves some form of integrated representation of the world over time.

The crucial step in the argument is (6), the claim that place reidentification involves a primitive grasp of the first-person concept. There seem to be two ways in which this could be argued. The first would be that the conscious registration of places requires the capacity to entertain thoughts or proto-thoughts of the sort "I have been to this place before." It is in virtue of this capacity that place reidentification is to be distinguished from simply finding one's way back to a place, and it seems plausible that entertaining such proto-thoughts requires possessing the first-person concept. A second line of argument here would be that one can build up an integrated representation of the environment over time only if one has a grip on one's own location in it. An integrated representation of the environment is only possible if one is capable of a representation of one's actual and previous locations, as well as of understanding the role that changes in one's own location contribute to one's changing perceptual experience. None of these would be possible, Peacocke would argue, in the absence of some form of the first-person concept.

There might seem to be a difficulty here, however. The defense of (4) that has been attributed to Peacocke rests on a claim about propositional attitudes—namely, that it is impossible to bear propositional attitudes to just one place. But why, one might ask, should this be thought relevant to a discussion of scenario content? Scenario content is supposed to be nonconceptual content, and it is often thought (surely correctly) that one of the distinctive features of nonconceptual content is that the constraints appropriate at the level of conceptual content just do not apply.[6] There seems to be no contradiction in granting that one cannot have attitudes to just one place, without this carrying any implications for the possibility of ascribing genuinely spatial scenario content.[7] In which case, then, there seems to be a confusion of levels involved in the argument against AT—a constraint appropriate to the level of conceptual content is being applied at the level of nonconceptual content. Why does this not amount to making nonconceptual content into a form of conceptual content?

I suspect that Peacocke would respond that this is not a confusion of levels at all. Rather, it is precisely a sign of how conceptual and nonconceptual content need to be elucidated simultaneously. Because scenario content is genuine spatial content, its conditions of possibility involve the perceiver's being capable of holding propositional attitudes to more than one place. In the absence of this capacity there can be no genuine spatial content at all. And that, Peacocke would claim, is a further reason why AT is unacceptable. Rejecting AT in this way, he would stress, does not involve tacitly transforming scenario content into a type of conceptual content. The explanatory distinctiveness of nonconceptual scenario content is preserved, even though its autonomy is denied.

I think, however, that although this objection does not work, it is on the right lines, and that a successful response to Peacocke's argument against AT will proceed by showing that Peacocke's argument obliterates the distinction between conceptual and nonconceptual content. In the next section I would like to outline such a response.

4 Is Scenario Content Nonconceptual Content?

Nonconceptual content is a type of content that can be attributed to a creature without thereby attributing to that creature a mastery of any of the concepts involved in specifying that content (I will henceforth abbreviate this to "relevant concept mastery"). What I would like to suggest, however, is that Peacocke's argument against AT effectively makes it a condition of attributing scenario content to a creature that that creature should have mastery of at least one of the concepts involved in canonically specifying any possible scenario content. In which case, then, there can be no nonconceptual scenario contents.

Consider stage (6) in the argument against AT. The claim there is that the rei-dentification of places requires a rudimentary form of first-person thought. The conscious registration of places as places that have already been encountered requires the capacity to entertain thoughts or proto-thoughts of the form "I have been to this place before," and this is conditional upon mastery of the first-person concept, as is the reasoning about one's own location involved in building up an integrated representation of the environment. It might initially seem tempting to assume that this mastery of the first-person is itself sufficient to contravene the requirement that scenario content attribution not involve attribution of relevant concept mastery. If scenario content is specified in terms of an egocentrically cen-tered origin and axis, then, it might appear, the first-person concept will be involved in that specification. If so, however, scenario content would be con-ceptual rather than nonconceptual content, because it would only be available to creatures on the condition that they possessed one of the concepts involved in the specification of any possible scenario content. This would not be quite right, however. The fact that the origin and axis are egocentrically centered on the per-ceiver does not mean that they have to be specified egocentrically. It is perfectly possible to specify an egocentric spatial framework without employing any first-person notions. As Evans puts it, an egocentric spatial vocabulary refers to points in public space (1982, p. 157) [essay 2, p. 52]. The distinction between egocentric and public space is at the level of sense rather than of reference, and so it remains possible to give a specification of egocentric space that does not involve first-person notions. It might, for example, proceed with reference to impersonally specified body parts.

This does suggest a further line of argument, however. Suppose, for example, that we stress other aspects of the putative proto-thoughts involved in place rei-dentification. It has been suggested that such a proto-thought will be of the form "I have been to this place before." Clearly, the possibility of this type of thought requires attributing to the subject not just the capacity for primitive first-person thought, but also a mastery of the concept of "place." The first-person component here is relatively innocuous, but the notion of a place seems more problematic. The concept of a place is part of a family of related concepts, such as "location," "point," "position," etc. Mastery of any one of them cannot be divorced from mastery of the others, so that attributing to a thinker the concept of one of them is effectively to attribute to him the concept of any of them. Any specification of scenario content will employ at least one of these concepts, most prominently the concept of a point, as should be clear from the outline of scenario content given in section 2.

This creates a significant tension within Peacocke's characterization of scenario content. According to the argument against AT, if a subject is to have experiences with scenario content he must be capable of place reidentification, and that requires possessing the concept of a place, or one of the related concepts in the family. At the same time, however, it follows from Peacocke's description of how scenarios are fixed that one or more of these concepts must feature in any speci-fication of a scenario content. This makes scenario content into a form of concep-tual rather than nonconceptual content, because any subject who is in a state with scenario content will be required to possess at least one of the concepts required to specify that content.

If this is so, then the rejection of AT creates problems for Peacocke's position. On the one hand we have the general requirement on nonconceptual content that it can be attributed to a creature without thereby attributing to that creature mastery of any of the concepts required to specify that content. On the other hand, however, we have the specific requirements for scenario content to be genuine spatial content, and these specific requirements entail that the subject possess at least one concept involved in specifying any possible scenario content. This tension will not be an easy one to resolve. Nonetheless, there are several lines of defence available here, which need to be considered before the conclusion is drawn that Peacocke's rejection of AT effectively transforms scenario content into a form of conceptual content.

5 Objections Considered

(1) An initial response might be to deny that place reidentification requires the concept of a place. The sort of proto-thoughts implicated in place reidentification do not, the defence might run, necessarily involve mastery of a concept from the relevant family. It is worth pointing out, however, that this strategy is a danger-ous one for anybody concerned with denying AT, because what must at all costs be avoided is making the proto-thoughts so innocuous that they no longer require possession of a primitive form of the first-person content, and hence do not permit the move to (6) in the argument against AT. This certainly rules out the option of construing place reidentification as a practical capacity manifested in sufficiently sophisticated navigational abilities. Bearing this in mind, then, it would seem that the only way of construing the proto-thoughts would be via some sort of demon-strative—perhaps of the form "I have been here before." The difficulty with this, however, is that it seems to contravene Peacocke's claims about the holistic nature of place identification. The argument against AT has depended crucially upon the idea that it is unintelligible that a subject should have thoughts about just one place in his environment, because places are essentially spatially related to other places. Consider, however, a subject only capable of demonstrative thought about places of the form "I have been here before." That subject would be incapable of having thoughts about more than one place in his environment at any given moment, thereby falling foul of the intelligibility requirement.

(2) It was argued in section 4 that Peacocke's argument against AT made the pos-sibility of being in states with scenario content dependent upon possession of a concept necessarily involved in the specification of any possible scenario content.

The conclusion drawn from this was that that was sufficient to make scenario content conceptual content. The previous reply attacked the initial claim. It could also be objected, however, that the conclusion rests upon a crucial equivocation in the conception of conceptual content.

When it was argued in section 4 that scenario content was conceptual content, the operative notion of conceptual content was this: a given content is conceptual just in case that content can only be canonically specified by means of concepts at least one of which must be possessed by any subject who is in a state with that content. The notion of possession here is ambiguous, however. On one reading the requirement could just be that the subject has to possess the concept, irrespective of whether or not it is employed in the relevant experience. Alternatively, it could mean not only that the subject has to possess the concept, but also that his possession of the concept must play an explanatory role in that experience being the experience that it is. With this distinction in mind, then, it could be pointed out that the argument in section 4 depends upon the first reading—whereas if the second reading is adopted it fails to go through. The point is this. The necessity of possessing the concept of a place for scenario content to be possible should not be taken to imply that any experience with scenario content will involve the subject's employing the concept of place. Rather, the thesis is much more general. What it amounts to is the idea that experiences with scenario content are only available to creatures capable of more general forms of spatial representation (including, for example, thought about places). Although these more general forms of spatial representation involve the concept of place, this does not entail that the concept of place is involved in scenario contents. Because of this scenario content remains nonconceptual content.

The following passage seems to suggest that Peacocke does not clearly distinguish between these two readings (1992b, p. 68) [essay 5, p. 112]:

> [I]t is crucial to observe that the fact that a concept is used in fixing the scenario does *not* entail that the concept itself is somehow a component of the representational content of the experience, nor that the concept must be possessed by the experiencer.[8]

What makes content conceptual on this account (as opposed, for example, to Cussins' 1990, p. 383 [essay 6, p. 135]) is that its appearance in a specification of the scenario entails its possession by the subject. This is neutral, however, on the issue raised by the second reading, which makes the stronger demand that the possession of the relevant concept play an explanatory role in the representational content of the experience being as it is.

We can begin by considering Peacocke's position as specified in the passage quoted. As it stands, Peacocke's position does not rule out my argument for scenario content being conceptual content. Consider the following reformulation of the argument in section 4. The fact that the concept of a place/point can be employed in fixing a scenario entails that the scenario content is genuine spatial content. The fact that a perceiver is in states with genuine spatial content entails that the perceiver possesses the concept of a place/point. This argument certainly seems to satisfy his conditions upon a content being conceptual content.

But the question remains: can Peacocke retreat to the second reading of conceptual content in the manner suggested earlier? The additional requirement that this second reading imposes is that the possession of the relevant content should play an explanatory role in that content's being the content that it is. It would seem, however, that this requirement is also met by the argument in the previous paragraph. Presumably it is part of what it is for a given scenario content to be the scenario content that it is that it should be genuinely spatial content.[9] But the central claim of Peacocke's argument against AT was that a given scenario content was genuinely spatial content in virtue of the perceiver's being capable of place reidentification, and hence in virtue of their possessing the concept of place. If so, it seems clear that possession of the concept of place/point is playing the sort of genuine explanatory role required for conceptual content.

(3) This last response suggests a final defense that a defender of Peacocke might adopt. It is open to him to modify the first premise of his argument against AT. That premise, it will be remembered, was that scenario content is genuine spatial content. This could be modified to the claim that, although scenario content itself does not qualify as genuine spatial content, only creatures that are capable of being in states with genuine spatial content can be in states with scenario content. What might make this move seem appealing is the idea that, once it is denied that scenario content is genuine spatial content, the argument that scenario content is conceptual content could be defused along the following lines. Certainly, it might be argued, scenario content is only available to creatures capable of being in states with genuine spatial content, and, moreover, creatures capable of being in such states must possess the concept of a place. But it is nonetheless important to distinguish between the levels of scenario content and genuine spatial content. Although the level of genuine spatial content does indeed require the possession of certain concepts, this does not entail that the level of scenario content requires the possession of those concepts. In which case, the argument that scenario content effectively becomes conceptual content fails to go through.

One question that anybody arguing in this direction must answer, however, is precisely what the connection is between the two levels of content: why, that is, should experiences with scenario content only be available to creatures capable of experiences with genuine spatial content? What is needed is a substantive reason for the interdependence of scenario content and genuine spatial content. And it would seem that the only non-question-begging way of doing this would be to argue that scenario content would be impossible in the absence of genuine spatial content. This, however, amounts to the claim that there are aspects of scenario content that are made possible by genuine spatial content. Or, in other words, that certain features of genuine spatial content make possible certain features of scenario content.[10] Amongst those features of genuine spatial content will presumably be some that implicate grasp of the concept of place/point. If this is granted, however, then it becomes possible to run the earlier argument that possession of the concept of place/point is playing the sort of genuine explanatory role required for conceptual content.

6 Conclusion

This places Peacocke in a difficult position. His argument against the Autonomy Thesis places such strong conditions of possibility upon scenario content that it effectively transforms scenario content into conceptual content. Apart from making AT rather nugatory, this endangers the project of grounding the possession conditions of certain primitive concepts in nonconceptual scenario content. He seems to have a choice between giving up his attack on AT, on the one hand, and giving up his suggestion that scenario content is nonconceptual, on the other. Given the crucial role that nonconceptual, scenario content plays in his account of possession conditions, as well as the more general theoretical uses it has in both philosophy and psychology, the wisest course of action would seem to be to abandon his attack on the Autonomy Thesis and admit the possibility of a creature being in states with nonconceptual content even though not possessing any concepts at all.

Rejecting the argument against AT, however, means rethinking some of the issues opened up by that argument. In particular, the existing account of place reidentification will have to be modified. There seem to be two theoretical options open to Peacocke here. The first would be to lighten the constraints that he places upon genuine place reidentification. It is the reflective and disengaged elements in his understanding of spatial representation that are creating difficulties, and so it might seem sensible to get rid of them. He could do this by withdrawing the requirement that any creature capable of genuine place reidentification be capable of spatial reasoning, and placing much more stress on the importance of navigational abilities and practical capacities.[11] In terms of his argument against AT, this would be to reject at least premise (5), thereby blocking the move to (6) and hence to the conclusion that a primitive form of the first-person concept is required. And clearly it would also have the effect of not making possession of the concept of a place a necessary condition of being capable of genuine place reidentification, thus keeping nonconceptual content independent of conceptual content. One problem with this approach, however, is that it might be thought to beg the question of why we are talking here about content at all. Certainly some sort of account would have to be given of the correctness conditions of spatial representation. What would it be to reidentify a place correctly as opposed to incorrectly, if the connection between spatial representation and spatial reasoning is severed?

The second general strategy open here would be to try to preserve this connection between spatial representation and spatial reasoning, but without making it dependent upon possession of the appropriate concepts. This would require developing a theory that would allow for a nonconceptual analogue of proto-thoughts like "I have been to this place before," and that would explain how such nonconceptual proto-thoughts could feature in primitive forms of spatial reasoning to build up an integrated representation of the environment over time. In particular such a theory would have to explain how a creature can represent itself first-personally without that requiring possession of even a primitive form of the first-person concept.[12] It would also have to explain the possibility of a creature's reasoning and reflecting about places even though it did not possess the concept of a place, or any of the associated concepts. In terms of the argument against AT, if this could be done then it would be possible to preserve all the steps except for the last two. Although adopting this strategy would concede the autonomy of nonconceptual content, it would nonetheless preserve the nonconceptual nature of scenario content.

What both these strategies have in common, however, is that they leave open the possibility that a creature might be in states with content despite not possessing any concepts at all, and this, as pointed out earlier, greatly widens the explanatory scope of the notion of nonconceptual content within both psychology and philosophy. Peacocke's notion of scenario content has a vital role to play in the (relatively) narrow project of explaining what it is to possess a concept. But if its potential autonomy is conceded then it can have an equally important role to play elsewhere in the philosophy and psychology of conceptual content.[13]

Notes

1. It should be noted that this paper is concerned only with ascriptions of content at what might be termed the personal level. The notion of nonconceptual content is also employed in the context of subpersonal computational states, the idea being, for example, that early visual processing involves representations of the environment that do not implicate mastery of the relevant concepts (e.g. the concept of binocular disparity). Although I do think that the notion of nonconceptual content can be legitimately employed in the subpersonal context, my interest, and that of Peacocke in the argument under discussion, is with the content of experience.

2. Of course, there are other ways of accommodating this point. One could maintain, as McGinn does (1989, pp. 59ff), that the similarities in perceptual experience are a function of the basic observational concepts they have in common. Alternatively, one could hold that the similarities are qualitative features of the experience, rather than representational features.

3. There seem, however, to be possible versions of developmental explanation that are compatible with denying AT. For example, it could be argued that, although in general nonconceptual and conceptual contents form a holism, there are certain conceptual contents that develop out of nonconceptual contents.

4. There remains an ambiguity of scope. Should the definition of a nonconceptual property be taken in a strong or weak sense, where the strong reading means that the subject is not required to possess *any* of the concepts involved in characterizing the property, and the weak reading means that the subject is not required to possess all of the concepts involved in the characterization. I take it that the strong reading is correct, and that requiring the possession of even one of the concepts involved in the canonical characterization of a property is sufficient to make that property count

as a conceptual property. I also take it that the strong reading is equally appropriate at the level of content. If the specification of a content involves just one conceptual property, it will *ipso facto* count as a conceptual content.

5. Or rather: it does so in conjunction with a further level of nonconceptual representational content, which Peacocke terms "protopropositional content" (1992b, chap. 3) [essay 5]. The protopropositional content of experience specifies the relational aspects of experience. I am not mentioning it specifically because it does not affect the argument of this paper. However, when the term "scenario content" is employed below, this should not be taken to exclude protopropositional content.

6. This is certainly the way that Evans saw the matter in his seminal discussion of nonconceptual content in *The Varieties of Reference*. "It is one of the fundamental differences between human thought and the information-processing that takes place in our brains that the Generality Constraint applies to the former but not the latter. When we attribute to the brain computations whereby it localizes the sounds it hears, we *ipso facto* ascribe to it representations of the speed of sound and of the distance between the ears, without any commitment to the idea that it should be able to represent the speed of light or the distance between anything else" (Evans 1982, p. 104, n. 22) [essay 2, appendix, p. 74, n. 47]. Admittedly, Evans is discussing subpersonal nonconceptual content, whereas Peacocke's nonconceptual content is a personal-level notion, but the point holds in virtue of the type of content, rather than the level of processing. The Generality Constraint is a condition upon concept possession, not upon any type of mental representation—but see Davies 1986, pp. 145–146.

7. Although the traditional notion of content holds it to be whatever is specified in a "that" clause when attributing a propositional attitude (from which it would seem to follow that constraints on propositional attitudes are *ipso facto* constraints on content), Peacocke characterizes content in terms of states that have "correctness conditions"—where having correctness conditions is a sufficient condition for representing the world in a particular way.

8. And also the following: "There is no requirement at this point that the conceptual apparatus used in specifying a way of filling out the space be an apparatus of concepts used by the perceiver himself. Any apparatus we want to use, however sophisticated, may be employed in fixing the spatial type, however primitive the conceptual resources of the perceiver with whom we are concerned" (1992b, p. 63) [essay 5, pp. 108–109].

9. And presumably part of what it is for something to be genuinely spatial content is that there should be a determinate answer to the question Peacocke poses in *Transcendental Arguments and the Theory of Content*: "Why is it correct to take an experience as representing the existence of various features, surfaces and solids as at various distances and directions, rather than as representing the same features, etc., as at angles rotated around the direction of straight by a certain quantity?" (p. 13) Clearly, however, the existence of an answer to this question is part of what it is for the scenario content to be the content that it is.

10. Perhaps the answer to the question mooted in n. 11.

11. This would be in the spirit of the notion of causal indexicality developed in Campbell 1993.

12. I have attempted to make some headway on this problem in my "Ecological Perception and the Notion of a Nonconceptual Point of View."

13. I am very grateful to Julie Jack and an anonymous reader for comments on earlier versions.

Chapter 16

Nonconceptual Content: Kinds, Rationales, and Relations (1994)

Christopher Peacocke

José Bermúdez's critique has a quite specific target, but the important issues raised by his discussion range more widely [essay 15; see also essay 8, pp. 187–191]. His specific target is my rejection, in *A Study of Concepts* [essay 5, pp. 124–130], of the Autonomy Thesis, which states that a creature could be in states with nonconceptual content while possessing no concepts at all. The wider issues raised by Bermúdez's critique include the following: Are there more varieties of nonconceptual content than I distinguished in *A Study of Concepts* [see essay 5]? How are any further kinds related to those already acknowledged? Do the explanatory purposes served by nonconceptual contents require acceptance of the Autonomy Thesis?

Bermúdez reaches two main conclusions. The first is about the notion of scenario content I introduced, and which I regard as a form of nonconceptual content (Peacocke 1989b, 1992a, 1992b) [essay 5]. Bermúdez summarizes his first conclusion thus: "[I]t follows from Peacocke's description of how scenarios are fixed that one or more of these concepts [*location, point, position*] must feature in any specification of a scenario content. This makes scenario content into a form of conceptual rather than nonconceptual content, because any subject who is in a state with scenario content will be required to possess at least one of the concepts required to specify that content" (p. 412) [pp. 301–302]. Bermúdez's point is that my reasons for rejecting the Autonomy Thesis entail that anyone enjoying experiences with scenario content will have certain concepts used in specifying scenarios. In arguing for his first conclusion, Bermúdez aims to make use of a characterization of a conceptual property developed by Adrian Cussins (1990) [see essay 6]. Bermúdez's second conclusion, or family of conclusions, concerns the Autonomy Thesis. Developmental and phylogenetic explanations of the acquisition of concepts will involve transitions from prior states with only nonconceptual content to those with conceptual content, Bermúdez holds, but such prior states would be an impossibility if the Autonomy Thesis fails. Bermúdez concludes that the idea of experiential states with nonconceptual content "can only be of theoretical use if AT (the Autonomy Thesis) is accepted" (p. 406) [p. 296].

From *Mind and Language*, vol. 9 (1994), pp. 419–429. Reprinted with the kind permission of the author and Blackwell Publishers. The postscript is published here for the first time.

Against these points, I will argue:

(1) It is a nonsequitur to argue from the premise that the subject must possess some of the concepts used in specifying a scenario content to the conclusion that scenario content is conceptual content.

(2) The characterization of a conceptual state on which Bermúdez relies in his argument is too weak, for it counts some nonconceptual states as conceptual. His characterization is also not the notion formulated by Cussins, and indeed Cussins' actual criterion cannot be used in support of Bermúdez's conclusion.

(3) Bermúdez writes as if scenario content and the notion of nonconceptual content introduced by Cussins are identical, and as if there were merely disagreement about what theses are true of a single type of content. In fact, the types of nonconceptual content introduced by me and by Cussins are to be sharply distinguished, both in respect of their nature, and in respect of the motivation for their introduction. The relations between them are complex. In the limited space available, I will very briefly discuss these relations, in a way I hope makes clear that the whole issue merits further investigation. I will also argue that explanations of the acquisition of concepts do not require the Autonomy Thesis. Further, once scenario content and Cussins' notion are kept separate, rejection of the Autonomy Thesis does not even appear to be in conflict with the project of explaining the emergence of conceptual mastery from states that are nonconceptual in Cussins' sense.

(1) Scenario content is essentially the notion of a spatial type, a type an experience can represent as instantiated in the volume of space around the subject of the experience. In the literature that introduced scenario content, there was emphasis on the distinction between the spatial type itself, and the infinitely many ways there are of picking out that type by description. The way the experience represents the world as being is given (in part) by the type itself, not descriptions of the type. If we respect the distinction between the type and its descriptions, it is clear that one cannot establish that scenario content is conceptual content simply from the fact that the subject of experience must possess such concepts as *location* and *position*. It would have additionally to be established that using only such concepts we can give an exhaustive statement of the way the experience represents the world as being (i.e. of the type itself), and can do so without any reliance on nonconceptual content.

Such concepts as *location* and *position* are by themselves too general to capture uniquely the fine-grained content of experience, the content that scenarios help to capture. We need something more detailed. A specification that uniquely fixes a particular scenario content will contain, *inter alia*, such material as this (for instance): the particular scenario is a type that requires for its instantiation that there be a triangular surface with vertices at egocentric coordinates (a,b,c), (a',b',c'), (a'',b'',c''), where the coordinates are given in metric units. Clearly such a description as this does not normally enter the representational content of an experience, and is not required to do so for the experience to have spatial content.

A more promising direction for the critique to take would be to appeal to demonstrative modes of presentation, which are certainly conceptual. These do not feature crucially in Bermúdez's discussion, but it would have been natural for him to bring them in. After all, my reasons, in *A Study of Concepts* [see essay 5], for rejecting the Autonomy Thesis entail that the subject of experience must be capable of such thoughts as "This place is the same as such-and-such place I encountered before." Anything in the (anchored) scenario content of an experience can be made the subject of a perceptual demonstrative, such as *that edge*, *that surface*, *there*, and the like. So does this not show that scenario content is fully capturable by conceptual contents after all?

It does not. We must remember the clause above, to the effect that the relevant concepts must exhaustively give the content of the perceptual experience without any reliance on nonconceptual content. The defender of nonconceptual content will say that these perceptual demonstratives do not meet this last condition. The natural account of the individuation of these perceptual demonstratives is that, in addition to the general concepts they respectively involve (*surface*, *edge*, etc.), they are also individuated in part by a spatial type. This is the type that is involved in giving the spatial content of the experience that makes available the perceptual demonstrative to the subject. This spatial type contributes to the cognitive significance of the perceptual demonstrative. This contribution is represented in such a notation as (*that F, W*) for a perceptual demonstrative "*that F*" where the way *W* in which the (apparently) presented object is perceived would involve at least part of the scenario content of the experience that makes available the demonstrative.[1]

Of course this natural account needs defense against the various considerations that, elsewhere in the literature, are alleged to show that nonconceptual content is impossible. But the mere existence of a natural position in logical space with the properties I have advocated is enough to show that someone can consistently accept Bermúdez's conclusion that the experiencer must have some of the concepts in a specification of the scenario, without thereby abandoning the scenario's fundamentally nonconceptual character. It is true, and true for constitutive reasons, that a state is an experience with a scenario content only if it has various connections with other, conceptual states of the thinker. This is consistent with the way it represents the world as being having an irreducibly nonconceptual component.

(2) What makes a property of a thinker a conceptual property? Bermúdez's argument employs a criterion that he ascribes to Cussins, and formulates thus: "A property is a conceptual property if, and only if, it is canonically characterized, relative to a theory, by means of concepts which are such that a creature must have those concepts in order to instantiate the property" (p. 406) [p. 296]. Bermúdez makes clear that it is the canonical characterizations given in a correct theory of

content that are to be employed in applying this criterion. But the considerations in (1) above suggest that the criterion captures too much. The scenario content of an experience is canonically characterized in part by some concepts that a thinker must have in order to enjoy experiences with scenario contents. If the considerations under (1) above are correct, then this criterion will count enjoyment of a state with fundamentally nonconceptual content as a conceptual property.

In fact, to ascribe the quoted criterion to Cussins is a misattribution. Bermúdez omits the word "only" from Cussins' criterion, which reads as follows (Cussins 1990, pp. 382–383) [essay 6, p. 134]:

> A property is a conceptual property if, and only if, it is canonically characterized, relative to a theory, *only* by means of concepts which are such that an organism must have those concepts in order to satisfy the property. [Italicization added by Peacocke to emphasize the present point, with Cussins' own emphases removed.]

When the word "only" is included in the criterion, no one could have thought that the resulting criterion would count having an experience with scenario content as a conceptual property. The canonical specification of such a property involves the sort of material concerning the metric-coordinate specification of a triangular surface we gave above. Cussins' criterion would count this as an example of a conceptual property only if the subject of the experience had to have *all* of the concepts involved in the canonical specification.

Cussins' actual criterion, however, with the word "only" included in the characterization, seems to be too strong. There are two problems. The first can be illustrated by Cussins' own example of the operation of his criterion: "Consider the property of thinking of someone as a bachelor. A specification of what this property is will use the concepts *male*, *adult*, and *unmarried*. But nothing could satisfy the property unless it possessed these concepts. . . . So the property of thinking of someone as a bachelor (unlike the property of being a bachelor) is a conceptual property" (Cussins 1990, p. 383) [essay 6, p. 135]. It is, though, equally true that nothing could satisfy the property without having the property of thinking. But a creature can think without having the concept of thinking. Since the criterion demands that a conceptual property be canonically characterized *only* by concepts the organism must have in order to satisfy the property, the criterion will count the property of thinking of someone as a bachelor as nonconceptual. A similar point applies to beliefs, desires, fears, intentions and other attitudes with conceptual contents if we allow, as it seems we should, that a creature can be in these states without having concepts of these states.

The second problem is raised by the level of analysis attained by "the" theory of concepts which is to provide the canonical characterization of conceptual properties. Believing that all banknotes are rectangular is a conceptual property. The content of the belief may involve the observational concept *rectangular*. This concept is individuated in part by its links with perceptions with a certain kind of nonconceptual content, which in turn will be characterized by concepts the thinker need not possess. So if the theory of content proceeds to that level of analysis of observational concepts, then believing that all banknotes are rectangular will not be classified as a conceptual property. It is not tempting to make the notion of a conceptual property relative to a level of theoretical analysis.

Bermúdez's aim was to introduce the notion of conceptual content via Cussins' definition of a conceptual property. There is something puzzling about this procedure. Cussins' definition itself uses the notion of a concept. So the definition can be applied only if we already have some account of what a concept is. But if we do already have some account of which contents are conceptual, we do not need to proceed via Cussins' definition of a conceptual property. We can say simply that a conceptual content is one which is a concept, or is composed solely of concepts. A conceptual property is then one which consists of a relation to a conceptual content, where the relation itself does not involve any other contents. A criterion for which contents are conceptual must, though, be formulated in the context of a consideration of the nature of nonconceptual content, and that is our next task.

(3) As Bermúdez notes, Cussins' nonconceptual content—his construction-theoretic content, henceforth "CT content"—is pre-objective. States with CT content can, in Cussins' account, be enjoyed by creatures in advance of their having any grasp of some states of affairs as objective. Such states are intended to be a resource that can be used in the explanation of the emergence of a grasp of objectivity, without presupposing the creature is already capable of some minimal form of objective thought.

Scenario content, by contrast, cannot be pre-objective. The scenario content of an experience captures part of its phenomenological representational content, and a scenario content requires for its correctness that the world around a certain location be a certain way in respect of the surfaces, events and movements there. Scenario content is used in the description of the conscious states of someone who has already acquired at least some rudimentary conception of the objective world. Part of the motivation for employing it is that if we do not, we will not have fully captured one of the kinds of way in which our perceptual experience represents the world to be. States with scenario content cannot, then, precede objective thought, and it would be a mistake to try to explain the emergence of objective thought by supposing that they do.[2]

A related difference between scenario content and CT content is that states with only CT content do not really have correctness conditions. They cannot have correctness conditions that concern the objective, spatial world, since they are supposed to be pre-objective. They should also not be regarded as having correctness conditions that concern only mental states. Thought about mental states itself presupposes an objective/subjective distinction, and cannot be given in advance of it.[3]

Since CT content is distinct from scenario content, and my rejection of the Autonomy Thesis is a rejection of a thesis about scenario content, that rejection poses no obstacle to those who see either a developmental or a phylogenetic progression from states with only CT content to states with conceptual content. Rejection of the Autonomy Thesis entails only that where there is scenario content, there must also be certain conceptual contents. It does not entail that where there is CT content, there is also conceptual content. (The issue of acquisition does of course also arise for states with scenario content, and I return to it below.)

Given what I have said about scenario content, I am committed to disagreeing with the thesis that all objective contents are conceptual. What then for me distinguishes some contents as conceptual? The overarching claim of *A Study of Concepts* was that concepts are individuated by their possession conditions, and so I am naturally attracted to the following thesis: conceptual contents are those that are wholly composed of contents that are individuated by their possession conditions. The fact is, though, that one does not have to accept the overarching claim of *A Study of Concepts* in order to give an adequate answer to the question. One could equally answer that conceptual contents are those that are individuated by considerations of epistemic possibility, or informativeness, along the lines of Frege's original criterion for the identity of senses. This counts scenario contents as squarely nonconceptual. A scenario content is just an (anchored) spatial type— its individuation has nothing to do with informativeness or epistemic matters. Perceptual demonstratives which are conceptual are made available by experiences with scenario contents, to suitably conceptually equipped thinkers, but the individuation of the scenario itself remains an entirely nonepistemic matter. Cussins does develop a theory on which all objective contents are conceptual (Cussins 1990, p. 381) [essay 6, p. 133]. But as far as I can see, there would be nothing fundamentally inimical to the general project of explaining conceptual content in terms of CT content, or to the other explanatory uses to which he wishes to put the notion of CT content, to recognize a distinction, within the class of objective representational contents, between those that are classified as conceptual by the criteria endorsed in this paragraph and those that are not.

What is the relation between scenario content and CT content? This question is particularly pressing because, for Cussins, CT content is involved in conscious, personal-level states. "The notion of nonconceptual content is a notion which must ultimately be explained in terms of what is available in *experience*. If the content is canonically characterized as a complex disposition of some specified sort, then the claim is that this disposition is directly available to the person in his or her experience, and that the content of the experience consists in this availability." (Cussins 1990, p. 397) [essay 6, p. 145]. For spatial contents, Cussins' view is that the relevant disposition of which the subject is aware is a spatial disposition. He endorses the idea that the spatial content of an auditory perception "consists in the experiential availability to the subject of a dispositional ability to move" (1990, p. 396) [essay 6, p. 144]. "My knowledge of where the sound is coming from consists in, say, knowledge of how I would locate the place . . . I may have that knowledge even though I am unable to entertain any thoughts about the way of moving in question; I require no concepts of my ability to find my way in the environment, in order to have an experience whose content consists in presenting to me a way of moving" (1990, p. 395) [essay 6, pp. 143–144]. One proposal we should consider about the relations between the two kinds of content is then this:

> For a creature capable of objective thought about the world, to have an experience in which *that F* is represented as being at a certain distance and egocentric distance from it is for there to be some movement-type M such that the thinker is aware in experience that a movement of type M would take him to the thing presented as *that F*.

This proposal is multiply flawed.

(a) There are places presented in the scenario content of experience that are places to which no active movement of the subject would take him, nor need he be under any experiential illusion that some such movement would take him there. You perceive such a place when, standing on its floor, you see the join of two vaults in the ceiling of a Gothic cathedral, more than fifty feet above you. No active movement of yours will take you there, nor does it seem to you as if any will. The join is nevertheless presented as being a certain distance and direction from you.

(b) It seems that we can conceive of two creatures who have very different repertoires of active movements, and are consciously aware from the first-person perspective only of movements within their respective repertoires, but who yet have overlapping egocentric spatial contents of experience. We can consider two unfortunate individuals. The first is a person congenitally paralyzed from below the waist, and who moves in a wheelchair, while the second person is congenitally paralyzed from the waist up. It seems to me that they can both, when seated, on different occasions see a mark on the wall as the same particular distance and direction from them. For each of them, there are movements of which he is aware that they would take him to that mark. But the set of movements for which one of them has such an awareness is totally disjoint from the set for which the other has such an awareness.

It might be replied that the movements mentioned in the displayed proposal need not be active movements of the subject. Perhaps the subject needs only to be aware of which movements of his body, possibly induced by something else, would take him to the place at which he perceives something to be located. But in the example in which you see the join in the vaulting of the cathedral roof, the only way you might have of thinking of the movement which would get you there is something tantamount to "a movement *that* far in *that* direction," or even just "a movement to *there*," where all the italicized demonstratives are made available by the scenario content of the perceptual experience. Far from providing an analysis of the possession by states of scenario content, these ways of thinking of movements simply presuppose what is made available by scenario content.

Alternatively, it may be said that in experiencing something as at a certain distance and direction from you, you have the impression (correct or incorrect) that you could keep track of it if you were passively moved towards it, and would know when you have reached it. But there are many examples in which it is hard to believe that there is any such impression. You may see a drop of water fall from a melting icicle into a pool, and follow its path as it falls. Does this mean that you also have to have the impression that you could keep track of it if you were to speed through space in time to reach it before it hits the pool? No such impressions are required.

If we accept the points of these past few paragraphs, are we thereby committed to denying that there are any special connections between scenario content and certain kinds of actions? We are not. There are some such special connections, but the point is that the types of actions that, in suitable circumstances, are produced by states with scenario content are ones that are produced by intentions and tryings with an egocentric spatial content. It is because you have a basic ability to move your head in a direction, egocentrically thought about, that you can, without further inference at a personal level, move your head in the direction from which your experience presents it as coming—as Evans, the great pioneer of non-conceptual content, emphasized (Evans 1982, pp. 154–157) [essay 2, pp. 50–53]. If the ways in which places are given in experience, and thought about in the formation of intentions and tryings, were different, then some personal-level reasoning would be necessary. But they are not different, and so no such reasoning is needed. What we have here is a conditional necessity: there will be such links to a certain type of action provided that some aspects of scenario content feature in the basic intentions and tryings controlling actions of that type. When that condition is not met for a given kind of action, either temporarily or permanently, the links will be absent too. For a temporary case, we can consider your situation when your arms and hands are intertwined behind your back, in such a way that when you point with your right index finger, you do not know which direction, relative to your torso, is the direction in which you are pointing. When in this state, you cannot, without further personal-level thought and reasoning, point at will in the direction of a heard sound. For a more permanent case: I can move my ears, and my doing so is intentional under the basic description "moving my ears" (I do not do it by forming the intention to do it by means of doing something else). In fact I do not know whether my ears move up/down or back/front when I move them. I could not, without further thought, reliably and knowledgeably follow the command to move my ears in the direction of a heard sound—even if that direction is one in which I can move my ears.

Just as for other states with content, a positive account of states with scenario content will say that they have that content in part by virtue of their power to explain, and be explained by, certain environmental states of affairs (Peacocke

1993). For the possession of scenario content, what matters is the power to explain and be explained by spatial states of affairs, egocentrically characterized. One way this power can be manifested is by these states' explaining active movements relationally and spatially characterized. But it does not seem to be the only way. We can make sense of the possibility of creatures with only very minimal control over their bodily movements still having perceptual states with scenario contents. We can make sense of it provided that the states play a role in the explanation of the spatial properties of actions, even if the actions are not themselves bodily movements. The creature which changes color, or its electric charge, or the odor it emits, because it is a certain distance from a perceived position can meet this condition even though none of these actions is a bodily movement. From this theoretical standpoint, then, a connection with active bodily movements provides one, but not the only, kind of way in which the conditions for attributing scenario content can be met. Moreover, when the conditions are met by bodily movements, the actions must be controlled by states that themselves have contents with some of the features of scenario content. When the actions are so controlled, they cannot be used in a reductive explanation of the possession of scenario content. The overlapping contents mean that we have at best a simultaneous elucidation of how, for such a creature, the conditions for ascribing scenario content to experience, and spatial content for the states which control bodily movements, are simultaneously met.

I conclude by identifying and commenting on two other issues. Though none of our knowledge in these areas is notably secure, these two issues are particularly wide open. The first concerns the issue of acquisition of states with scenario content, a problem Bermúdez rightly emphasizes. Possible models of acquisition are constrained in any case in which, like that of scenario content and other spatial representations, we have a local holism. Local holisms preclude any treatment of acquisition in which it is alleged that one of the states in the local holism is fully acquired before the others. The genuine need for an account of acquisition cannot force us into a general atomism about mental states, for the local holisms are real, and here to stay. But the connectionist literature certainly contains models that give us at least the beginnings of an account of how states forming a local holism can be acquired. Consider the example of identifying the Case of some part of a sentence—identifying it as the Agent, the Patient or the Instrument. I doubt that someone could have the ability to identify something as the Agent without having the resources to identify Patient and Instrument, so inextricably involved with one another are these notions. Yet there are connectionist models of the acquisition of Case classifications (McClelland and Kawamoto 1986). A network can be trained to yield almost entirely correct Case classifications. The gradual acquisition of the correct classifications does not at all proceed by first fully mastering Agent, and then moving on to mastery of Patient (nor could it). Nor is the acquired state one in which Case classifications coincide with very simple classifications of position in a sentence. As grammarians have long emphasized, the grammatical subject may be classified as Agent in one sentence ("The boy broke the plate"), Patient in another ("The plate broke"), and Instrument in a third ("The hammer broke the plate"). I would be the first to emphasize that this model is a limited and restricted case in all sorts of respects, even within the particular domain it treats. Its existence is enough, though, to show that models of acquisition, and in particular computational models, are in no way excluded by recognition of a local holism. What we need now are models of possible routes to the acquisition of scenario content and the other spatial contents to which it has internal links.[4]

Those who accept Cussins' suggestion about the particular way in which CT content can be used in the explication of objective content must in any case already be committed to the possibility of accounts of acquisition for holistically interrelated states. For on Cussins' theory, the crucial step from CT content to objective content is perspective-independence (1990, pp. 423–429). This too, given the nature of perspective-independence, is a holistic condition. Since a conception of the objective world is certainly something that can be acquired, there cannot be insuperable obstacles to acquisition of states involved in an interlocking holistic structure.

The second issue I wish to identify is that of whether an approach to the acquisition of states with representational contents that proceeds via CT content would, at best, in the very nature of the case, give us only a partial solution to the problem of acquisition. Cussins fends off the charge that his approach is really behavioristic by emphasizing that his CT content is to be explained in terms of what is available in conscious perceptual experience (1990, p. 397 [essay 6, p. 145], and see above). This answers the objection, but leaves us with the problem of the emergence of conscious states. If the explanation of the emergence of states with conceptual content cannot presuppose prior possession of conceptual states, then equally the explanation of the emergence of conscious states cannot presuppose prior possession of conscious states. The explanation of the emergence of perceptual states with scenario content must include an explanation of the emergence of conscious states, if it is to be a full explanation. For this explanation, some new approach is needed. The problem goes far beyond what can be solved just by constructing states with one kind of content from states with another kind of content.

Postscript: The Relations between Conceptual and Nonconceptual Content (2002)

Does the enjoyment by a creature of perceptual states with nonconceptual representational content require that creature also to possess concepts? I used to answer this question in the affirmative. That is, I disputed the Autonomy Thesis, which holds that such nonconceptual states can exist in the absence of conceptual states (Peacocke 1992b, 1994b [essays 5 and 16]). In this note I explain why I have come to think that this was the wrong answer, and to think that the Autonomy Thesis is correct.

To give it in the shortest possible compass, the argument I gave for rejecting the Autonomy Thesis ran thus:

> A state has objective content (has a correctness condition concerning the objective world) only if the creature can use it in the construction of a representation of the layout of the world in which the creature is embedded.
> To have that capacity, the creature must be able to keep some track of his changing spatial relations to objects, processes, or places presented in the states with objective content.
> This requires the use of representations with first-person contents, for example, such contents as are roughly captured as "That tree is in front of me," "Now that same tree is behind me."

There are two reasons this argument fails to establish the Autonomy Thesis. First, even if it were sound, nothing in the argument shows that the first-person notion it mentions must be conceptual. Nor need the other contents mentioned in the argument be conceptual. Second, the argument is not sound. It is right to hold that the capacity to keep track of changing spatial relations to the environment is required for objective spatial content of perceptions. It is wrong to hold that this can be done only by use of a first-person notion, even a nonconceptual one. The most that is true is this: when there is objective spatial content of perception, there will be the possibility of introducing a first-person notion, when certain additional conditions are met.

To elaborate this second reason further, we can start by noting that the resources for supporting it are already present in the account I developed of one kind of nonconceptual content, scenario content (Peacocke 1992b [essay 5]). A scenario has an origin. In a particular spatial experience, the perceived things, events, and places are experienced as bearing particular spatial relations to this location, the origin. A fuller account would bring in axes and the possibility of multiple origins. Using this apparatus, we can characterize mastery of an auxiliary nonconceptual notion *hier*. In an account of mastery of *hier*, we distinguish two components.

> (1) To possess *hier*, a creature must form representations of the world in the following way: if the creature's perception represents there as being something F that bears R to the origin, then the thinker comes to represent the following as being the case: "That's F and it's R to *hier*." The demonstrative "that" is individuated in part by the egocentrically identified location by which the perceived object is given in perception.
> (2) To possess *hier*, there must be a range of spatial relations R of which the following is true. If the creature initially represents it as being the case that some object, continuing event, or location bears R to *hier*, and then moves in such a way that its spatial relation to it becomes R', then the creature updates its representation to the content that that same object, continuing event, or location bears R' to *hier*.

The updating may proceed via map-like representations, either at a conscious or at an unconscious level. It would be too strong to require that the updating proceed in response to changing features of a concurrent experience with scenario content. A blind creature can employ such a *hier* notion and engage in such updating, without there needing to be such concurrent experiences of distal arrays of objects.

The possibility of *hier* contents, the account of which does not even mention any first-person notion, shows that the spatial updating requirements can be met by a creature without that creature exercising first-person notions. This is a very primitive level of content, perhaps the most primitive that still counts as objective content.

Suppose that a creature usually perceives something—its body—as located at the origin of the scenario. When this additional condition is met, there is the possibility of introducing a first-person notion *Ich* as follows:

> To possess *Ich*, a creature must form representations with the content "That's *F* and it's *R* to *Ich*" when it forms representations with the content "That's *F* and it's *R* to *hier*."

This requirement then combines with the second component (2) in mastery of *hier*. Given (2), the updating of spatial relations to the place represented as *hier* carries over to the updating of spatial relations to the object represented as *Ich*. When the creature moves, and updates his information about a tree recently seen to represent "It's now behind *hier*" as correct, it correspondingly updates its *Ich*-representations. They will now include the content "It (that tree) is now behind *Ich*" as correct. Enthusiasts for these issues will know there are a thousand interesting complexities here. For instance, although we have spatial updating, so far we have provided only for present-tense contents involving *Ich*. There are some resources here for introducing past and future-tense contents, resources that are not yet exploited. But for the immediate purpose of assessing the argument against the Autonomy Thesis, these points will suffice.

Why are *hier* and *Ich* not concepts? I offer three reasons.

(i) Intuitively, an organism without any concepts at all could employ representations whose content contains *hier* and *Ich*. John O'Keefe (1989) has described a computational system that may be employed in the hippocampus of rats. In this system, the egocentrically characterized layout of objects or features in the environment of the rat can be represented by a matrix (ibid., pp. 242ff.). The matrix captures the locations of the objects or features relative to the location of the rat itself; but there does not need to be any representation of the rat as an object in the world. As the rat moves, the rat's spatial translation and rotation can be represented by a transform matrix. The resulting egocentrically characterized layout after movement can then be computed by multiplying the pre-movement matrix by the transform matrix (ibid., p. 243). This kind of computational mechanism could underlie possession of representations with constituents meeting the conditions on *hier*. I am neutral on the conceptual capacities or otherwise of rats; but I do say that this computational mechanism by itself is not enough to ensure the possession of concepts, and certainly not the possession of the first-person concept. (If rats have concepts, they must have something more too.)

(ii) *Hier* and *Ich* do not have the guaranteed recombinability distinctive of concepts. This is in essence the recombinability that Evans (1982) (essay 2, appendix) captured in his Generality Constraint, and which is agreed on by very different theories of concepts (Peacocke 1992b, Fodor 1998). The only contents that must be capable of entering the representations of a creature who has *hier* and *Ich* are those that the creature can perceive to be the case, or which can be reached by (possibly iterated) applications of the updating procedure, starting from contents that are perceived to be the case. So, suppose that, like humans, a creature cannot perceive colors at low levels of illumination, even though it can still see things and their shapes at that same level of illumination. This means that it will be unable to form a perceptual representation with the content "That's green in a dark region and it's in such-and-such a direction from *hier*." Nor does anything in the description of the capacities required for possession of *hier* require that there be any other kind of mental state in which this complete content features. Conceptual competence and conceptual thought is not so restricted, and this is a matter of its nature. Anyone capable of entertaining the thoughts "That's green" and "That's square and it's in the dark" must be capable of entertaining the thought "That's green and it's in the dark." That content, even if it cannot be perceived to hold, may be used in spatial, causal, and counterfactual reasoning by the thinker capable of conceptual thought.

(iii) Concepts are individuated by their canonical role in judgments. Judgment is not just an automatic endorsement of the content of a perceptual or other informational state. Though the content of an informational state may be taken at face value, a thinker can also assess whether it should be taken at face value. That is, the thinker may engage in critical reflection. Such critical assessment may take place at various levels of depth. It would be too strong to require for conceptual thought the capacity for critical assessment at every, or even at any very great, level of depth. But a creature employing *hier* and *Ich* need not have any critical abilities whatsoever. A wholly uncritical acceptance of perceptual representations, together with the capacity to update, suffices for the possession of those notions. The creature need not even have any representation, conceptual or nonconceptual, of the notion of perception, nor of its own states, nor even of contents currently or potentially endorsed but now up for assessment. Having at least one of these kinds of representation is a precondition of any critical assessment of what it accepts or is disposed to accept.

Going hand-in-hand with the possibility of critical assessment of one's own informational states is the capacity not just for objective representation, but the ability to appreciate the content of some of one's mental states *as* objective. To have the idea that one's methods may be incorrect is to have a notion of correctness that does not immediately consist in what can be reached by one's current methods.

What is the relation between (ii) and (iii)? Recombinability and the possibility of critical assessment may not seem to have much to do with one another, and their presence together may give the impression of an ad hoc list of criteria for concept-hood that lacks any underlying unity. There are, however, deeper connections between them. The recombinability, which implies that the subject is capable of the thought that "That's green and it's in the dark," in such a way that it can be true, means that the subject has some implicit conception of a categorical property. The idea of the categorical is an indispensable element in possession of the idea of what is objectively the case. The idea of what is objectively the case is the essential background without which critical assessment of one's own informational states could not take place. Recombinability, the categorical, objectivity and critical assessment are essentially intertwined.[5]

Notes

1. It would also involve some of the protopropositional content of the experience, in the terminology of *A Study of Concepts* [essay 5]. The notation [*that F, W*] is found in Peacocke (1981), but the point is an old one: see Kaplan (1989, pp. 514–516). The point is implicit in many discussions of informative identities.

2. Cussins himself explicitly distinguishes scenario content from CT content (1990, p. 392, n. 48) [essay 6, pp. 161–162, n. 25].

3. If there are conscious states with CT content, as Cussins holds, then content as something with a correctness condition and content as one kind of "object" of a conscious state come apart. It is natural to be uncomfortable with a notion of content divorced from any correctness condition, but the fact is that "content" has also regularly been used in the philosophical literature for the content of awareness. If Cussins is right, we cannot always hang on to both of the conventional associations of "content."

4. Bermúdez also writes that my rejection of the Autonomy Thesis "endangers the project of grounding the possession conditions of certain primitive concepts in nonconceptual scenario content" (p. 416) [p. 305]. Grounding is an asymmetrical relation, but no relevant asymmetrical relation needs to hold between a concept and some kinds of scenario content for the latter to illuminate the possession conditions of the former. If the Autonomy Thesis is false, then all that follows is that possession of the primitive concepts in question and enjoyment of experiences with scenario content have to be elucidated simultaneously.

5. I thank York Gunther for the opportunity to include a brief postscript in this collection. I also wish to acknowledge squarely that the reasons from animal perception to accept the Autonomy Thesis were pressed on me in Bermúdez (1994) and I ought to have accepted them. (For the record, I stand by the other parts of my reply [1994b] to his paper.) The position necessarily so briefly and dogmatically outlined in the present postscript is intended to be consistent with the position on nonconceptual content outlined in Peacocke 2001a. The significance of the possibility of new methods as distinctive of conceptual contents, emphasized late in that paper, could be added to the reasons (i)–(iii) above. For more defense of the notion of the categorical, see Peacocke 2001b.

References

Anderson, J. R. and Bower, G. H. 1973. *Human Associative Memory*. Washington: V. H. Winston.

Anscombe, G. E. M. 1981. On Sensations of Position. *Metaphysics and the Philosophy of Mind: Collected Papers, Vol. 2*. Minneapolis: University of Minnesota Press.

Armstrong, D. 1962. *Bodily Sensations*. London: Routledge & Kegan Paul.

Armstrong, D. 1969. *A Materialist Theory of Mind*. London: Routledge & Kegan Paul.

Aune, B. 1967. *Knowledge, Mind, and Nature*. New York: Random House.

Austin, J. L. 1962. *Sense and Sensibilia*. Oxford: Clarendon Press.

Averbach, E. and Coriell, A. S. 1960. Short-Term Memory in Vision. *Bell System Technical Journal*, vol. 40, no. 196.

Averbach, E. and Coriell, A. S. 1961. Short-Term Storage of Information in Vision. *Information Theory: Proceedings of the Fourth London Symposium*, C. Cherry (ed.). London: Butterworths.

Baillargeon, R. 1987. Object Permanence in 3.5- and 4.5-Month-Old Infants. *Developmental Psychology*, vol. 23.

Baker, L. 1994. Instrumental Intentionality. *Mental Representation*, S. Stich and T. Warfield (eds.). Oxford: Blackwell.

Barwise, J. 1987. Unburdening the Language of Thought. *Two Replies*, CSLI Report no. 87–74.

Bell, D. 1990. How "Russellian" was Frege? *Mind*, vol. 99.

Bennett, J. 1976. *Linguistic Behaviour*. Cambridge: Cambridge University Press.

Berkeley, G. 1713. The First Dialogue between Hylas and Philonous. Reprinted in *A Modern Introduction to Philosophy*, P. Edwards and A. Pap (eds.). New York: The Free Press, 1973.

Bermúdez, J. L. 1994. Peacocke's Argument Against the Autonomy of Nonconceptual Content. *Mind and Language*, vol. 9.

Bermúdez, J. L. 1995a. Syntax, Semantics, and Levels of Explanation. *Philosophical Quarterly*, vol. 45.

Bermúdez, J. L. 1995b. Transcendental Arguments and Psychology. *Metaphilosophy*, vol. 26.

Bermúdez, J. L. 1995c. Ecological Perception and the Notion of a Nonconceptual Point of View. *The Body and the Self*, J. Bermúdez, A. Marcel, and N. Eilan (eds.). Cambridge, MA: The MIT Press.

Bermúdez, J. L. 1995d. Nonconceptual Content: From Perceptual Experience to Subpersonal Computational States. *Mind and Language*, vol. 10, no. 4.

Bermúdez, J. L. 1998. *The Paradox of Self-Consciousness*. Cambridge, MA: The MIT Press.

Blackmore, C. 1973. The Baffled Brain. *Illusion in Nature and Art*, E. Gombrich and R. Gregory (eds.). London: Duckworth.

Block, N. 1981. *Readings in Philosophy of Psychology, Vol. 2*. London: Methuen.

Block, N. 1983. Mental Pictures and Cognitive Science. *Philosophical Review*, vol. 93.

Boden, M. 1990a. *The Philosophy of Artificial Intelligence*. Oxford: Oxford University Press.

Boden, M. 1990b. *The Creative Mind: Myths and Mechanisms*. London: Weidenfeld & Nicholson.

Bonaventure. 1882–1902. *Doctoris Seraphici S. Bonaventurae . . . Opera Omnia. . . .* Ad Claras Aquas, Quaracchi: Ex Typographia Collegii S. Bonaventurae.

Bower, T. G. R. 1972. The Visual World of Infants. *Perception: Mechanisms and Models*. San Francisco: W. H. Freeman.

Bower, T. G. R. 1975. Infant Perception of the Third Dimension and Object Concept Development. *Infant Perception From Sensation to Cognition, vol. 2: Perception of Space Speech and Sound*, L. Cohen and P. Salapatek (eds.). New York: Academic Press.

Brentano, F. 1874. *Psychology from the Empirical Standpoint*, Rancurello, Terrell, and McAlister (trs.). London: Routledge & Kegan Paul, 1973.

Brewer, B. 1993. The Integration of Spatial Vision and Action. In Eilan, McCarthy, and Brewer 1993.

Burge, T. 1974. Demonstrative Constructions, Reference, and Truth. *Journal of Philosophy*, vol. 71.

Burge, T. 1979. Individualism and the Mental. *Midwest Studies in Philosophy*, vol. 4, P. French, T. Uehling, and H. Wettstein (eds.). Minneapolis: University of Minnesota Press.

Burge, T. 1986. Individualism and Psychology. *Philosophical Review*, vol. 95.

Campbell, J. 1989. Review of Evans 1985. *Journal of Philosophy*, vol. 86.

Campbell, J. 1993. The Role of Physical Objects in Spatial Thinking. In Eilan, McCarthy, and Brewer 1993.

Chisholm, R. M. 1958. Sentences About Believing. *Minnesota Studies in the Philosophy of Science*, vol. 2, H. Feigl, M. Scriven, and G. Maxell (eds.). Minneapolis: University of Minnesota Press.

Church, A. 1956. Propositions and Sentences. *The Problem of Universals*. Notre Dame, IN: University of Notre Dame Press.

Churchland, Patricia. 1986. *Neurophilosophy*. Cambridge, MA: The MIT Press.

Churchland, Paul. 1981. Eliminative Materialism and the Propositional Attitudes. *Journal of Philosophy*, vol. 78.

Clark, A. 1989. *Microcognition: Philosophy, Cognitive Science, and Parallel Distributed Processing*. Cambridge, MA: The MIT Press.

Clark, A. 1990. Connectionism, Competence, and Explanation. *British Journal for the Philosophy of Science*, vol. 41. Reprinted in Boden 1990a.

Clark, A. 1991. Radical Ascent. *Proceedings of the Aristotelian Society*, supp. vol. 65.

Clark, A. 1993. *Associative Engines: Connectionism, Concepts, and Representational Change*. Cambridge, MA: The MIT Press.

Clark, A. 1994. Connectionism and Cognitive Flexibility. In Dartnall 1994.

Clark, A. and Karmiloff-Smith, A. 1993. The Cognizer's Innards: A Psychological and Philosophical Perspective On the Development of Thought. *Mind and Language*, vol. 8, no. 4.

Copleston, F. 1962–1977. *A History of Philosophy*. New York: Image Books.

Coren, S. and Girgus, J. 1978. *Seeing is Deceiving*. London: Wiley.

Craig, E. J. 1976. Sensory Experience and the Foundations of Knowledge. *Synthese*, vol. 33.

Crane, T. 1988. The Waterfall Illusion. *Analysis*, vol. 48.

Crane, T. 1992. The Nonconceptual Content of Experience. *The Contents of Experience*, T. Crane (ed.). Cambridge: Cambridge University Press.

Crowder, R. G. and Morton, J. 1969. Precategorical Acoustic Storage (PAS). *Perception and Psychophysics*, vol. 5.

Cussins, A. 1987. Being Situated Versus Being Embedded. *CSLI Monthly*, vol. 2, no. 7.

Cussins, A. 1990. The Connectionist Construction of Concepts. In Boden 1990a.

Cussins, A. 1992. The Limitations of Pluralism. *Reduction, Explanation, and Realism*, D. Charles and K. Lennon (eds.). Oxford: Oxford University Press.

Dallet, K. 1974. Transactional and Probabilistic Functionalism. *Handbook of Perception*, E. Carterette and M. Friedman (eds.). New York/London: Academic Press

Dartnall, T. (ed.) 1994. *Artificial Intelligence and Creativity*. Netherlands: Kluwer Academic Publishers.

Davidson, D. 1967. Truth and Meaning. Reprinted in Davidson 1984.

Davidson, D. 1973. Radical Interpretation. Reprinted in Davidson 1984.

Davidson, D. 1979. Mood and Performances. Reprinted in Davidson 1984.

Davidson, D. 1982. *Essays on Actions and Events*. Oxford: Clarendon Press.

Davidson, D. 1984. *Inquiries into Truth and Interpretation*. Oxford: Clarendon Press.

Davies, M. 1986. Tacit Knowledge and the Structure of Thought and Language. *Meaning and Interpretation*, C. Travis (ed.). Oxford: Oxford University Press.

Davies, M. 1990. Thinking Persons and Cognitive Science. *AI and Society*, vol. 4. Reprinted in *Connectionism in Context*, A. Clark and R. Lutz (eds.). London: Springer-Verlag, 1992.

Davies, M. 1991. Individualism and Perceptual Content. *Mind*, vol. 100.

Davis, S. (ed.) 1992. *Connectionism: Theory and Practice*. New York: Oxford University Press.

de Beauvoir, S. 1989. *The Prime of Life*. London: Penguin.

DeBellis, M. 1995. *Music and Conceptualization*. New York: Cambridge University Press.

Dennett, D. 1969. *Content and Consciousness*. New York: Routledge & Kegan Paul.

Dennett, D. 1981a. Towards a Cognitive Theory of Consciousness. In Dennett 1981c.

Dennett, D. 1981b. Intentional Systems. In Dennett 1981c.

Dennett, D. 1981c. *Brainstorms*. Montgomery, VT: Bradford Books.

Dennett, D. 1987a. True Believers. In Dennett 1987b.

Dennett, D. 1987b. *The Intentional Stance*. Cambridge, MA: The MIT Press.

Dennett, D. 1991. *Consciousness Explained*. Boston: Little, Brown and Company.

Dennett, D. 1996. Evolutionary Intentionality. *Proceedings from the Third European Conference on Systems Science* (Rome, October 1–4), E. Pessa, A. Montesanto, and M. Penna (eds.). Rome: Edzioni Kappa.

de Sousa, R. 1987. *The Rationality of Emotion*. Cambridge: Cambridge University Press.

Dewey, J. 1934. *Art as Experience*. New York: Minton.

Dickinson, A. 1980. *Contemporary Animal Learning Theory*. Cambridge: Cambridge University Press.

Dickinson, A. 1988. Intentionality in Animal Conditioning. In Weiskrantz 1988.

Donnellan, K. 1972. Proper Names and Identifying Descriptions. *Semantics of Natural Language*, D. Davidson and G. Harman (eds.). Dordrecht: Reidel.

Dretske, F. 1969. *Seeing and Knowing*. Chicago: University of Chicago Press.

Dretske, F. 1981. *Knowledge and the Flow of Information*. Cambridge, MA: The MIT Press.

Dretske, F. 1990. Misrepresentation. In Lycan 1990.

Dretske, F. 1992. *Explaining Behavior: Reasons in a World of Causes*. Cambridge, MA: The MIT Press.

Dreyfus, H. 1991. *Being in the World*. Cambridge, MA: The MIT Press.

Dummett, M. 1973. *Frege: Philosophy of Language*. London: Duckworth.

Dummett, M. 1975. What Is a Theory of Meaning? (I). Reprinted in Dummett 1993.

Dummett, M. 1976. What Is a Theory of Meaning? (II). Reprinted in Dummett 1993.

Dummett, M. 1991. *The Logical Basis of Metaphysics*. Cambridge, MA: Harvard University Press.

Dummett, M. 1993. *The Seas of Language*. Oxford: Clarendon Press.

Dummett, M. 1994. *The Origins of Analytical Philosophy*. Cambridge, MA: Harvard University Press.

Egan, F. 1992. Individualism, Computation, and Perceptual Content. *Mind*, vol. 101.

Eilan, N., McCarthy, R. and Brewer, B. 1993. *Spatial Representation*. Oxford: Basil Blackwell.

Elster, J. 1985. *Sour Grapes*. New York: Cambridge University Press.

Epstein, W. 1967. *Varieties of Perceptual Learning*. New York: McGraw-Hill.

Evans, G. 1975. Identity and Predication. Reprinted in Evans 1985.

Evans, G. 1980. Things Without the Mind. Reprinted in Evans 1985.

Evans, G. 1982. *The Varieties of Reference*, J. McDowell (ed.). Oxford: Oxford University Press.

Evans, G. 1985. *Collected Papers*, A. Phillips (ed.). Oxford: Oxford University Press.

Evans, G. and McDowell, J. (eds.). 1976. *Truth and Meaning*. Oxford: Clarendon Press.

Fodor, J, 1975. *The Language of Thought*. New York: Thomas Crowell.

Fodor, J. 1978. Propositional Attitudes. *Monist*, vol. 61.

Fodor, J. 1983. *The Modularity of Mind*. Cambridge, MA: The MIT Press.

Fodor, J. 1986. Why Paramecia Don't Have Mental Representations. *Midwest Studies in Philosophy*, vol. 10, P. French, T. Uehling, and H. Wettstein (eds.). Minneapolis: University of Minnesota Press.

Fodor, J. 1987. *Psychosemantics*. Cambridge, MA: The MIT Press.

Fodor, J. 1995. *The Elm and the Expert*. Cambridge, MA: The MIT Press.

Fodor, J. 1998. *Concepts: Where Cognitive Science Went Wrong*. Oxford: Oxford University Press.

Fodor, J. and Lepore, E. 1993. Is Intentional Ascription Intrinsically Normative? *Dennett and His Critics*, B. Dahlbom (ed.). Oxford: Blackwell.

Fodor, J. and Pylyshyn, Z. 1988. Connectionism and Cognitive Architecture: a Critical Analysis. *Cognition*, vol. 28.

Føllesdal, D. 1982. Brentano and Husserl on Intentional Objects and Perception. *Husserl, Intentionality and Cognitive Science*, Dreyfus (ed.). Cambridge, MA: The MIT Press.

Freedman, S. J. and Rekosh, H. 1968. The Functional Integrity of Spatial Behavior. *The Neuropsychology of Spatial Oriented Behavior*, S. Freedman (ed.). Homewood, IL: Dorsey Press.

Frege, G. 1879. *Begriffschrift*. Reprinted in Frege 1997.

Frege, G. 1891. Function and Concept. Reprinted in *Philosophical Writings of Gottlob Frege*, P. Geach and M. Black (eds.). Oxford: Blackwell, 1985.

Frege, G. 1892. On Sense and Reference. Reprinted in Frege 1997.

Frege, G. 1918a. Thought. Reprinted in Frege 1997.

Frege, G. 1918b. Negation. Reprinted in Frege 1997.

Frege, G. 1979. *Posthumous Writings*. Chicago: The University of Chicago Press.

Frege, G. 1997. *The Frege Reader*, M. Beaney (ed.). Oxford: Blackwell.

Frisby, J. P. 1979. *Seeing*. Oxford: Oxford University Press.

Geach, P. T. 1957. *Mental Acts*. London: Routledge & Kegan Paul.

Gibson, E. 1969. *Principles of Perceptual Learning and Development*. New York: Appleton-Century-Crofts.

Gibson, J. J. 1950. *The Perception of the Visual World*. Boston: Houghton Mifflin.

Gibson, J. J. 1966. *The Senses Considered as Perceptual Systems*. London: Houghton Mifflin.

Goodwin-Austen, R. 1965. A Case of Visual Disorientation. *Journal of Neurology, Neurosurgery, and Psychiatry*, vol. 28.

Gregory, R. L. 1966. *Eye and Brain*. London: Weidenfeld & Nicolson.

Gunther, Y. 1995. Perceptual Content and the Subpersonal. *Conference: A Journal of Philosophy and Theory*, vol. 6, no. 1.

Gunther, Y. 1999. *Nonconceptual Content: A Critique and Defense*. Columbia University dissertation.

Gunther, Y. 2000. Response-Dependence and the Emotions. *Southwest Philosophy Review*, vol. 16, no. 1.

Gunther, Y. 2001. Content, Illusion, Partition. *Philosophical Studies*, vol. 102, no. 2.

Gunther, Y. (under review). A Theory of Emotional Content.

Haber, R. N. (ed.) 1969. *Information Processing Approaches to Visual Perception*. New York: Holt, Rinehart and Winston.

Haber, R. N. and Hershenson, M. 1973. *The Psychology of Visual Perception*. New York: Holt, Rinehart and Winston.

Hamblin, C. 1973. Questions in Montague English. *Foundations of Language*, vol. 10.

Hamlyn, D. W. 1957. *The Psychology of Perception*. London: Routledge & Kegan Paul.

Hamlyn, D. W. 1969. Seeing Things As They Are. In Hamlyn 1957 (3rd impression).

Hamlyn, D. W. 1971. *The Theory of Knowledge*. London: Macmillan.

Hamlyn, D. W. 1977. The Concept of Information in Gibson's Theory of Perception. *Journal for the Theory of Social Behavior*, vol. 7, no. 1.

Hamlyn, D. W. 1983. *Perception, Learning, and the Self*. London: Routledge & Kegan Paul.

Hamlyn, D. W. 1990. *In and Out of the Black Box*. Oxford: Basil Blackwell.

Hamlyn, D. W. 1994. Perception, Sensation, and Nonconceptual Content. *Philosophical Quarterly*, vol. 44, no. 175.

Hare, R. 1952. *The Language of Morals*. Oxford: Oxford University Press.

Harman, G. 1973. *Thought*. Princeton, NJ: Princeton University Press.

Harman, G. 1990. The Intrinsic Quality of Experience. *Philosophical Perspectives*, vol. 4, J. Tomberlin (ed.). Atascadero, CA: Ridgeview Publishing.

Hebb, D. O. 1974. Summation and Learning in Perception. *Readings in Perception*, P. Fried (ed.). Lexington, MA: D. C. Heath.

Heidegger, M. 1927. *Being and Time*, J. Macquarrie and E. Robinson (trs.). Oxford: Basil Blackwell, 1962.

Heidegger, M. 1936. The Origin of the Work of Art. Reprinted in *Basic Writings*. San Francisco: Harper, 1993.

Helm, B. 1994. The Significance of Emotions. *American Philosophical Quarterly*, vol. 31, no. 4.

Hoffmann, E. T. A. 1810. Review of Beethoven's Fifth Symphony. *Allgemeneine musicalische Zeitung*, July 4 and 11.

Holland, P. C. 1979. Differential Effects of Omission Contingencies on Various Components of Pavlovian Appetitive Responding in Rats. *Journal of Experimental Psychology*, vol. 5.

Horgan, T. and Tienson, J. 1992. Structured Representations in Connectionist Systems. In Davis 1992.

Husserl, E. 1901. *The Logical Investigations*, Findlay (tr.). London: Routledge & Kegan Paul, 1970.

Jackson, F. 1977. *Perception*. Cambridge: Cambridge University Press.

James, W. 1890. *The Principles of Psychology*, vol. II. Dover Publications, 1950.

Johansson, G. 1977. Spatial Constancy and Motion in Visual Perception. *Stability and Constancy in Visual Perception*. W. Epstein (ed.). New York: Wiley.

Kant, I. 1790. *Critique of Judgment*, W. Pluhar (tr.). Indianapolis: Hackett Publishing, 1987.

Kaplan, D. 1989. Demonstratives. *Themes from Kaplan*, J. Almog, J. Perry, and H. Wettstein (eds.). New York: Oxford University Press.

Karmiloff-Smith, A. 1979. Micro- and Macro-Developmental Changes in Language Acquisition and Other Representational Systems. *Cognition Science*, vol. 3, no. 2.

Karmiloff-Smith, A. 1986. From Meta-Processes to Conscious Access: Evidence From Children's Metalinguistic and Repair Data. *Cognition*, vol. 23.

Karmiloff-Smith, A. 1988. The Child Is a Scientist, Not an Inductivist. *Mind and Language*, vol. 3, no. 3.

Karmiloff-Smith, A. 1990. Constraints on Representational Change: Evidence From Children's Drawing. *Cognition*, vol. 34.

Karmiloff-Smith, A. 1992. *Beyond Modularity: A Developmental Perspective on Cognitive Science*. Cambridge, MA: The MIT Press.

Karttunen, L. 1977. The Syntax and Semantics of Questions. *Linguistics and Philosophy*, vol. 1.

Katzky, R. 1975. *Human Memory*. San Francisco: W. H. Freeman.

Kelly, S. 2001. The Nonconceptual Content of Perceptual Experience: Situation Dependence and Fineness of Grain. *Philosophy and Phenomenological Research*, vol. 62, no. 3.

Kierkegaard, S. 1843. *Fear and Trembling*, H. Hong and E. Hong (eds., trs.). Princeton, NJ: Princeton University Press, 1983.

Kirsh, D. 1987. Putting a Price on Cognition. *Southern Journal of Philosophy*, suppl. vol. 26.

Kosslyn, S. 1980. *Image and Mind*. Cambridge, MA: Harvard University Press.

Kusch, M. 1995. *Psychologism*. New York: Routledge.

Lange, C. 1885. The Emotions. Reprinted in *The Emotions*, Lange and James (eds.). New York: Harner Publishing, 1967.

Langer, S. 1953. *Feeling and Form*. New York: Scribner.

Lenat, D. and Feigenbaum, E. 1987. On the Thresholds of Knowledge. *MCC-AI Non-Proprietary Technical Report*.

Lennon, K. 1990. *Explaining Human Action*. London: Duckworth.

Lewis, D. 1983a. Individuation by Acquaintance and Stipulation. *Philosophical Review*, vol. 92.

Lewis, D. 1983b. General Semantics. *Philosophical Papers*, vol. 1. Cambridge: Cambridge University Press.

Lindsay, P. H. and Norman, D. A. 1972. *Human Information Processing*. New York: Academic Press.

Loewer, B. and Rey, G. 1991. *Meaning in Mind*. Oxford: Basil Blackwell.

Lopes, D. 1996. *Understanding Pictures*. Oxford: Oxford University Press.

Lycan, W. (ed.) 1990. *Mind and Cognition*. Oxford: Basil Blackwell.

Mach, E. 1914. *The Analysis of Sensations*. Chicago: Open Court.

Malcolm, N. 1963. Three Forms of Memory. *Knowledge and Certainty*. Englewood Cliffs, NJ: Prentice-Hall.

Margolis, E. and Laurence, S. (eds.). 1999. *Concepts: Core Readings*. Cambridge, MA: The MIT Press.

Marks, J. 1982. A Theory of Emotion. *Philosophical Studies*, vol. 42.

Marr, D. 1982. *Vision*. San Francisco: W. H. Freeman.

Martin, C. B. and Deutscher, M. 1966. Remembering. *Philosophical Review*, vol. 75.

Martin, M. G. F. 1992. Perception, Concepts, and Memory. *Philosophical Review*, vol. 101.

McClelland, J. and Kawamoto, A. 1986. Mechanisms of Sentence Processing: Assigning Roles to Constituents. *Parallel Distributed Processing: Explorations in the Microstructure of Cognition. Vol. 2: Psychological and Biological Models*, J. McClelland, D. Rumelhart, and the PDP Research Group (eds.). Cambridge, MA: The MIT Press.

McDowell, J. 1977. On the Sense and Reference Of a Proper Name. *Mind*, vol. 86.

McDowell, J. 1986. Singular Thought and the Extent of Inner Space. *Subject, Thought, and Context*, J. McDowell and P. Pettit (eds.). Oxford: Oxford University Press.

McDowell, J. 1994a, The Concept of Perceptual Experience. *Philosophical Quarterly*, vol. 44.

McDowell, J. 1994b. *Mind and World*. Cambridge, MA: Harvard University Press.

McDowell, J. 1998. Reply to Commentators. *Philosophy and Phenomenological Research*, vol. 58, no. 2.

McGinn, C. 1989. *Mental Content*. Oxford: Blackwell.

Melzack, R. 1961. The Perception of Pain. *Scientific American*, vol. 204.

Melzack, R. 1973. How Acupuncture Can Block Pain. *Impact of Science on Society*, vol. 23.

Melzack, R. and Wall, P. 1965. Pain Mechanisms: A New Theory. *Science*, vol. 150.

Merleau-Ponty, M. 1962. The Thing and the Natural World. *Phenomenology of Perception*, C. Smith (tr.). London: Routledge & Kegan Paul.

Millar, A. 1985–1986. What's In a Look? *Proceedings of the Aristotelian Society*, vol. 86.

Millar, A. 1991a. Concepts, Experience and Inference. *Mind*, vol. 100, no. 4.

Millar, A. 1991b. *Reason and Experience*. Oxford: Clarendon Press.

Miller, G. 1956. The Magical Number Seven, Plus or Minus Two: Some Limits on Our Capacity For Processing Information. *The Psychological Review*, vol. 63.

Millikan, R. 1984. *Language, Thought, and Other Biological Categories*. Cambridge, MA: The MIT Press.

Millikan, R. 1991. Speaking Up for Darwin. In Loewer and Rey 1991.

Montague, R. 1974. *Formal Philosophy*. New Haven, CT: Yale University Press.

Moore, G. 1918–1919. Some Judgments of Perception. *Proceedings of the Aristotelian Society*, vol. 19.

Neisser, U. 1967. *Cognitive Psychology*. New York: Appleton-Century-Crofts.

Neisser, U. 1977. Gibson's Ecological Optics: Consequences of a Different Stimulus Description. *Journal for the Theory of Social Behavior*, vol. 7, no. 1.

Neumann, O. and Prinz, W. 1990. *Relationships Between Perception and Action: Current Approaches*. Berlin: Springer.

Ockham, W. 1967–1979. *Scriptum in Librum Primum Sententiarum*. St. Bonaventure, NY: Editiones Instituti Franciscani Universitatis S. Bonaventurae.

O'Keefe, J. 1989. Computations the Hippocampus Might Perform. *Neural Connections, Mental Computation*, L. Cooper, P. Culicover, R. Harnish, and L. Nadel (eds.). Cambridge, MA: The MIT Press.

O'Keefe, J. and Nadel, L. 1978. *The Hippocampus as a Cognitive Map*. Oxford: Clarendon Press.

O'Shaughnessy, B. 1980. *The Will, Vol. 2*. Cambridge: Cambridge University Press.

Palmer, S. 1983. The Psychology of Perceptual Organization: A Transformational Approach. *Human and Machine Vision*, J. Beck, B. Hope, and A. Rosenfeld (eds.). New York: Academic Press.

Papineau, D. 1987. *Reality and Representation*. Oxford: Basil Blackwell.

Peacocke, C. 1979. *Holistic Explanation*. Oxford: Clarendon Press.

Peacocke, C. 1981: Demonstrative Thought and Psychological Explanation. *Synthese*, vol. 49.

Peacocke, C. 1983. *Sense and Content: Experience, Thought, and Their Relations*. New York: Oxford University Press.

Peacocke, C. 1984. Colour Concepts and Colour Experience. *Synthese*, vol. 58.

Peacocke, C. 1986a. Explanation and Computational Psychology: Language, Perception, and Level 1.5. *Mind and Language*, vol. 1.

Peacocke, C. 1986b. *Thoughts: An Essay on Content*. Oxford: Basil Blackwell.

Peacocke, C. 1986c. Analogue Content. *Proceedings of the Aristotelian Society*, supp. vol. 60.

Peacocke, C. 1987. Understanding Logical Constants: A Realist's Account. *Proceedings of the British Academy*, vol. 73.

Peacocke, C. 1989a. What Are Concepts? *Midwest Studies in Philosophy*, vol. 14, P. French, T. Uehling, and H. Wettstein (eds). Minneapolis: University of Minnesota Press.

Peacocke, C. 1989b. *Transcendental Arguments in the Theory of Content*. Oxford: Oxford University Press.

Peacocke, C. 1989c. Perceptual Content. *Themes from Kaplan*, J. Almog, J. Perry, and H. Wettstein (eds.). New York: Oxford University Press.

Peacocke, C. 1989d. When Is a Grammar Psychologically Real? *Reflections on Chomsky*, A. George (ed.). Oxford: Blackwell.

Peacocke, C. 1992a: Scenarios, Concepts and Perception. *The Contents of Experience*, T. Crane (ed.). Cambridge: Cambridge University Press.

Peacocke, C. 1992b. *A Study of Concepts*. Cambridge, MA: The MIT Press.

Peacocke, C. 1993. Externalist Explanation. *Proceedings of the Aristotelian Society*, vol. 93.

Peacocke, C. 1994a. Content, Computation and Externalism. *Mind and Language*, vol. 9.

Peacocke, C. 1994b. Nonconceptual Content: Kinds, Rationales and Relations. *Mind and Language*, vol. 9.

Peacocke, C. 1998. Nonconceptual Content Defended. *Philosophy and Phenomenological Research*, vol. 58, no. 2.

Peacocke, C. 2001a. Does Perception Have a Nonconceptual Content. *Journal of Philosophy*, vol. 98.

Peacocke, C. 2001b. Understanding the Past Tense. *Time and Memory*, C. Hoerl and T. McCormack (eds.). Oxford: Oxford University Press.

Pennebaker, J. and Lightner, J. 1980. Competition of Internal and External Information In an Exercise Setting. *Journal of Personality and Social Psychology*, vol. 39.

Perenin, M. and Vighetto, A. 1988. Optic Ataxia: A Specific Disruption in Visuo-Motor Mechanisms. *Brain*, vol. 111.

Perkins, M. 1962. Emotion and Feeling. *The Philosophy of Mind*, Englewood Cliffs, NJ: Prentice Hall.

Perry, J. 1979. The Problem of the Essential Indexical. *Nous*, vol. 13.

Piaget, J. 1954. *The Construction of Reality in the Child*. New York: Basic Books.

Piaget, J. 1969. *The Mechanisms of Perception*. London: Routledge & Kegan Paul.

Pierce, J. R. 1961. *Symbols, Signals and Noise*. New York: Harper.

Pinker, S. and Prince, A. 1989. Rules and Connections in Human Language. *Transactions in the Neurosciences*, vol. 11. Reprinted in *Language and Cognition*, J. Higginbotham (ed.). Cambridge: Blackwell, 1993.

Pitcher, G. 1971. *A Theory of Perception*. Princeton, NJ: Princeton University Press.

Pitson, A. E. 1984. Basic Seeing. *Philosophy and Phenomenological Research*, vol. 45.

Platts, M. 1980. Introduction. *Reference, Truth and Reality*, Platts (ed.). London: Routledge & Kegan Paul.

Poincaré, H. 1958. *The Value of Science*. New York: Dover.

Premack, D. 1988. Minds With and Without Language. In Weiskrantz 1988.

Pribram, K. H. 1971. *Languages of the Brain*. Englewood Cliffs, NJ: Prentice-Hall.

Prinz, W. 1990. A Common Coding Approach to Perception and Action. In Neumann and Prinz 1990.

Quine, W. v. O. 1960. *Word and Object*. Cambridge, MA: The MIT Press.

Quine, W. v. O. 1969. *Ontological Relativity and Other Essays*. New York: Columbia University Press.

Ramsey, W. 1992. Connectionism and the Philosophy of Mental Representation. In Davis 1992.

Reifel, S. 1987. The Sri Mobile Robot Testbed: A Preliminary Report. Technical note 413, SRI International, Menlo Park, CA.

Robinson, H. G. 1980. *Matter and Sense*. Cambridge: Cambridge University Press.

Rock, I. 1975. *An Introduction to Perception*. New York: MacMillan.

Russell, B. 1905. On Denoting. Reprinted in Russell 1957.

Russell, B. 1912. *The Problems of Philosophy*. Oxford: Oxford University Press.

Russell, B. 1957. *Logic and Knowledge*, R. Marsh (ed.). London: Allen & Unwin.

Ryle, G. 1949. *The Concept of Mind*. Chicago: The University of Chicago Press, 1984.

Sartre, J. 1938. *Nausea*, Alexander (tr.). New York: New Directions, 1964.

Schiffer, S. 1978. The Basis of Reference. *Erkenntnis*, vol. 13.

Schopenhauer, A. 1819. *The World as Will and Representation*, Payne (tr.). New York: Dover, 1958.

Searle, J. 1979. *Expression and Meaning*. Cambridge: Cambridge University Press.

Searle, J. 1980. Minds, Brains and Programs. *Behavioral and Brain Sciences*, vol. 3, no. 3.

Searle, J. 1983. *Intentionality*. New York: Cambridge University Press.

Searle, J. 1992. *The Rediscovery of the Mind*. Cambridge, MA: The MIT Press.

Sedivy, S. 1990. *The Determinate Character of Perceptual Experience*. University of Pittsburgh dissertation.

Segal, G. 1989. Seeing What Is Not There. *Philosophical Review*, vol. 98.

Sejnowski, T. and Rosenberg, C. 1986. NETtalk: A Parallel Network That Learns To Read Aloud. *John Hopkins University Electrical Engineering and Computer Science Technical Report*, January.

Seng-ts'an, C. 1991. *The Eye Never Sleeps*, Merzel (tr.). Boston: Shambhale Publications.

Shepard, R. 1981. Psychophysical Conplementarity. *Perceptual Organization*, M. Kubovy and J. Pomerantz (eds.). Hillsdale, NJ: Lawrence Erlbaum Associates.

Shoemaker, S. 1984. Persons and Their Pasts. *Identity, Cause, and Mind*. Cambridge: Cambridge University Press.

Sibley, F. 1971. Analyzing Seeing. *Perception*, F. Sibley (ed.). London: Methuen.

Smart, J. 1959. Sensations and Brain Processes. *Philosophical Review*, vol. 68.

Smith, B. 1987. *The Correspondence Continuum*. CSLI, Report no. 87–71.

Smith, D. and McIntrye, R. 1982. *Husserl and Intentionality*. Dordrecht, Holland: D. Reidel Publishing Company.

Smolensky, P. 1987. On Variable Binding and the Representation of Symbolic Structures in Connectionist Systems. *Department of Computer Science, University of Colorado at Boulder, Technical Report CU-CS*.

Smolensky, P. 1988. On the Proper Treatment of Connectionism. *Behavioral and Brain Sciences*, vol. 2.

Smolensky, P. 1991. Connectionism, Constituency, and the Language of Thought. In Loewer and Rey 1991.

Solomon, R. 1976. *The Passions*. Garden City, NY: Anchor Press.

Sosa, E. 1995. States of Affairs. *The Cambridge Dictionary of Philosophy*, R. Audi (ed.). Cambridge: Cambridge University Press.

Spelke, E. S. 1990. Principles of Object Perception. *Cognitive Science*, vol. 14.

Spelke, E. S. and van de Walle, G. A. 1993. Perceiving and Reasoning about Objects: Insights from Infants. In Eilan, McCarthy, and Brewer 1993.

Sperling, G. 1960. The Information Available in Brief Visual Presentations. *Psychological Monographs*, vol. 74, no. 11.

Stalnaker, R. 1998. What Might Nonconceptual Content Be? *Philosophical Issues*, vol. 9, E. Villanueva (ed.). Atascadero, CA: Ridgeview Publishing.

Stalnaker, R. 1999. Indexical Belief. Reprinted in *Context and Content*. Oxford: Oxford University Press.

Steinfeld, G. J. 1967. Concepts of Set and Availability and Their Relation to the Reorganization of Ambiguous Pictorial Stimuli. *Psychological Review*, vol. 74, no. 6.

Stenius, E. 1967. Mood and Language-Game. *Synthese*, vol. 17.

Stephens, L. and Graham, G. 1987. Minding Your p's and q's: Pain and Sensible Qualities. *Nous*, vol. 21.

Sterelny, K. 1990. *The Representational Theory of Mind*. Oxford: Basil Blackwell.

Stich, S. 1969. Beliefs and Subdoxastic States. *Philosophy of Science*, vol. 45.

Stich, S. 1981. Dennett on Intentional Systems. *Philosophical Topics*, vol. 12.

Stich, S. 1983. *From Folk Psychology to Cognitive Science*. Cambridge, MA: The MIT Press.

Strawson, P. F. 1959. *Individuals*. London: Methuen.

Strawson, P. F. 1966. *The Bounds of Sense*. London: Methuen.

Strawson, P. F. 1974. Imagination and Perception. *Freedom and Resentment*. London: Methuen.

Taylor, C. 1964. *The Explanation of Behaviour*. London: Routledge & Kegan Paul.

Taylor, C. 1978–1979. The Validity of Transcendental Arguments. *Proceedings of the Aristotelian Society*, vol. 79.

Touretzky, D. and Hinton, G. 1985. Symbols among the Neurons: Details of a Connectionist Inference Architecture. *Proceedings of the Ninth International Joint Conference on Artificial Intelligence*. Los Altos, CA: Morgan Kaufmann.

Triesman, A. and Gelade, G. 1980. A Feature-Integration Theory of Attention. *Cognitive Psychology*, vol. 12.

Triesman, A. and Schmidt, H. 1982. Illusory Conjunctions in the Perception of Objects. *Cognitive Psychology*, vol. 14.

Tsu, Lao. *Hua Hu Ching*, Walker (tr.). New York: Harper Collins, 1992.

Tye, M. 1991. *The Imagery Debate*. Cambridge, MA: The MIT Press.

Tye, M. 1992. Naturalism and The Mental. *Mind*, vol. 101.

Tye, M. 1995. *Ten Problems of Consciousness*, Cambridge, MA: The MIT Press.

Tye, M. 1996. The Function of Consciousness. *Nous*, vol. 30.

Tye, M. 1997. A Representational Theory of Pains and Their Phenomenal Character. *The Nature of Consciousness*, N. Block, O. Flanagan, and G. Guzeleve (eds.). Cambridge, MA: The MIT Press. An earlier version was published in *Philosophical Perspectives*, vol. 9, J. Tomberlin (ed.). Atascadero, CA: Ridgeview Publishing.

Uhr, L. 1973. *Pattern Recognition, Learning, and Thought*. Englewood Cliffs, NJ: Prentice-Hall.

van Gulick, R. 1990. Functionalism, Information and Content. In Lycan 1990.

Vendler, Z. 1972. *Res Cogitans*. Ithaca: Cornell University Press.

Walker, S. 1983: *Animal Thought*. London: Routledge & Kegan Paul.

Wallace, J. 1979. Only In the Context of a Sentence Do Words Have Any Meaning. *Midwest Studies in Philosophy*, vol. 4, P. French, T. Uehling, and H. Wettstein (eds.). Minneapolis: University of Minnesota Press.

Warga, C. 1987. Pain's Gatekeeper. *Psychology Today*, August.

Warren, R. M. 1970. Perceptual Restoration of Missing Speech Sounds. *Science*, vol. 167.

Weiskrantz, L. (ed.) 1988. *Thought Without Language*. Oxford: Clarendon Press.

Weiskrantz, L., Warrington, E. K., Saunders, M. D., and Marshall, J. 1974. Visual Capacity in the Hemianopic Field Following a Restricted Occipital Ablation. *Brain*, vol. 47.

Wiggins, D. 1967. *Identity and Spatio-Temporal Continuity*. Oxford: Blackwell.

Williams, B. 1973. Morality and the Emotions. *Problems of the Self*. Cambridge: Cambridge University Press.

Winograd, T. 1973. A Procedural Model of Language Understanding. *Computer Models of Thought and Language*, R. Schank and K. Colby (eds.). San Francisco: W. H. Freeman.

Wittgenstein, L. 1921. *Tractatus Logico-Philosophicus*, Ogden (tr.). London: Routledge & Kegan Paul, 1922.

Wittgenstein, L. 1951. *Philosophical Investigations*, G. Anscombe (tr.). Oxford: Basil Blackwell.

Wittgenstein, L. 1980. *Philosophy of Psychology, Vol. 1*, G. Anscombe and G. von Wright (trs.). Oxford: Blackwell.

Wollheim, R. 1993. Pictures and Language. *The Mind and Its Depths*. Cambridge, MA: Harvard University Press.

Wright, C. 1993. Eliminative Materialism: Going Concern or Passing Fancy? *Mind and Language*, vol. 8, no. 2.

Index